T0375241

DEMOCRACY BEYOND ATHENS

What was ancient democracy like? Why did it spread in ancient Greece? An astonishing number of volumes have been devoted to the well-attested Athenian case, while non-Athenian democracy – for which evidence is harder to come by – has received only fleeting attention. Nevertheless, there exists a scattered body of ancient material regarding democracy beyond Athens, from ancient literary authors and epigraphic documents to archaeological evidence, out of which one can build an understanding of the phenomenon. This book presents a detailed study of ancient Greek democracy in the Classical period (480–323 BC), focusing on examples outside Athens. It has three main goals: to identify where and when democratic governments established themselves in ancient Greek city-states; to explain why democracy spread to many parts of Greece in this period; and to further our understanding of the nature of ancient democracy by studying its practices beyond Athens.

ERIC W. ROBINSON is Associate Professor in the Department of History, Indiana University. He has published widely on ancient democracy, and previous books include *The First Democracies* (1997), *Ancient Greek Democracy: Readings and Sources* (2003) and *Oikistes: Studies in Constitutions, Colonies, and Military Power in the Ancient World Offered in Honor of A. J. Graham* (co-edited with Vanessa Gorman, 2002).

DEMOCRACY
BEYOND ATHENS

Popular Government in the Greek Classical Age

ERIC W. ROBINSON

CAMBRIDGE
UNIVERSITY PRESS

CAMBRIDGE UNIVERSITY PRESS
Cambridge, New York, Melbourne, Madrid, Cape Town,
Singapore, São Paulo, Delhi, Mexico City

Cambridge University Press
The Edinburgh Building, Cambridge CB2 8RU, UK

Published in the United States of America by Cambridge University Press, New York

www.cambridge.org
Information on this title: www.cambridge.org/9780521843317

First published 2011
Reprinted 2012

A catalogue record for this publication is available from the British Library

Library of Congress Cataloguing in Publication data
Robinson, Eric W.
Democracy beyond Athens : popular government in classical Greece / Eric Robinson.
p. cm.
Includes bibliographical references and index.
ISBN 978-0-521-84331-7 (hardback)
1. Democracy – Greece – History – To 1500. 2. Greece – Politics and
government – To 146 B.C. I. Title.
JC75.D36R6 2011
320.938 – dc23 2011021229

ISBN 978-0-521-84331-7 Hardback

Contents

Figures

Acknowledgments

This book has been a long time in the making, and I have many people to thank for help along the way.

Colleagues at the University of North Florida, Harvard University, and Indiana University have been very supportive, and research money received from all three institutions, including from the Loeb Classical Library at Harvard, has been invaluable. A summer's work years ago at the Center for Hellenic Studies in Washington, DC provided a congenial setting and welcome resources for launching the project. Among the many peers and mentors who have heard or read various pieces of the work in progress over the years I would like especially to thank for their thoughts Kurt Raaflaub, Mogens Hansen, Nino Luraghi, Donald Kagan, Martin Ostwald, Harvey Yunis, Robert Wallace, Anna Missiou, Jürgen Mejer, Vanessa Gorman, Greg Anderson, and Chloe Balla. Naturally, they are not to be held responsible for persisting flaws. I would also like to thank Susanne Carlsson and Andrei Zaikov for their help from great distances. My copy-editor, Jan Chapman, and the anonymous readers for Cambridge University Press saved me from many an error with their meticulous comments and turned me in some helpful directions. I am further grateful for the many stimulating contributions of graduate students in my classes at Harvard University and Indiana University over the years, and especially for the excellent research assistance carried out by Patrick Baker, Chris Molnar, Xin Fan, Charles Aull, and, above all, Heather Roberts.

In two instances versions of text and arguments presented in this book have previously appeared in print elsewhere. In both cases the relevant chapter sections here have been revised and expanded. Chapter 2's treatment of Syracuse in the fifth century owes much to "Democracy in Syracuse, 466–412 BC," *HSPh* 100 (2000): 189–205; and the portion of Chapter 5 dealing with the sophists draws heavily upon "The Sophists and Democracy Beyond Athens," *Rhetorica* 25.1 (2007): 109–22.

I dedicate this book in love and gratitude to my wife, Carwina Weng.

Abbreviations

Abbreviations of classical periodicals follow those in *l'Année Philologique*. Ancient authors and texts are abbreviated according to the *Oxford Classical Dictionary*. The following is a list of further books and series found in the notes to come.

Buck	C. D. Buck, *The Greek Dialects*. Chicago, 1955.
CAH	*Cambridge Ancient History*, 2nd edn. Cambridge, 1961–; 1st edn. Cambridge, 1923–39
FGH	F. Jacoby, *Die Fragmente der griechischen Historiker*, 3 vols. Berlin and Leiden, 1923–58
HCT	A. W. Gomme, A. Andrewes, and K. J. Dover, *A Historical Commentary on Thucydides*, 5 vols. Oxford, 1945–81
Heracl. Lemb.	Heraclidis Lembi, *Excerpta politiarum*, ed. and trans. M. R. Dilts. Durham, NC, 1971
IG	*Inscriptiones Graecae*. Berlin, 1873–
IGDS	L. Dubois, *Inscriptions grecques dialectales de Sicile. Contribution à l'étude du vocabulaire grec colonial*. Rome, 1989
Inventory	M. H. Hansen and T. H. Nielsen, eds., *An Inventory of Archaic and Classical Poleis*. Oxford, 2004; entries are cited by author and page number
IvO	*Inschriften von Olympia*, ed. W. Dittenberger and K. Purgold. Berlin, 1896
ML	R. Meiggs and D. Lewis, *A Selection of Greek Historical Inscriptions to the End of the Fifth Century BC*, rev. edn. Oxford, 1988

RE	A. Pauly, G. Wissowa, and W. Kroll, *Real-Encyclopaedie d. klassischen Altertumswissenschaft*. Stuttgart, 1893–
Rhodes and Osborne	P. J. Rhodes and R. Osborne, *Greek Historical Inscriptions 404–323 B.C.* Oxford, 2003
SEG	*Supplementum epigraphicum Graecum*. 1923–
*Syll.*³	W. Dittenberger, *Sylloge Inscriptionum Graecarum*, 3rd edn. Leipzig, 1915–24
Tod	M. N. Tod, *A Selection of Greek Historical Inscriptions to the End of the Fifth Century B.C.* Oxford, 1933

Introduction

This book seeks to answer vital questions about the establishment and practice of democracy (Greek *demokratia*) in the Greek world during the Classical period (480–323 BC). Its focus is not on Athens, the democracy for which the ancient testimony is most plentiful and about which there is an embarrassment of modern scholarly books. Instead, this study aims to take a comprehensive look at Classical democracies outside Athens, which are relatively rarely studied. If we are to understand the true nature of Greek democracy – a political legacy that is revered above all others from antiquity in contemporary politics, to such an extent that almost any non-democratic form of government is delegitimized – we need to know the range of possibilities for its practice, not just how things took shape in one city. Occasional comparison of the communities studied here with the Athenian democracy will be inevitable, but it will not happen systematically or frequently. One of the goals of this study, in fact, is to create a kind of database that in future will allow more detailed comparison of Athenian and non-Athenian practice than has been heretofore possible. It does not aim to do so comprehensively itself.

My previous book-length work on non-Athenian democracies, *The First Democracies*, was a very different project. There, the goal was simply to determine where and when the first democracies appeared in Greece. It covered the Archaic period (*c.* 700–480 BC) and concluded that by the middle of the sixth century *demokratiai* had formed in a number of city-states, though the thinness of the evidence precluded certainty about exactly how many there were or which had come first. But in the Classical period literary and epigraphic evidence for political history improves dramatically, enabling me to ask deeper questions in this study. The two central lines of inquiry that have driven it are: (1) how and why *demokratia* expanded as it did in the Greek world during the Classical period, and (2) what was the nature of democratic practice outside Athens.

I

To gather the material needed to answer these broad questions the first three chapters of this book discuss the evidence for likely democracies in fifty-four different city-states, organized by region (mainland Greece, western Greece, and eastern Greece, in Chapters 1–3, respectively). These cases do not represent every possible Classical democracy, but only those for which the available literary, epigraphic, and archaeological evidence presents a compelling case that popular government existed in the city-state in question at some point during the period from 480 to 323 BC. Each treatment discusses the evidence for when and how the *demokratia* came to be, with what subsequent constitutional changes, followed by consideration of the nature of its institutions and practices. Following the case studies in these three chapters are two more chapters tackling the larger issues. Chapter 4 explores the extent of and reasons for the spread of Classical democracy, considering arguments for and against seeing a preeminent Athenian role in the process and suggesting possible alternative drivers of the expansion. Chapter 5 seeks to assess the functioning of non-Athenian *demokratiai*, noting commonalities and variations among attested institutions and practices.

In identifying which states were democratic, one inevitably runs into the problem of definition. What constitutes democracy? Various criteria may be used, and one suspects that almost as many definitions can be found as there are political theorists who write on the subject.[1] Agreement might be reached on some of the general principles that a democratic order should embody – for example, decisive power in the hands of the people as a whole; a community that promotes the ideals of political freedom and equality; an inclusive citizen body – but when examining historical cases one can quickly reach the point where some tenets of democracy seem to be present and others absent, where theoretical perspective A would see democracy and B would see something else. In the ancient Greek setting the problem is compounded not just by the insufficiency of evidence (more on that below) but also by the area of overlap that existed between broad oligarchies and "moderate" democracies.[2] Such orders could share many of the same institutions, including sizable assembly meetings

---

[1] In *The First Democracies: Early Popular Government outside Athens* (Stuttgart, 1997), 13–16, I discussed just a few theoretical approaches, settling eventually on criteria for a democratic process worked out by Robert Dahl. These criteria include effective citizen participation, voting equality at the decisive stage, access to good information, and control of the agenda. S. Carlsson has since adopted the same criteria for evaluating Hellenistic democracies: *Hellenistic Democracies. Freedom, Independence, and Political Procedure in Some East Greek City-States* (Stuttgart, 2010), 47–9, 291–3.

[2] On oligarchy, see the brief but excellent study by M. Ostwald, *Oligarchia: The Development of a Constitutional Form in Ancient Greece* (Stuttgart, 2000).

with decisive power, property qualifications for offices, and representative councils. This overlap is illustrated and exacerbated by Aristotle's flexible use of the term *politeia*, which in the *Politics* – the single best Classical source for constitutional analysis – serves triple duty as a generic term for any kind of constitutional government, a more specific one denoting a liminal order that mixes oligarchic and democratic elements (*Pol.* 1293b33–4), and one indicating an unusually responsible form of democracy.[3]

Because of the inevitable difficulties in trying to settle on a modern-theory-derived definition of democracy that would apply in all cases, a better approach (and the one followed in this study wherever possible) is to allow Greek contemporaries to decide the issue. Did they, as far as we can tell, label city-state x a *demokratia*? If so, then we should assume it was a *demokratia* (= democracy).[4] Naturally, it is not always so easy. Sometimes no contemporary author specifically identifies a state as being democratic, but only an author writing decades later (e.g., Aristotle in the *Politics* concerning a fifth- or early fourth-century *polis*). Worse, the designation might only come from an author writing centuries later (e.g., Diodorus), or *no* author uses the term *demokratia* about the state in question, but there are other reasons to believe it was democratic: it belonged to a group of states that a contemporary source implies was democratic, or demonstrated institutions and practices typically associated by Classical authors with *demokratia*. On other occasions it is possible that the constitutional term is being used tendentiously, or the term is *not* being used for tendentious purposes.

Whatever the complications are, the principle that I will follow here in trying to decide whether *demokratia* existed is whether or not contemporary Greeks *did* call or *would have* called (as best we can determine) such a state *demokratia*, not whether we from our own perspective would deem the state to have exhibited a sufficient level of popular power and participation to merit our term "democracy." The characteristics of *demokratia* according to Classical authors are critical for this approach. In *The First Democracies* I devoted a chapter to ancient definitions of *demokratia*, drawing heavily

---

[3] The last meaning arises when Aristotle compares correct (*orthai*) and deviant (*parekbaseis*) forms of constitutions in the *Politics* and the *Nicomachean Ethics*: the philosopher refers to *politeia* and *demokratia* as counterparts, the good and bad versions of rule by the mass (*plethos*) of the citizens (*Pol.* 1279a22–b19; *Eth. Nic.* 1160a31–1161b11). See under Syracuse in Chapter 2 for a discussion of what to make of Aristotle's use of the term *politeia*, especially as regards that city-state.

[4] I will use the English word democracy as a convenient synonym for *demokratia*, i.e., a governmental order the Greeks considered to be democratic, since the only cases of democracy that matter here are the ancient variety. In doing this I certainly do not mean to equate modern democratic practice with the ancient. On comparing the two, see Robinson, *First Democracies*, 25–33.

on Aristotle's *Politics* and also surveying key passages from earlier authors.[5] A fairly consistent picture emerges regarding the institutions and ideals of *demokratia*. Commonly attested elements in definitions of *demokratia* include the primacy of the *demos* (the people), freedom and equality as guiding principles of the order, low property qualifications, use of the lot for some offices, and on occasion public pay for participation of the commons. Ostracism and accountability of the magistrates through procedures such as the *euthuna* (scrutiny of those leaving office) were also associated with *demokratia*, though not uniquely (*euthuna*) or universally (ostracism). In the opening of Chapter 5 in this book I revisit the issue, considering again Aristotle's treatment and the corroboration for it that we find in other Classical-era authors. I then go on to consider the degree to which the specified practices are collectively attested in the cases studied in Chapters 1 through 3.

The evidence for *demokratia* must be sifted on a case-by-case basis. If the only claims for *demokratia* in a particular city-state come from late authors, we should consider their likely sources and their understanding of earlier democratic practice. Allowances should be made for authorial bias and the positive or negative connotations of particular terms. Importantly, we must also expect that we will not have anything close to the full spectrum of evidence that we would like. Though the situation is better than for the Archaic period, the source material for the constitutional history of Classical states outside Athens is still spotty at best and nearly non-existent much of the time. This means emphasizing results gained from critical assessment of the evidence that we *do* have and not allowing the absence of other potentially useful information to deter us from coming to a reasonable judgment.[6] In doing all of this, one can usually arrive at a satisfactory conclusion, at least in the fifty-four cases examined here, about whether the Greeks considered (or would have considered) a state's constitution to have been a *demokratia*. Of course, scholarly opinions may still vary.[7]

It is surprising the degree to which the larger questions considered in Chapters 4 and 5 – why democracy spread and what it looked like outside Athens in the Classical period – have been quietly ignored by scholars. The

---

[5] *First Democracies*, 35–64.

[6] For example, it is unfortunate that we typically lack indications about the presence or absence of property qualifications for citizenship in specific city-states. According to Aristotle and other authors, high qualifications would indicate non-democracy, low or non-existent ones would suggest *demokratia*. But since we simply do not know anything about this in the vast majority of cases, the silence of the sources in any one case ought not to be taken as evidence one way or the other.

[7] A good example of the necessary juggling of many factors – and disagreements about how to interpret them – comes in the case of fifth-century Syracuse (see Chapter 2, opening).

issues seem central to a proper understanding of the general phenomenon of Greek democracy. No doubt the paucity of evidence mainly explains this, though one also suspects that the sheer convenience of letting the iconic Athenian example stand in for *demokratia* overall has also played a role. Each of the last two chapters begins with discussions of previous scholarly approaches, which inevitably show Athenocentric tendencies. My conclusions place more emphasis on non-Athenocentric explanations, with what success the reader may judge. But whatever one thinks of the ideas presented here, my hope is that by collecting the material I have and asking the larger questions I do subsequent discussions may be sparked in which the large body of non-Athenian *demokratiai* will receive their due consideration.

CHAPTER I

Classical demokratiai *on the Greek mainland (central Greece and the Peloponnese)*

This chapter discusses the appearance and nature of democracies to be found outside Athens on the Greek mainland from 480 to 323 BC. Each state considered separately below either *certainly* or *probably* experienced at least one episode of democratic government during this time period. While it is always possible – indeed, it is likely – that further examples of *demokratia* cropped up on occasion in these or other communities of the mainland, the following represent the only cases for which we have compelling evidence.

With the exception of a few of the better-attested examples, treatments are brief. The primary purpose here is to come to an understanding of how democracies arose in these places and, at least generally, how they functioned. Usually more can be said about the former than the latter. This chapter engages in very little comparison or synthesis: the fourth and fifth chapters of the book, drawing on the previous sections including this one, will pursue these goals.

The order of discussion is roughly alphabetical, though we begin with Argos owing to its importance and follow with Corinth because of the close association of its brief period of democracy with the Argive state.

ARGOS

Argos and its environs loom large in any proper reckoning of Greek history and the Greek imagination, from heroic myths to the realities of the Mycenaean age to the political, social, and economic history of the city-state in the Archaic and Classical eras. It also holds a central place in the study of Classical democracy: excepting only Athens, the Argive democracy stands above all others in terms of the quantity and variety of information available, and thus in our ability to picture what *demokratia* could look like outside Attica. Literary evidence, while scattered about in brief segments, includes some valuable testimony from such authors as Herodotus, Thucydides, Euripides, Xenophon, Aristotle, Aeneas Tacticus, and Diodorus Siculus. Moreover, a number of inscribed decrees and other texts survive from the fifth and fourth centuries and later; and the archaeological excavations of the city carried out in recent decades have been very revealing too. From these various types of material one can glean much about how the Argive democracy functioned, institutionally and culturally.

That Argos was a *demokratia* during most of the Classical period is not in any doubt. Thucydides, for one, repeatedly labels Argos a democracy in his fifth book, commenting on how the shared democratic forms of government at Mantinea and Argos, and at Argos and Athens, encouraged alliances among these states between 421 and 418 BC; he further notes that the democracy at Argos discouraged military ties between Argos and then-oligarchic Boeotia and Megara (5.29, 5.31, 5.44). Later, he describes an oligarchic coup, followed quickly by a democratic resurgence, after the battle of Mantinea (5.81–2). Various passages in Xenophon, Diodorus, and Aristotle confirm the existence of this democracy and make clear that it persisted until late in the fourth century.[1]

Exactly when Argos first became democratic presents more of a challenge, however. I have argued elsewhere that Argos achieved its earliest democratic government soon after its disastrous battle with the Spartans at Sepeia, customarily dated to 494 BC.[2] While it is possible that Argos had a moderately democratic government already in the sixth century – literary sources talk of a popular revolution overthrowing the last king of Argos, and mid-sixth-century epigraphic documents would seem to confirm that a constitutional government of some kind with regular boards of magistrates was in place – the evidence is too vague to insist on democracy. It perhaps best suits a moderate oligarchy or an Aristotelian *politeia* (a mixture between democracy and oligarchy).[3]

After the battle of Sepeia, however, popular government more obviously takes hold at Argos. Thanks to the terrible losses in that battle, a political revolution took place, our sources tell us, one involving the inclusion of

---

[1] Arist. *Pol.* 1302b18, 1303a6–8, 1304a27; Diod. Sic. 12.80.23, 15.58; Xen. *Hell.* 7.1.44. On Aeschylus' *Suppliants* see below. The democracy was replaced by an oligarchy in 322 but seems to have returned by the end of the century (Diod. Sic. 17.57.1; M. Piérart, "Argos. Un autre democratie," in P. Flensted-Jensen, T. H. Nielsen, and L. Rubinstein, eds., *Polis & Politics: Studies in Ancient Greek History* (Copenhagen, 2000), 297–314, at 309–10).

[2] Robinson, *First Democracies*, 82–8. On the date, see below.

[3] Paus. 2.19.2; Diod. Sic. fr. 7.13.2; Robinson, *First Democracies*, 82–4. Wörrle favors a hoplite *politeia* over *demokratia*; M. Wörrle, *Untersuchungen zur Verfassungsgeschichte von Argos im 5. Jahrhundert vor Christus* (Erlangen, 1964), 101–2.

many new citizens from previously disenfranchised classes of inhabitants. Details vary by author: Herodotus (6.83) calls the newly dominant citizen body "slaves" (*douloi*), while Aristotle (*Pol.* 1303a6–8) and Plutarch (*De mul. vir.* 4) describe them as *perioikoi*, dwellers in dependent lands nearby. We probably ought to associate the newly included inhabitants with the *gumnetes*, Argives whose status has been described as "between free and slave" (Pollux, *Onom.* 3.83). This newly expanded *demos* took full control of the affairs of state, pushing Argos in a democratic direction.[4] Some features familiar to us from the mature Argive democracy (see below) probably had their start at this time, but our sources for the post-Sepeia events do not discuss institutions.

A greater uncertainty, however, concerns the exact date of the battle of Sepeia itself, and with it the timing of the consequent democratic revolution. The 494 date which I and others have used depends on rather vague implications in Herodotus' account: we know it occurred during the reign of the Spartan king Cleomenes (*c.* 525–488), and not too long before the Persian invasion of 480, when the losses at Sepeia could still be considered "recent" according to Herodotus.[5] A date in the later 490s would make good sense, therefore. But some scholars have proposed that the battle took place earlier: Aubonnet in the Budé, for example, would put it in 519 or 509; Vollgraff offers 520.[6] Nothing about these dates would surprise in constitutional terms – the earliest instances of popular governments occurred earlier still in the sixth century – but they do seem to overstretch Herodotus' use of "recent" (*neosti*). We also do not know the exact fate of the newly inclusive post-Sepeia constitutional order: it may have steadily progressed into the fully democratic state we see later in the fifth century, or the road might have been rockier, given the subsequent

---

[4] Robinson, *First Democracies*, 84–8; Wörrle, *Verfassungsgeschichte von Argos*, 101–11; H.-J. Gehrke, *Stasis. Untersuchungen zu den inneren Kriegen in den griechischen Staaten des 5. und 4. Jahrhunderts v. Chr.* (Munich, 1985), 24–6; F. Ruzé, *Délibération et pouvoir dans la cité grecque* (Paris, 1997), 254–64; H. Leppin, "Argos. Eine griechische Demokratie des fünften Jahrhunderts v. Chr.," *Ktema* 24 (1999), 297–312, at 300–3. Cf. D. Lotze, "Zur Verfassung von Argos nach der Schlacht bei Sepei," *Chiron* 1 (1971), 95–109.

[5] 7.148, with 6.19, 6.77. Robinson, *First Democracies*, 84, n. 76. A date in the late 490s would also allow for the expiration of a (putative) fifty-year peace treaty with Sparta after the battle of champions.

[6] J. Aubonnet, *Aristote Politique*, vol. II.2 (Paris, 1973), 157–8; G. Vollgraff, "Ad titulos Argivos," *Mnemosyne* 58 (1930), 20–40, at 27. Ch. Kritzas suggests 505 or 494, but prefers 494, in "Aspects de la vie politique et économique d'Argos au Ve siècle avant J.-C.," in M. Piérart, ed., *Polydipsion Argos* (*BCH* Supplement 22; Paris, 1992), 231–40, at 231. D. M. Lewis offers 494 or a few years earlier in "Mainland Greece, 479–451 B.C.," in D. M. Lewis *et al.*, eds., *CAH²*, vol. V (Cambridge, 1992), 96–120, at 101 with n. 16.

social strife mentioned by Herodotus when the sons of the fallen came of age.[7]

But by 470 or 460 the Argive democracy was undoubtedly firmly established and in full swing. Aeschylus' *Suppliants*, produced in the 460s, portrays a popularly managed heroic-age Argos, using phrases such as *to demion, to ptolin kratunei* ("the people, which rules the city," 699).[8] Inscriptions dated by letter forms to 475 or 450 also begin to employ the phrase "decreed by the assembly" (*aliaiai edoxe*) and other democratic formulae.[9] The practice of ostracism is attested for Argos,[10] and a potsherd possibly used in one can be dated to the second quarter of the century (see below). Around this time Argos engaged in the conquest of formerly independent states in nearby areas, including Tiryns and Mycenae, annexing the territory and resettling the lands; combined with the evidence for mid-century creation of a fourth tribe and reorganization of the phratry system, the evidence suggests that a newly aggressive Argos was attempting to integrate more closely an expanding citizen population into the political order.[11] Finally, Argos engaged in a major public building campaign around the middle of the century in and around the agora, including the "theater with straight tiers," where the assembly no doubt met, and a meeting hall (probably for a council) known as the Hypostyle Hall, among other new structures.[12] Taken together, the above evidence strongly indicates that the Argive democracy was coming into its own in the second quarter of the fifth century.

[7] 6.83 refers to the overthrow of the *douloi* by the sons of the fallen, possibly indicating that a backlash returned Argos to a more conservative political order for a time.

[8] Cf. D. Lotze, "Zum Begriff der Demokratie in Aischylos' 'Hiketiden,'" in E. G. Schmidt, ed., *Aischylos und Pindar* (Berlin, 1981), 207–16.

[9] *SEG* 13.239; ML 42. Jameson's suggestion that ML 42 may not be Argive has been firmly rejected: M. Jameson, "A Treasury of Athena in the Argolid (*IG* 4.554)," in D. W. Bradeen and M. F. McGregor, eds., *Phoros* (Locust Valley, 1974), 67–75; *SEG* 49.351.

[10] Arist. *Pol.* 1302b18–19; scholion to Aristophanes, *Knights*, 855.

[11] Kritzas, "Aspects de la vie politique et économique d'Argos"; M. Piérart and G. Touchais, *Argos: un ville grecque de 6000 ans* (Paris, 1996), 42.

[12] Leppin, "Argos," 299–303; K. Barakari-Gléni and A. Pariente, "Argos du VIIième au IIième siècle av. J.-C.: synthèse des données archéologiques," in A. Pariente and G. Touchais, *Argos et l'Argolide: topographie et urbanisme* (Paris, 1998) 165–78 at 166; and A. Pariente, M. Piérart, and J.-P. Thalmann, "Les recherches sur l'agora d'Argos: résultats et perspectives," in Pariente and Touchais, *Argos et l'Argolide*, 211–31 at 213; Piérart and Touchais, *Argos*, 42–52; J.-F. Bommelaer and J. Des Courtils, *La salle hypostyle d'Argos* (Athens, 1994); J. Des Courtils, "L'architecture et l'histoire d'Argos dans la première moitié du Ve siècle avant J.-C.," in M. Piérart, ed., *Polydipsion Argos* (Paris, 1992), 241–51; R. Ginouvès, *Le théatron à gradins droits et l'odéon d'Argos* (Paris, 1972); J.-C. Moretti, with S. Diez, *Théâtres d'Argos* (Athens, 1993), 30–2. Cf. I. Morris, "Beyond Democracy and Empire: Athenian Art in Context," in D. Boedeker and K. A. Raaflaub, eds., *Democracy, Empire, and the Arts in Fifth-Century Athens* (Cambridge, MA, 1998), 59–86 at 82; and T. Hölscher, "Images and Political Identity: The Case of Athens," in Boedeker and Raaflaub, eds., *Democracy, Empire*, 153–84 at 163–9.

The nature of Argive democracy

The institutions and procedures of the democracy at Argos have recently become a matter of some debate. Wörrle's comprehensive 1964 study of the constitution is still the standard work on the subject, but the picture it paints has had to be modified in important ways by the archaeological discoveries made since then. Studies by Piérart, Kritzas, Ruzé, and others have built on Wörrle's treatment to add new detail and depth to our understanding of the Argive system of government.[13] Basic features of the constitution included a popular assembly, called the *aliaia*, a council (*bola*), and another group or council called the Eighty with financial and judicial responsibilities. There was also a variety of officials, including the prominent *artunai* – possibly the chief magistrates, though the word is most often used generically – and treasurers, generals, secretaries, religious and tribal officials, ad hoc boards, and others, including a *basileus* chosen annually and used to date years.[14] The exciting find of numerous Classical-era financial documents from the treasury in an Athena sanctuary – only partly published at the time of this writing – has already deepened our understanding of important aspects of the constitution, especially as concerns different officials.[15]

Deliberation in the state appears to have been handled probouleutically. That is, a council discussed topics first, which were then passed on to the *aliaia* for a final decision. Inscribed documents of official enactments from the fifth and fourth centuries usually begin or end with the phrase *aliaiai edoxe*, "decreed by the assembly." *Damos* appears intermittently as part of the formulae used (e.g., *edoxe toi damoi*, "decreed by the people") only in the later fourth century. Importantly, documents sometimes also contain information about who was president of the council – "X presided (*areteue*)" or "X presided over the council (*areteue bolas*)" – which would seem to confirm prior consideration of these matters by the council.[16]

---

[13] Kritzas, "Aspects de la vie politique et économique d'Argos"; Ruzé, *Délibération et pouvoir*, 241–88; Piérart, "Argos"; Leppin, "Argos." More generally, M. Piérart in *Inventory*, 604–5.

[14] *Artunai* as the name of magistrates is unusual (though Epidaurus once had councilors called *artunoi*, Plut. *Quaest. Graec.* 291E); it is possible that the *artunai* at Argos replaced as top officials the *damiourgoi*, who appear in archaic Argive inscriptions but not in Thucydides 5.47.9 (Gomme, *HCT* and S. Hornblower, *A Commentary on Thucydides*, 3 vols. [Oxford, 1991–2008], ad loc.)

[15] See below. Ch. Kritzas, "Nouvelles inscriptions d'Argos: les archives des comptes du trésor sacré (IVe s. av. J.-C.)," *CRAI* (2006), 397–434, and "Literacy and Society: The Case of Argos," *Kodai Journal of Ancient History* 13/14 (2003/4), 53–60.

[16] P. J. Rhodes, with D. M. Lewis, *The Decrees of the Greek States* (Oxford, 1997), 67–8, 70–1, 476, with 475–8 generally. Ruzé, *Délibération et pouvoir*, conveniently tabulates the most relevant documentary data at pp. 265–6.

To flesh out the evidence from decrees one may turn to Thucydides' brief but informative literary description at 5.27–8 of how decision-making could take place. Of course, constitutional procedure is not Thucydides' subject here (rather, the various interstate negotiations in which Argos took part in 421) but thanks to the historian's precision we gain a glimpse into how matters could proceed in Argos:

27 [2] The Corinthian [ambassadors] first turned aside to Argos and opened negotiations with some of the men in office there (*tinas ton en telei onton*), pointing out that the Spartans could have no good end in view... [and that] Argos should immediately pass a decree inviting any Hellenic state that chose... to make a defensive alliance with the Argives; appointing a few individuals with plenipotentiary powers, instead of making the people (*ton demon*) the medium of negotiation, in order that, in the case of an applicant being rejected, the fact of his overtures might not be made public... [3] After this explanation of their views the Corinthians returned home. 28 [1] The persons with whom they had communicated reported the proposal to the magistrates (*tas archas*) and the people, and the Argives passed the decree and chose twelve men to negotiate an alliance for any Hellenic state that wished it, except Athens and Lacedaemon, neither of which should be able to join without reference to the Argive people.[17]

The order of events is revealing: the Corinthians approached a few Argive officials, who then reported the matter to a larger group of officials, "*tas archas*," which can perhaps be taken to mean (or to include) the council.[18] These *archai* seem to have put the matter before the "*demos*" (no doubt the *aliaia*), which voted on the matter. They approved of the alliance plan and empowered a board of twelve to implement their decision – unless Athens or Sparta should try to join the alliance, in which case the matter must be referred back again to the assembly.

[17] R. Crawley translation (*Thucydides*, New York, 1982), modified. Κορίνθιοι δὲ ἐς Ἄργος τραπόμενοι πρῶτον λόγους ποιοῦνται πρός τινας τῶν ἐν τέλει ὄντων Ἀργείων ὡς χρή, ἐπειδὴ Λακεδαιμόνιοι οὐκ ἐπ' ἀγαθῷ, ἀλλ' ἐπὶ καταδουλώσει τῆς Πελοποννήσου σπονδὰς καὶ ξυμμαχίαν πρὸς Ἀθηναίους τοὺς πρὶν ἐχθίστους πεποίηνται, ὁρᾶν τοὺς Ἀργείους ὅπως σωθήσεται ἡ Πελοπόννησος καὶ ψηφίσασθαι τὴν βουλομένην πόλιν τῶν Ἑλλήνων, ἥτις αὐτόνομός τέ ἐστι καὶ δίκας ἴσας καὶ ὁμοίας δίδωσι, πρὸς Ἀργείους ξυμμαχίαν ποιεῖσθαι ὥστε τῇ ἀλλήλων ἐπιμαχεῖν, ἀποδεῖξαι δὲ ἄνδρας ὀλίγους ἀρχὴν αὐτοκράτορας καὶ μὴ πρὸς τὸν δῆμον τοὺς λόγους εἶναι, τοῦ μὴ καταφανεῖς γίγνεσθαι τοὺς μὴ πείσαντας τὸ πλῆθος· ἔφασαν δὲ πολλοὺς προσχωρήσεσθαι μίσει τῶν Λακεδαιμονίων. καὶ οἱ μὲν Κορίνθιοι διδάξαντες ταῦτα ἀνεχώρησαν ἐπ' οἴκου· οἱ δὲ τῶν Ἀργείων ἄνδρες ἀκούσαντες ἐπειδὴ ἀνήνεγκαν τοὺς λόγους ἔς τε τὰς ἀρχὰς καὶ τὸν δῆμον, ἐψηφίσαντο Ἀργεῖοι καὶ ἄνδρας εἵλοντο δώδεκα, πρὸς οὓς τὸν βουλόμενον τῶν Ἑλλήνων ξυμμαχίαν ποιεῖσθαι πλὴν Ἀθηναίων καὶ Λακεδαιμονίων· τούτων δὲ μηδετέροις ἐξεῖναι ἄνευ τοῦ δήμου τοῦ Ἀργείων σπείσασθαι (Thuc. 5.27–8).

[18] Councilors in Greek cities can be referred to as *archai*. Hornblower believes that the council is precisely what Thucydides means here: Hornblower, *Commentary*, vol. III, 62. See further discussion below.

It is worth noting that the Corinthians explicitly sought to avoid having the *demos* involve itself in the individual negotiations with potential allies. The stated reason is to enable greater secrecy, but one may perhaps infer that the oligarchic Corinthians also mistrusted the ruling *demos* at Argos and sought to restrict its involvement as much as possible.[19] In any case, their request for a special board with plenipotentiary powers presupposes that the normal procedure at Argos would have been to allow the *demos* to control the negotiations at every stage. And even though the assembly approved this board of twelve to manage the details, it made a point of requiring reference back to the *demos* in the most important potential cases (i.e., Sparta or Athens).

Regarding the assembly, it met regularly, at least once a month, and possibly more.[20] Documents refer to it in three different guises: simply as the *aliaia* (twice, *c.* 475 and 350–325); as the *Aliaia* for Sacred Matters (*aliaia ton iaron, c.* 450); and, most frequently, as the Principal *Aliaia* (*aliaia teleia*, fourth century and thereafter). These different names and the relative dates of their reference suggest that at some point after 475 what was originally referred to simply as a meeting of the *aliaia* became the *aliaia teleia*, and a separate meeting could be called for dealing with sacred matters.[21] Whether this *Aliaia* for Sacred Matters happened every month in addition to the principal meeting, or regularly but less frequently, or only as needed, is unknown. Ad hoc meetings of the *aliaia* were certainly possible: a passage from Aeneas Tacticus (11.7–10) describes an incident in the early fourth century in which a popular leader (*tou demou prostates*) calls an assembly suddenly and without advance notice (*tachisten ekklesian sunagagein kai to mellon me proeipein*) in order to foil an oligarchic plot.

---

[19] Corinthian distaste for Argive democracy is also inferred by G. T. Griffith, "The Union of Corinth and Argos (392–386 B.C.)," *Historia* 1 (1950), 236–56, at 237–8. For a comparable case, see Thuc. 4.22.3: in 425 Spartan envoys at Athens to negotiate a truce request that specific terms be discussed quietly with a few Athenians commissioned for the purpose, worrying (Thucydides tells us) that open discussions in assembly will reveal details to their allies that would prove embarrassing should the negotiations fall through. The populist Cleon, however, casts this request in a negative light, suggesting a nefarious Spartan preference for secrecy instead of honest discussion before all the people. Thucydides' presentation is not favorable to Cleon here, but of course it never is where that particular politician is concerned. Spartan discomfort with democratic assemblies may indeed have been a factor on this occasion, as at Argos.

[20] Wörrle, *Verfassungsgeschichte von Argos*, 33–43; Ruzé, *Délibération et pouvoir*, 245–9; Rhodes, *Decrees*, 71. Inscribed decrees usually refer to the month in which the assembly meeting took place, but sometimes the day as well: see Inv F 95 in M. Piérart and J.-P. Thalmann, "Nouvelle inscriptions argiennes (I) (Fouilles de l'agora)," *Études argiennes* (BCH Supplement 6; Paris, 1980), 255–78.

[21] Wörrle, *Verfassungsgeschichte von Argos*, 35–9. For the Argolic dialect see C. D. Buck, *The Greek Dialects* (Chicago, 1955), 162–4.

Archaeological investigation has helped to establish where and in what numbers the people met in assembly. Built into a hillside less than 200 meters to the west of the agora is the so-called theater with straight tiers ("théatron à gradins droits"), the earliest sizable gathering place found in Argos and one of the oldest in Greece. Though the date of construction cannot be precisely established, it goes back to the fifth century, probably the middle decades, and may be best associated with the new construction around the general area of the agora in that period.[22] This meeting place had at least thirty-seven rows of straight-cut tiers carved into the rock of the hill facing the city on the west. The precise dimensions of the area and what it looked like near the base cannot be worked out from the present remains – an odeon built over it in the Roman era has obliterated crucial parts of the original construction, and it is poorly preserved in the upper reaches and to the sides. One estimate suggests that 2,300–2,500 people could sit on the carved seats;[23] others would put the seating capacity at 2,770 to 3,000.[24] These may seem rather small numbers of seats for the popular assembly of a substantial state such as Argos, with an adult male citizen population of ten to twenty thousand.[25] It must be borne in mind that many more could have fit standing instead of sitting, and higher up on the slope of the hill beyond the last currently apparent tier numerous others could sit or stand and (as my own experiments there demonstrated to me) still hear a speaker at the base. So for especially important meetings one imagines that a thousand or more additional citizens might easily have

---

[22] Ginouvès, *Le théatron à gradins droits*, 61–2, 76–7; J. C. Moretti, *Théâtres d'Argos*, 23, 30.

[23] J. C. Moretti, *Théâtres d'Argos*, 31. Cf. W. A. McDonald, *The Political Meeting Places of the Greeks* (Baltimore, 1943), 80–4 (guesses 1,800).

[24] Based on seat width of 37 or 40 cm; M. H. Hansen and T. Fischer-Hansen, "Monumental Political Architecture in Archaic and Classical Greek *Poleis*," in D. Whitehead, ed., *From Political Architecture to Stephanus Byzantinus. Sources for the Ancient Greek Polis* (Stuttgart, 1994), 23–90, at 57 with n. 134.

[25] Reliable evidence is scarce on Argos's population in the Classical period, but it is probably right to conclude that it varied between being roughly half that of Athens to something much closer. The figure of 20,000 adult male citizens (for the late fifth century) should probably be seen as an upper limit. Beloch estimates there were 10,000 hoplites and 20,000 citizens based on Lysias 34.7 and the size of the land area around Argos; *Die Bevölkerung der griechisch-römischen Welt* (Leipzig, 1886), 116–23. Jameson *et al.* estimate for the fourth century 15,000 citizens based on the epigraphically attested grain gifts from Cyrene in 330–326, the proportions of which given to Athens and Argos suggest that Argos's population was half that of Athens; M. H. Jameson, C. N. Runnels, and T. H. van Andel, *A Greek Countryside: The Southern Argolid from Prehistory to the Present Day* (Stanford, 1994), 559–61; Tod 196. M. H. Hansen, using calculations based on intramural space within the city, estimates a total population (including citizens and non-citizens) of 31,050 but considers this figure too low, since the presence of 7,000 Argive hoplites at Nemea (Xen. *Hell.* 4.2.17) would seem to imply roughly twice that many; *The Shotgun Method: The Demography of the Ancient Greek City-State Culture* (Columbia, 2006), 94.

been able to fit into or around the venue. Nevertheless, that regular seating for at most only around 2,500 participants was carved into the rock in Argos's earliest large assembly space is revealing: it suggests that, as with the Pnyx at Athens, normal attendance at mass deliberative meetings was expected to involve only a fraction of the total citizen population.[26]

Archaeologists made a notable discovery in the year 2000 that, among other things, further suggests active citizen involvement in state administration. They found in what appears to have been a treasury of Pallas Athena, which doubled as the state treasury, a collection of about 134 small bronze (and two lead) strips or plaques with inscriptions on them in the Argive alphabet, the majority dating roughly to the first half of the fourth century. The inscriptions include names, phratries, places of origin, and numerous offices, some of which are familiar, but a great many we read about for the first time. Letter forms might suggest dates for the plaques as early as the second half of the fifth century, but internal references in the documents point to dates (for many if not all of them) within the time of the Corinthian War and the years following, perhaps 390–360 BC. All the plaques appear to contain accounts of a financial nature, disclosing deposits and withdrawals from the treasury for a variety of public activities, including festivals, athletics, construction, and war financing. Though they have yet to be fully published, many of the tablets have undergone detailed preliminary analysis by Charalambos Kritzas and already shed extraordinary new light on Argive official bodies.[27]

Perhaps the most striking single thing we learn from the new documents is that the majority of officials at Argos served only six-month terms. The only exceptions appear to be the *iaromnamones*, *athlothetes*, and certain ad hoc colleges. That the council (*bola*) operated on a six-month cycle had been suspected before, based on a lone fourth-century document (*IG* 12.3.1259 = Tod 179/Buck 86). This has been dramatically confirmed and shown to have applied broadly among regular magistrates of the state. A six-month term is, of course, extremely brief; but rapid turnover of officials

---

[26] At Athens in the fifth century no more than roughly a seventh of the citizens could have attended meetings at the Pnyx; after the enlargement of the Pnyx and the decline in population in the fourth century, a quarter or a third might have attended. At Argos the fraction would seem to have varied between a quarter and an eighth of the voting populace, depending on the population figures one adopts (see previous note). On the Pnyx see M. H. Hansen, *The Athenian Ecclesia* (Copenhagen, 1983), 16–18, 25–6; cf *The Athenian Democracy in the Age of Demosthenes* (Oxford, 1991), 128–32. Compare also the theater at Mantinea, which probably could accommodate 3,000 people, out of a citizen population up to an estimated 18,000 (see discussion under Mantinea below). This issue is further discussed in Chapter 5.

[27] Kritzas, "Nouvelles inscriptions" and "Literacy and Society."

is appropriate within a *demokratia*, where the idea was to allow the people to rule in turn, and not to entrench magisterial authority anywhere for very long.[28] Other important discoveries from the bronze documents include many new magistracies that we previously knew nothing about, such as the eight *sunepignomenes* of the *epignoma*, who controlled deposits and distribution of money at the temple treasury, and the *anelateres*, who may have been collectors of fines. The Eighty, a rather mysterious body before, are everywhere in the documents, and always mentioned first, indicating their importance. They work in groups of ten (*dekades*) and withdraw money from the treasury as loans. In all, Kritzas concludes from the documents that Argos operated with an impressive transparency of financial transactions and much rotation of citizen participants, demonstrating in detail a routine democratic functioning.

But much remains unknown about other aspects of the constitution, including the council (*bola*). For example, we do not know if councilors were elected or allotted, or how many there were. They may have met in the Hypostyle Hall, an apparent bouleuterion in the agora.[29] Thuc. 5.47.9 mentions the Eighty, which was called on to administer treaty oaths to the council, the *artunai*, and themselves in 420. Given the four Argive tribes, it has been conjectured that the Eighty were a kind of tribal prytany for a council of 320 men; this could work, especially since in the word order of Thucydides' treaty the Athenian counterpart to the Eighty was the prytany; but there is no way to be sure, and the Eighty could have formed an entirely separate body, perhaps one with judicial responsibilities in addition to the financial ones repeatedly attested in the new bronze documents. Indeed, an unedited inscription from the third quarter of the fourth century also mentions the body and shows that it could be called upon to arbitrate legal cases.[30]

Recently Hartmut Leppin has challenged standard views about the council and other aspects of the Argive democracy.[31] He believes that Wörrle's influential analysis relies too much on comparisons with the Athenian democracy, resulting in some dubious assumptions. In particular, Leppin questions the importance of the council in the Argive democracy. According to Herodotus (7.148), during the time of the Persian Wars (and thus

---

[28] Aristotle emphasizes this in the *Politics*: 1308a13–16 (which specifically mentions six-month terms), 1317b19–25; also 1261a32–7. See Cos (Chapter 3), where six-month terms obtained for the democracy from the Hellenistic period. Kritzas, "Nouvelles inscriptions," 421, n. 84.

[29] Pariente, Piérart, and Thalmann, "Les recherches sur l'agora d'Argos," 213.

[30] Piérart, "Argos," 304–5; Ruzé, *Délibération et pouvoir*, 267–9; Kritzas, "Nouvelles inscriptions," 413.

[31] Leppin, "Argos."

before the democracy had fully developed) the Argive council wielded great authority, deciding entirely on its own the question of whether Argos would aid the Greek cause. In contrast, one is hard-pressed to discover a visible role for the council thereafter. The formula of Argive decrees reads *aliaia edoxe*, with no mention of the council. The word is also absent from literary descriptions where we would have reason to expect it to appear, such as Thucydides' account of Argive alliance-seeking in 421 (5.27–8), and also at Thucydides 5.61.1 and relevant sections in Aeneas Tacticus (11.7ff.) and Diodorus (15.57.3ff.). Leppin concludes that *probouleusis* itself – assumed by Wörrle to be universal in Greek democracies – cannot be proven to have operated in Argos. Instead, he believes that as the democracy developed, the council lost power to officials who, while not without supervision from the *demos*, were able to assert remarkable authority, especially with regard to foreign policy.[32] Leppin sees this increased authority in the surprising appointment of the twelve men with full diplomatic powers in 421 (Thuc. 5.28). Leppin also proposes that the Eighty may have been a collection of officials rather than a council and debunks the idea that they corresponded to the Athenian Areopagus.

Leppin's approach is refreshing, and he is certainly right to be suspicious of assuming at every opportunity parallels between Athenian and Argive institutions. Trying to make the Eighty correspond to the Athenian Areopagus is indeed most dubious, especially given the role attested in the new bronze tablets. He also makes a reasonable case for a decline in council authority over time. The Herodotus passage is crucial here. While it is possible, of course, that Herodotus, disinterested in constitutional niceties, simply left out of his story a referral of the issue to the assembly in which the *demos* approved the council's recommendations, the historian's account repeatedly specifies the council and council chamber as the locus of action. It would therefore seem more prudent to take Herodotus at his words than to presume that essential details have dropped out.[33] The barely visible role

---

[32] R. A. Tomlinson, *Argos and the Argolid* (Ithaca, 1972), makes similar points about officials seeming to have a relatively free hand at Argos, 198–9. But he puts this in the context of the overall "moderation" of the Argive democracy as compared with the Athenian one (a claim he underpins by speculating, with no supporting evidence, that Argos required a hoplite property census for its citizens).

[33] For what it is worth, this *logos* is one of those occasions on which Herodotus goes out of his way to make clear that he is reporting what was told to him (without necessarily believing in one version instead of another); 7.152. Compare what happens at Hdt. 9.5 when a matter is brought to the Athenian *boule*, where a councilor duly proposes to forward a motion to the assembly (though the proposer comes to regret it in this extreme case). The suggestion in W. W. How and J. Wells, *A Commentary on Herodotus* (Oxford, 1912), ad loc. that the aristocratic-seeming *boule* referred to here (149.1) might be the Eighty makes little sense: that body, whatever its precise role and duties,

of the council in later literary sources (though, admittedly, accounts are few) could indeed reflect a loss of its independent authority and an Argive transition to a more populist government over time.

Leppin goes too far, however, in suggesting an absence of *probouleusis* altogether at Argos. The epigraphic evidence alone strongly implies that decrees normally went from council to assembly. What better explanation is there for the prominent reference to the president (and sometimes the secretary) of the council in decrees of the assembly, starting with the Argos–Knossos–Tylissos agreement in the 450s and occurring regularly by the later fourth century?[34] Moreover, the council does, in fact, appear in literary sources after Herodotus in significant roles. In Thucydides' description of the oaths to be taken on the occasion of the treaty between Argos, Athens, Mantinea, and Elis in 420, the text lists the *boule* first among those swearing at Argos, just like the *boule* at Athens (for the Mantineans the *boule* is listed second; no *boule* is mentioned at all for the Eleans) (5.47.9). Leppin's arguments against the council being included under the rubric *archai* – thus denying a probouleutic role for the council in the events described at Thucydides 5.27–8 – do not convince. Athenian orators and Aristotle, for example, are quite clear in saying that *boule* members in a city could count as *archai*, even if the council can sometimes be separated out (along with the assembly, the courts, and magisterial boards) as a distinct organ of state.[35] More to the point for the Argos evidence, Thucydides also seems to consider council members to be *archai*: at 5.47.9 he lists the Mantinean oath-takers as "the demiourgoi and the council and the *other* magistrates (*hai allai archai*)" [my emphasis].

One might also question Leppin's thesis that over time the council lost power to the officials. The council's role may indeed have diminished from the early, seemingly independent authority attested by Herodotus, but if so it was the assembly rather than magistrates that more obviously gained in clout.[36] Leppin finds it illustrative of his thesis that twelve officials were granted plenipotentiary powers in 421 to negotiate alliances with other states. I would draw rather different conclusions from the same episode. As noted above, Thucydides' text makes it clear that these arrangements were unusual, and thus that the *demos* in the 420s normally involved itself

is only attested after Argos was fully democratized and thus seems a peculiar choice for an early elite-dominated council. As Leppin argues, it may not even have been a council.
[34] Also noted by Piérart, "Argos," 303. And one might note that not all Athenian decrees mention the council in the opening formula.
[35] E.g., Arist. *Pol.* 1317b30–1. See Hansen's discussion in *Athenian Democracy*, 226–7. Hornblower, *Commentary*, vol. III, 60, 62 for Argive officials at Thuc. 5.27–8.
[36] Ruzé also sees a strong assembly at Argos: *Délibération et pouvoir*, 277–88.

directly in foreign affairs rather than leaving them to the *archai*. And even in this exceptional case the scope of activity of the twelve is carefully limited: the *demos* apparently granted them authority to negotiate *defensive* alliances (*hoste te allelon epimachein*, 5.27.2), and pointedly excluded from their purview Athens and Sparta, the most important states; alliances with these two required the direct involvement of the people. And in truth the people (*toi plethei*) do take the reins when a diplomatic agreement with Sparta was initially negotiated the following year by ambassadors: ultimately they cancelled the nascent deal, and the Argives turned instead toward Athens, in part through a desire to associate with a fellow democracy (5.41.3, 5.44.1).

Furthermore, all officials at Argos operated under a watchful and sometimes suspicious demotic eye. A document from the early to mid fifth century (*IG* 4.554) makes clear that auditing by *euthuna* of outgoing officials was normal[37] and lawsuits could be expected, for a particular group of councilors, *artunai*, treasurers, and their legislative actions was decreed in this document to be exempt from auditing or legal charges. Argos also practiced ostracism, a device used to keep the most influential politicians of a community under the control of the democracy. More than one source attests the practice for Argos.[38] Moreover, an intriguing potsherd turned up in the 1985 excavations at the southern end of the agora area: the piece resembles *ostraka* at Athens, with a name ("Alkandros," otherwise unattested at Argos) written on it. Letter forms date the writing to the second quarter of the fifth century; the pot dates to the first quarter.[39] One named ostrakon cannot be taken as final proof of the existence of the practice but, given that there is no particular reason to doubt the literary testimony for ostracism at Argos, it is a valuable discovery.

Moreover, literary sources emphasize that the Argive *demos* could be quick to punish officials or other important leaders whom it thought had harmed or intended to harm the *polis*. Thucydides recounts (with obvious distaste) the treatment of the general Thrasyllus after he avoided a risky battle with the Spartans and made a truce in 419:[40]

[37] The *euthuna*, while not a uniquely democratic institution, was associated with democracy: Hdt. 3.80.6. *Pace* P. J. Rhodes, who downplays this association: "Nothing to Do with Democracy: Athenian Drama and the Polis," *JHS* 123 (2003), 104–19 at 116.

[38] Arist. *Pol.* 1302b18–19; scholion to Aristophanes, *Knights*, 855.

[39] A. Pariente, M. Piérart, and J. P. Thalmann, "Rapport sur les travaux de l'École française d'Athènes en 1985; Argos; the Agora," *BCH* 110 (1986), 764–5. The authors note that the first ostraka found at Athens were isolated ones (in 1870 and 1887); it was not until 1910 that large deposits of them turned up.

[40] See also Diod. Sic. 12.78.4–6. On the continuing effects of the *demos*'s reprimands, Thuc. 5.64.5–6.

[Thrasyllus and other Argives present] did so upon their own authority, not by order of the people; and Agis on his authority accepted their proposals... and granted the Argives a truce for four months, in which to fulfill their promises; after which he immediately led off the army... [2] The Lacedaemonians and allies followed their general out of respect for the law, but amongst themselves loudly blamed Agis for going away from such a strong position... [5] The Argives however blamed still more loudly the persons who had concluded the truce without consulting the people, themselves thinking that they had let escape with the Lacedaemonians an opportunity such as they should never see again... [6] On their return accordingly they began to stone Thrasyllus in the bed of the Charadrus, where they try all military cases before entering the city. Thrasyllus fled to the altar, and so saved his life; his property however they confiscated.[41]

As Thucydides presents it this might seem to be an emotional overreaction by the Argive *demos*, especially given the historian's description in the previous section of the dangerous (*deinon*) situation the Argive army had found itself in. But Thucydides, in presenting the Argive *demos*'s reaction in this way, may have had in mind his own bitter experience with the Athenian *demos* after his less than successful generalship a few years earlier, which resulted in his exile.[42] It is, in fact, plain that the Argive *demos* had reason to be concerned. Whether or not it was the right thing to do in military terms, Thrasyllus blatantly overstepped his authority in entering into these agreements with the Spartans. And given that within two years the Argives would suffer an oligarchic revolution at the hands

---

[41] 5.60, trans. Crawley, modified. καὶ οἱ μὲν ταῦτα εἰπόντες τῶν Ἀργείων ἀφ' ἑαυτῶν καὶ οὐ τοῦ πλήθους κελεύσαντος εἶπον: καὶ ὁ Ἆγις δεξάμενος τοὺς λόγους αὐτός, καὶ οὐ μετὰ τῶν πλεόνων οὐδὲ αὐτὸς βουλευσάμενος ἀλλ' ἢ ἑνὶ ἀνδρὶ κοινώσας τῶν ἐν τέλει ξυστρατευομένων, σπένδεται τέσσαρας μῆνας, ἐν οἷς ἔδει ἐπιτελέσαι αὐτοὺς τὰ ῥηθέντα. καὶ ἀπήγαγε τὸν στρατὸν εὐθύς, οὐδενὶ φράσας τῶν ἄλλων ξυμμάχων. οἱ δὲ Λακεδαιμόνιοι καὶ οἱ ξύμμαχοι εἵποντο μὲν ὡς ἡγεῖτο διὰ τὸν νόμον, ἐν αἰτίᾳ δ' εἶχον κατ' ἀλλήλους πολλῇ τὸν Ἆγιν, νομίζοντες ἐν καλῷ παρατυχὸν σφίσι ξυμβαλεῖν καὶ πανταχόθεν αὐτῶν ἀποκεκλῃμένων καὶ ὑπὸ ἱππέων καὶ πεζῶν οὐδὲν δράσαντες ἄξιον τῆς παρασκευῆς ἀπιέναι. στρατόπεδον γὰρ δὴ τοῦτο κάλλιστον Ἑλληνικὸν τῶν μέχρι τοῦδε ξυνῆλθεν: ὤφθη δὲ μάλιστα ἕως ἔτι ἦν ἁθρόον ἐν Νεμέᾳ, ἐν ᾧ Λακεδαιμόνιοί τε πανστρατιᾷ ἦσαν καὶ Ἀρκάδες καὶ Βοιωτοὶ καὶ Κορίνθιοι καὶ Σικυώνιοι καὶ Πελληνῆς καὶ Φλειάσιοι καὶ Μεγαρῆς, καὶ οὗτοι πάντες λογάδες ἀφ' ἑκάστων, ἀξιόμαχοι δοκοῦντες εἶναι οὐ τῇ Ἀργείων μόνον ξυμμαχίᾳ ἀλλὰ κἂν ἄλλῃ ἔτι προσγενομένῃ. τὸ μὲν οὖν στρατόπεδον οὕτως ἐν αἰτίᾳ ἔχοντες τὸν Ἆγιν ἀνεχώρουν τε καὶ διελύθησαν ἐπ' οἴκου ἕκαστοι, Ἀργεῖοι δὲ καὶ αὐτοὶ ἔτι ἐν πολλῷ πλέονι αἰτίᾳ εἶχον τοὺς σπεισαμένους ἄνευ τοῦ πλήθους, νομίζοντες κἀκεῖνοι μὴ ἂν σφίσι ποτὲ κάλλιον παρασχὸν Λακεδαιμονίους διαπεφευγέναι: πρός τε γὰρ τῇ σφετέρᾳ πόλει καὶ μετὰ πολλῶν καὶ ἀγαθῶν ξυμμάχων τὸν ἀγῶνα ἂν γίγνεσθαι. τόν τε Θράσυλον ἀναχωρήσαντες ἐν τῷ Χαράδρῳ, οὗπερ τὰς ἀπὸ στρατείας δίκας πρὶν ἐσιέναι κρίνουσιν, ἤρξαντο λεύειν. ὁ δὲ καταφυγὼν ἐπὶ τὸν βωμὸν περιγίγνεται: τὰ μέντοι χρήματα ἐδήμευσαν αὐτοῦ.

[42] See T. Rood, *Thucydides, Narrative and Explanation* (Oxford, 1998), 104, with Hornblower, *Commentary*, vol. III, 157, for the idea that Thucydides is here contrasting democratic regimes such as Argos and Athens with non-democracies.

of elite leaders who plotted their actions with the Spartans,[43] we cannot consider suspicions that the *demos* had about collusion or treachery by their generals to have been unreasonable. The statement about the Charadrus being the designated place where the Argives judge cases arising from military expeditions (*houper tas apo strateias dikas prin esienai krinousin*) shows that close scrutiny of generals by the people was no aberration.[44]

Less easy to fathom, but further illustrating both popular domination and suspicion of elites at Argos, is the famous *skutalismos* incident of the year 370 or 369. According to Diodorus, demagogues whipped up the masses (*to plethos*) by making accusations against certain wealthy, leading citizens, who then began to plot to overthrow the democracy. The conspirators were caught, resulting in further accusations, leading to thirty executions and seizures of property. From here things continued to spiral out of control – ultimately 1,200 were slaughtered, and before it was over the mob had turned on the demagogues who had fomented the trouble, until finally the *demos* recovered its senses.[45] Diodorus' account may exaggerate the madness of the episode or its murderous extent, but it cannot be dismissed. Aeneas Tacticus (11.7–10) describes a portion of the same or (perhaps more likely) a different occasion at Argos where paranoia by popular politicians about a planned oligarchic coup sets in.[46] In his account a popular leader (*tou demou prostates*) heard that the rich would bring in mercenaries to accomplish a revolution and so calls a meeting of the assembly to prepare military action in response. Years earlier, not long after the democratic counter-revolution of 417, vague suspicions resulted in hundreds of citizens being rounded up and turned over to Alcibiades and the Athenians for safekeeping; later, these were returned to the Argive people for execution.[47] And in 416 the Argives again suspected some of their number of planning treasonous action in conjunction with an (ultimately aborted) invasion by the Spartans; some were seized, others fled the city.[48] In these various cases the abiding interest of the Argive *demos* in keeping a close eye on leaders,

---

[43] Thuc. 5.76, 5.81–2, 5.84, 6.61.3; Diod. Sic. 12.75.7, 12.79.6–80.3; Plut. *Alc.* 15.2; Paus. 2.20.2; Arist. *Pol.* 1304a25–7; Aen. Tact. 17.2–4. On this revolution and its sources see E. David, "The Oligarchic Revolution in Argos, 417 B.C.," *AC* 55 (1986), 113–24.

[44] Also noted by Leppin, "Argos," 307.

[45] Diod. Sic. 15.57–8. (See also Isoc. 5.52; Dion. Hal. 7.66.5; Plut. *Mor.* 814B; Aelius Aristides, *Panathenaic Oration* 273.) Diod. Sic. 15.62.1 also notes the presence of 500 Argive refugees fighting for the Spartans soon thereafter.

[46] D. Whitehead, *Aineias the Tactician* (Oxford, 1990), 130; E. David, "Aeneas Tacticus, 11.7–10 and the Argive revolution of 370 B.C.," *AJPh* 107 (1986), 343–9; Ruzé, *Délibération et pouvoir*, 286 with n. 21.

[47] Thuc. 5.84.1, 6.61.3; Diod. Sic. 12.81.   [48] Thuc. 5.116.1.

elites, or anyone disaffected with the democratic constitution is taken to extremes of mistrust and violence.

Conclusion (Argos)

The power of the *demos* over its officials is one of the clear themes to emerge from both the literary and the documentary evidence for the Classical Argive democracy. Institutionally this is apparent from the attestation of *euthunai*, ostracism, and short (six-month) terms of office. In practice we find historical accounts of the *demos* acting jealously to safeguard its power and to chastise leaders who exceed their authority. Physical evidence of a politically active *demos* includes the public buildings of the mid fifth century, especially the assembly place and the recently discovered bronze tablets illustrating the myriad officials involved in public spending and accounting. A weakness in the bouleutic function in the Argive state has been posited, and a real decline in the council's importance as *demokratia* took root may be traceable. But *probouleusis* itself did operate at Argos, and the council continued to be active. Making more specific judgments about the council's relative weight in the constitution, given the limitations of our sources, is mostly a matter of guesswork.

Was Argos an especially volatile democracy? One might think so from the descriptions of the aftermath of Sepeia, the oligarchic revolution of 417, and the infamous *skutalismos*. But these few events took place in the course of a long stretch of time, comparable to that in which (supposedly stable) Athens underwent the Cleisthenic revolution, the violence around Ephialtes, the oligarchic coup of 411, and the Thirty Tyrants. As democracies go (or indeed most other forms of *polis* government), such turmoil does not appear extraordinary. These Argive events, and the actions of the Argive *demos* at other times, point therefore not so much to an unusually violent or chaotic system as to a vibrant democracy, one which mixed an active assembly protective of its power with other populist institutions and with elite leaders not always content to work solely within the existing constraints.

CORINTH

Ever since the overthrow of the Cypselid tyrants and for most of the Classical period Corinth appears to have been reliably oligarchic in government.[49]

---

[49] See summary of the evidence in J. B. Salmon, *Wealthy Corinth: A History of the City to 338 B.C.* (Oxford, 1997), 231–9. On deliberation at Corinth after the Bacchiad tyranny, see Ruzé, *Délibération et pouvoir*, 297–307.

Our sources are few, but all tend in the same direction. Plutarch describes fourth-century Corinth (of Dion's time) as being an oligarchic state in which the *demos* in assembly conducted little business (*Dion* 53.4). Consistent with this, no fifth-century author ever mentions a popular assembly taking place at Corinth. *Probouloi*, officials characteristic of oligarchies according to Aristotle, are attested in one source, together with a smallish council of eighty (or perhaps two hundred) men.[50] For the mid fourth century Diodorus writes of a prominent *gerousia* and *sunedrion*, which no doubt largely controlled affairs (16.65–6; but cf. Plut. *Tim.* 3.2, 5.2, and 7.2 for the *demos* and once, vaguely, even *demokratia*). Inscriptions contribute little before the Hellenistic period.[51]

Nevertheless, in spite of its long history of oligarchy Corinth did experience a significant episode of democratic rule. In around 392 Corinth underwent a violent political crisis that resulted in democracy and even isopolity and union with Argos, lasting until 386. Xenophon provides the fullest account, a few paragraphs in the course of his narrative of the Corinthian War, at *Hellenica* 4.4.1–8. According to him, "the most and best" of the Corinthians were tiring of the war against Sparta but were prevented from making peace by a combination of Corinth's allies in the war (Argives, Athenians, Boeotians) with those Corinthians who had received Persian bribes (see 3.5.1) and those who had been most responsible for the war. Fearing that the would-be peacemakers might turn the city over to the Spartans, the others concocted and executed a murderous plan, killing many of them in the agora and driving others of the "best men" (*beltistoi*) into retreat and potential exile. Upon invitation, some of those driven away returned to the city, only to find it governed (as Xenophon conveys from their perspective) "tyrannically" with metics holding greater influence than themselves and, even worse, with Corinthians having to share citizenship with Argos. (Whether we are to understand these metics to have been Argive newcomers or previously disenfranchised Corinthians is unclear.)[52] Some of these *beltistoi* found the situation intolerable and determined to free their city, to return Corinth to

---

[50] Nic. Dam. *FGH* 90 F60; Diod. Sic. 7.9.6. On *probouloi* generally, Arist. *Pol.* 1299b30–5. Ruzé proposes a 200-person council rather than the more usually supposed 80: *Délibération et pouvoir*, 297–302.

[51] Rhodes, *Decrees*, 72–3 and 476. The place where the Corinthian assembly met is also a matter of dispute. G. R. Stanton, "The Territorial Tribes of Korinth and Phleious," *ClAnt* 5 (1986), 139–53, argues that one can use tribal boundary markers to locate where the assembly met and deduce that citizens gathered in it according to tribal subdivisions (*trittues*).

[52] Griffith, "The Union of Corinth and Argos," 236–56, at 247; M. Whitby, "The Union of Corinth and Argos: A Reconsideration," *Historia* 33 (1984), 295–308, at 296, n. 3.

itself and bring *eunomia*. They thus attempted to betray their city to the Spartans.

Xenophon writes tendentiously here, clearly favoring the faction of the *beltistoi* over their scheming, murdering opponents; he apparently seeks to justify as good and noble the exiles' decision to help Sparta against their own city. One wonders how far the anti-war party had gone before the plot to kill or drive them off hatched.

Xenophon never actually states that democracy replaced oligarchy at Corinth after the *stasis*, or that political ideology had anything to do with the struggle, but that is the clear implication given the author's juxtaposition of *beltistoi* favoring *eunomia* on the one side and, on the other, revolutionaries who govern like tyrants, exalt metics, and seek to merge the *politeia* with that of (democratic) Argos.[53] Diodorus offers a much briefer picture of events, but his text – if it has been properly emended – shows that an explicit desire for democracy had motivated the revolutionaries from the start (14.86.1).[54] So also implies the Oxyrhynchus historian, who at 10.2–3 (Chambers) describes Corinthians who wished to bring political change to their city (*metastesai ta pra[gm]ata zetountes*) and were hostile to Sparta, much like the Athenians and Boeotians who hated Sparta because of the Laconian practice of supporting opposing political factions within their cities. Political ideology, therefore, seems to have played a major role in the upheaval at Corinth.[55]

Both Xenophon and Diodorus make clear that at some point after the initial revolution, probably two years later in 390, Argos took firmer

---

[53] His use of the words *oi pleistoi kai oi beltistoi* at 4.4.1 to describe those sick of the war with Sparta cannot be taken to indicate that the majority of Corinthians opposed the populist revolution to come: the *pleistoi* is dropped when it comes to describing who was targeted in the violence or forced to withdraw. Indeed, this expression should probably be taken as a hendiadys born of Xenophon's bias – "the most and the best men" really means "most of the best men."

[54] This emendation – altering the nonsensical *en de tei Korintho tines ton epithumiai kratounton sustraphentes ktl.* in the text to the more reasonable *en de tei Korintho tines ton demokratias epithumounton sustraphentes* – has been challenged by Ruzé, *Délibération et pouvoir*, 307–9, among others. While Ruzé does not doubt that internal politics were involved in this episode, she sees no reason to bring in the word *demokratia* here and considers J. B. Salmon's alternative emendation (*en de tei Korintho tines ton kratounton epi thusia sustraphentes*, *Wealthy Corinth*, 355–7) to be a better solution. Her objection is reasonable, and though it seems to me that the content of the Xenophon and *Hellenica Oxyrhynchia* passages are in fact suggestive of democratic motivation, it is perhaps adventurous to insert the word here. Other emendations seem possible as well: for example, *en de tei Korintho tines ton kratous epithumounton sustraphentes, ktl.*

[55] *Contra* S. Perlman in "The Causes and Outbreak of the Corinthian War," *CQ* (1964), 64–81, and J. Buckler in "A Note on Diodorus 14.86.1," *CPh* 94 (1999), 210–14. Perlman sees fear of Sparta as the only motivator for the Corinthian alliance with Argos. (Cf. Ruzé, *Délibération et pouvoir*, 288.) Buckler may well be right to doubt the emendation of the text of Diod. Sic. 14.86.1 (see previous note), but his denial of democratic/oligarchic conflict in Corinth before the Argive alliance and takeover is less convincing.

control of Corinth, marching in a large army and effectively uniting the two polities. This union lasted until the terms of the King's Peace were enforced in 386.[56]

Scholars have argued vigorously over the chronology of the union with democratic Argos, the factions involved, and, to a lesser degree, about the nature of the resulting government.[57] G. T. Griffith's influential article proposed a two-stage process, whereby an agreement of *isopoliteia* linked Corinth and Argos soon after the democratic faction won out in Corinth, allowing citizens of each state to exercise their civic rights when present in the other, but the two states retained their own sovereignty. The real union of the two states, in which Corinth was subsumed into the Argive territory, was delayed until perhaps 389, and probably came about because of the desire of the Corinthian democrats for more support in the war against Sparta on the one hand and the expansionist desires of Argos on the other. Most scholars have accepted this basic scheme for understanding the union, though contradictions in Xenophon's account make matters uncertain and invite argument. For example, does *Hellenica* 4.4.6 describe full union between the two states already in 392, or merely movement and further planning in that direction? Probably the latter is correct, given the notices elsewhere in Xenophon and in other authors implying the continued existence of a sovereign Corinthian state between 392 and 390, though one cannot be sure.[58]

The institutions at work in Corinth during this period of democracy cannot be pinned down. We may presume from the unhappy reaction of Xenophon's *beltistoi* to the power of "metics" that large numbers of ordinary Corinthians – or perhaps large numbers of Argive soldiers in concert with friendly Corinthians – were able to outvote what was left of the conservative faction in the city in an enlarged and newly important assembly. There is no indication that peculiarly Argive institutions were imported or Corinthian ones disbanded, and so it is perhaps easiest to believe that existing institutions (such as the *boule* and a more active assembly) continued on but were employed in a more democratic fashion.

---

[56] Xen. *Hell.* 4.8.34, 5.1.34, 5.1.36; Diod. Sic. 14.91–2.

[57] Griffith, "The Union of Corinth and Argos"; D. Kagan, "Corinthian Politics and the Revolution of 392 B.C.," *Historia* 11 (1962), 447–57; Perlman, "Corinthian War"; Tomlinson, *Argos and the Argolid*, 129–38; C. D. Hamilton, "The Politics of Revolution in Corinth, 395–386 B.C.," *Historia* 21 (1972) 21–37 (= ch. 9 in *Sparta's Bitter Victories* [Ithaca, 1979], 260–78); C. Tuplin, "The Date of the Union of Corinth and Argos," *CQ* 32 (1982), 75–83; Whitby "Union of Corinth and Argos"; Ruzé, *Délibération et pouvoir*, 307–10; R. Legon in *Inventory*, 467.

[58] Whitby convincingly defends Griffith's basic hypothesis against the textual and chronological objections of Tuplin (see previous note).

One doubts, however, that *probouloi* played any prominent role. That the closeness of relations with Argos was a live issue among the Corinthians is signaled by a report in Xenophon that the Athenian Iphicrates at one point actually killed some Corinthians who especially favored Argos (*tinas ton argolizonton*) before the Argives took firmer control of the city themselves.[59] The new government once in place was loathe to give up its authority, even after the King's Peace had been made: Xenophon tells us at 5.1.34–6 that the Corinthians refused to dismiss the Argive garrison in the city. They ultimately caved in only under direct threat of renewed war from Sparta. At this point, and once the perpetrators of the *stasis* of the 390s left the city and the exiles returned, Corinth returned to its old identity and renewed its traditional alliance with Sparta.

The significance of Corinth's brief episode of democracy lies less in the nature of its popular government (about which we know so little) than how it came to be. It is a remarkable example of how factional politics, when combined with outside support and/or pressure, could result in a major reversal of the traditional political alignment of a city-state. Corinth had for so much of its history been both an ally of Sparta and oligarchically governed: when the first element was removed (in part thanks to money coming from Persia) the second soon followed, thanks to a combination of internal political maneuvering[60] and the reliance over a period of years on assistance from a coalition of mostly democratic states. The alignment of the city switched back only when Sparta, in effect, won the war. We see therefore that even in the Peloponnese, oligarchic Sparta's region of greatest influence, and among Sparta's oldest friends, *demokratia* could win through.

ACHAEA

In the early history of Achaea there is some evidence of political progressiveness. As argued in *The First Democracies*, one could accept Polybius' general statement (2.41.5–6) that the Achaeans had changed their constitution to *demokratia* early in their history after the fall of their dynasty of kings (dates unknown). Combined with some evidence from Achaean colonies in southern Italy, a fair case for early Achaean democracy

---

[59] Xen. *Hell.* 4.8.34. This seems to have been part of an attempt by Iphicrates to take control of the city on Athens' behalf, though Athens itself did not support the effort: Diod. Sic. 14.91–2.

[60] See the pieces by Kagan and Hamilton in n. 57 above for possible reconstructions of the internal factions at Corinth prior to the *stasis*.

(presumably of a moderate, agricultural variety) can be made.[61] However, the sources are mostly late, and there is no corroborating evidence, as direct testimony about Achaean politics is very hard to come by for the Archaic or indeed the early Classical period. In fact, scholars continue to dispute whether one can speak of a unified Archaic Achaea at all, with recent views tending to the negative.[62]

For the Classical period evidence remains scarce. Polybius' passage about Achaean democratization goes on to claim that, despite various troubles, Achaea attempted to keep its *koinon politeuma* democratic through to the time of Alexander and Philip (2.41.6). This might suggest that democracy was the norm for most of the fifth and fourth centuries, but a problem arises: unless one wishes to put great weight on the word "attempted" (*epeironto*), the presence of a dominating Achaean oligarchy from perhaps 417 to 366 directly contradicts Polybius' statement. We know Achaea was oligarchic by 366: in that year Epaminondas led the Thebans in an invasion of Achaea with the goal of making the cities their allies. Initial successes led to negotiations with aristocratic leaders (*beltistoi*) from the Achaean cities. The Achaeans agreed to support the Thebans, who in return did not exile anyone or make changes in what must have been oligarchic *polis* constitutions. But complaints soon arose from populist opponents of the Achaean aristocrats and from the (democratic) Arcadian allies, prompting the Theban assembly to reverse Epaminondas' policy: they helped local popular groups drive out the aristocrats and set up *demokratiai*. This situation did not last, however, as the aristocratic exiles banded together and launched a successful military campaign, one by one capturing the cities and bringing about the elites' restoration, after which Achaea pursued a strongly pro-Spartan foreign policy.[63] The oligarchy thus attested for 366 may have had its start in 417, for according to Thucydides (5.82.1) in that year the Spartans – who had just effected an oligarchic coup to topple the *demokratia* in Argos – "settled Achaean affairs, which previously had not been favorable" (*ta en Achaiai ouk epitedeios proteron echonta kathistanto*), strongly implying the establishment of a pro-Spartan oligarchy.[64] Thus Polybius' general statement about a continuous reign of democracy in Achaea loses much of its credibility, certainly as regards the late fifth and early fourth centuries.

---

[61] Robinson, *First Democracies*, 73–8.

[62] C. Morgan, *Early Greek States beyond the Polis* (London, 2003), 196–202; C. Morgan and J. Hall in *Inventory*, 472–8.

[63] Xen. *Hell.* 7.1.41–3; Diod. Sic. 15.75.2; *FGH* 70 F84. J. Buckler, *The Theban Hegemony, 371–362 BC* (Cambridge, MA, 1980), 185–93. See also the subsection on Thebes and Boeotia in this chapter. Pellene may have briefly returned to democracy in the next year or so: Xen. *Hell.* 7.2.11–14, 7.4.17–18.

[64] See Gomme, Andrewes, and Dover, *HCT* and Hornblower, *Commentary*, vol. III, ad loc.

Only for the later fourth century does he receive a hint of corroboration: Pseudo-Demosthenes 17.10, which states outright that Achaea generally and Pellene specifically were democratically governed (*edemokratounto*), probably originates in Athens in the 330s. The text implies either that the government of Achaea underwent a democratic change again at some point after 366, or that the author used the term loosely, seeking to exaggerate what was in fact a contrast between constitutional government (whether democratic or oligarchic) with Macedonian-imposed tyranny.[65]

But even if one dismisses fourth-century democracy in Achaea as too brief (366) or too uncertain (330s), one must acknowledge the strong possibility that democracy did hold sway earlier in the fifth century. After all, Thucydides' statement implying a change to oligarchy in Achaea after 417 implies just as strongly that a more populist government preceded it. We should also note further statements of Polybius on the ancestry of Achaean democracy in which he notes the role of Achaea in settling the constitutional crises among Achaean colonials in southern Italy during the Pythagorean upheavals of (perhaps) the mid-to-late fifth century.[66] Polybius claims that the admirable qualities of the democratic Achaean system helped to resolve the troubles there and even led to that governing system being copied. Dating these events with any precision is impossible, but most scholars would put them in the range of 454 to 420.[67]

Between Polybius and Thucydides, then, one can surmise that Achaea employed a democratic order of one kind or another before the Spartan intervention of 417. From Polybius' discussions one assumes that this applied to league arrangements binding the various Achaean cities together, not to internal constitutions of the cities themselves (though Thuc. 5.82.1 could be interpreted either way). However, corroborating evidence for such a fifth-century league – of whatever political stripe – from other sources is very hard to come by. Only by the first third of the fourth century do implications of dual citizenship and the issuing of joint coinage make clear the existence of a league; the necessity of accepting that there had been an earlier, fifth-century confederacy has therefore been vigorously challenged.[68] The constitutional history of individual Achaean cities cannot help with

---

[65] H. Beck treats Achaea in the fourth century as an oligarchic league of cities: *Polis und Koinon* (Stuttgart, 1997), 63–6. J. A. O. Larsen is willing to contemplate a moderately democratic league even much later; *Greek Federal States: Their Institutions and History* (Oxford, 1968), 232.

[66] 2.38.6–39.8, with Strabo 8.7.1. Gehrke, *Stasis*, 13–15, with caution in n. 2.

[67] See the chronological discussions in F. W. Walbank, *A Historical Commentary on Polybius*, vol. 1 (Oxford, 1957), 222–6.

[68] C. Morgan and J. Hall in *Inventory*, 474–7, carefully distinguish assertions of a common Achaean ethnicity in the fifth century (plentiful) from assertions that must imply an overarching political

this conundrum, as almost nothing is known of them before the fourth century. We are left, then, with the probability that Achaea participated in democracy in some fashion in the fifth century (prior to 417) based on the vague testimony of Thucydides and Polybius, but whether this participation came in the form of an early Achaean confederacy or the constitutions of individual cities cannot be ascertained.

As a result, little can be said regarding the nature of the Achaean democracy, either that of the fifth century or the briefer interlude(s) in the fourth (one in 366, gained with the help of Theban arms, and possibly one in the 330s). Of the fourth-century democracies the main thing to note is that, short-lived as they were, they involved the individual cities of Achaea, not (or not just) the league structure. Institutionally, the fourth-century oligarchic league featured a college of *damiourgoi* and a council, as attested by an inscription from the end of the century. These bodies may well have been held over from earlier democratic days but, if so, will have no doubt possessed lessened authority under the *demokratia* in the face of a popular assembly of some kind.[69] As for Polybius' glowing description of early Achaean democracy, it is very generalized, and thus not especially helpful in divining the government's nature. The only specific principles he names in praising Achaea's democracy are *isegoria* and *parresia* (2.38.6, 2.38.10);[70] these certainly suit democracy, and, if they reflect historical reality, might be taken to suggest a truly open environment for political debate with no bar on popular participation in assemblies and courts.

ELIS

On the basis of inscriptions found at Olympia which date at the latest to the last quarter of the sixth century or the first quarter of the fifth, I argued in *The First Democracies* that Elis was practicing popular government by around the turn of the century, years before the state's synoecism of 471.[71]

---

structure at that time (negligible). Cf. Beck, *Polis und Koinon*, 62–3; Larsen, *Greek Federal States*, 80–9.

[69] *SEG* 14.375. Larsen, *Greek Federal States*, 86–8.

[70] It should be noted that later in the same discussion Polybius also claims *pistis* and *kalok'agathia* as having served Achaea well in the years after 371: hardly typical democratic traits, and ones named for a time when Achaea was certainly oligarchic; 2.39.10.

[71] Robinson, *First Democracies*, 108–11. For the synoecism, Strabo 8.3.2; Diod. Sic. 11.54.1. Neither ancient source refers to democratization at that time, though the consolidation has been taken by scholars as a likely time for the fixing of the democratic government in Elis: *RE* s.v. Elis (vol. v, 1905), 2392–3; G. Busolt and H. Swoboda, *Griechische Staatskunde*, vol. I, 47–8; Gehrke, *Stasis*, 365–7. More recently, J. Roy, "The Synoikism of Elis," in T. H. Nielsen, ed., *Even More Studies in the Ancient Greek Polis* (Stuttgart, 2002), 249–64, thoroughly investigates all aspects of the synoecism

The early inscriptions are full of populist terms and institutions and repeatedly highlight the decisive role played by the *damos*: broad categories of laws could not be changed or punishments rescinded without its approval, or without the approval of the *damos plethuon* and the *awlaneos*[72] (fully assembled?) Council of 500. The lack of confirming literary testimony for this early period makes certainty impossible, but the provisions bear the hallmarks of *demokratia*.[73] Indeed, the echoes of terms often associated only with democratic Athens (*demos plethuon*, a Council of 500) have led scholars to posit direct Athenian influence on Elis by means of Themistocles' presence in the Peloponnese in the late 470s. However, the date of the inscriptions and lack of evidence for a Themistoclean program of spreading democracy work strongly against this hypothesis.[74]

That Elis was (still) democratically governed later in the fifth and early in the fourth centuries is implied, though not directly stated, in literary sources. Thucydides describes the negotiations leading up to the treaty made between Argos, Mantinea, Elis, and Athens in 420, in which the first three are frequently grouped together, for Elis and Mantinea were quick to join Argos in the alternative Peloponnesian alliance that Corinth was encouraging at the time as a ploy against Sparta. Democracy is mentioned twice as a reason to join or not join the Argive alliance: Mantinea is said to have signed on in part because of having a democratic government like that of Argos (5.29.1), whereas we are told that then-oligarchic Megara and Boeotia chose *not* to join the alliance because of Argos's *demokratia* (5.31.6). Elis's governmental form is never mentioned, but the implication is that it posed no compatibility problems constitutionally with the other allies.[75] In addition, the description of the eventual treaty with Athens is suggestive: the Elean officials who swore to the alliance include the Six

and concludes, among other things, that there was no discernible connection between the synoecism and constitutional change at Elis.

[72] *W* representing *digamma*.

[73] Arist. *Pol.* 1306a12–19 does refer to a former oligarchic government at Elis that was overthrown thanks to being too narrow. We can perhaps assume that it was replaced with a *demokratia*. The event is undated, however.

[74] Argued in Robinson, *First Democracies*, 108–11, following the lead of J. L. O'Neil, "The Exile of Themistokles and Democracy in the Peloponnese," *CQ* 31 (1981), 335–46, *contra* W. G. Forrest, "Themistokles and Argos," *CQ* n.s. 10 (1960), 221–41 at 221–9. The inscriptions are collected in W. Dittenberger and K. Purgold, eds., *Inschriften von Olympia* (*IvO*) (Berlin, 1896), nos. 3, 7, 9, 11, and reexamined with up-to-date discussions in S. Minon, *Les inscriptions éléennes dialectales*, vol. 1 (Geneva, 2007), nos. 4, 10, 12, 13.

[75] Thucydides implies that Elis joined the Argive alliance because of Elis's ongoing feud with Sparta over Lepreum: he raises this dispute when Elis joined with Argos, and he returns to it repeatedly in the narrative (5.31.1–5, 5.49.1–5, 5.62.1). Having such a dispute with Sparta neither supports nor undermines the notion of Elean democracy at the time.

Hundred. This would appear to represent an enlarging of the old Council of 500 known from one of the early inscriptions.[76] Such an increase implies more democracy rather than less. The other groups mentioned in the treaty (*demiourgoi, thesmophulakes*) are constitutionally indeterminate.

Xenophon's *Hellenica* also testifies in uncertain terms to a continuing Elean democracy, at 3.2.21–31. A few years after the end of the Peloponnesian War, Sparta, angry about past Elean transgressions (including the brief alliance with Argos, Mantinea, and Athens), made war on the state.[77] In the second year of the war factional violence ensued within Elis itself when certain men, hoping to turn the city over to Spartans by themselves, began a massacre and made a point of trying to kill Thrasydaeus, the popular leader (*prostates tou demou*). The wrong man was slain however, and when the *demos* learned that Thrasydaeus still lived, they rallied around him and he led them into a victorious battle against the killers.[78] Meanwhile the Spartan and allied forces plundered the country all around. The next year Thrasydaeus opened negotiations with the Spartans: after the Eleans made a number of concessions (though they managed to retain control of Olympia), the Spartans came to terms with them and the two sides agreed to peace and renewed alliance. Importantly, no change in the government of Elis is reported. This fact, plus the triumph of the *demos* and their leader Thrasydaeus in the plot against them, strongly implies that democracy continued at Elis all through this period.[79]

J. L. O'Neil agrees that democracy continued at Elis after the war but does not think it lasted long.[80] Following older scholars, he maintains that the only way contingents from towns liberated from Elean control by the

---

[76] *IvO* 7 = Minon, *Inscriptions*, no. 10.

[77] Cf. Diod. Sic. 14.17.4–12 and 14.34.1; Paus. 3.8.3–5. For other, strategic reasons for the Spartan aggression against Elis, see C. Falkner, "Sparta and the Elean War, ca 401/400 B.C.: Revenge or Imperialism?," *Phoenix* 50 (1996), 17–25, with elaboration and support from J. Roy, "Spartan Aims in the Spartan–Elean War of *c.* 400: Further Thoughts," *Electronic Antiquity* 3.6 (1997). On the date of the war (most probably 401–399/8), see R. K. Unz, "The Chronology of the Elean War," *GRBS* 27 (1986), 29–42. Generally, Gehrke, *Stasis*, 53–4.

[78] See also Paus. 3.8.4, 5.4.8, 7.10.2, where the leader of the attackers/betrayers is identified as Xenias, head of a faction of wealthy Eleans and a man with ties of *xenia* and *proxenia* to Sparta. It is, of course, entirely possible that the Spartans encouraged this coup attempt from the start. See the discussion in Roy, "Spartan Aims."

[79] Compare Xenophon's use of similar terms describing internal politics in Mantinea, a democracy at the time, at 5.2.3–7. On Thrasydaeus as a supporter of Athenian democrats in 404/3, see Plut. *Mor.* 835r.

Roy, "Spartan Aims," does not doubt this, considering that "democracy was solidly rooted among Elean citizens." He further theorizes that Sparta may have hoped to lessen democracy's influence by taking control of Elis's ports and navy.

[80] *The Origins and Development of Ancient Greek Democracy* (Lanham, MD, 1995), 79–81.

Spartans would be found as part of Elean contingents just a few years later in 394 (Xen. *Hell.* 4.2.16) was if an oligarchic party gained control of the state and convinced the Spartans to return the territories to Elean control. However, no evidence exists for any such change in the Elean government; the appearance of troops from formerly dependent territories fighting alongside the Eleans in cooperation with ally Sparta means nothing constitutionally.

Later in the fourth century, we learn from Xenophon, Elis once again experienced internal dissension in the context of a foreign war (*Hell.* 7.4.12–16). In 365 while fighting a war with the Arcadians two parties competed for control internally: one was attempting to "lead the city to democracy" (*eis demokratian egon ten polin*), the other "to oligarchy" (*eis oligarchian*). Xenophon's phrasing raises the question of what their government was at the moment – a strict reading would seem to require something other than either *demokratia* or *oligarchia* (perhaps a mixture like an Aristotelian *politeia*?). However, such a reading is probably oversubtle. The economical expression of Xenophon is surely designed to relate the sympathies and programs of the two factions, nothing more. The government going into the conflict could have been either democratic or oligarchic, perhaps more likely democratic given what we know of Elis's history to this point.[81] This time, however, democracy did not survive the internal and external struggles: the populist faction, encouraged by the support of the (democratic) Arcadians, failed in an attempt to seize control of the city outright, were exiled, and later soundly defeated by their opponents (Xen. *Hell.* 7.4.16, 7.4.26). One can only assume that an oligarchy now governed Elis, if it had not before.[82]

More upheavals came in the following decades. At some point democracy returned, for Demosthenes states in a speech from 343 that the *demos* had recently been overthrown in Elis – possibly thanks to bribes from Philip of Macedon (19.294; Paus. 4.28.4–5, 5.4.9). This *stasis* may have resulted in a civil war mentioned in Diodorus at 14.63.4, in which exiled Eleans hired mercenaries to help in their fight. An inscription from the middle of the century describes terms relating to the restoration of exiles (Buck 65 = Minon, *Inscriptions*, no. 30). This may belong to the war reported in Diodorus, or perhaps to another recall of exiles that took place

---

[81] I.e., Elis's long tradition of democracy, plus the fact that Elis had been working closely with democratic Argos and Arcadia in opposing Sparta in the recent past (e.g., Diod. Sic. 15.68). J. Roy in *Inventory*, 497, considers that Elis was democratic through to 365.

[82] As it is typically restored, *IG* 2² 112 (= Rhodes and Osborne 41) would seem to confirm the absence of an Elean democracy in 362/1.

in 335 (Arrian, *Anab.* 1.10.1).[83] At some point in this general period (mid fourth century) we should probably place the overthrow of a narrow Elean oligarchy attested by Aristotle (*Pol.* 1306a12–16). Such timing would match with the reported activities of Phormio of Elis, a student of Plato's, who won renown for dismantling a narrow oligarchy at Elis and establishing a new constitution (Plut. *Mor.* 805D, 1126C).

A number of the institutions of the Elean democracy are known to us, at least in general terms. Early inscriptions show the central importance of the *demos* in assembly, as noted above. A Council of 500 had apparently grown to 600 members by the last quarter of the fifth century: this body swore to the treaty with Athens, Argos, and Mantinea in 420, just as a *boule* did for each of the other states (Thuc. 5.47.9). Various officials are attested for Elis, including the *thesmophulakes* who administered the treaty oaths of 420 and the *demiourgoi* who both administer and swear to them and are also attested epigraphically. Some inscriptions refer to *hellanodikai*, the Olympic judges, and an early one notes *basilaes*.[84] An inscription from the early fourth century also mentions the names of several *prostatai*, whose function is unclear.[85] At least some officials are subject to regular scrutiny (*en mastraai*) and can be fined for inappropriate action or inaction.[86]

Fourth-century inscriptions from the Pisatans and Triphylians in Elis show remarkable village autonomy in making law for the local community and even in fashioning outside agreements.[87] Indeed, Robin Osborne argues that such inscriptions and the archaeology of Classical Elis suggest vigorous independent activity in the villages of Elis and thus a relatively loose overall political organization in the state. The land was rich and well populated and, while not always peaceful internally, generally showed egalitarian rather than domineering relations between city and countryside, especially as compared with other democratic communities such as Athens and especially Thasos.[88]

Democracy in Classical Elis comes across in our sources as having a long history but also eventually becoming unstable, in large part thanks

[83] J. Roy in *Inventory*, 497, associates the exiles' recall with a democratic/oligarchic reconciliation *c.* 350. Minon will only confidently put the date somewhere between 370/365 and *c.* 324.

[84] *IvO* 2 = Minon, *Inscriptions*, no. 20.   [85] *SEG* 15.241 = Minon, *Inscriptions*, no. 27.

[86] *IvO* 2 (= Minon, *Inscriptions*, nos. 20), as noted by Rhodes, *Decrees*, 93–5, 529.

[87] *IvO* 36, *SEG* 29.405 (though this last requires much restoration) Cf. *IvO* 11, 16 (= Minon, *Inscriptions*, nos. 12, 22).

[88] *Classical Landscape with Figures: The Ancient Greek City and Its Countryside* (New York, 1987), 123–32. Caution is in order, however, in the use of a Polybian passage (4.73–4) that Osborne cites in support of these conclusions as it probably refers to a much later period in Elis's history.

to external pressures. In the fifth century popular government seems to have persisted and continued to develop straight through to the end of the century, surviving even defeat in war by Sparta. But as the fourth century progressed, internal factions agitating for and against *demokratia* made themselves ever more apparent, resulting in occasional periods of oligarchic rule from the mid-360s on down, if not before. Elis's proximity to politically conservative Sparta often required alliance with it, and sometimes encouraged internal dissent against the popular order but for most of the period did not prevent democracy itself from continuing.

LEUCAS

The island *polis* of Leucas transitioned to democracy at some point in the late Archaic or the Classical era, though neither the date nor the duration of the democratic government can be pinned down. The only evidence comes from Aristotle, *Politics* 1266b21–4, where, in the context of a discussion of laws regulating property and their effects on the state, the philosopher notes that at Leucas when laws protecting the old, presumably colonial land allotments (*palaious klerous*) were removed, the constitution became too populist (*lian demotiken*) since the established property qualifications for office no longer applied. The context of the overall discussion is historical, at times distantly so: Solon's laws are mentioned at one point, as illustration of the idea that even those of old (*ton palai*) understood the political significance of leveling out property ownership. But Plato's *Laws* and especially Phaleas of Chalcedon (date uncertain, perhaps late fifth or early fourth century) also feature in the discussion. It would seem that Aristotle here, as often in the *Politics*, simply pulls examples from wherever he can to make his points without worrying much about chronology. A fifth-century date might make the best guess as to when this constitutional change occurred, but a late Archaic or early fourth-century event could equally be referred to; no corroborating evidence from other sources exists to refine the date.[89]

Little can be said about the nature of the Leucadian democracy. In fact, given that the adjective *demotikos* translates more properly as "populist" than "democratic" (*demokratikos* means "democratic"), it is possible that Aristotle did not intend to signal a Leucadian *demokratia*. However, given the rest of Aristotle's statement – that the constitution was made too

---

[89] H.-J. Gehrke and E. Wirbelauer in *Inventory*, 364–6; Gehrke, *Stasis*, 101; T. J. Saunders, *Aristotle: Politics Books I and II* (Oxford, 1995), 135; W. Nestle, "Phaleas," *RE* 38 (1938), 1658–9.

demotikos because of the absence of the old property qualifications – and the constitutional importance Aristotle attaches to the issue of who gets to participate in the running of the state,[90] there can be little doubt that he does in fact mean that Leucas remains or, more probably, becomes a *demokratia* as a result of the repeal of the old property law.[91] What is not clear is how exactly the breaking up of the old estates led to the end of *timema* for office-holding. The implication is that the requirement was given up altogether, which would have been very *demotikos* indeed (and thus perhaps makes the best sense of the passage). It is possible, however, that once the traditional qualifications based on the old *kleroi* became untenable, new, lower ones were created.

MANTINEA AND THE ARCADIANS

The Arcadians occupied numerous settlements in a mountainous portion of the central Peloponnese. Written sources mention a total of seventy settlements, thirty-nine of which are identifiable as *poleis*.[92] While the Arcadians shared a unique dialect, a mythical founder, and on occasion a common coinage, for most of the Classical period individual Arcadian *poleis* seem to have remained autonomous.[93] Only after the Theban Epaminondas' crushing defeat of Sparta at Leuctra in 371 and his subsequent sponsorship of a strong Arcadia with a new common city of Megalopolis did the region unite politically by means of a democratic federal league.

But the earliest democracy in Arcadia appeared long before, in Mantinea, one of the more influential cities in the region. Mantinea developed a remarkable form of popular government by the last quarter of the fifth century, and perhaps much earlier. Thucydides provides us with a *terminus ante quem* when he states at 5.29.1 that one of the reasons why the Mantineans decided to join the new Argive alliance in 420 was that the Argives,

---

[90] E.g., *Pol.* 1291b21–34, 1317a40–b24. The last passage also shows how Aristotle will sometimes use *demotikos* as almost a synonym for *demokratikos*.

[91] Note the similar case in archaic Ambracia, where property qualifications for office also erode, resulting in *demokratia*: 1303a22–4, 1304a31–3, and 1311a39–b1; Robinson, *First Democracies*, 80–2.

[92] T. H. Nielsen in *Inventory*, 506–35.

[93] *Pace* W. P. Wallace, "Kleomenes, Marathon, the Helots, and Arkadia," *JHS* 74 (1954), 32–5. Wallace (among others) argues that the coins with the legend *ARKADIKON* (or abbreviations) from early in the fifth century, when combined with Herodotus 6.74–5 and 9.35 (on troubles caused for Sparta by Arcadians working together against them), suggest to the author that the Arcadians formed a political league around this time. Even if we accept this rather shaky evidence, the nature of the league is impossible to know, and at least one major Arcadian city was not part of it – Mantinea – for Herodotus excludes it at 9.35, and the city continued to produce its own coinage during this time. For a detailed, highly skeptical discussion of a possible fifth-century league, see T. H. Nielsen, *Arkadia and Its Poleis in the Archaic and Classical Periods* (Göttingen, 2002), 121–41.

like themselves, practiced democracy (*demokratoumenen hosper kai autoi*).[94] But how long the Mantineans had done so before the late 420s is unknown. Two dates advanced by scholars as possible starting points are *c.* 471, and *c.* 425. The latter date approximates the era of the legislation of Nicodorus, an athlete turned lawgiver, who, with the help of Diagoras of Melos, did great service to Mantinea (according to Aelian, *Varia historia* 2.23). The problem here is that neither Aelian nor any other source suggests that Nicodorus' laws had anything to do with democracy; furthermore, the chronology of the activities of Nicodorus (and Diagoras) is most uncertain.[95]

The other date sometimes advanced is 471, assumed to be the time of Mantinea's incorporation (*sunoikismos*). Here is an occasion of major change in the state in which Argos – probably democratic itself by this time – played a large role, and during which time Themistocles probably lived at Argos. Putting these points together, it is not hard to imagine that Mantinean *demokratia* began at this time.[96] However, chronological uncertainty about when the synoecism took place – Strabo (8.3.2) suggests the years soon after the Persian Wars (*c.* 471?) for Elis but no date for Mantinea – and regarding Themistocles' movements, makes the potential coincidence in timing impossible to be sure of. Also, there is no hint of testimony anywhere that Themistocles had a program of promoting democracies.[97] Hence, it is speculative at best to assume a Themistocles-inspired democratic movement in Arcadia, especially one coinciding with a synoecism in 471.[98]

A third possibility is that Mantinea first turned to popular government during the sixth century, a time when the earliest democracies were emerging in Greece. Aristotle, at *Politics* 1318b6–27, prominently raises a previous Mantinean democracy as an example of what he calls the oldest (and best) kind of democracy, that in which the *demos* is agricultural (*georgikos*) and spends more time at work in the fields than worrying about politics and

---

[94] Hornblower, *Commentary*, vol. III, 66–7.

[95] Dates for Nicodorus are in fact unknown. It is his alleged amorous relationship with Diagoras of Melos that suggests a date at some point in the fifth century, but whether early (Diagoras fl. 482 or 468 according to late chronographers) or late (exiled in 415 according to scholia to Aristophanes) is not well established. For rather confident assessments favoring a late date, see O'Neil, "Exile of Themistokles," 335–46, esp. 336–7, relying on L. Woodbury, "The Date and Atheism of Diagoras of Melos," *Phoenix* 19 (1965), 178–211.

[96] A. Andrewes, "Sparta and Arcadia in the Early 5th Century," *Phoenix* 56 (1952), 1–5, followed by Forrest, "Themistokles and Argos," 221–41.

[97] Sparta will have had plenty of other reasons for directing its animus toward him for his various post-Persian Wars activities without having to imagine that he also championed a populist movement in the Peloponnese (*pace* Andrewes, "Sparta and Arcadia," 3).

[98] For a similar skepticism regarding Themistocles and 471, argued in full detail, see O'Neil, "Exile of Themistokles," 335–46.

government. (Aelian, it might be noted, also associates Mantinea with states famous for early legal reforms, including Solonian Athens: *VH* 2.22.) If Aristotle's connection of Mantinea to the oldest forms of *demokratia* was not fortuitous, the mid sixth century would offer an appropriate context for the Mantinean system's beginnings.[99]

In any case, the fact remains that we do not have a firm idea of when the Mantinean democracy began, other than prior to 421. As for the nature of this *demokratia*, let us begin with a closer look at Aristotle's discussion in the *Politics*. The philosopher raises the case of Mantinea to illustrate how the oldest and best kind of *demokratia*, one with an agricultural *demos* too busy working on the land to spend much time on politics, might function with respect to offices.

And also, if [the people] have any ambition, to have control over electing magistrates and calling them to account makes up for the lack of office, since in some democracies even if the people have no part in electing the magistrates but these are elected by a special committee selected in turn out of the whole number, as at Mantinea, yet if they have the power of deliberating on policy, the multitude are satisfied. (And this too must be counted as one form of democracy, on the lines on which it once existed at Mantinea.) Indeed it is for this reason that it is advantageous for the form of democracy spoken of before, and is a customary institution in it, for all the citizens to elect the magistrates and call them to account, and to try law-suits, but for the holders of the greatest magistracies to be elected and to have property-qualifications, the higher offices being elected from the higher property-grades, or else for no office to be elected on a property-qualification, but for officials to be chosen on the ground of capacity.[100]

The need to underscore that this sort of system is democratic probably comes from the fact that it does not fit especially well with Aristotle's statement in the *Politics* that *demokratia* means everyone ruling and being ruled by turns.[101] Aristotle, in effect, is defending the novel idea of representative democracy against Greeks who might object that such hardly counts as true democracy.

---

99 It might also be noted that Demonax, the arbiter of popular reforms at Cyrene *c.* 550, came from Mantinea. See Robinson, *First Democracies*, 113–14 (Mantinea) and 105–8 (Cyrene).

100 *Pol.* 1318b22–33, trans. H. Rackham (Cambridge, MA, 1932). ἔτι δὲ τὸ κυρίους εἶναι τοῦ ἑλέσθαι καὶ εὐθύνειν ἀναπληροῖ τὴν ἔνδειαν, εἴ τι φιλοτιμίας ἔχουσιν, ἐπεὶ παρ' ἐνίοις δήμοις, κἂν μὴ μετέχωσι τῆς αἱρέσεως τῶν ἀρχῶν ἀλλά τινες αἱρετοὶ κατὰ μέρος ἐκ πάντων, ὥσπερ ἐν Μαντινείᾳ, τοῦ δὲ βουλεύεσθαι κύριοι ὦσιν, ἱκανῶς ἔχει τοῖς πολλοῖς· καὶ δεῖ νομίζειν καὶ τοῦτ' εἶναι σχῆμά τι δημοκρατίας, ὥσπερ ἐν Μαντινείᾳ ποτ' ἦν. διὸ δὴ καὶ συμφέρον ἐστὶ τῇ πρότερον ῥηθείσῃ δημοκρατίᾳ καὶ ὑπάρχειν εἴωθεν, αἱρεῖσθαι μὲν τὰς ἀρχὰς καὶ εὐθύνειν καὶ δικάζειν πάντας, ἄρχειν δὲ τὰς μεγίστας αἱρετοὺς καὶ ἀπὸ τιμημάτων, τὰς μείζους ἀπὸ μειζόνων, ἢ καὶ ἀπὸ τιμημάτων μὲν μηδεμίαν, ἀλλὰ τοὺς δυναμένους.

101 *Pol.* 1317b23–6.

The electoral system described does seem a special one and is otherwise unattested among Greek democracies. Instead of the people in assembly electing officials themselves, a subset chosen "in turn" (or "by section" – see below) from the whole citizen body (*hairetoi kata meros ek panton*) does all the choosing. The *demos* as a whole, occupied with their own affairs most of the time, remain satisfied because they retain control over deliberation in the state and also hold to account (*euthunein*) the officials selected by their representatives. Nevertheless, men of relatively greater wealth and capacity will tend to hold office more than one would expect in a typical democratic system that features use of the lot or direct election by the masses.

Evidence for the existence of the special electoral scheme has been found on the ground in Mantinea. In and around the theater in town, where the public assemblies probably met and accommodated perhaps 3,000 people, roughly 200 circular coin-sized clay tesserae (tokens) have been found dating from the fifth to the third centuries BC.[102] Among the legible ones, each has on one side a name and patronymic, and on the other side one of twenty-five letters of the alphabet. The tokens also come in one of five different shapes, probably corresponding to the five demes or five phylae known to exist in Mantinea,[103] and the mixing in of demes/phylae across the letter-based divisions suggests an effort to distribute members of one set of civic divisions across another set.[104] These tokens, it would seem, belonged to citizens, identifying them by name, family, civic organization, and some further division based on the alphabet. Identification tokens like these of one kind or another seem not uncommon in Greek democracies: they are attested for Athens, Argos, Rhodes, Iasus, and Camarina, for example (see discussions under each state), and could serve varying public functions, including jury selection and assembly attendance. The connection of the Mantinean ones to Aristotle's electoral process comes with the interpretation of a brief inscription also found in the theater – *ME H* – as standing for *meros eta*. This ties the rows of seats in the theater, which were inscribed with letters, to the *mere* in Aristotle. So *kata meros* means the electors were chosen not "in turn," but according to *mere*, civic

---

[102] *IG* 5.2, 323. See G. Fougères, *Mantinée et l'Arcadie orientale* (Paris, 1898), 530–4; I. N. Svoronos, "ΤΑ ΠΗΛΙΝΑ ΕΙΣΙΤΗΡΙΑ ΤΟΥ ΘΕΑΤΡΟΥ ΤΗΣ ΜΑΝΤΙΝΕΙΑΣ," *Journal International d'Archéologie Numismatique* 3 (1900), 197–228; M. Amit, *Great and Small Poleis* (Brussels, 1973), 141–7; N. F. Jones, *Public Organization in Ancient Greece* (Philadelphia, 1987), 132–5, 150 n. 4.

[103] N. F. Jones, *Public Organization*, 150, favors phylae; Amit, *Great and Small Poleis*, 141–5, demes.

[104] Amit, *Great and Small Poleis*, 144, invokes the logic of the Cleisthenic tribal reform, to which I might add the Cyrenean one and Aristotle's general dictum (*Pol.* 1319b19–27) that democracies seek to mix together their citizenry across new and different civic organizations (see Robinson, *First Democracies*, 105–8).

divisions given physical form by the sections of the theater marked off to seat members of each one. If this is right, one imagines that during a special assembly meeting all citizens attending would bring their tokens with them (if they did not always do so) and the tokens of those in each seating section would be collected and a certain number randomly selected. The men indicated, *hairetoi kata meros ek panton*, would then serve as electors for however long the Mantinean official cycle lasted, probably a year.[105]

The only problem with this clever reconstruction is that the phrase *kata meros* is quite common in Aristotle, especially in contexts such as this one where democracy and/or political offices are involved, and the meaning "in turn" or "by turns" is well established.[106] It seems unlikely that Aristotle in this one instance meant *meros* to refer rather to the seating arrangements of the Mantinean theater or the specific civic divisions to which these sections gave physical form. But such doubts do not affect the interpretation of the tokens and their use in the theater – the letters on the tokens matching the letters for seating rows seems too great a coincidence – only the direct connection of them to the use of the word *meros* in the *Politics*. For Aristotle, the important thing about the Mantinean elector system was the fact that people chosen "in turn" (by whatever method) from the whole *demos* determined the officials of the state.

The picture that emerges from the evidence, then, is of an unusual Mantinean system for magistrate selection and a relatively conservative kind of *demokratia*, but a *demokratia* nonetheless. The people do meet *en masse* in assembly on occasion, for they jealously guard their privileges of controlling deliberation in the state and supervising their officials. (They were apparently helped in these tasks by *prostatai tou demou* and *demagogoi*, the latter of whom were especially resented by the wealthy land owners, according to Xenophon.)[107] The people also had to gather periodically (once per year?) for the selection of the electors. The identifying tokens for citizens that would prove so useful for this task might also have served in

---

[105] Svoronos, who made the initial connection of the tokens to the theater rows and thence to Aristotle's *kata meros*, thought that the tokens would belong only to the electors. But Amit (*Great and Small Poleis*, 144–7) is surely right in thinking that *all* citizens were divided into *mere* and had tokens. The clay tokens would have been cheap to make, easy to collect and distribute, and useful for the selection of electors, not to mention jury selection, as attendance tokens at public meetings, or for other public purposes.

[106] E.g., 1252a15–16 (*kata meros archon kai archomenos*); 1279a9 10 (*hotan ei kat' isoteta ton politon sunestekuia kai kath' homoioteta, kata meros axiousin archein*); perhaps most revealingly, 1298a15–17 (*eis de tas archas badizousi pantes kata meros ek ton phulon kai ton morion ton elachiston pantelos heos an dielthei dia panton*).

[107] Xen. *Hell.* 5.2.7.

other democratic exercises, such as random juror selection or public pay for attendance at meetings, though no direct evidence demonstrates these practices.

Thucydides' description of the oath-swearing for the 421 treaty of alliance with Athens, Elis, and Argos (5.47.9) adds a few important constitutional details: "the *demiourgoi* and council and the other officers" are to swear the oaths, while "the *theoroi* and the *polemarchoi*" will administer them. The specification of a council confirms what we might otherwise expect, that a smaller deliberative body operated at Mantinea as well as the assembly. The variety of different officials mentioned here is interesting but does not amount to an especially unusual list: all can be found in various other states as titles of offices of one kind or other, *theoroi* being religious in nature and *polemarchoi* military. One cannot hazard much of a guess about the duties of the *demiourgoi*, other than that they may have been the chief magistrates.[108] An early fourth-century decree describing the joining of Helisson to Mantinea as a subordinate town confirms aspects of Thucydides' material and adds further details: a *boleion* (council hall) is mentioned where public lists or announcements might be published on whitened boards by a college of officials named *thesmotoaroi* (law-watchers/guardians); Helisson was to have a *thearos* at Mantinea "like the other towns," suggesting that membership in this important group of officials (the *theoroi* noted in Thucydides) was composed of men from the constituent towns; and procedures are detailed for trying certain legal disputes (*imphaseis*) before the Three Hundred, possibly the council or a dedicated judicial body.[109]

J. L. O'Neil reads into Thucydides' listing of officials signs of greater power for Mantinean leaders than for those in other democracies, since the *demiourgoi* are listed before the council when Thucydides records the Mantinean oath-takers, whereas for the Athenians and Argives Thucydides lists the council first. Relying on the word order here, however, is a dubious basis on which to conclude anything about relative constitutional authorities. O'Neil also points to a passage in Xenophon's *Hellenica* (6.5.4–5) in which Agesilaus, sent on a diplomatic mission from Sparta, meets Mantinean officials who refuse to summon an assembly meeting for him to address; they further tell him that his request (that the Mantineans cease building fortifications just started) flew in the face of a decree already voted

---

[108] See Gomme, *HCT* and Hornblower, *Commentary*, vol. III, ad loc., and the Helisson inscription noted in the text, at line 23.

[109] See the text and discussion of this document in Rhodes and Osborne 14.

on by the whole people and thus was impossible. O'Neil considers that such actions by officials at Athens would have been considered "a violation of the people's sovereignty."[110] While there is more to go on here than with Thucydides' word order, the passage does not really signal greater authority for Mantinean officials. For one thing, just a little bit earlier in the *Hellenica* (at 6.4.19–20) Xenophon notes an occasion when *Athenian* officials (the Council of 500) acted similarly, dismissing a foreign envoy and his request without summoning a meeting of the assembly. Surely it was up to the discretion of officials in any democracy when to call an assembly of the citizens to hear foreign deputations and when not to do so.[111] When a state is united behind a particular course of action (as the Mantineans seem to have been in building their fortifications) one would hardly expect their officials to grant public hearings to foreigners bent on changing it.

But if O'Neil overstates the case for unusually great magisterial authority in the Mantinean democracy, he is correct in his larger point, that the Mantinean system as we know it does not well fit an Athenian model (imported via Themistocles or anyone else). He notes that the elector system for magistrate selection bears no resemblance to Athenian practice.[112] I would add the following as well. The titles of the most prominent officials – *demiourgoi, theoroi, polemarchoi, thesmotoaroi*, the Three Hundred – do not square with Athenian ones, which one might have expected if one system brought forth the other. The five demes and phylae and the twenty-five letter-based divisions bear no resemblance to Athenian civic organization, though both post-Cleisthenic Athens and democratic Mantinea seem to have shared the generic democratic preference for mixing citizens through memberships across different groups.[113] Furthermore, according to Aristotle, there were relatively few assembly meetings in democracies of the Mantinean variety,[114] something which cannot be said about Athens.

---

[110] O'Neil, "Exile of Themistokles," 337.

[111] For discussions of who summoned assemblies at Athens, see Hansen, *Athenian Democracy*, 132–4, 264–5; D. Hamel, *Athenian Generals: Military Authority in The Classical Period* (Leiden, 1998), 6–12.

[112] O'Neil, "Exile of Themistokles," 337; *Origins and Development*, 45–7. In the latter O'Neil also argues that the expulsion of a mere sixty Argolizers and popular leaders when Sparta dismantled the Mantinean democracy in 385 (Xen. *Hell.* 5.2.7) shows how limited was active participation in the government. I do not concur: sixty *prostatai tou demou* sounds like a rather healthy crop of populist politicians for a moderately sized citizen body, and that this many were exiled tells us nothing about the overall level of participation in the democracy.

[113] Arist. *Pol.* 1319b19–27. It must be added, however, that a degree of mixing could take place in non-democracies: e.g., tribes and obes in Sparta, *hemiogdoa* and *triakades* in Corinth.

[114] Arist., *Pol.* 1318b11–12.

The Arcadian confederacy and demokratia

In 385 the Spartans brought an end to the Mantinean democracy through military force. After accusing Mantinea of disloyalty and failing to induce the city to meet their various demands, the Spartans invaded and prevailed in the ensuing war. As part of the peace settlement, Mantinea had to accept *aristokratia* and surrender into exile sixty of its "Argolizers and popular leaders." But Sparta went further still: it also insisted on breaking down the Mantinean state into its constituent four or five villages (*komai*).[115] This "dioikism" would last until the crushing defeat of Sparta by the Thebans at the battle of Leuctra in 371, after which the Mantineans revived their united state. This reunification seems to have brought with it revived *demokratia* as well, given the prominent role of the *demos* of Mantineans according to Xenophon (*Hell.* 6.5.3–5). Moreover, just after this (in late 370)[116] came the movement and realization of a unified Arcadian state, a *koinon* driven by populist nationalism and based on democratic principles. Both Tegea and Mantinea played prominent roles in the league's formation. At the same time as Mantinea was reunifying and redemocratizing its own *polis*, civil strife broke out in Tegea between a conservative party favoring Tegea's traditional laws (*patrious nomous*) and a popular, nationalistic party in favor of all Arcadians coming together *en toi koinoi* to make common decisions. The populists won, but only after they armed the *demos* and gained the aid of Mantineans who arrived in force at Tegea to help them (Xen. *Hell.* 6.5.5–9). Both Xenophon and Diodorus highlight the subsequent role of one Lycomedes – a Tegean according to Diodorus 15.59, probably in error; he is a Mantinean in *Hellenica* 7.1.23 and Diodorus 15.62[117] – who persuaded the Arcadians to govern themselves collectively (*es mian sunteleian*), appointing federal officials and convening the Ten Thousand (*hoi murioi*) as the main decision-making body for the league.[118] Thebes, while it helped to defend the new ethnic confederation once formed and assisted in founding a new capital at Megalopolis, does not seem to have had any role in setting up its political institutions.[119] Not all Arcadian cities joined the league at once: Lepreon, Heraea, and Orchomenus initially

---

[115] Xen. *Hell.* 5.2.1–7; Diod. Sic. 15.5, 15.12; Paus. 8.8.7–10; Isoc. 4.126, 8.100; Polyb. 4.27.6, 38.2.11–12.

[116] P. J. Stylianou, *A Historical Commentary on Diodorus Siculus Book 15* (Oxford, 1998), 415–16.

[117] Stylianou, *Commentary*, 416.

[118] Xen. *Hell.* 7.4.2–3; Diod. Sic. 15.59. On the terms "league" vs. "confederacy" (which I use interchangeably here) and the arrangements in Arcadia at this time, see Nielsen, *Arkadia and Its Poleis*, 474–7.

[119] H. Beck, "Thebes, the Boeotian League, and 'The Rise of Federalism,'" in P. A. Bernardini, ed., *Presenza e funzione della città di Tebe nella cultura greca* (Pisa, 2000), 331–44, at 340–3.

resisted and fought alongside the Spartans.[120] Eventually, however, all seem to have joined. A federal decree granting proxeny to an Athenian dated to the mid-360s lists participating officials from the major cities of Arcadia, and other sources fill in the gaps for most other Arcadian communities.[121]

During the decade of the 360s the Arcadian confederacy acted as one of the most powerful political and military forces in the Peloponnese, working actively to protect its cities' territories and oppose the Spartans. Indeed, combating Sparta was a *raison d'être* of the league itself. In doing so, it often promoted democracies, democratic factions, and democratic alliances: it was the motivating force behind the coalition of Arcadia, Argos, Elis, and Thebes in 370 (it had sought out the Athenians as well), and worked for democratic ends in Sicyon *c.* 367 and Elis and Pellene *c.* 365.[122] Arcadian unity did not last long, however. By 363 or 362 the league seems to have split in two or dissolved altogether (our failing sources do not permit certainty on the matter), and the Arcadians' influence in the Peloponnese declined precipitously thereafter.[123]

How democratic were the federal arrangements of the Arcadians? The populist origins of the confederacy and its frequent support of democratic causes in the Peloponnese during the 360s strongly imply that the governing spirit of the union was that of *demokratia*. The institutions we know about support this conclusion, but information is limited and, of course, the matter is complicated because the structure spanned many cities, not just a single *polis* as was the norm for a *demokratia*; nor did all the constituent cities have democratic histories.[124]

The most important federal body was that of the *Murioi* (or Ten Thousand). It was the decisive deliberative agent in the confederacy, with full responsibility for league affairs, most especially defense and foreign policy. The huge number named in its title suggests a broad membership of all

---

[120] Xen. 6.5.11, 6.5.22.

[121] *IG* 5.2.1 (= Rhodes and Osborne 32); Nielsen, *Arkadia and Its Poleis*, 477–8.

[122] Diod. Sic. 15.62; Xen. *Hell.* 7.1.44–6; 7.4.15–18. Nielsen, *Arkadia and Its Poleis*, 485–90. On the constitution of Elis in the 360s, see entry in this chapter.

[123] J. Roy, "Problems of Democracy in the Arcadian Confederacy 370–362," in R. Brock and S. Hodkinson, eds., *Alternatives to Athens* (Oxford, 2000), 308–26; T. H. Nielsen in *Inventory*, 490–9. Cf. M. Piérart, "Argos, Cleonai, et le Koinon des Arcadiens," *BCH* 106 (1982), 119–38, for the probable existence of an Arcadian league after the Lamian War.

[124] Indeed, Tegea and Orchomenus seem to have had oligarchic periods and traditions prior to the formation of the Arcadian League: Thuc. 5.62.2, 5.64.1; Xen. *Hell.* 6.5.6–10; on oligarchy in Orchomenus, see Osborne, *Classical Landscape with Figures*, 118–23. Arcadian cities that had experience with democracy before the league, in addition to Mantinea, probably include Heraea (Arist. *Pol.* 1303a15) and Phigaleia (Diod. Sic. 15.40.2, with Stylianou, *Commentary*, 330–4). See discussions by T. H. Nielsen in *Inventory*, 512–33.

citizens of Arcadian cities, with few or no property qualifications.[125] Even if there were minor property qualifications, policing of them at meetings – with Arcadians streaming in from cities all across the region – would have been problematic. Ancient sources claim that the *Murioi* met in Megalopolis, the new city built as the federal capitol of the Arcadians, in a building called the Thersilium.[126] Remains presumed to be those of the Thersilium found at the site of Megalopolis suggest that at maximum perhaps 6,000 could sit in the building. That 10,000 would have to stand in order to fit, or might not have fit in the space at all, means little: the term *murioi* implies a grandly large number encompassing the mass of Arcadians and need not be taken as a literal guide to the membership or expected attendance at meetings.[127] Indeed, as we have seen at Argos (and Athens), assembly space in Greek *demokratiai* tended to fall well short of the amount needed to accommodate the total membership. But there are indications that meetings of the *Murioi* could happen elsewhere in Arcadia than Megalopolis.[128] This may reflect the time that it took to construct the city and its public buildings, or a desire to rotate meetings of its decisive bodies between different host cities of the league.

An inscription testifies to the existence of a federal council as well, beginning *edoxe tei boulei ton Arkadon kai tois muriois*, but we have no further information about the membership or activities of this presumably probouleutic council. The same inscription, however, informs us about a board of fifty *damiourgoi* that served the league. These collectively might have served as the council, though this is hypothetical. It would seem that member cities each contributed a certain number of *damiourgoi*: according to the list at the bottom of this decree, the Megalopolitans provided ten, the Tegeans five, the Mantineans five, and so on, numbers which seem contrived to measure carefully the participation of each community. Fifty is also a nice, round number. Not all the member cities of the league are represented in this document's list, however: if the proportions and total number were fixed and served a representative function within the league structure, one would expect to find cities such as Stymphalos having a

---

[125] Rhodes, *Decrees*, 507; T. H. Nielsen in *Inventory*, 479; Roy, "Democracy in the Arcadian Confederacy," 313–14.

[126] Dem. 19.11; Harpocration s.v. *murioi en Megalei Polei*; Paus. 8.32.1. On the founding of Megalopolis, Diod. Sic. 15.72.4; Paus. 8.27.1–8.

[127] McDonald, *Political Meeting Places*, 106–7; Roy, "Democracy in the Arcadian Confederacy," 315. The Thersilium is listed as a *bouleuterion* in Hansen and Fischer-Hansen, "Monumental Political Architecture," 40.

[128] Xen. *Hell.* 7.4.36 has the body meeting in Tegea, and the federal proxeny decree mentioned above was found in Tegea. Roy, "Democracy in the Arcadian Confederacy," 315.

share as well, but they are absent from the list. Xenophon's text talks of Arcadian *archontes*, which may or may not refer to these *damiourgoi*, being elected by the *Murioi* and subject to *euthuna* (7.1.23–5, 7.4.34). The only other important federal official we know about is the *strategos*, who served alone as commander of the league forces, probably elected annually by the *Murioi*.[129]

In sum, the narratives of the formation of the league, its foreign policy actions, and the limited information available about the federal arrangements, including the very large and powerful primary assembly the *Murioi*, with its decisive powers and control over election and supervision of the magistrates, all point to a strong spirit of *demokratia* guiding the new confederacy. Nevertheless, the application of *polis* democratic principles to a larger ethno-regional community fighting for its survival against hostile neighbors results in peculiarities. The exact nature of contributions of magistrates remains unclear, with an apparently representative system put in doubt by the non-participation of important cities according to our key document. And the use of a lone, powerful *strategos* (even if annually selected) to command league forces is unusually autocratic for a popular government.

MEGARA

Megara practiced one of the first known democracies in Greece in the early-to-mid sixth century, but, as Aristotle notes in the *Politics*, that government was overthrown by a group of former exiles and replaced with an oligarchy.[130] We have nothing to go on regarding the Megarian constitution from this point until the era of the Peloponnesian War, when in

---

[129] Constitutional discussions: Nielsen, *Arkadia and Its Poleis*, 477–81; Roy, "Democracy in the Arcadian Confederacy," 310–16; Larsen, *Greek Federal States*, 186–95. On the evidence for the supposed involvement of Plato or an associate in the organization of the league (not a very probable scenario), see Diog. Laert. 3.23; Aelian, *VH* 2.42; and Plut. *Mor.* 1126c with Roy, "Democracy in The Arcadian Confederacy," 311–12.

[130] Arist. *Pol.* 1300a16–19, 1302b30, 1304b34–40; *Poet.* 1448a; Plut. *Quaest. Graec.* 18, 59; Robinson, *First Democracies*, 114–17. S. Forsdyke, "Revelry and Riot in Archaic Megara: Democratic Disorder or Ritual Reversal?," *JHS* 125 (2005), 73–92, challenges the idea that *demokratia* truly existed in sixth-century Megara, arguing *inter alia* that Aristotle and Plutarch were probably drawing on well-worn anti-democratic traditions in constructing their accounts and that other explanations are possible to elucidate the disruptive events in Megara at the time. These arguments are not especially convincing, and though this is not the place for a full refutation, I would simply point out that (1) there is no reason to think that Aristotle's belief in early Megarian *demokratia* rested exclusively on the curiosities that we may currently read in Plutarch, as Forsdyke apparently assumes; and (2), anti-democratic traditions can be employed just as easily to attack *actual* democracies as they can be to attack non-democratic social disruptions.

the opening years the city was an oligarchy and a member of the Peloponnesian League: perhaps it had remained steadfastly oligarchic for longer than a century; perhaps there had been revolutions about which we know nothing.[131]

In any case, Thucydides informs us in his account for 424 that earlier (probably in 427) the Megarian *plethos* had, during *stasis* in the city, exiled a number of citizens, citizens who eventually would return and change the government to a narrow oligarchy. Sparta temporarily settled the exiles in Plataea after the successful Spartan siege there, but before long most seem to have ended up in Pegae, whence they began to harass the Megarians in the city. In 424 the *prostatai tou demou*, fearing that the *demos* would waver under their hardships and not continue to support them, secretly contacted the Athenians with a plan to betray the city to their control. The attempt failed, and in the aftermath the main conspirators fled the city; a compromise agreement between the now-returned exiles and others in the city broke down, and an extreme oligarchy (*oligarchian ta malista*) was established and lasted a long time (comments Thucydides) for how few were behind it.[132]

Thucydides' account leaves little doubt that *demokratia* took over after the *stasis* of *c.* 427 and the expulsion of the oligarchic party, but that the popular leaders could not rest easy in their accomplishment. The *demos* was willing to look for compromise or change to escape their troubles, and neither would bode well for the leaders of the democratic camp. This suggests that, unlike the narrow oligarchy that followed it, the *demokratia* of *c.* 427–424 was no extreme government in which the radicals of a single faction controlled affairs, at least not in 424.[133] If the democracy had been more united in its purpose, one expects that the *prostatai* would not have needed to be so secretive about courting Athenian aid, nor so worried about the shifting opinions of the *demos*.[134] It is also worth pointing out that while the democratic leaders turned to Athens for help when their personal political futures began to look tenuous, there is no evidence that Athens had anything to do with the initial revolution against the oligarchs, nor did the Megarian revolutionaries or *demos* seem to think that the new democracy meant they should affiliate with Athens and its cause in the larger war. Internal politics caused the change, and similarity of government type did not trump Megarian hostility towards the Athenians.

---

[131] For speculations about the Megarian constitution in the early and mid fifth century, see R. Legon, "Megara and Mytilene," *Phoenix* 22 (1968), 200–25, at 212–13, and *Megara* (Ithaca, 1981), 183–4.

[132] Thuc. 3.68.3, 4.66–8, 4.73–4. Gomme, *HCT*, ad loc.   [133] Gomme, *HCT*, at 4.66.1.

[134] Legon, "Megara and Mytilene," 214–21.

Megara seems to have had further democratic interludes in the fourth century, though we are less well informed about the surrounding events. The Sparta-aligned oligarchy established in 424 may have continued into the early fourth century (Thuc. 4.74.4; Plato, *Crito* 53b; Dem. 18.96), but how long it lasted thereafter is unclear. Some have supposed that Megara fought against Sparta in the Corinthian War and democratized at this time, but positive evidence for this is completely lacking.[135] More concretely, Diodorus reports that in the time after the general peace of 375 (or perhaps after 371)[136] some Megarians tried to change their constitution but were defeated by the *demos* and killed or driven out of the city (15.40.4). The implication is that democracy controlled affairs then and remained dominant afterward. This conclusion is reinforced by Diodorus' introduction to this section, where he claims that at this time cities were misusing the powers afforded by *demokratia* to condemn and drive out "good" citizens (*agathon andron*) (15.40.1). Though not all of the examples Diodorus then lists follow this thesis, that of Megara certainly does.[137] Later, for the 350s, Isocrates hints at a moderate, perhaps broadly oligarchic (?) Megarian constitution when he uses the word *sophrosune* to characterize the state's approach to policy.[138] Political disturbances are reported for the 340s involving a threat from partisans of Philip of Macedon, but, aside from mentioning a trial before a body of Three Hundred (a democratic court? An oligarchic council?), little can be gleaned from this episode constitutionally (Dem. 19.294–5; Plut. *Phocion* 15).[139] In sum, Megara probably had at least one period of *demokratia* in the fourth century, but the constitutional picture is murky.

As for the institutions of Megara's Classical democracies, we have some interesting pieces of evidence. An assembly of the *demos* had ultimate authority, not surprisingly, but it may also have voted with a secret ballot: soon after the oligarchic exiles had returned to power in 424 they compelled the *demos* to approve the execution of a hundred men thought to have been involved in negotiations with the Athenians, making the people vote openly (*anankasantes ton demon psephon phaneran dienenkein*). The compulsion here implies a change from past procedures, suggesting that the *demos*

---

[135] Gehrke, *Stasis*, 110; Legon, *Megara*, 264–5.
[136] See Stylianou, *Commentary*, 330–2 for a defense of the dating of this episode to the years post-375 as Diodorus' account indicates. Cf., however, Legon, *Megara*, 276–8.
[137] Legon, disagreeing with earlier scholars, argues that Diod. Sic. 15.40.4 need not indicate *demokratia* in Megara, noting that the *demos* could have acted in defense of an oligarchy as well as a democracy; *Megara*, 277–8. While this is true, 15.40.1 so clearly indicates a democratic context for Diodorus' thought as to render the reference to the *demos*'s actions in 15.40.4 less than ambiguous.
[138] Isoc. 8.117–19. Legon, *Megara*, 277–8.   [139] Legon, *Megara*, 290–4; Gehrke, *Stasis*, 110.

had voted more secretively under the democracy. Tokens of some kind could have been employed to make a truly secret ballot, as was required on specific occasions in the Athenian assembly. It is also possible, however, that voting during the democracy was handled in a more typical manner, say by show of hands, with the simultaneity and sheer number involved providing a degree of anonymity, while the oligarchs for the aforesaid vote arranged a special procedure whereby each person's vote could be seen by the leadership (e.g., voters might one by one file past two containers, putting a simple stone in one or the other, thereby revealing their vote). We know that voters during the Megarian democracy used tokens at least sometimes, for the ostracism procedure is attested there, a very powerful tool in the hands of the *demos* to give it control of its leaders. A scholion to Aristophanes' *Knights*, 855, lists Megara as one of the states engaging in the practice, and the discovery at Megara of an inscribed ostrakon would seem to confirm it.[140]

Inscribed documents are not very helpful in terms of the offices and procedures of the Classical Megarian democracies since the earliest date (perhaps) to the end of the fourth century. A number of proxeny decrees from this period show a democratic-style motion formula (*dedochthai tai boulai kai toi damoi*) and list annual officials including a "king" (*basileus*), a college of five generals, a secretary of the council and the assembly. Curiously, a few of these documents seem to show a board of six generals serving multiple years. One supposes that the probouleutic process exemplified here also existed under the democracies of the fifth and earlier fourth centuries, with similar officials, but it is only a supposition.[141] *Aisimnatai* forming the council or an executive committee are referred to in a late (second century BC) inscription (*Syll.*[3] 642), with further brief reference to the title in a document from sixth-fifth-century Olympia that may or may not involve Peloponnesian Megara (*IvO* 22; Jeffery, *LSAG* 271, 277; *IGDS* 28).

PHLIUS

The constitutional situation of Classical Phlius before the fourth century is unknown, though its friendship in the Peloponnesian War with Sparta, hostility to Argos, and especially its reception of Argos's oligarchic exiles

---

[140] Ch. Kritzas, "*To proto megariko ostrakon*," *Horos* 5 (1987), 59–73; R. Legon in *Inventory*, 464.
[141] Rhodes, *Decrees*, 109–12.

in 417 (Thuc. 5.83.3) hint at oligarchy rather than democracy.[142] But by the early fourth century things must have changed. The Corinthian War found Phlius initially neutral, and a number of pro-Spartan citizens had been exiled. When the Spartans had the opportunity in around 391 to restore the exiles (whom the Spartans themselves favored) and to settle the state however they wished, Xenophon makes a point of noting that they did neither, leaving the laws (*tous nomous*) as they found them (*Hell.* 4.4.15). That this forbearance seemed remarkable to Xenophon implies that the constitution had become something the oligarchic Spartans found distasteful. A few years later, in 384, Sparta did demand the exiles' return. Fearing that in a conflict some in the city would want to overthrow the current government, the Phliasians voted (*epsephisanto*) to restore the exiles and their lost property (*Hell.* 5.2.8–10). The presumption that a *demokratia* held sway in this period is bolstered by what followed. In 381 Sparta attacked and besieged Phlius, responding to complaints from the restored exiles about unfair treatment in Phliasian courts. In the course of the siege, the Phliasians held assembly meetings (*ekklesiazon*) in full view of the Spartans with 5,000 men attending (*Hell.* 5.3.16) – a very large number for a relatively small state, implying an inclusive citizen body with little or no property qualification.[143] When in the end the Phliasians had to give in to the Spartans, the Spartan king established a board of a hundred Phliasians (including fifty former exiles) to establish new laws. Putting such a small group in charge is in itself oligarchic, and an oligarchic constitution apparently resulted. Later in Xenophon's account one reads of a new group of exiles working with (democratic) Argos, Thebes, and others in the 360s to bring about their own restoration (*Hell.* 7.2.1–23, 7.4.11; cf. Diod. Sic. 15.40.5). It seems safe to say, then, that democracy lasted in Phlius from some point in the 390s until 379.[144]

The nature of the democracy at Phlius is hard to measure, however. No decrees survive from the period to tell us about magistracies, councils, or

---

[142] R. Legon, "Phliasian Politics and Policy in the Early Fourth Century B.C.," *Historia* 16 (1967), 329–37, at 325–6; M. Piérart in *Inventory*, 613–14.

[143] Procles of Phlius called it one of the *mikrai poleis* (Xen. *Hell.* 6.5.44). However, the context here compares it to Athens, Sparta, and Thebes, next to which most Greek cities would seem small. A century earlier 1,000 Phliasians fought at Plataea, a middling tally (Hdt. 9.28). It seems not unreasonable that once the democracy opened up citizenship to the poorer classes, 5,000 adult males might be available to attend the assembly in time of war (and 1,000 oligarchic exiles might flee to Sparta). Even if the physical territory of the city was limited, we need not reject the numbers in Xenophon as inflated. See discussion in M. Piérart in *Inventory*, 613–14.

[144] The best discussion of the constitutional evidence is Legon, "Phliasian Politics," 326–8.

legislative procedures.[145] Archaeological investigation has revealed buildings that may have been used in governing in the early fourth century, including a theater and a courtroom/council chamber, though uncertainties in their dating, extent, and purpose limit their illustrative value.[146] More useful constitutionally are the occasional comments by ancient writers already noted above, mostly from Xenophon. The willingness of the Phliasians to risk repeatedly Sparta's displeasure and ultimately undergo a twenty-month siege to retain its government suggests a strong commitment to democracy. They also insisted on using their internal, populist litigation procedures to resolve property disputes when the exiles returned, thanks to Spartan pressure, in 384. The exiles detested these procedures since, in their view, they allowed the "wrongdoers" to decide the cases – meaning, no doubt, that the *demos* of Phliasians made up the juries, and members of the *demos* (or the *demos* collectively?) had taken over the property of the exiles. The exiles wanted some special, outside procedure set up, but the *demos* refused to consider the idea. When the exiles went again to Sparta to complain – in essence undertaking a foreign mission without the permission of the *demos* – the Phliasians punished them in a manner typical of a litigious democratic community: they imposed fines. Not surprisingly, to the oligarchic sensibilities of the exiles and their Spartan backers all these actions together could be described as overbearing (*biazomenoi*) and insolent (*hubrizein*).[147]

R. Legon, noting the fierceness with which the Phliasian *demos* defended its prerogatives against the oligarchic Spartans, but also the determination with which the Phliasian citizens later fought off the democratic exiles in league with Argos in 369 (Xen. *Hell.* 7.2.5–9), asserts that the Phliasian *demos* must have simply been fighting hard for *polis* integrity and autonomy, not for this or that constitutional type. But G. E. M. de Ste. Croix rightly counters that the citizen body of 369 was not the same as that during

---

[145] Stanton, "Tribes of Korinth and Phleious," 139–53, argues that a Dorian decree found at Delos (*SEG* 30.990) belongs to Phlius, not to Corinth as others have surmised. The prescript reads *edoxe tai ekklesiai* (with no mention of a probouleutic council, though a *boula* is given responsibilities at the end of the decree), and the contents indicate that civic subdivisions to which citizens were assigned included tribes, phratries, *triakades*, and *hemiogdoa* (half-eighths).

[146] There are, in close proximity to one another, the "Hypostyle Hall" (possibly archaic in date), the Palati (a possible bouleuterion built in the second half of the fifth century), a theater with a listening area of uncertain size (fourth century), and the agora; W. R. Biers, "Excavations at Phlius, 1970," *Hesperia* 40 (1971), 424–47 and "Excavations at Phlius, 1972," *Hesperia* 42 (1973), 102–19; P. C. Rossetto and G. P. Sartorio, eds., *Teatri greci e romani* (Rome, 1994), vol. II, 117; M. Piérart in *Inventory*, 614.

[147] Xen. *Hell.* 10–13.

the democracy: it was surely much smaller.[148] Xenophon talks of citizens (*politai*) who bravely fight off the democratic exiles (*polemioi*), but he gives us no hint about who made up the citizen group – except, one might argue, when horsemen (surely members of the elite) ride out to win the battle for the "citizens" in the end. In any case, we should not think of these *politai* as being the same (or a similarly numerous) group of 5,000 defiant assembly-goers attested as standing in defense of the city from Phlius's democratic period.

SICYON

In the fifth century Sicyon may have practiced democracy for an unknown period of time before Spartan intervention changed the situation, but the source material is exceedingly thin and ambiguous. In the fourth century oligarchy at first prevailed as one democratic coup failed, but later the city clearly did become democratically governed for a brief time.

Thucydides reports at 5.81.2 that the Spartans (after defeating the Argives at the battle of Mantinea) marched to Sicyon with 1,000 soldiers and rendered things "more oligarchic" there (*ta t' en Sikuoni es oligous mallon katestesan*). This was part of a general effort by Sparta at this time to remove unfavorable governments, for as part of the same expedition to Sicyon the Spartans also overthrew the democracy at Argos and replaced it with an oligarchy. (See also the ensuing intervention in Achaea, 5.82.1.) One can interpret the statement that Sicyon was rendered *es oligous mallon* as indicating the removal of a democratic government and replacement of it with oligarchy, just as the Spartans were doing elsewhere, with the differing language an example of Thucydidean *variatio*. Alternatively, one can envision something else: a "tightening up" of an existing oligarchy into a narrower and more phil-Laconian government.[149] Unfortunately, no decisive evidence can be brought to bear on the question. Sicyon had long been an ally of Sparta, so, given the Laconian preference for oligarchic governments among its friends, one might suppose an oligarchic constitution more likely. But democratic allies of Sparta existed in the Peloponnese at this time (e.g., Mantinea, Elis), so such a consideration cannot settle the issue. It is also possible that Sicyon, which apparently sent no troops to fight

---

[148] G. E. M. de Ste. Croix, *The Class Struggle in the Ancient Greek World* (Ithaca, 1981), 296 with n. 49. He suggests that the citizen group may have approximated the 1,000 oligarchic exiles from the siege of 381–379.

[149] Andrewes, *HCT* vol. IV, 149 (followed by Hornblower, *Commentary*, vol. III, 207) assumes without argument a prior Sicyonian oligarchy.

with the Spartans at the battle of Mantinea 418, may have been drifting from Sparta's control.[150] Was a Sicyonian democracy tempted by the new alliance of democracies (Argos, Mantinea, Elis, Athens) then threatening Sparta's power in the Peloponnese, or was a Sicyonian oligarchy simply showing more independence than the Spartans liked to see from their allies? In either case, Sparta fixed things more to its liking in 417.[151]

Euphronian tyranny or democracy?

The next notice about the Sicyonian constitution crops up for the year 375 or a few years later in the account of Diodorus, who briefly describes the deaths of some men who attempted a coup (*tines neoterizein epibalomenoi*). If the government were still oligarchic – a strong probability given statements regarding events after 369[152] – we ought to assume that these plotters aimed for democracy.[153] In any case, the attempted revolution failed. But change threatened again in *c*. 368 when Euphron, a leading citizen, plotted with the Argives and Arcadians (both democratically governed; see sections above) to install a democracy. Sicyon had remained a loyal ally to Sparta after the disastrous defeat at Leuctra in 371, but Epaminondas' invasion of 369 resulted in its coming over to the side of the Theban coalition.[154] Despite this change in alliance, the traditional oligarchy persisted, and perhaps the next year[155] Euphron made his proposal to bring democracy to the city (*ean de demokratia genesthai*), citing to the Argives and Arcadians the danger of Sicyon's return to Sparta's side should an oligarchy remain in charge. Not surprisingly, the democratic allies were in favor of Euphron's proposal; Euphron, then, in their presence proceeded to summon the Sicyonian *demos* to the agora, intending to make the constitution operate on the basis of equality (*hos tes politeias esomenes epi tois isois kai homoiois*). He invited open elections to the generalship; five men were chosen and he was one of them (Xen. *Hell.* 7.1.44–5).

Thus it appears that Sicyon adopted democratic government in a bloodless revolution from within with symbolic assistance (or pressure) from democratic allies Argos and Arcadia. The constitutional picture, however,

[150] Thuc. 5.64.4, 5.67.1; A. Griffin, *Sikyon* (Oxford, 1982), 65 and 68, n. 19, citing the work of E. Frolov.

[151] R. Legon in *Inventory*, 469–70, and Gehrke, *Stasis*, 146–7, see a prior moderate oligarchy; P. A. Brunt, "Spartan Policy and Strategy in the Archidamian War," *Studies in Greek History and Greek Thought* (1993), 85 (= *Phoenix* 19 [1965], 256), considers a prior democracy probable.

[152] Xen. *Hell.* 7.1.44.   [153] Griffin, *Sikyon*, 67–8; Stylianou, *Commentary*, 336.

[154] Diod. Sic. 15.69.1; Xen. *Hell.* 7.1.18, 7.1.22.

[155] On the uncertain chronology of these events, see Griffin, *Sikyon*, 68–73, esp. 71, n. 5.

is complicated by the subsequent actions of Euphron and his condemnation by Xenophon (and more briefly, Diodorus) as a tyrant. We read that Euphron appointed his own son to be commander of an existing force of mercenaries and went to great lengths to befriend them; he banished pro-Spartan Sicyonians and made use of their wealth; he also banished or killed fellow officials, to the point where he "clearly" was a tyrant (*hoste panta huph' heautoi epoiesato kai saphos turannos en*).[156] In the end (*c.* 366) he was driven out of the city by an Arcadian general, managed a return with the help of both the Sicyonian *demos* and mercenaries gathered in Athens, and was assassinated while in Thebes attempting to get back into the good graces of the Thebans.[157]

Despite the label of tyrant that Xenophon applies to him, there is good reason to suspect that Euphron did indeed bring *demokratia* to Sicyon and for much of his ascendancy controlled affairs more like a dominant popular leader such as Pericles than an actual tyrant. For one thing, our chief source, Xenophon, disliked democracy and was prone to dismiss its practice as tyrannical – see, for example, the description *tous turanneuontas* he applies to those in control during the Corinthian democracy of *c.* 392–386.[158] The very fact that Xenophon felt the need to say Sicyon "clearly" (*saphos*) became a tyranny after listing Euphron's deeds suggests that to others' eyes it may not have been so clear. He also demonstrably exaggerates the autocratic nature of Euphron's power in at least one respect: at *Hellenica* 7.1.46 he attributes to Euphron alone the banishment of wealthy Sicyonians, but at 7.3.1 he implies that some of them were exiled by means of popular decree (*dogmati*). Indeed, many of the supposedly damning actions carried out by Euphron were not necessarily sinister or even autocratic (if we allow that Xenophon may not have informed us that the *demos* voted its approval), such as spending public monies on mercenaries, appointing his son to help command them, or ejecting hostile, pro-Laconian elites from the city. The people certainly seemed to approve of Euphron's leadership: not long after his removal by the Arcadian general, *stasis* in Sicyon between the elites and the *demos* broke out anew, and the latter enabled Euphron (with mercenaries from democratic Athens) to return to power (*kai tou*

---

[156] 7.1.45–6. Cf. Diod. Sic. 15.70.3, which presents a condensed version, noting Argive involvement in a plan for tyranny, the banishment of forty wealthy men, and the use of their property to gather mercenaries, all resulting in autocratic rule (*tes poleos edunasteusen*).

[157] Xen. *Hell.* 7.3.1–5. Griffin, *Sikyon*, 70–5; H. Berve, *Die Tyrannis bei den Griechen*, vol. 1 (Munich, 1967), 305–7; J. Mandel, "Zur Geschichte des coup d'état von Euphron I in Sikyon," *Euphrosune* 8 (1977), 93–107; Gehrke, *Stasis*, 147–9; Stylianou, *Commentary*, 464.

[158] *Hell.* 4.4.6. See the entry on Corinth, this chapter.

men asteos ekratei sun toi demoi). He was also given extraordinary honors after his death by the citizens (*politai*).[159]

Sicyon around 368–366 therefore presents a more complicated constitutional picture than one might first suppose. Diodorus' agreement with Xenophon about a Euphronian tyranny lends some weight to the charge, and Euphron's frequent association with mercenaries is at least suspicious; also, the fact that a general of the Arcadian League felt compelled to intervene and drive out Euphron suggests that something had gone wrong since the coalition of democratic allies had encouraged a popular revolution in the city. Nevertheless, we need not doubt that at least initially Euphron brought democracy to Sicyon, and that the line the politician walked between democratic revolutionary leader and popular tyrant came to be a very thin one.

It is difficult to say much about the nature of Sicyon's government during its periods of likely democracy. No contemporary decrees survive epigraphically to flesh out procedures. Extrapolating from the brief accounts of events during Euphron's ascendancy, we learn only that there were voting assemblies; that five generals served at any one time, elected by the people; and that the people had the power to banish and confiscate the property of fellow citizens suspected of pro-Spartan sympathies or activities, property which may have been appropriated by Euphron himself.

THEBES AND BOEOTIA (INCLUDING PLATAEA)

For such a large and important city and region as Thebes and Boeotia our sources for their political history in the Classical era are relatively sparse, excepting brief periods in the fourth century. Nevertheless, we can safely draw at least a broad constitutional picture.

For most of the fifth century oligarchy of one kind or another dominated at Thebes. Thucydides provides a Theban speech after the fall of Plataea in which the speaker claims that during the era of the Persian Wars a narrow oligarchy (*dunasteia oligon andron*) ruled Thebes autocratically (3.62.3; though cf. Hdt. 9.86–7), a tyrannical government he compares unfavorably to *oligarchia isonomos* and *demokratia*. He claims this *dunasteia* ended with the withdrawal of the Persians and that then Thebes' "laws" (*tous nomous*) were attained; the implication is that one of the other, more legitimate governments mentioned took over. One might hypothesize that it was an oligarchy of some kind that continued, given that the rhetorical need

---

[159] Xen. *Hell.* 7.3.4, 7.3.12.

to account for Thebes' Medism probably resulted in an exaggeration of the difference between Theban governments before and after the Persian Wars. But really there is nothing solid to go on regarding the Theban government before the aftermath of the Athenian victory in the battle of Oenophyta in *c.* 457. At this point, as Aristotle makes clear (at *Pol.* 1302b25), a democracy was in control until it succumbed to *stasis* in the face of disgust by the wealthy (*euporoi*) at its chaos and disorder. The Athenians may have been able to impose a democratic government for a time after their victory in 457, which could be the one that disintegrated, though such an assumption is complicated by Pseudo-Xenophon's notation of Athenian support for aristocrats (*tous beltistous*) in Boeotia that resulted in enslavement of the *demos* (Thuc. 1.108, 113; Ps.-Xen. *Ath. pol.* 3.11). It might make the most sense of the sources, in fact, if we posit a feckless Theban democracy, discredited by the result at Oenophyta in 457, being undermined by native elites with new support from a victorious Athens looking to establish its influence among local leaders. If true, this would mean that a native Theban democracy took hold sometime after the fall of the *dunasteia* of the Persian Wars (which, incidentally, would make sense of the Theban speaker's otherwise odd, vaguely approving reference to *demokratia* in his speech to the Spartans at Thuc. 3.62.2) and lasted until the middle of the century, rather than just being a brief, failed experiment in the 450s.[160] But in either case, by the battle of Coronea *c.* 447, in which the Thebans and Boeotians triumphed over the Athenians and reclaimed their autonomy, oligarchy was in place again (Thuc. 1.113, 3.62.5, 5.31; with Arist. *Pol.* 1302b25). This oligarchy lasted until the 380s (see below).[161]

As for the other individual Boeotian cities, the few indications we have all point to oligarchic governments in the later fifth and early fourth centuries. Prior to describing Boeotia's federal system, the Oxyrhynchus Historian specifies the internal arrangements within the cities in the year

---

[160] Busolt assumed a Theban democracy followed the Persian War; Busolt and Swoboda *Griechische Staatskunde*, vol. 1, 438. D. M. Lewis proposed that a "hoplite democracy" assumed power after the fall of the medizing government; "Mainland Greece," 96.

[161] On the Theban constitution in the fifth century, see N. Demand, *Thebes in the Fifth Century: Heracles Resurgent* (London, 1982), 16–17; Gehrke, *Stasis*, 372–5; O'Neil, *Origins and Development*, 50; Hornblower, *Commentary*, vol. 1, 456–7; M. H. Hansen in *Inventory*, 455. P. Salmon, *Étude sur la Confédération béotienne (447/6–386)* (Brussels, 1976), 27, n. 2; E. M. Walker, "The Political Situation in Boeotia in 457 B.C.," in J. B. Bury, S. A. Cook, and F. E. Adcock, eds., *CAH*, vol. v (Cambridge, 1927), 469. Walker rejects the straightforward source interpretation of earlier scholars that results in the assumption of a Theban democracy (opposed by the Athenians) before 457 BC, basing the argument on the improbability of Athenian support for democrats in some places and oligarchs in others. The argument is flawed: at this early date, a pattern of consistent Athenian support for democrats and Spartan for oligarchs had not yet developed. See Chapter 4 for refutation of Walker's related idea that Athens established democracy throughout its fifth-century empire.

395: each maintained four councils, with property qualifications for members, to deliberate over affairs in turn, enacting resolutions that all four approved; no place is left, it appears, for a public assembly of ordinary citizens (*Hell. Oxy.* 19.2–3 [Chambers]).[162] The claim that Boeotian cities generally employed this same conservative system suggests that oligarchy was imposed uniformly at the time the league took formal hold (probably soon after 447). Other episodes appear to confirm this picture. In 424 the Athenian general Demosthenes plotted with certain Boeotians to transform their governments to *demokratia* as part of his invasion plan: Thucydides names Siphae and Chaeronea as targets, with exiles from Orchomenus and Thebes participating as well (4.76; the plot did not succeed, 4.89, 101). Further, in 414 the *demos* at Thespiae attempted to overthrow the government there but failed after help arrived from Thebes (Thuc. 6.95). The only known exception to the oligarchic pattern was Plataea, which had defected from the league earlier and apparently turned to democracy, given the way the *plethos* was consulted constantly for major decisions (Thuc. 2.2, 272–4; 3.65).[163]

Of course, the first manifestation of the Boeotian federal league operated all through this era and itself functioned oligarchically. Lasting from perhaps just after 447 to its dissolution with the King's Peace in 386, the federal government drew councilors and other officials (boeotarchs, jurors, etc.) from the different parts of Boeotia according to a fixed representative pattern. Four councils carrying supreme authority, and probably the other federal boards, met on the Cadmea at Thebes. Over time Thebes increasingly dominated from the center, providing the location for meetings and contributing an outsized proportion of the magistrates. In general, the ruling councils acted in favor of oligarchic interests, at one point turning down an otherwise attractive alliance with Argos on the grounds that the Argives' democratic constitution seemed less compatible than the conservative Spartan system (Thuc. 5.31).[164]

In the late 380s division among leaders in Thebes led to *stasis* that the Spartans famously settled by seizing the Cadmea. From 382 to 379 Thebes

---

[162] P. Salmon, *Confédération béotienne*, 60–2.

[163] On the governments of the individual Boeotian cities: M. H. Hansen in *Inventory*, 437–59; R. J. Buck, *A History of Boeotia* (Edmonton, 1979), 159–60. For signs of oligarchic laws (often of uncertain date) in some of the cities, see P. Salmon, *Confédération béotienne*, 53–5.

[164] On the first Boeotian League: *Hell. Oxy.* 19.3–4; Thuc. 5.38.2. P. Salmon, *Confédération béotienne*; M. H. Hansen in *Inventory*, 432; Rhodes, *Decrees*, 480–1; O'Neil, *Origins and Development*, 50–2; R. J. Buck, *History of Boeotia*, 154–62; Demand, *Thebes in the Fifth Century*, 34–7; P. R. McKechnie and S. J. Kern, *Hellenica Oxyrhynchia* (Warminster, 1988), 152–61; P. Roesch, *Études béotiennes* (Paris, 1982), 266–7; Hamilton, *Sparta's Bitter Victories*, 137–45.

was controlled by a narrow, pro-Laconian oligarchy (called a *dunasteia* or even a tyranny in our sources) secured by a Spartan garrison on the citadel (Xen. *Hell.* 5.2.25–6, 5.4.1–2, 5.4.13, 5.4.46). Exiles from Thebes went to Athens to plot their return, and when they succeeded in overthrowing the now-discredited oligarchs and freed the Cadmea, they established a *demokratia*. Athenians had helped the exiles, providing a force that approached later to help retake the Cadmea and oppose the Spartan army; but the revolution had internal democratic roots, as our sources talk of the populist (*demotiken*) exiles rallying all the Thebans in the name of freedom (*eleutheria*), the *demos* meeting in the *ekklesia* to take decisive action, and the masses (*tous plethous*) being armed for battle.[165]

The Theban hegemony in Greece arose during the period of this democracy – indeed, the new constitution of the city and (soon) the Boeotian League arguably made the hegemony possible[166] – but the constitution outlasted Theban preeminence in Greece, continuing into the time of Philip of Macedon's domination. From the start the Thebans employed the trappings of the Boeotian League in their revolution, as the Theban *demos* meeting in *ekklesia* elected Pelopidas boeotarch before the assault on the Cadmea (Plut. *Pel.* 12–13). Thebes rapidly reassumed its dominant position at the center of the league (usually described as a *koinon* or *sunteleia* in the sources), but did not have an entirely simple task in bringing the oligarchic Boeotian cities into newly populist arrangements. The Thebans had to fight battles with pro-Spartan factions and the Spartans themselves around cities such as Orchomenus, Tanagra, and Thespiae. According to Xenophon, the *demos* (presumably meaning the populist factions) of Thespiae and other cities nearby withdrew to Thebes to escape the *dunasteiai* that had been established in the towns (*Hell.* 5.4.46, 5.4.49; also Plut. *Pel.* 15.4). But Thebes did succeed eventually in subduing the Boeotian cities (Xen. *Hell.* 6.1.1), and from this point onward dominated the league. In fact, so closely does Thebes direct affairs that it becomes very hard to separate "Theban" from "league" business when our sources present narratives of political events. Only after 338 do decrees of the

[165] Diod. Sic. 15.25–7; Plut. *Pel.* 5–15; Xen. *Hell.* 5.4.1–19; Arist. *Pol.* 1306a33–b3. We do not hear of any property qualifications for citizens and should assume that any that had existed under the oligarchy were abolished. J. Buckler argues that the democratic leaders must have been influenced in their political thinking by their time spent in exile witnessing the Athenian democracy and the debates held there; *The Theban Hegemony, 371–362 BC* (Cambridge, MA, 1980), 44–5 (cf. P. J. Rhodes, "On Labelling 4th Century Politicians," *LCM* 3 [1978], 207–11). This was no doubt true. In this way, Athens can be seen as indirectly influencing the rise of *demokratia* in Thebes. But as for direct causes, Thebans, not Athenians, sparked the revolution and made the decisions to move toward popular government there.

[166] Buckler, *Theban Hegemony*, 34–45.

league adopt the formula *edoxe toi koinoi Boioton*; earlier ones simply used the *edoxe toi demoi*.[167] All league meetings were held in Thebes, which now meant even greater power for the city than it had exercised under the previously oligarchic league arrangements, since popular assemblies (not councils of the wealthy) wielded decisive authority and denizens of Thebes and areas close by surely predominated among those attending. The number of boeotarchs also declined from eleven before 478, of which Thebes had contributed four, to seven afterwards, all of which seem to have been Theban if the lack of ethnics given in contemporary inscriptions is any guide.[168] Hence the democracy strengthened Thebes' control over league dealings.[169]

It is not clear, however, to what extent Thebes encouraged or installed democratic regimes in the individual cities of Boeotia. Exiles from Plataea and Thespiae complained at Athens of the loss of their cities (Xen. *Hell.* 6.3.1), and some Athenian orators bemoaned Theban aggression in Boeotia,[170] all of which may imply that Thebes intervened constitutionally. The apparent pro-democratic interventionist policy, however, did not mean that oligarchic factions lost their power entirely: in 364 Theban exiles persuaded the cavalrymen (*hippeis*) at Orchomenus to help them bring about an aristocratic revolution in Thebes. Was Orchomenus itself therefore still oligarchic? Probably, since even though the knights could have been acting on their own without the city's complicity, the Theban *demos* clearly believed otherwise: the attempted revolution failed, and the Theban *demos* reacted violently to the endeavor, voting in assembly to raze Orchomenus and kill or sell into slavery its inhabitants, a plan that was carried out (Diod. Sic. 15.79.3–6).

We have certainly seen such fear-induced, harsh reactions before from large democracies under threat (e.g., Athens dealing with rebellious allies in wartime, or Argos quelling revolution through the *skutalismos*). The Theban democracy of the fourth century is typical in other ways as well. In external affairs it could often be found fighting alongside other democracies and supporting democratic factions, as it did in the Peloponnese

[167] Rhodes, *Decrees*, 121–4.
[168] D. Knoepfler, "La loi de Daitondas," in P. A. Bernardini, ed., *Presenza e funzione della città di Tebe nella cultura greca* (Pisa, 2000), 345–66, at 351–2.
[169] On Thebes and the Boeotian League during the democracy: Beck, "The Rise of Federalism," 332–8; Rhodes, *Decrees*, 119–22; Buckler, *Theban Hegemony*, 15–45. Nepos (*Pelopidas* 3.3) describes people streaming into an assembly meeting from the fields all around, not just the city itself, when Thebes was on the verge of liberation, but such an exceptional occasion hardly undermines the notion of Thebes-dominated assembly meetings in the normal course of events.
[170] E.g., Isoc. 14.9, 14.19, 14.35. See discussion in Buckler, *Theban Hegemony*, 20–2.

during its long conflict with Sparta. The most dramatic case involved Achaea, a longtime ally of Sparta into which Epaminondas, in 366, led an invasion to turn its cities toward the Theban coalition. After initial successes, Epaminondas met with oligarchic leaders (perhaps representatives of the Achaean League). They promised Achaean support for the Thebans in future, and in return Epaminondas agreed to make no constitutional changes in the (presumably oligarchic) cities. However, when complaints arose from populist opponents of the Achaean aristocrats and from the (democratic) Arcadians, the assembly in Thebes voted to reverse Epaminondas' policy: they sent harmosts into the Achaean cities who, with the help of local popular groups, drove out the aristocrats and set up *demokratiai*.[171] We do not know if Epaminondas was skirting an established Theban policy of democratic support, or if the *demos* on this occasion simply overruled its chief general, persuaded by the pleas of outside groups (or rival Theban politicians).[172] Thebes did have a habit of promoting the establishment of other federal states when given the opportunity – in Thessaly, Arcadia, and Messenia – but of these only the Arcadians clearly adopted democratic institutions, and even here the evidence for Theban influence in this choice is negligible.[173] More meaningful, perhaps, was Thebes' leading role in a coalition of democratic states opposed to Sparta formed in 370.[174] Either way, in the case of the Achaean intervention, the Theban *demos* asserted its preeminence in foreign policy matters and did so to promote other democrats.

In other respects too our evidence suggests a lively, assertive democratic system at work in Thebes and the Boeotian confederacy in this period. The *demos* meeting in assembly had supreme authority, naturally, and could be found involving itself in a variety of different kinds of business, from electing the highest officials (the boeotarchs), setting them tasks to accomplish, removing them from office, initiating spending measures, overseeing foreign policy, and conducting trials.[175] Courts were active in keeping officials held to account. In 370–369, for example, after a brilliantly successful winter campaign in the Peloponnese resulting in a friendly Arcadian League,

---

[171] Xen. *Hell.* 7.1.41–3; Diod. Sic. 15.75.2; *FGH* 70 F84. Buckler, *Theban Hegemony*, 185–93.

[172] Buckler believes Menecleides, Epaminondas' chief political opponent, was at the center of the reversal of his Achaean policy; *Theban Hegemony*, 191 with 145–50.

[173] Arguing against the common idea that Thebes had a "federal program" in its dealings with other states is Beck, "The Rise of Federalism," 331–44. Cf. H. Beister, "Hegemoniales Denken in Theben," in H. Beister and J. Buckler, eds., *Boiotika* (Munich, 1989), 131–53.

[174] Argos, Elis, and Arcadia, although the Arcadians took the leading role in forming the coalition: Diod. Sic. 15.62.

[175] E.g., Diod. Sic. 15.72.2, 15.78.4–79.1, 15.79.5; Xen. *Hell.* 7.1.41–3; Plut. *Pel.* 12–13.

a refounded Messenia, and a humiliated Sparta, Epaminondas and other boeotarchs for the year were put on trial for remaining in office beyond the end of their term.[176] The defendants prevailed at trial, unsurprisingly, but the fact that gloriously popular generals could be successfully brought to trial on such charges bespeaks the seriousness with which rules for official conduct were taken in the democracy and the eagerness of the *demos* to consider charges that magistrates overstepped their authority. More generally, despite the concentration of our source material on just two Theban politicians of the era – Epaminondas and Pelopidas – the accounts make clear that others competed with them for favor with the people. Different strategies for advancement were possible. Pelopidas, for example, a very popular politician, was said to be extremely generous with his wealth to the poor and less fortunate. Plutarch reports this as a matter of character and philosophy, but one does not have to read too imaginatively between the lines to see a democratic political program at work (Plut. *Pel.* 3.1–3, 25.4). Epaminondas made his great mark as an inspired general and statesman, but even he fell out of favor with the *demos* at times and suffered political defeat (Diod. Sic. 15.72.2; Plut. *Pel.* 25.4). Menecleides, a sometime opponent of both of these leaders, spoke often *pros ton demon* using his great rhetorical skill (*deinotatos legein*) to attack his adversaries (Plut. *Pel.* 25.3). Pelopidas was able to bring him down in the end by charging and convicting him of moving an unconstitutional measure (*psephisma graphetai paranomon*), resulting in a crushing fine – a suitably legalistic, litigious way of removing an opponent in a democracy (Plut. *Pel.* 25.7).[177]

For the most part in texts and documents for this period a council is missing. Probouleusis is attested in Diodorus, who describes how in 335 *hegemones* met to prepare a resolution that the *plethos* in due course approved (17.9.1). Could these *hegemones* refer to councilors? The very few Theban decrees from the period (if they are from the period) use the formula *edoxe toi demoi* with no *boule* included;[178] all narratives also omit any mention of a council, referring only to officials or the people or

---

[176] On the episode, Plut. *Pel.* 25.

[177] One should also mention Daitondas, a known boeotarch in the era of Epaminondas and Pelopidas, and a potentially significant politician thanks to his law regulating the conduct of women – assuming he can be identified with Cicero's Diagondas, as would D. Knoepfler, "Un legislateur thébain chez Cicéron (*De legibus*, II xv 37)," in M. Piérart and O. Curty, eds., *Historia Testis: Mélanges d'epigraphie, d'histoire ancienne et de philologie offerts a Tadeusz Zawadzki* (Fribourg, 1989), 37–60. The thesis is further defended at Knoepfler, "La loi de Daitondas."

[178] *IG* 7.2407/8; *SEG* 50.481; Rhodes, *Decrees*, 119–22. On probouleusis and the varying decree formulae in Boeotian decrees of the Hellenistic period, see J. Tréheux, "La 'prise en considération' des décrets en Grèce à l'époque hellénistique," in C. Nicolet, ed., *Du pouvoir dans l'antiquité: mots et réalités* (Geneva, 1990), 117–27, at 117–23.

assembly meetings, except for one: Xenophon states that the *boule* was in session with some officials on the Cadmea when some Sicyonians killed their onetime leader Euphron there while waiting to plead their respective cases. Xenophon then has Theban *archontes* bring the killers before the council, accuse them of wrongdoing, and say that it is up to them (the councilors, it seems) to decide their punishment. Next the Sicyonians make a stirring speech in self-defense. At the end Xenophon becomes more vague, saying only that "the Thebans" decided Euphron had met a just end (*Hell.* 7.3.5–12).[179] While it is possible to imagine that Xenophon's abbreviated account masks a referral of the trial from the council to the assembly,[180] at the very least the description here shows that Thebes did have a deliberative council that worked with magistrates on judicial and foreign policy matters; it is therefore likely that the Diodorus reference to *hegemones* engaging in probouleusis in 335 describes the action of the *boule*. The failure of other narratives to mention it does not mean it did not exist or that it was unimportant.

Finally, the question arises of the relationship of the Theban constitution to the contemporary Athenian one. That there were some connections is entirely likely: the conspirators who spearheaded the democratic revolution at Thebes spent their exile in Athens, where they will have been able to see at first hand how a democracy could harness and inspire the people of a large state. But, as far as we can tell, what they learned and instituted at Thebes had more to do with democracy generally than the specific Athenian version. One finds there what one finds in many democracies: a powerful assembly and the desire to keep a tight leash on magistrates. One also finds a less visible council. Few details we know about the Theban government of the period match specifically Athenian practices: the Boeotian league employed an eponymous archon, an inscription shows;[181] and, as we saw above, the Thebans had a law resembling the Athenian *graphe paranomon*. Differences include decree formulae, tribal/district arrangements, and the politically important offices, which at Thebes were the boeotarchs, seven in number. The differing relationship of Thebes with the Boeotian League (as compared with Athens with Attica or with its allies) would have complicated direct importation of some Athenian practices, but one imagines that Thebes' and Boeotia's own legal traditions, *polis*

---

[179] Xenophon also mentions a functioning Theban council at 5.2.29, it should be noted, but this passage refers to events during the previous oligarchic era.

[180] So O'Neil, *Origins and Development*, 94.

[181] *IG* 7.2407. On the archonship in the Hellenistic period, when it is much more thoroughly attested, see Roesch, *Études béotiennes*, 282–6.

pride, and longstanding rivalry with Athens would have proved equally high barriers.[182]

THESSALY

For most of the Classical period Thessaly and its major cities appear to have been dominated by powerful aristocratic families. Specific constitutional information is limited, but most of what there is indicates oligarchy. For example, Thucydides (4.78) describes Thessalian political affairs in 424 as narrowly oligarchic rather than egalitarian (*dunasteia mallon e isonomiai echronto to enchorion hoi Thessaloi*), while Aristotle uses the Thessalian cities of Larisa and Pharsalus as examples in his discussions of oligarchic government (*Pol.* 1305b28–30, 1306a9–12). Together with the well-attested wealth and power of Thessalian noble families from the Archaic into the Classical period (especially the Aleuadae from Larisa), such references suffice to indicate government generally in the hands of the few.[183]

Nevertheless, there were signs that during the fifth century popular politics began to make inroads, possibly even resulting in brief episodes of democracy. Scholars have seen a pattern of significant political change that included the *c.* 457 BC replacement of lifetime tetrarchs with more temporary, probably annually elected, military officials (the polemarchs), as attested by an inscription (*SEG* 17.243). This suggests a move away from narrow oligarchy. Aristotle quotes a punning line by Gorgias about officials in Larisa making new citizens as craftsmen make pots, hinting at a broadening of citizenship as well, at least in Larisa (*Pol.* 1275b26–30). Even the passage that most firmly attests the Thessalian predilection for oligarchy – Thucydides 4.78, noted above – also makes obvious that this tendency had come to be challenged forcefully: when Brasidas was leading a Spartan force through Thessaly under the guidance of certain distinguished Thessalians, others in the opposition (*alloi ton t'anantia toutois bouleuomenon*) stopped the Spartan and criticized him for proceeding without the common consent of all (*aneu tou panton koinou*). Thucydides had just noted a few lines before that the *plethos* of the Thessalians had long favored the Athenians, adding further flavor to the political tensions implied. The increasing populist influences may be connected with the growing power of cities

---

[182] Buckler, *Theban Hegemony*, 44–5, is too quick to attribute general democratic practices to specific borrowing from Athens.

[183] J.-C. Decourt, T. H. Nielsen, and B. Helly *et al.* in *Inventory*, 696, 703; Larsen, *Greek Federal States*, 19–22; H. D. Westlake, *Thessaly in the Fourth Century* (London, 1935), 31–7, 47–8. On Philostratus, *VS* 1.16, which mentions Thessalian oligarchies at the end of the fifth century, see below.

at the expense of the Thessalian confederacy at this time, suggested by Thucydides' description of individually commanded city contingents (as opposed to a united federal force) when Thessaly aided Athens during the Peloponnesian War (2.22.3), and by epigraphic evidence for city control over import and export duties (*Syll.*³ 55, of fifth-century date).[184]

For all these indications of political change, however, the only ancient report of actual *demokratia* appearing in Thessaly occurs in Xenophon's *Hellenica*, at 2.3.36. There, Theramenes, denounced by Critias in a meeting of the (oligarchic) council at Athens in 404, declares that during the Arginusae trial at Athens Critias was not present, but off in Thessaly "establishing *demokratia* with Prometheus and arming the serfs against their masters" (*en Thettalia meta Prometheos demokratian kateskeuaze kai tous penestas hoplizen epi tous despotas*). If Xenophon's Theramenes is to be believed here, this would prove that the political agitations in Thessaly had by the end of the fifth century risen to the level of democratic revolution on at least one occasion. However, there are obstacles to taking this passage at face value. First, this was a speech to oligarchs by an oligarch trying to slander another oligarch – a likely occasion for false or exaggerated claims regarding democratizing activities of an opponent. Second, Critias himself has to be one of the last people one might imagine to bring about *demokratia* anywhere, given his actions and opinions in this period (e.g., Xen. *Hell.* 2.3.15, 2.3.25–6).

Two other texts bear on Critias' time in Thessaly: at *Memorabilia* 1.2.24, Xenophon remarks on how Critias, separated from Socrates after fleeing to Thessaly, fell in with a bad crowd, men employing lawlessness rather than justice (*anomiai mallon e dikaiosunei chromenois*). Given Socrates' and Xenophon's political biases, such a description could easily apply to democratization and serf-arming, though it need not. A passage from Philostratus (*V S* 1.16), on the other hand, flatly contradicts Theramenes' accusations in the *Hellenica*, stating that Critias strengthened the oligarchies in Thessaly, criticizing *demokratia* generally and Athenians in particular.[185] The reference to multiple oligarchies is interesting, suggesting that – if this passage is to be preferred over those of Xenophon – in multiple Thessalian

---

[184] M. Sordi, *La lega tessala fino ad Alessandro Magno* (Rome, 1958), 106–7, 109–23; Larsen, *Greek Federal States*, 20–6, and "A New Interpretation of the Thessalian Confederacy," *CPh* 55 (1960), 229–48. Cf. B. Helly, *L'état thessalien* (Lyons, 1995), 226–37, 338–45. Helly differs sharply with Sordi (and Larsen) over the nature of the *tagos* and the interpretation of *SEG* 17.243, among other things, but nevertheless accepts the thesis of the growing power and (to some degree) democratization of Thessalian cities in the course of the fifth century.

[185] βαρυτέρας δ' αὐτοῖς ἐποίει τὰς ὀλιγαρχίας διαλεγόμενος τοῖς ἐκεῖ δυνατοῖς καὶ καθαπτόμενος μὲν δημοκρατίας ἁπάσης, διαβάλλων δ' Ἀθηναίους, ὡς πλεῖστα ἀνθρώπων ἁμαρτάνοντας.

cities aristocrats retained control despite the ongoing disputes and changing political landscape.

H.-J. Gehrke firmly rejects the idea that Critias helped to establish *demokratia* in Thessaly in 406. He is skeptical about the *Hellenica* passage for the reasons already noted, and also because (1) the *anomia* (and lack of *dikaiosune*) characterizing the men Critias joined with according to the *Memorabilia* passage is a topos for tyranny, and (2) the arming of slave populations (to include the Thessalian *penestai*) against their masters is also a typical mark of tyranny.[186] Tyranny appears soon enough in Thessaly, of course, with the emergence of Lycophron in 404 (Xen. *Hell.* 2.3.4), so Gehrke's association of Critias' actions with a rising tyrant's bag of tricks has some appeal.[187] We have plenty of reasons, therefore, to reject Xenophon's Theramenean accusation against Critias. However, this does not mean that *demokratia* did not appear in Thessaly around this time. Indeed – and this is crucial – if Theramenes planned to blacken Critias' reputation in the eyes of Athenian oligarchs by associating him with the establishment of *demokratia* on some occasion, the charge would be far more persuasive were it generally known that democracy *had actually come about in that time or place*, whether or not Critias had anything to do with it. Note that Theramenes feels compelled to include the name of a Thessalian co-revolutionary in his accusation. Quite possibly this Prometheus (about whom we know nothing further) truly did lead a movement to arm *penestai* and bring about a democratic revolution. Critias may have known or befriended him at some point, providing Theramenes with his opportunity to associate the two; or maybe the association was wholly manufactured and Critias' only connection to him was his presence in Thessaly at the time. Regardless, most of the objections to the use of Xenophon's passage to indicate *demokratia* in Thessaly at this time disappear if we do not insist on the actual participation of Critias. Furthermore, while it may be true that terms such as *anomia* and the mass arming of excluded classes can be associated with tyranny, they most certainly could also apply to democratic revolutions and their portrayal in our sources.[188]

---

[186] Gehrke, *Stasis*, 375–6. J. Ducat, *Les pénestes de Thessalie* (Paris, 1994), 54–63; Helly, *L'état thessalien*, 307; Westlake, *Thessaly*, 47–8; G. Rechenauer, "Zu Thukydides II 22,3," *RhM* 136 (1993), 238–44, at 240–1. Cf. Sordi, *Lega tessala*, 141–6.

[187] Berve, however, considers a moderate democracy could have arisen in Larisa with Lycophron's victory, *Tyrannis*, 284.

[188] The association of *demokratiai* with disorder is a commonplace in authors such as Plato, Isocrates, and Aristotle (to name a few); on democratic revolutions involving the arming of non-citizen lower classes, consider, e.g., Argos *c.* 494.

One might further note the possible significance of a passage from Aristotle's *Politics* sometimes associated with this period, though its dating is not certain. At 1305b22–30 Aristotle is discussing the ways in which oligarchies can be overthrown and notes that such can occur whenever the oligarchs themselves engage in demagoguery, such as when in Larisa "the *polis* Guardians played demagogues to the common mob because it elected them" (*hoi politophulakes dia to haireisthai autous ton ochlon edemagogoun*, b29–30). This passage has often been taken to reflect a moderately oligarchic regime thought to have been established in Larisa after Lycophron's victory in 404.[189] But it is worth emphasizing that whatever the nature of the oligarchic regime initially depicted, the point of the *Politics* passage is that it failed, and given that it failed thanks to "demagoguery before the *ochlos*" it is quite possible that the resulting revolution led to the introduction of *demokratia* – perhaps on the occasion to which Theramenes refers.

In the end, we cannot be certain that democracy appeared in Thessaly near the close of the fifth century. One source claims that it did, and the dubiousness of Critias' own leadership in the events hardly disproves that a revolution took place. There are certainly plentiful indications that Thessaly in the later fifth century was riven by factional discord and responding to pressures to change its traditionally oligarchic ways. But if *demokratia* did make an appearance federally or in one or more cities in Thessaly, it did not last: Lycophron and then resurgent oligarchs in Larisa emerged to compete for dominating roles, after which little is known politically until the rise of Jason of Pherae.

The nature of any Thessalian democracy is even harder to judge. Scholars have argued for and against the existence of a federal assembly in fifth-century Thessaly primarily on the basis of Thucydides' reference to a *panton koinon* at 4.78.3.[190] The passage is not decisive either way. But if there were indeed a *demokratia* in fifth-century Thessaly, such a popular body will have no doubt existed and proved very important. Perhaps, like the *Murioi* of the Arcadian federal democracy in the fourth century (see discussion in this chapter), it met only occasionally and left much of the business to the discretion of its officials, whom it elected.

---

[189] E.g., Geluke, *Stasis*, 189–90; Westlake, *Thessaly*, 51–6. Ps.-Herodes Atticus, *Peri politeias* 30–1 is typically associated with events in Larisa at the end of the century, though this too is uncertain.

[190] Also, Hdt. 5.63.3. Larson, *Greek Federal States*, 19, n. 4, and "Thessalian Confederacy," 243–4; Gomme, *HCT* vol. III, 544; Hornblower, *Commentary*, vol. II, 260; J. Tréheux, "Koinon," *REA* 89 (1987), 39–46, at 39–41; J.-C. Decourt, T. H. Nielson, B. Helly, *et al.* in *Inventory*, 680.

ZACYNTHUS

The island *polis* of Zacynthus and its factions went back and forth between Athenian and Spartan alliances for much of the fifth and fourth centuries, and its constitutional status can sometimes be tied to these changes.

During the Peloponnesian War and the conflicts leading up to it, Zacynthus frequently aided the Corcyreans and the Athenians, becoming firm allies of the latter.[191] No evidence exists for its constitutional situation, however. While one might hypothesize that its consistent support for democratic Corcyra and Athens suggests democracy rather than oligarchy, such cannot be proven. In the early fourth century Zacynthus seems to have turned to oligarchic government, for a passage in Diodorus describes the *demos* there suffering under the rule of those in charge during the period of Sparta's predominance (15.45.2). It seems probable, then, that after the Peloponnesian War the Spartans, preeminent in Greece, were able to make sure that political affairs in Zacynthus suited their conservative constitutional tastes.

But this changed again, for the *demos* managed to drive out the oligarchs (15.45.2). When did this happen? Diodorus' treatment of the episode and its aftermath is not very illuminating, as the historian seems to have compressed the chronology of a long sequence of events. In the same passage as the demotic victory is asserted, after a presumed lacuna, the historian describes a reversal of roles, where an exiled popular faction receives Athenian aid from Timotheus who helps them fortify a base nearby from which they can raid those in the city. These events described by Diodorus belong to the period after the Peace of 375, probably just after.[192] How long before this the *demos* had been in control, before being exiled themselves, cannot be ascertained, but the episode may go back as far as the Corinthian War.[193] In any event, in 375 the Athenian aid to the democratic exiles led to appeals from Zacynthus for Spartan assistance, which were granted, resulting in further Athenian military involvement (Diod. Sic. 15.45.4–15.46.3; Xen. *Hell.* 6.2.2–3). The Athenians committed themselves to the populist

---

[191] Thuc. 1.47.2, 2.7.3, 2.9.4, and many more. See H.-J. Gehrke and E. Wirbelauer in *Inventory*, 374.

[192] 15.45.2–3; Xen. *Hell.* 6.2.2–3. On Diodorus' text and the chronology of events see the extended discussion in Stylianou, *Commentary*, 348–63.

[193] H.-J. Gehrke and E. Wirbelauer in *Inventory*, 374. F. W. Mitchel, however, would date the expulsion of the oligarchs by the *demos* to 376/5 or a little earlier, based on a reevaluation of the Zacynthian *demos* entry in the document proclaiming the Second Athenian League (see next note) and the differing locations of where these exiles were in the inscription and the texts. "The Nellos (*IG* II2 43 B 35–38)," *Chiron* 11 (1981), 73–7. If his hypothesis is correct (which is far from certain) the *demos* will have held power for at most a year or two before being overthrown.

exiles to the point of admitting them into their Second Athenian League (*Zakun[th]ion ho demos ho en toi Nelloî*).[194] The result of the conflict as regards Zacynthus is not reported in our sources, however, and we cannot judge what happened constitutionally.[195] That Dion in 357 launched his expedition to Sicily from the island indicates little (Plut. *Dion* 22).

The limit of what can be said about a Zacynthian *demokratia*, therefore, is that one almost certainly held sway for a limited time in the first quarter of the fourth century after the *demos* had driven out its opposition; there may also have been democracy in the fifth century during Zacynthus' alliance with Athens and in the fourth after 374 if the Athenian support of the exiled *demos* won out, but evidence to confirm either proposition is lacking.

[194] *IG* 2² 43, in the margins at lines 79–82, evidently an additional entry. The decree dates to 378/7.
[195] Gehrke, *Stasis*, 198–9.

CHAPTER 2

Classical demokratiai *in western and northwestern Greece (plus Cyrene)*

This chapter discusses democracies located in Sicily and southern Italy, as well as Corcyra, Epidamnus, and Cyrene, from 480 to 323 BC. The treatment covers all the examples for which there is strong evidence of *demokratia* at some point during this period, resulting in certainty or probability of democracy in each case. Further cases (for which there is less available evidence) could have existed as well, of course.

Sicilian cities come up first for discussion, followed by Italian ones,[1] then Corcyra, Epidamnus, and Cyrene. Within the subsections a roughly alphabetical order will be followed, though I begin the chapter with Syracuse owing to its importance.

SICILIAN CITIES

Syracuse[2]

Scholars have reached conflicting conclusions about Syracusan democracy in the fifth century BC. Late in the century things become clear, for in 412 the politician Diocles persuaded the citizens in the assembly to enact new laws including a provision for the use of the lot for choosing officials, thereby enhancing the democratic nature of the constitution.[3] From this point until Dionysius' assumption of tyranny in 406 the existence of *demokratia* in Syracuse seems certain.[4] But how should we describe the

---

[1] Messana, though a Sicilian city, is discussed together with Rhegium in the Italian subsection.

[2] The treatment of Syracuse in this chapter represents a revision and substantial expansion of "Democracy in Syracuse, 466–412 BC," *HSPh* 100 (2000), 189–205 (which was reprinted in *Ancient Greek Democracy* [Malden, MA, 2004], 140–51).

[3] The most important sources are Diod. Sic. 13.34.4–35.5 and Arist. *Pol.* 1304a27–8. See below for discussion of how great a change this was. On the possibility of a slightly later date for the Diocles reforms, see A. W. Gomme, A. Andrewes, and K. J. Dover, *A Historical Commentary on Thucydides*, vol. IV (Oxford, 1970), 430–1.

[4] Cf., however, Arist. *Pol.* 1305b39–1306a2, with discussion below at note 23.

government of the preceding several decades, the crucial stretch of years between 466 and 412 BC? Some consider that a democracy existed then as well, while others would deny that title. Even those who accept the ancient testimony for *demokratia* sometimes assert that the popular government was of a moderate or even aristocratic kind, and it was certainly not as radical as the contemporary Athenian variety.

In terms of the history of ancient democracy, this issue is an important one to settle. Few classical *poleis* outside Athens offer more testimony about the history of their government than Syracuse, and in western Greece Syracuse is unique in having both a fair amount of narrative extant about its political history and to have been repeatedly labeled a *demokratia*. It was also a major power that exerted enormous influence in the region. If we are to understand the phenomenon of classical democracy in western Greece, then it is essential to clarify how fifth-century Syracuse fits into the picture.

Syracusan democracy had its start – albeit a false one – in the early fifth century. As argued in *The First Democracies*, from *c.* 491 until Gelon's seizure of power in 485 our sources indicate that Syracuse came to be democratically governed after a violent revolution carried out against the wealthy landowning class, the *gamoroi*. Participating in this upheaval were the *Kyllyrioi*, a servile population probably deriving from conquered native populations, who gained a role in the governing (*politeuma*) of the state in consequence of the revolution.[5] There is little to go on about the nature of the resulting popular constitution, and its rapid replacement at the hands of Gelon with dynastic tyranny means that any continuity of traditions or institutions between this government and the democracy that came after would be difficult to posit. Gelon allowed meetings of the assembly to continue, it is true, but he also restored the elite families of the *gamoroi*, thereby reversing a central aspect of the revolution.[6]

With the fall of the Deinomenid tyrants in the 460s BC, popular government returned to Syracuse, though its precise nature has been disputed. The following analysis of the period from 466 to 412 proceeds from two different perspectives. First we will look at the direct constitutional evidence,

---

[5] Hdt. 7.155; Arist. *Pol.* 1302b25–33; see also Diod. Sic. 10.28 and Photius s.v. *Killyrioi*. Robinson, *First Democracies*, 120–2; N. K. Rutter, "Syracusan Democracy: Most Like the Athenian?," in R. Brock and S. Hodkinson, eds, *Alternatives to Athens* (Oxford, 2000), 137–51, at 138–41. On the *Politics* passage, N. Luraghi, "Crollo della democrazia o sollevazione anti-oligarchica? Syracusa e Rodi in Aristotle, *Politica* 5 1302 b15–33," *Hermes* 126 (1998), 117–23.

[6] Hdt. 7.155; Diod. Sic. 11.26.5–6. On Gelon and the *demos*, Berve, *Tyrannis*, 142–4.

statements by ancient historians and others that one constitution or other came into being by revolution or legislation. Scholars have naturally looked primarily to this kind of testimony to sort out the issue. The evidence is not unequivocal: while it seems to support the contention that democracy held sway, there are elements which prompt some commentators to question the popular nature of the government. That Syracuse possessed a vigorous *demokratia* at this time emerges most clearly only after considering more indirect evidence as well, to include the attitude displayed by the ruling *demos*, demagoguery in the assembly, and the fostering of political rhetoric. Exploration of these topics suggests the existence of a vibrant democratic ideology comparable in some ways to that of fifth- and fourth-century Athens.

Constitutional testimony

The most important accounts concerning the Syracusan government after 466[7] come in Aristotle's *Politics* and Diodorus' and Thucydides' histories. At 11.67–8 Diodorus, who probably drew on Timaeus for this portion of his narrative,[8] states that when the Deinomenid tyrant Thrasybulus came to power he showed himself to be an even more cruel ruler than his brother Hieron had been, murdering and exiling many Syracusans while bringing in numerous mercenaries to maintain his control. The citizens soon banded together to oust him: the entire *polis* was united in the effort, and Thrasybulus was forced to gather an army of allies and mercenaries to fight the Syracusans. He seized parts of the city and waged war until, defeated in battles on land and sea, he negotiated his withdrawal to Locri.

---

[7] Diod. Sic. 11.38.7, 11.86.6 and Arist. *Pol.* 1315b34–8 combine to suggest a date for the overthrow of Thrasybulus in 466 or 465. W. S. Barrett argues convincingly that it must have been 466 in "Pindar's Twelfth *Olympian* and the Fall of the Deinomenidai," *JHS* 93 (1973), 23–35.

[8] K. Meister, *Die sizilische Geschichte bei Diodor von den Anfängen bis zum Tod des Agathokles* (diss. Ludwig-Maximilians-Universität, Munich, 1967), 47; D. Asheri, "Sicily, 478–431 BC," in D. M. Lewis *et al.*, eds., *CAH²*, vol. v (Cambridge, 1992), 147–70, at 165.

K. Sacks, in the course of his argument for a more independently minded Diodorus than hitherto accepted, notes that the Sicilian historian did not always despise democracy even though he seems to have considered the system vulnerable to demagoguery; *Diodorus Siculus and the First Century* (Princeton, 1990), 167. There is little reason to think Diodorus' lateness has impaired his understanding of *demokratia*: other portions of his history show a clear enough understanding of the government involved (though a few sections are suspicious – see Rutter, "Syracusan Democracy," 144–5); but in any case fifth- and fourth-century sources corroborate his use of the term here (see below). On the sometimes slippery nature of the term in the Hellenistic period and beyond, see J. A. O. Larsen, "Representation and Democracy in Hellenistic Federalism," *CPh* 40 (1945), 65–97, esp. 88–91, and de Ste. Croix, *Class Struggle*, 321–6. But cf. P. Gauthier, "Les cités hellénistiques," in M. H. Hansen, ed., *The Ancient Greek City-State* (Copenhagen, 1993), 211–31.

Diodorus states that from this time the city enjoyed peace and prosperity and "guarded its *demokratia* for almost sixty years, until the tyranny of Dionysius."[9]

At this point the Syracusans made a number of key decisions. They liberated and restored democracies to other Sicilian cities that had also been under tyranny (11.68.5).[10] They also held an assembly meeting (*ekklesia*) in Syracuse at which the citizens took counsel about their own democracy (11.72). Ceremonial matters were voted on, including the commissioning of a colossal statue to Zeus Eleutherios (the Liberator) and the institution of annual games and sacrifices in honor of Eleutheria.[11] The assembly also decided to restrict office-holding to those who had been citizens before the Deinomenid tyranny – for during his reign Gelon had made 10,000 foreign mercenaries citizens, and the original Syracusans did not trust the 7,000 or so mercenary-citizens who were still around.[12] The denial of access to office sparked a nasty rebellion; the foreigners (*xenoi*, as Diodorus calls them) were defeated only after a difficult fight.[13]

Diodorus describes another significant episode for the new democracy, this in his account for the year 454 (11.86–7). After a man named Tyndarides attempted a coup, and other would-be tyrants threatened now and again,

---

[9] ἀπὸ δὲ τούτων τῶν χρόνων εἰρήνην ἔχουσα πολλὴν ἐπίδοσιν ἔλαβε πρὸς εὐδαιμονίαν, καὶ διεφύλαξε τὴν δημοκρατίαν ἔτη σχεδὸν ἑξήκοντα μέχρι τῆς Διονυσίου τυραννίδος (11.68.6).

[10] This statement becomes especially important with respect to the emergence of other Sicilian democracies in this period: see their individual case studies later in this chapter. On Sicilian coinages at this time, which do not always reflect the political changes manifestly underway, see N. K. Rutter, *Greek Coinages of Southern Italy and Sicily* (London, 1997), 132–9.

[11] καταλύσαντες τὴν Θρασυβούλου τυραννίδα συνήγαγον ἐκκλησίαν, καὶ περὶ τῆς ἰδίας δημοκρατίας βουλευσάμενοι πάντες ὁμογνωμόνως ἐψηφίσαντο Διὸς μὲν ἐλευθερίου κολοττιαῖον ἀνδριάντα κατασκευάσαι, κατ᾿ ἐνιαυτὸν δὲ θύειν ἐλευθέρια καὶ ἀγῶνας ἐπιφανεῖς ποιεῖν κατὰ τὴν αὐτὴν ἡμέραν, ἐν ἧ τὸν τύραννον καταλύσαντες ἠλευθέρωσαν τὴν πατρίδα· θύειν δ᾿ ἐν τοῖς ἀγῶσι τοῖς θεοῖς ταύρους τετρακοσίους καὶ πεντήκοντα, καὶ τούτους δαπανᾶν εἰς τὴν τῶν πολιτῶν εὐωχίαν (11.72.2).

[12] τὰς δὲ ἀρχὰς ἁπάσας τοῖς ἀρχαίοις πολίταις ἀπένεμον· τοὺς δὲ ξένους τοὺς ἐπὶ τοῦ Γέλωνος πολιτευθέντας οὐκ ἠξίουν μετέχειν ταύτης τῆς τιμῆς, εἴτε οὐκ ἀξίους κρίναντες, εἴτε καὶ ἀπιστοῦντες μήποτε συντεθραμμένοι τυραννίδι καὶ μονάρχῳ συνεστρατευμένοι νεωτερίζειν ἐπιχειρήσωσιν· ὅπερ καὶ συνέβη γενέσθαι (11.72.3).

[13] Diod. Sic. 11.73. Arist. *Pol.* 1303b1–2 apparently refers to the same incident but with a notable discrepancy. During his discussion of how faction can be caused in cities by the admission of additional citizens, he states that "the Syracusans after the tyrannical period, having made citizens of foreigners and mercenaries, fell into stasis and battle." This summary version implies that the outsiders were made citizens *after* the fall of the Deinomenids, not by them. No explanation is offered as to why faction then broke out (denial of offices? Perhaps the new *demos* voted to confirm only partially a previous grant of citizenship, prohibiting them from office, which sparked the fighting). On the whole the much fuller Diodoran account is to be preferred, though one is left to wonder whether Aristotle made an error in his rush to offer a condensed example of *stasis*-by-citizenship or was working from a slightly different tradition. See also D. Keyt, *Aristotle* Politics *Books V and VI* (Oxford 1999), 91–2.

the Syracusans instituted the practice of petalism, a sort of Syracusan ostracism.[14] The goal was to protect against tyranny by countering the presumption and influence of the most powerful.[15] Leaders could now be exiled by a simple popular vote; the exile was for a period of five years (instead of Athens' ten), and votes were recorded on olive leaves rather than ostraka. However, after a short period of time the Syracusans discontinued the practice. According to Diodorus, the best and most prominent men were avoiding public affairs for fear of petalism, leaving matters in the hands of less capable, troublesome leaders, which resulted in factional conflict (*stasis*). So the Syracusans repealed the law.[16] (The Athenians eventually stopped their practice as well, of course, though only after several decades of use and without taking it off the books.)

Aristotle in the *Politics* seems to confirm Diodorus' assertion of democratic revolution in 466: at 1316a32–3 the philosopher lists the end of the tyranny of Gelon's family in Syracuse as an example of transition from tyranny to *demokratia*.[17] But this testimony is confused by his claim at 1304a27–9 that after the victory over the Athenians in 413, a triumphant Syracusan *demos* changed the government from a *politeia* to a *demokratia*.[18] This assertion implies that the government down to 413 had been a *politeia*, or polity, a system which the philosopher says mixes oligarchic and democratic elements (*Pol.* 1293b33–4). Aristotle certainly seems to contradict

[14] Diodorus claims the Syracusans were copying Athenian practice. For problems with this assertion, see S. Forsdyke, *Exile, Ostracism, and Democracy* (Princeton, 2005), 285–7.

[15] τούτῳ γὰρ τῷ τρόπῳ διελάμβανον ταπεινώσειν τὰ φρονήματα τῶν πλεῖστον ἰσχυόντων ἐν ταῖς πατρίσι (11.87.2). Tyndarides had collected a sizable bodyguard from among the poorest (*ton peneton*), a common practice for seekers of tyranny. It is risky to read a genuine political program into this power play: Diodorus does not describe Tyndarides as leader of the people or demagogue, only as a person of presumptuous daring. No aristocratic crackdown results from his defeat, but rather petalism, specifically aimed at the high and mighty of the city.

[16] Diodorus does not tell us whether another marker of *demokratia*, pay for public service, was enacted at Syracuse in addition to petalism. It may or may not have been: given the meager evidence for Syracusan history in this era, the negative *argumentum e silentio* is particularly weak. Sortition for offices other than the generalship apparently begins only in 412 after Diocles' legislation (Diod. Sic. 13.34).

[17] ἀλλὰ μεταβάλλει καὶ εἰς τυραννίδα τυραννίς, ὥσπερ ἡ Σικυῶνος ἐκ τῆς Μύρωνος εἰς τὴν Κλεισθένους, καὶ εἰς ὀλιγαρχίαν, ὥσπερ ἡ ἐν Χαλκίδι ἡ Ἀντιλέοντος, καὶ εἰς δημοκρατίαν, ὥσπερ ἡ τῶν Γέλωνος ἐν Συρακούσαις, καὶ εἰς ἀριστοκρατίαν, ὥσπερ ἡ Χαρίλλου ἐν Λακεδαίμονι (1316a 30–4). Cf. *Pol.* 1312b10–16.

[18] καὶ ἐν Συρακούσαις ὁ δῆμος αἴτιος γενόμενος τῆς νίκης τοῦ πολέμου τοῦ πρὸς Ἀθηναίους ἐκ πολιτείας εἰς δημοκρατίαν μετέβαλεν. Cf. W. L. Newman, *The Politics of Aristotle*, vol. IV (Oxford, 1902), 328–9; Aubonnet, *Aristote Politique*, 168, 233.

Diodorus also mentions important political changes at Syracuse soon after the Athenian expedition, changes instituted by Diocles and including the choosing of offices by lot. He does not, however, apply a label to either the old or the new political order (13.33–5), leaving us with his earlier statement that the *demokratia* in Syracuse continued for sixty years.

himself with these statements – did he consider Syracuse a *politeia* or a democracy? One cannot get around the problem by supposing that sometime between 466 and 413 there was another constitutional revolution, omitted in all our sources, in which the post-Deinomenid democracy became a *politeia*. There is simply no evidence for this; moreover, Thucydides, our only contemporary source for these events, clearly identifies Syracuse as a *demokratia* during Athens' Sicilian Expedition of 415–413.[19] This testimony is crucial. On the one hand, it rules out a shadowy prior revolution from *demokratia* to *politeia* (unless we want to imagine a *second* unattested revolution back to *demokratia* before 415), thus retaining the contradiction in Aristotle. On the other hand, and more importantly, it offers powerful evidence that Syracuse was indeed democratic during the period claimed by Diodorus.

Interpretations

It is perhaps surprising, then, that a number of scholars confidently conclude from the available testimony that the Syracusan state was *not* democratic after the fall of the Deinomenid tyranny, at least not until the reforms of Diocles many decades later in 412. H. Wentker in his 1956 book *Sizilien und Athen* asserted that a *politeia* was installed, one dominated by wealthy landowners. Despite a scathing rebuttal by P. A. Brunt in a review of Wentker's book, others have since voiced similar interpretations. A. Lintott, for example, claims that a "broad oligarchy" took over affairs after the tyrants fell, with an aristocratic elite retaining substantial control thereafter. B. Caven makes similar statements. In a book on Syracusan imperialism and government, S. Consolo Langher maintains that power was in the hands of the knightly and hoplite classes: *politeia*, not full democracy, held sway in Syracuse after the revolution. And M. Hofer believes that, at least in its initial stages, the new order resembled a "gemässigten Aristokratie."[20]

---

[19] [Describing Athenian despair after a Syracusan naval victory in 413:] πόλεσι γὰρ ταύταις μόναις ἤδη ὁμοιοτρόποις ἐπελθόντες, δημοκρατουμέναις τε, ὥσπερ καὶ αὐτοί, καὶ ναῦς καὶ ἵππους καὶ μεγέθη ἐχούσαις, οὐ δυνάμενοι ἐπενεγκεῖν οὔτ᾿ ἐκ πολιτείας τι μεταβολῆς τὸ διάφορον αὐτοῖς, ᾧ προσήγοντο ἄν, οὔτ᾿ ἐκ παρασκευῆς πολλῷ κρείσσονος, σφαλλόμενοι δὲ τὰ πλείω, τά τε πρὸ αὐτῶν ἠπόρουν, καὶ ἐπειδή γε καὶ ταῖς ναυσὶν ἐκρατήθησαν, ὃ οὐκ ἂν ᾤοντο, πολλῷ δὴ μᾶλλον ἔτι (7.55.2). See also 6.39, where two years earlier Athenagoras uses the name *demokratia* in his defense of the government at Syracuse.

[20] H. Wentker, *Sizilien und Athen. Die Begegnung der attischen Macht mit den Westgriechen* (Heidelberg, 1956), 52–3; P. A. Brunt, review of Wentker in *CR* n.s. 7 (1957), 243–5; A. Lintott, *Violence, Civil Strife, and Revolution in the Classical City* (London, 1972), 187–91; B. Caven, *Dionysius I, Warlord of Syracuse* (New Haven, 1990), 15; S. N. Consolo Langher, *Un imperialismo tra democrazia e tirannide. Siracusa nei secoli V e IV a.C.* (Rome, 1997), 51–3; M. Hofer, *Tyrannen, Aristokraten, Demokraten* (Bern, 2000), 151, cf. 182. More thorough is Rutter, "Syracusan Democracy." Earlier standard works

At least one non-classicist has used such views to fuel sweeping conclusions: S. Weart declares in his book *Never at War* that no well-established democracy, ancient or modern, has *ever* made war on another one. He can make this startling argument only because of the occasionally voiced notion that Syracuse, before and during the time of its war with Athens, was not really a democracy.²¹

To reach such conclusions scholars primarily rely upon Aristotle's passage stating that Syracuse went from *politeia* to democracy in 412.²² But as we have seen, Aristotle compromises his statement by elsewhere describing the revolution against Thrasybulus as resulting precisely in democracy. The contradiction renders his testimony a dubious basis for assertions of an undemocratic Syracuse, while Diodorus' and Thucydides' statements that *demokratia* existed are unambiguous.²³ If but one of the Aristotle passages is to be plucked out and given credence, it ought to be the one confirmed by the other sources.

such as W. Hüttl's *Verfassungsgeschichte von Syrakus* (Prague, 1929) accept the ancient testimony for democracy in Syracuse during this time (65–99). More recent authors who concur, though not all to the same degree, include: M. Giangiulio, "Gli equilibri difficili della democrazia in Sicilia: il caso di Siracusa," in L. Canfora, ed., *Venticinque secoli dopo l'invenzione della Democrazia*, (Paestum, 1998), 107–23; O'Neil, *Origins and Development*, 43–4, 73–5; Asheri, "Sicily, 478–431 B.C.," 165–70; D. M. Lewis, "Sicily, 413–368 B.C.," in D. M. Lewis *et al.*, eds., *CAH²*, vol. vi (Cambridge, 1994), 120–55, esp. 125–6; M. I. Finley, *Ancient Sicily* (2nd edn; Totowa, NJ, 1979), 58–73; Gomme, Andrewes, and Dover, *HCT*, vol. iv, 430–1; T. Fischer-Hansen, T. H. Nielsen, and C. Ampolo in *Inventory*, 226–7; Brunt, review cited above.

²¹ S. Weart, *Never at War: Why Democracies Will Not Fight One Another* (New Haven, 1998), esp. 1–37, 298–9. For the debate over his and others' theories of an ancient "democratic peace," see Chapter 5.

²² One can also look to *Pol.* 1312b4–9, where Aristotle can be taken to imply that Syracuse around this time was governed "*kalos*" by a *politeia*. (So Rutter, "Syracusan Democracy," 142.) However, two problems attend this reading: (1) The period to which Aristotle refers is uncertain, as all he says is that this was "during the time when the Syracusans were governed well," *kai Syrakousioi kata ton chronon hon epoliteuonto kalos*; and (2) Aristotle actually seems to imply that the government at this (unspecified) time was a *basileia* or *aristokratia*, not a *politeia* (or *demokratia* for that matter).

²³ In fact, Aristotle's apparent confusion and self-contradiction continues past Diocles' reforms. At *Pol.* 1305b39–1306b2, in the course of discussing ways in which oligarchies can incur revolution by extravagant spending and licentious living, resulting in attempts at tyranny for oneself or others, he gives as an example Hipparinus' promotion of Dionysius at Syracuse (on Hipparinus see also Plut. *Dion*, 3). Thus Aristotle would seem to be claiming that the government from 412 to 406 was oligarchic, in direct contradiction of his statement at 1304a27–9. That he is wrong is strongly signalled by Diodorus' description of events leading up to the tyranny of Dionysius, which make clear the dominating role of the people in asserting their will over the magistrates and overseeing the conduct of the war with the Carthaginians with many meetings of the *ekklesia*, 13.91.3–5 and 13.92.4 (plus the use of the lot, 13.34.4–35.5; and Plato's condemnation of excessive freedom among the populace before the tyranny, pl., *Letters* 8.353–4). Perhaps Aristotle did not mean to imply that Syracuse was truly an oligarchy at the time, but only that would-be oligarchs, men of that class – such as Hipparinus – can be led to foment revolution in any government thanks to their own profligate ways. Or maybe he mentions Hipparinus as an example of someone helping someone else to tyranny, not as an example of oligarchies destroying themselves. Either solution would save Aristotle from error, but neither seems a natural reading.

Moreover, even though the *Politics* does not lack contradictions within its pages, it might be possible to save Aristotle in this instance to the following degree: in the *Politics* and the *Nicomachean Ethics* when comparing correct (*orthai*) and deviant (*parekbaseis*) forms of constitutions, he refers to *politeia* and *demokratia* as counterparts, the good and bad versions of rule by the mass (*plethos*) of the citizens.[24] Perhaps in using *politeia* at *Politics* 1304a27–9 Aristotle merely meant that in 412 the legislation pushed through by the demagogue Diocles[25] turned a relatively responsible popular government into an irresponsible one – not that it became popular for the first time. Such a reading would elide the apparent contradiction and accord more neatly with the other sources.[26] Furthermore, Aristotle's use of *politeia* in this sense could have been contextually determined: since Diocles had convinced the people to adopt another trademark democratic institution, sortition for officials, Aristotle naturally labeled the post-412 government *demokratia*. He then needed, however, another term to describe the earlier democracy. In the philosopher's vocabulary of constitutional types, *politeia* came the closest.

Some scholars analyzing post-Deinomenid Syracuse take a somewhat more careful path than those who doubt democracy altogether. S. Berger and N. K. Rutter do not quite deny the title of *demokratia* but contend that aristocratic elements remained highly influential. This conclusion, while still open to debate, at least does not fly in the face of the majority of the testimony. Berger points to two incidents in mid-fifth-century Syracusan history as particularly revealing: the *demos*'s denial of full participation to the mercenary-citizens of Gelon, and the brief duration of petalism at

---

[24] *Pol.* 1279a22–b19, esp. a37–9; *Eth. Nic.* 8.10–11 (1160a31–1161b11), esp. 10.3.

[25] See above note 23.

[26] Attractive as it is, this interpretation must remain uncertain because of the multivalent nature of the term for Aristotle. For example, in some places *politeia* denotes a government in which the hoplite class rules (*Pol.* 1265b26–9; 1279b2–4; 1288a6–15), a definition which sounds too restrictive even for Aristotle's favored, conservative forms of democracy (*Pol.* 1291b30–9, 1292b22–34, and 1318b6–1319a6). On the awkward double duty that *politeia* performs in the middle books of the *Politics*, caught between two conflicting analytical schemata, see R. Mulgan, "Aristotle's Analysis of Oligarchy and Democracy," in D. Keyt and F. D. Miller, Jr, eds., *A Companion to Aristotle's* Politics, (Oxford, 1991), 307–22, esp. 309–12.

Keyt, *Aristotle* Politics, 99–100 tentatively offers a different solution to the apparent contradiction: he points to Aristotle's statement at *Pol.* 1297b24–5 that in former times *politeiai* were called democracies. But the context of this statement, 1297b16–28, hardly suits Keyt's suggestion, for Aristotle is discussing times far earlier than fifth century Syracuse: he mentions the *first* Greek constitutions (after the fall of the primeval kings) and their development with the growth of cities and the emergence of heavily armed soldiers. Even if the statement could be taken to apply to our period, one would expect it to refer to writers other than Aristotle himself – would he not wish to correct source anachronisms in his own treatises, aware of the problem as he is?

Syracuse. These events Berger declares to be fundamentally undemocratic and to demonstrate the "pervasive power of the aristocracy."[27] Regarding the first incident, one might point out that there is nothing inherently undemocratic about restricting citizenship: famous democracies ancient and modern have done it frequently. The United States, for example, although priding itself on its immigrant heritage, has at times placed the severest limitations on which people from which countries might immigrate or be naturalized (consider the Chinese Exclusion Act of 1882, enforced well into the twentieth century); and in the "radical" Athenian democracy the very restrictive Periclean law of 451/0 significantly tightened access to citizenship.[28] Moreover, the original Syracusan citizens had good reason to be suspicious of foreign mercenaries brought into the city for the purpose of assuring a tyrant's power over them – why should the newly empowered *demos* respect such citizenship? That the people refused to do so should not be interpreted as the mark of political elitism. Secondly, regarding the duration of petalism, the fact that such a forceful populist tool was employed at all is a strong indicator of thorough-going democracy, even if after a time the citizens discontinued its use. Aristocratic power could not have been as dominant as Berger supposes for such a popular weapon to have been enacted and used with terrific effect against the elite of the city.

Rutter shares some of Berger's concerns about Syracusan citizenship and petalism but is even more troubled by inconsistency or unreliability in the ancient sources that claim *demokratia*, as well as on the lack of a visible role played by a probouleutic council and the absence of other constitutional details. Aristotle's obvious uncertainty about democracy or *politeia* (or oligarchy) at Syracuse probably signals some real difficulty in defining the system there, Rutter argues, while Diodorus' use of the term *demokratia* cannot always be trusted and Thucydides can sometimes blur distinctions between oligarchy and democracy when describing a community's decisions and actions. I have already discussed above the utility of Aristotle and

---

[27] S. Berger, *Revolution and Society in Greek Sicily and Southern Italy* (Stuttgart 1992 [*Historia* Einzelschriften 71]), 37–9; "Democracy in the Greek West and the Athenian Example," *Hermes* 117 (1989), 303–14.

[28] On US immigration law and the Chinese, L. E. Salyer, *Laws Harsh as Tigers: Chinese Immigrants and the Shaping of Modern Immigration Law* (Chapel Hill, 1995) and E. P. Hutchinson, *Legislative History of American Immigration Policy, 1798 – 1965* (Philadelphia, 1981).

Concerning the Periclean law, see generally C. Patterson, *Pericles' Citizenship Law of 451/0 B.C.* (New York, 1981). A. L. Boegehold offers some informed speculation about the popular politics behind the measure in "Pericles' Citizenship Law of 451/0 B.C." in A. L. Boegehold and A. C. Scafuro, eds., *Athenian Identity and Civic Ideology* (Baltimore, 1994) 57–66.

Diodorus as sources: Aristotle's self-contradictions are worrying, though his use of *politeia* at times to mean "correct" popular government provides a partial solution to his difficulties; Diodorus' distance from events (and potentially loose employment of *demokratia* in other parts of his history) does not invalidate his testimony.[29] The key author, however, is Thucydides, and here Rutter's concerns carry the least conviction. Of the three he is the author in the best position to have known how things stood in Syracuse, and his grasp of fifth-century Greek ideas about what constituted *demokratia* should be the most reliable. Even if his descriptions of a given state's actions can sometimes be constitutionally non-specific, in the case of Syracuse they most emphatically are not: he is explicit in his use of the terms *demokratia* and *demokratoumenai* for the Syracusans, and, further, as Rutter concedes, the picture that emerges from his account certainly appears democratic and in many ways comparable to contemporary Athenian practice.[30] The fact that our brief literary accounts, including that of Thucydides, fail to describe the actions of a probouleutic council or note such details as how often the assembly met – all of which would be nice to know more about, to be sure – cannot be taken as evidence that Thucydides (or others) misunderstood the basic nature of the Syracusan constitution.[31]

In sum, the *prima facie* case for the existence of democracy in Syracuse from 466 to 412 is more formidable than some commentators are willing to believe, and the available ancient testimony hardly seems to warrant reading aristocratic domination into the picture. However, one must concede that Aristotle's inconsistency opens the door for speculation about the constitution's nature, and the direct testimony is sparse enough to leave room for reasonable debate. Let us consider, then, other evidence that is not so much constitutional as ideological. Through more than one study Josiah Ober has established that a coherent popular ideology existed in Athens during its democracy, an ideology which successfully challenged the aristocratic values of the elites.[32] It is possible to identify a similar ideology at work in Syracuse, albeit from a much smaller store of available evidence. Peripheral passages not often taken into account show the Syracusan *demos* behaving in archetypically "democratic" ways between 466 and 412, bolstering the case for a radically popular government.

---

[29] See above, text and note 8.   [30] Rutter, "Syracusan Democracy," 148–50.
[31] See discussion below on Syracusan institutions.
[32] *Mass and Elite in Democratic Athens* (Princeton, 1989); *The Athenian Revolution* (Princeton 1996). For ideas on the shifting ideological equilibrium in democratic Syracuse, cf. Giangiulio, "Democrazia in Sicilia," 110–19.

Generals, demagogues, and the use of rhetoric

One of the reasons Diodorus gives for the enacting of petalism in Syracuse was to check the pride of the powerful (*tapeinosein ta phronemata ton pleiston ischuonton en tais patrisi*, 11.87.2). Another sign of a populist sentiment to bring the mighty low can be seen in the pattern of arbitrary and/or harsh punishment of generals which emerges in this period.[33] Throughout antiquity, of course, states of varying governments have at times accused failed generals of malfeasance; nevertheless, democracies seem to have been particularly enamored of this activity,[34] and Syracuse in our period shows a high number of incidents relative to the available testimony. Diodorus records for the year 453 that a man named Phayllus was elected navarch to lead an expedition against Tyrrhenian pirates. He took his forces as far as an island in the enemy sphere and ravaged it but did not seem to do anything else of significance. Upon his return, the citizens (*hoi Surakosioi*) convicted him of treachery and sent him into exile. A replacement was selected, who, not surprisingly, campaigned against the pirates much more aggressively (11.88). Though Diodorus accepts the verdict of the people, briefly stating that Phayllus did secretly (*lathrai*) take a bribe from the enemy, one cannot help wonder how he or his source knew the truth of the matter. Was clear proof of the "secret" bribery at hand, or was this just a case of public frustration with a dilatory commander who inspired charges from opponents? Two years later another unsuccessful general suffered the wrath of the people. Bolkon, acting in cooperation with allied forces, attempted to come to the aid of a city besieged by Ducetius and the Sicels. Bolkon was defeated and driven out of his camp by the enemy; with the onset of winter, he withdrew homeward as did his opponent. Once again the Syracusans read foul play into events: the general was accused of secretly acting in concert with Ducetius, convicted of treason – and executed. (Diodorus makes no comment as to the truth of the charges this time.) As one might expect, in the next summer Bolkon's successor, acting under clear orders to take the war to Ducetius, attacked straightaway (11.91).[35] Finally, Thucydides reports a similar episode. In 414, during the early stages of the Athenian siege against the city, the Syracusans sustained a number of defeats. They could not match the Athenian ground or sea

---

[33] On the number of generals at Syracuse and their significance, see below under Institutions.

[34] Hansen, *Athenian Democracy*, 215–18; Hamel, *Athenian Generals*, esp. 115–60. Cf. W. K. Pritchett, "Trials of Generals," in *The Greek State at War*, vol. II (Berkeley, 1974), 4–33.

[35] The tendency of the replacements to fall into line with the popular will is understandable, and it further indicates a *demos* fully in charge: consider Thucydides' praise of Pericles for bucking the trend of *demokratia* by daring to stand up to the whims of the people, something the ordinary democratic politician fails to do (2.65.8–10). See also Hamel, *Athenian Generals*, 118–21, 158–60.

forces, lost important skirmishes for control of the territory around the city, and seemed unable to stop the progress of the Athenian siege works (6.96–102). Their generals soon came under fire and were stripped of their office; new ones were elected. The reasoning, reported by Thucydides, is telling: the Syracusans considered that their recent woes resulted from the generals' bad luck *or* from their treachery (*e dustuchiai e prodosiai*, 6.103.4). Apparently it was unclear which was the cause, or the cause simply did not matter. The people were upset at the results of the campaign and took it out on the generals.[36]

Syracuse's harsh or vengeful behavior toward its generals does not in itself prove the existence of democracy, but it is suggestive of a populist attitude very much in line with the ancient stereotype – and sometimes the reality – of *demokratia*. Critics of democracy such as the "Old Oligarch" in his *Constitution of the Athenians* and Aristotle in the *Politics* take it as an established fact that in democracy the poor majority rule in their own interest and against the interest of the aristocrats. Elites suffer in public arenas such as the courts, where (lower-) class interest overwhelms justice; their political influence is often eclipsed by demagogues; and the assembled people blame leaders personally for failures of state policy.[37] To modern, democratically inclined ears this sort of whining from aristocratic circles may not arouse the intended sympathy. Nevertheless, occasions of victimization matching the accusations do occur. Consider the Old Oligarch's complaint, "If anything bad results from a decision taken by the *demos*, the *demos* charges that a few men acting against them corrupted things."[38] This allegation matches what we have seen happening in Syracuse, where unsuccessful generals were not merely disregarded or disadvantaged in the next election but were assumed to have committed treason and were punished on that basis. Democratic Athens, the target of the Old Oligarch's observations, also provides plentiful examples of generals finding themselves on trial or in flight from an angry *demos* after military debacles.

[36] Actual treason seems unlikely here: Thucydides, fascinated by the manner of warfare and the shifting tides of the battle for Syracuse, provides a detailed description of the fighting which led up to these events, yet at no point gives any hint of collusion or betrayal by Syracusan leaders.

[37] *Pol.* 1279b8–10, 1292a4–30, 1304b20–35, 1318b16–17; Ps.-Xen. *Ath. pol.* 1.3–9, 1.13–14, 2.9–10, 2.17–20. On these and other critics of democratic rule, see J. Ober, *Political Dissent in Democratic Athens* (Princeton, 1998). Affirming the truth of ancient assertions that the *demos* mistreated leaders at Athens is R. A. Knox, " 'So Mischievous a Beaste'? The Athenian *Demos* and Its Treatment of Its Politicians," *G&R* 32 (1985) 132–61. On generals as especially abused (two out of every board of ten may have faced prosecution during their careers), see Hansen, *Athenian Democracy*, 215–18 and other bibliography in note 34 above.

[38] καὶ ἂν μέν τι κακὸν ἀναβαίνη ἀπὸ ὧν ὁ δῆμος ἐβούλευσεν, αἰτιᾶται ὁ δῆμος ὡς ὀλίγοι ἄνθρωποι αὐτῷ ἀντιπράττοντες διέφθειραν (Ps.-Xen. *Ath. pol.* 2.17).

Thucydides himself, forced into exile after the fall of Amphipolis, makes an obvious case. Even more notable is Nicias' dread of slanderous political attack should he dare to give up the siege of Syracuse in 413 – indeed, what Nicias fears most of all is accusation that he was bribed to betray his men and withdraw.[39] The most infamous Athenian example comes with the actual execution, decreed by an overwrought assembly, of the generals in command at the battle of the Arginusae Islands in 406.[40] The Athenians later recognized the error of their rash act but of course could not put things right. One can only conclude that military leaders at Athens and Syracuse, usually members of the elite classes, served the *demos* at some personal risk: glory and popular influence could be theirs with success, but failure not uncommonly brought angry accusations of betrayal followed by dismissal, exile, or even execution. Ancient critics saw this as class-based injustice and – more importantly for our purposes – typical of democracy.

High-handed treatment of generals was not an anomalous populist feature within the broader picture of Syracusan politics. One finds further indications of typical democratic behavior in emotional or rash decision-making in the public assembly.[41] Some of the punitive actions already discussed resulted from demotic overexcitement, and other reports are worth noting, most particularly those indicating loud and boisterous *ekklesia* meetings at Syracuse.[42] Diodorus describes a meeting that took place just after the final defeat of the Athenians in which a popular demagogue spoke in favor of harsh punishment for captured Athenians. The proposal was well received; in fact, when Hermocrates took the floor and began to speak in opposition, "the *demos* made an uproar (*thorubountos*) and cut off his speech." The multitude only quieted itself down and allowed another person to present his views because it expected a more congenial opinion from

---

[39] ὡς ὑπὸ χρημάτων καταπροδόντες οἱ στρατηγοὶ ἀπῆλθον (Thuc. 7.48.4). See also the incident in 424 in which three Athenian generals were exiled or fined for alleged bribery after departing Sicily with their forces when peace broke out; Thuc. 4.65. Collecting and tabulating generals' depositions or prosecutions is Hamel, *Athenian Generals*, 136–57.

[40] Diod. Sic. 13.100–3; Xen. *Hell.* 1.6.33–1.7.35.

[41] Aristotle considers it the hallmark of the most radical kind of democracy when, as he puts it, "the multitude rule, and not the law," *Pol.* 1292a5; the irresponsibility of the *demos* in Athens (and Syracuse) is one of Thucydides' featured subjects. See also Ober, *Political Dissent*, ch. 2.

[42] Arguing persuasively for the essential connection between assembly *thorubos* and the democracy in Athens is J. Tacon, "Ecclesiastic *Thorubos*: Interventions, Interruptions, and Popular Involvement in the Athenian Assembly," *G&R* 48 (2001), 173–92. At p. 188: "Interruptions of the speaker by other speakers and by the *demos* at large with shouts, heckles, or cheers formed an integral part of Assembly debate and constituted a major aspect of the Athenian people's ability to communicate its collective views to the elite." See also the discussions in I. Sluiter and R. M. Rosen, eds., *Free Speech in Classical Antiquity* (Leiden, 2004), especially the treatments of R. W. Wallace, R. K. Balot, and J. Roisman at 221–78.

him.[43] After listening to all the speeches the crowd (*to plethos*) approved the severe punishments which the first demagogue had recommended (13.33). Plutarch also mentions this event, emphasizing the immoderate tumult and insolence (*hubris*) of the crowd (*Nic.* 28). We might imagine similar behavior at another *ekklesia* from a couple of years earlier. Thucydides in a brief account informs us that the Athenians, having arrived in Sicily, did not invade at once but kept their distance. This delay led the Syracusans to "despise their foe and order their generals to lead them out against" the enemy, "as the rabble (*ochlos*) tends to do when swelled with confidence."[44] Of course, marching out for battle played into Athenian hands and resulted in a major defeat. The use of *ochlos* here recalls Alcibiades' earlier sweeping characterization of the Sicilian population (surely aimed at the Syracusans most of all) as a mixed collection of mobs (*ochloi*) prone to disorder and disunity (Thuc. 6.17).[45]

The reported activities of demagogues at Syracuse further suggest a vibrant democracy, not only because they accord with Aristotle's comments on the subject (*Pol.* 1292a4–30), but also because potent demagoguery can exist only if the mass of ordinary people to whom demagogues make their appeals wield real power in the state. Diodorus says that starting in the 450s when petalism was employed, there arose a multitude of demagogues and sycophants (*demagogon plethos kai sukophanton*), and the young began to practice slick oratory (*logou deinotes*) (11.87). Some men became accustomed to demagoguery in speaking before the assembly (*enioi . . . ton demegorein eiothoton*, 11.92.3). We have seen one case already of demagogues at work among the people in the debate over Athenian prisoners reported

---

[43] Τότε μὲν οὖν τοῖς θεοῖς ἔθυσαν πανδημεί, τῇ δ᾽ ὑστεραίᾳ συναχθείσης ἐκκλησίας ἐβουλεύοντο, πῶς χρήσονται τοῖς αἰχμαλώτοις. Διοκλῆς δέ τις, τῶν δημαγωγῶν ἐνδοξότατος ὤν, ἀπεφήνατο γνώμην [to punish the Athenian captives harshly] . . . ἀναγνωσθέντος δὲ τοῦ ψηφίσματος Ἑρμοκράτης παρελθὼν εἰς τὴν ἐκκλησίαν ἐνεχείρει λέγειν, ὡς κάλλιόν ἐστι τοῦ νικᾶν τὸ τὴν νίκην ἐνεγκεῖν ἀνθρωπίνως. θορυβοῦντος δὲ τοῦ δήμου καὶ τὴν δημηγορίαν οὐχ ὑπομένοντος, Νικόλαός τις, ἐστερημένος ἐν τῷ πολέμῳ δυεῖν υἱῶν, ἀνέβαινεν ἐπὶ τὸ βῆμα κατεχόμενος ὑπὸ τῶν οἰκετῶν διὰ τὸ γῆρας· ὃν ὡς εἶδεν ὁ δῆμος, ἔληξε τοῦ θορύβου, νομίζων κατηγορήσειν τῶν αἰχμαλώτων (Diod. Sic. 13.19.4–6).

[44] ἔτι πλέον κατεφρόνησαν καὶ ἠξίουν τοὺς στρατηγούς, οἷον δὴ ὄχλος φιλεῖ θαρσήσας ποιεῖν, ἄγειν σφᾶς [the Syracusans] ἐπὶ Κατάνην, ἐπειδὴ οὐκ ἐκεῖνοι [the Athenians] ἐφ᾽ ἑαυτοὺς ἔρχονται (Thuc. 6.63.2).

[45] Alcibiades was doubtless exaggerating for political purposes, and Thucydides may have been trying to make subtle criticisms of *Athenian* democracy by highlighting Syracusan misadventures (cf. J. Ober, "Civic Ideology and Counterhegemonic Discourse: Thucydides on the Sicilian Debate," in A. L. Boegehold and A. C. Scafuro, eds., *Athenian Identity and Civic Ideology* [Baltimore, 1994], 102–26; Hornblower, *Commentary*, vol. III, 466, also sees an Athenian/Syracusan parallel being drawn). But such agendas are not important for the present argument: neither Thucydides nor Alcibiades could have been at all persuasive in making these statements if Syracuse was not generally known to be a democracy.

in Diodorus and Plutarch. There are other notable instances, including the inspiring of new popular legislation in 412. Diodorus describes Diocles, the prime mover, as a demagogue who "persuaded the *demos*" to make the reforms.[46] Then there was the famous assembly debate of 415, just before the Athenian expedition, featuring Hermocrates and a very shrill *prostates tou demou*, Athenagoras. The latter's speech, as reported by Thucydides (6.35–40), is remarkable for its fierce defense of popular rule and its vision of young oligarchic revolutionaries lurking in the shadows, waiting for an excuse to seize power. But most of all what strikes the reader is the speech's colossal wrong-headedness: Thucydides locates it, with its denial of a coming Athenian attack, immediately after his description of preparations for the very attack. The speech inevitably appears to the reader to be a blatant piece of demagoguery, a rant which spews groundless accusations and potentially endangers the state. It may be that Thucydides intended this episode as a commentary on the (mal)functioning of the democracy at Athens, and various theories have been proposed about which Syracusan speaker was meant to mirror whom at Athens.[47] But unless one is willing to take the extreme step of claiming that Thucydides invented the entire incident – particularly unlikely given Thucydides' obvious interest in and knowledge of Sicilian affairs – the debate adds further color to the picture presented in Diodorus of a Syracusan politics aflame with populist rhetoric and demagogic appeals.[48]

That political rhetoric should be widely practiced in a democracy is natural, for sovereign assemblies and popular courts provide numerous occasions for its use. It was certainly a fixture in fifth- and fourth-century Athens, which became a center for sophistic and rhetorical training. But, according to the ancient writers, Athens was not the first home of political oratory. In fact, it was generally agreed that the art of rhetoric arose in *Syracuse* at precisely the time under discussion. The sources are late but quite clear. Late antique rhetorical introductions called *Prolegomena* explain that a man named Corax invented rhetoric to help gain control over a disorderly *demos* after the fall of the Deinomenid tyranny. "Corax, having

---

[46] 13.34.6; cf. 13.19.4. As Diodorus continues on with his account in 13.35 he seems to confuse the person and actions of the popular politician Diocles with an earlier, legendary Syracusan lawgiver; E. Manni, "Diocles di Siracusa fra Ermocrate e Dionisio," *Kokalos* 25 (1979), 220–31.

[47] E.g., E. F. Bloedow, "The Speeches of Hermocrates and Athenagoras at Syracuse in 415 BC: Difficulties in Syracuse and in Thucydides," *Historia* 45 (1996), 141–58; G. Mader, "Strong Points, Weak Argument: Athenagoras on the Sicilian Expedition (Thucydides 6.36–8)," *Hermes* 121 (1993), 433–40; F. T. Hinrichs, "Hermokrates bei Thukydides," *Hermes* 109 (1981), 46–59.

[48] See Hornblower, *Commentary*, vol. III, 407–8 on the name Athenagoras and suspicions of Thucydidean invention.

demonstrated the works of rhetoric, was able to persuade the Syracusan *demos.*"[49] Some of these traditions suggest that Corax made his mark in the assembly; others say his activity focused on the courtroom. But all agree that the transition to democracy enabled, or indeed necessitated, the development of such arts. Corax spread his knowledge to students, including a certain Tisias, famous for initiating a lawsuit against his teacher and also authoring what may have been the first treatise devoted to rhetoric.[50]

Recent commentators have questioned the veracity of these traditions in terms of details about the earliest rhetoricians and the content of their works. One scholar, Thomas Cole, argues that the late traditions attributed theoretical advances to Tisias and Corax simply because it was assumed that Aristotle and other commentators *must* have been building on previous masters; in all likelihood the Syracusans' works were not nearly so extensive or fundamental. Cole even suggests that Corax and Tisias might have been the same person.[51] The state of the evidence makes such assertions difficult to prove: nothing directly contradicts the late testimonia, but neither is there any corroboration beyond the most elementary facts. However, for our purposes questions about precisely which theories Tisias and Corax developed and with what influence, or even whether they were one or two people, are not important. No one has questioned their existence in and association with Syracuse, nor is there any reason to do so. That the ancient traditions place the pioneers of rhetorical theory in Syracuse (whatever the

---

49 Κόραξ δέ τις ὄνομα, Συρακούσσιος τὸ γένος, σκοπήσας, ὡς ὁ δῆμος ἀστάθμητον καὶ ἄτακτον πέφυκε πρᾶγμα, καὶ ἐννοήσας, ὅτι λόγος ἐστίν, ᾧ ῥυθμίζεται ἀνθρώπου τρόπος, ἐσκόπησε διὰ λόγου ἐπὶ τὰ πρόσφορα τὸν δῆμον καὶ προτρέπειν καὶ ἀποτρέπειν. εἰσελθὼν οὖν ἐν τῇ ἐκκλησίᾳ, ἐν ᾗ ὁ πᾶς συνηθροίσθη δῆμος, ἤρξατο λόγοις πρότερον θεραπευτικοῖς καὶ κολακευτικοῖς τὴν ὄχλησιν καὶ τὸ θορυβῶδες καταπραϋναι τοῦ δήμου, ἅτινα καὶ προοίμια ἐκάλεσε... οὗτος τοίνυν ὁ Συρακούσσιος Κόραξ ἔργα ῥητορικῆς ἐπιδειξάμενος ἔπειθε τὸν τῶν Συρακουσσίων δῆμον, ὅπερ ἐστὶ τέλος τῆς ἡμετέρας τέχνης; Anonymous *prolegomena artis rhetoricae*, no. 4 in H. Rabe, ed., *Prolegomenon Sylloge* (Leipzig, 1931).

50 Rabe nos. 5, 7, 13, 17; Cic. *Brutus* 46. The last citation goes back to Aristotle, showing that at least some elements of the Tisias and Corax traditions described above were current in the Classical period. Other early references to the men or their work can be found in Plato, *Phaedrus* 267a, 273b, and Arist. *Rhet.* 1402a17, *Soph. el.* 183b29–34.

51 T. Cole, *The Origins of Rhetoric in Ancient Greece* (Baltimore, 1991) 22–9, 53–4, 82–3, and "Who was Corax?," *Illinois Classical Studies* 16 (1991), 65–84. In a similarly revisionist vein see now E. Schiappa, *The Beginnings of Rhetorical Theory in Classical Greece* (New Haven, 1999). For more conservative views see G. Kennedy, *The Art of Persuasion in Greece* (Princeton, 1963), 58–61 (slightly modified in *A New History of Classical Rhetoric* [Princeton, 1994], 11, 33–4); D. A. G. Hinks, "Tisias and Corax and the Invention of Rhetoric," *CQ* 40 (1934), 61–9. Wary of the contributions of Tisias and Corax but convinced that the circumstances of democracy powerfully encouraged the development of rhetorical art (at least in Athens) is H. Yunis, "The Constraints of Democracy and the Rise of the Art of Rhetoric," in D. Boedeker and K. A. Raaflaub, eds., *Democracy, Empire, and the Arts in Fifth-Century Athens* (Cambridge, MA, 1998), 223–40. On the importance of Tisias and Corax for Syracuse's political development, see also Hofer, *Tyrannen, Aristokraten, Demokraten*, 159–69.

content of their treatises or their actual impact on later theorists) and tie their activities to the democracy developing there remains very significant.

Democracy certainly existed in Syracuse from 466 to 412, and, indeed, following Diocles' reforms until Dionysius' rise to power in 406. The evidence presented above shows that the *demos* not only controlled the state – choosing and restraining their leaders, passing and revoking laws, and deciding the highest matters of state policy – but did so in a willful manner consistent with a deeply rooted populist ideology, one fitting the criticisms of aristocratic detractors of democracy. The people often treated their generals harshly or arbitrarily, seeing betrayal in every dilatory move or military setback; they let their passions spill over in raucous public assemblies, sometimes to the detriment of sober policy; they raised to prominence demagogues whose influence depended on their oratorical gifts or the fears they could stir up about oligarchic enemies of democracy; and in doing all this they provided the background for the first works of rhetorical theory. It seems entirely appropriate that all the most important ancient sources used the word *demokratia* in describing the government.

Institutions of the democracy
Unlike Argos – the other major democracy beyond Athens for which we have a fair quantity of literary evidence – Syracuse offers no extant contemporary epigraphic decrees to deepen our understanding of its governmental procedures. The closest we can come are passages from literary sources that might reflect actual Syracusan practice.[52] For example, at 11.92.2 Diodorus describes a meeting of the *ekklesia c.* 451 which was called by officials to consider an important matter after the people had already started to gather in the marketplace.[53] A regular assembly meeting ensued, with competing speeches made until a decision on the matter was reached. One might see here a hint of *probouleusis*, in that the *archontes* (a board of magistrates? a council? We cannot know) summoned the meeting and set the agenda for it.[54] This is a bare hint indeed. It suggests that some group of officials was responsible for calling and preparing assemblies at Syracuse, and yet the context of the passage (if Diodorus had the details right) indicates that very little time could have gone into this prior consideration. Was this unusual, or the norm for Syracuse? Combine this passage with the lack of epigraphic

---

[52] Noted in Rhodes, *Decrees*, 315–20.
[53] τοῦ δὲ πλήθους διὰ τὸ παράδοξον συρρέοντος εἰς τὴν ἀγοράν, οἱ μὲν ἄρχοντες συνήγαγον ἐκκλησίαν καὶ προέθηκαν βουλὴν περὶ τοῦ Δουκετίου τί χρὴ πράττειν.
[54] Rutter, "Syracusan Democracy," 145.

documents and the vivid literary picture we see of active, dominating assemblies (in both Diodorus and Thucydides), and one could wonder whether *probouleusis* – at least in the form of a council regularly preparing the assembly's business, the Greek *polis* standard – operated at all in Syracuse. Rutter notes the absence of an Athenian-style council in our sources, which adds to his concerns about how democratic Syracuse truly was. (For the reasons given above, I think such doubts can be dismissed. Indeed, Rutter's need to match Syracusan institutions to ones in Athens before being confident that *demokratia* could exist in Syracuse seems excessively Athenocentric.) We might recall the arguments of H. Leppin regarding the Argive democracy: the absence of a visible role for the council there in the later period could indicate an absence of *probouleusis* (see under Argos, in Chapter 1). In the case of Argos, contemporary epigraphic documents existed to undercut such a thesis with clear evidence of *probouleusis* and, in consequence, one could more easily interpret the *archai* noted in literary texts for having considered matters in advance to have been the council, especially given that one would not expect brief accounts in historians intent on other matters to dwell on constitutional details. For Syracuse, however, the lack of inscriptions means we cannot so easily find *probouleusis*; the *archontes* of Diodorus' passage above might be taken as a council, but the seemingly short time that elapsed between the triggering event and the summoning of the assembly make this hypothesis more difficult. Other sources fail even to hint at a fifth-century council. However, Plutarch does attest one in the fourth century (*Mor.* 825c).[55] The Argive parallel suggests caution in assuming that our sources' silence means no earlier council existed, but the supposition of at least a weaker council in Syracuse relative to those in other democracies is not unreasonable.

As for Syracusan offices, the one most prominent in our sources and clearly of great political consequence was the generalship. The size of the board of generals varied by date. Before and during the war with Athens (through 415) there were fifteen generals who served at a time – a very large number (compare Athens' ten). Indeed, after Syracusan forces fared poorly in the opening stages of the Athenian War, the conservative politician Hermocrates blamed in part "the number of the generals and the state

[55] A treaty between Athens and Syracuse during the reign of Dionysius I, perhaps in 368/7, may have required that a council at Syracuse swear to it, but the word *boulē* has to be restored to the text, and is thus uncertain. *IG* 2² 105.35–6 (= Rhodes and Osborne 34). Other general references to *archai* or those in office at Syracuse: Thuc. 7.73.3–4; Arist. *Pol.* 1303b23. T. Fischer-Hansen, T. H. Nielsen, and C. Ampolo, in *Inventory*, 227–8. For the possibility of a Council of 600 in the fourth century, see R. J. A. Talbert, *Timoleon and the Revival of Greek Sicily, 344–317 B.C.* (Cambridge, 1974).

of multiple command."[56] Hermocrates suggests not only electing fewer generals (three, to be exact), but also giving the generals full authority (*autokratoras*), complete with an oath from the voters to allow them to command as they see fit, which would enhance secrecy and orderliness.[57] Obviously a perception existed that the (highly democratic) Syracusan practice of electing a great many commanders and then micromanaging their actions in the assembly was getting in the way of battlefield success. (For more micromanagement of war fighting by the Syracusan *demos* a few years later, see Diodorus 13.92.4.) That Hermocrates was not alone in his view is indicated by the fact that he succeeded in persuading the Syracusan people to enact by popular vote (*epsephisanto*) all the changes he recommended. By 406 the number seems to have gone back up again, to judge by some passages that imply a good many generals in this time.[58]

Having fewer generals at a time with fuller battlefield authority naturally meant, in effect, a more powerful generalship.[59] But even before this change, generals at Syracuse were important. For one thing, the generalship could be an important stage in an ambitious man's career, as it proved to be for Hermocrates, Diocles, and Dionysius I.[60] But did Syracusan generals wield constitutional powers beyond military command? One episode has raised such questions: the closing of debate in the assembly meeting held before the arrival of the Athenian expedition in 415 and reported on in detail by Thucydides. At 6.41 we read that after Athenagoras' fiery speech rejecting Hermocrates' news of coming Athenian assault and making strident accusations of an oligarchic plot, one of the generals stood up and prevented anyone else from coming forward (*allon men oudena eti eiase parelthein*). He himself spoke a few words to the effect that (1) slanders were not helpful; (2) it could not hurt anything to make some basic preparations (as the generals could and were already doing); (3) information would be gathered; and (4) when the generals learned anything they would

---

[56] καὶ τὸ πλῆθος τῶν στρατηγῶν καὶ τὴν πολυαρχίαν (ἦσαν γὰρ πέντε καὶ δέκα οἱ στρατηγοὶ αὐτοῖς) (Thuc. 6.72.4). Some editors of the text would delete all here before *polyarchian*.

[57] Thuc. 6.72.5.

[58] Diod. Sic. 13.91.2–5, 13.92.1–2, 13.94.1–2, especially 94.2, where it is said that most of Dionysius' colleagues in the generalship (*plethos ton sunarchonton*) had adopted a particular course, indicating that at the very least there were four generals in total. The use of multiples of three in earlier periods (to match Syracuse's presumed three Dorian tribes?) might suggest that the number was actually six or nine or perhaps again fifteen. (In 356 they chose twenty-five generals: Plut. *Dion* 38.4.)

[59] But it hardly indicates a revolution in overall constitutional type. The changes were, after all, limited to the generalship, and the oversight authority of the *demos* to reprove and replace generals as desired was most emphatically retained (see Thuc. 6.103 with discussion above).

[60] On the importance of the generalship in the democracy, see Hofer, *Tyrannen, Aristokraten, Demokraten*, 192–6.

bring it back to the assembly. The decisive action by the general to end debate here could be taken to mean that a general or generals *presided* at Syracusan assemblies. However, no other evidence suggests this, and the Greek itself need hardly imply such authority.[61] Moreover, there is an obvious explanation for why the Syracusans might defer to their generals under the circumstances: during military crises democracies (ancient and modern) will often allow their chief military officials prerogatives they do not normally utilize. For example, one would seriously misunderstand the actual powers of the *Athenian* generalship if one were to judge its constitutional power by the fact that early in the Peloponnesian War, during the destructive initial invasion of Attica by Peloponnesian forces, the general Pericles would not summon any meetings of the assembly.[62] It is also worth emphasizing that, despite the atmosphere of crisis at Syracuse, the general there did not arrogate any powers to himself and his board, but simply promised to make basic preparations (already in the generals' purview) and to seek information – which would promptly be relayed to the assembly.

We learn some interesting tidbits about *thorubos* (uproar) and the Syracusan assembly from Diodorus. At 13.91–2 one reads about a meeting in 406 during which Dionysius whipped up an already angry crowd (*ta plethe*) by accusing the current generals of betraying the city and demanding that they be punished at once, a course of action that would go against existing law. At this point, the *archontes* fined Dionysius for violating the law about causing an uproar (*kata tous nomous hos thorubounta*). Philistus, the later historian and a very rich man, Diodorus tells us, paid this fine and promised to pay them all day long so that Dionysius could keep up his speaking. The demagoguery continued, including accusations of oligarchic sentiment (*oikeious ontas oligarchias*) among the generals' supporters, and in the end the assembly voted to depose some of the generals and to elect new ones, of whom one was Dionysius.

Assuming that Diodorus is accurate in his report here – and the direct reference to Philistus suggests he had access to a first-hand account – we may conclude a few things. First, we find further evidence for the claims

<hr/>

[61] See the discussion and references in *HCT*, vol. IV, 307 (Also Hornblower, *Commentary*, vol. III, 416). On *archontes* presiding at assembly meetings, see Diod. Sic. 13.91.4 and discussion below. For the possible case in a different city of a general exercising a veto over assembly decisions, see the Taras section in this chapter.

[62] Thuc. 2.22 and 2.59, with commentary by Gomme, *HCT*, vol. II, 76, and especially the discussion in Hamel, *Athenian Generals*, 8–12, 161–3. An example of the higher profile that generals could have during wartime is the practice of Athenian generals making decree proposals as a group, in a *gnome strategon*, on two occasions during the Peloponnesian War, as noted by P. J. Rhodes, "Who Ran Democratic Athens?," in P. Flensted-Jensen, T. H. Nielsen, and L. Rubinstein, eds., *Polis & Politics: Studies in Ancient Greek History* (Copenhagen, 2000), 465–77, at 466.

made earlier (for the period 466–412) about the sometimes emotional and impetuous behavior of the Syracusan *demos* during the democracy. Niceties of procedure are pushed aside when anger overflows. Demagoguery prevails in speeches, and suspicions about generals' treachery and shadowy oligarchs are used to score points with the mass of assembly-goers. Second, there was a law at Syracuse against *thorubos* or its incitement in assembly meetings, punishable by a fine. In all probability the fine was rather low, not because Philistus promised to keep paying it (Diodorus remarks upon his vast wealth), but because the officials presiding at the assembly – identity unknown, but presumably a board of some kind, possibly a subgroup of the council – had the power to levy the fines immediately.

We learn from Aeschines' speeches that Athens also had a law enjoining proper order (*eukosmia*) for those speaking before the *demos* and thereby discouraging *thorubos*. In the version of the law quoted in the text of one speech, the word *thorubos* does not appear. The provisions are aimed at *rhetores* who speak at the wrong time or to the wrong issue or slander (*loidoretai*) or shout approval (*parakeleuetai*); references to it, however, show that Aeschines saw its provisions as aimed at preventing *thorubos*, which was a common occurrence at Athenian assemblies.[63] We cannot compare the Syracusan law in any detail, of course. All we read is that the *archontes* levied a fine on Dionysius *hos thorubounta*. We might imagine an anti-*thorubos* law of the Athenian variety, aimed at preventing interruptions, shouting, and jeering (which we know happened at Syracuse) by punishing those who incite it. It is also possible, however, to interpret the charge of *thorubos* here as relating to Dionysius' proposal of an illegal motion. The object of Dionysius' speaking on this occasion – removing the generals at once – was illegal, after all, and its proposal immediately brought the fine. The Syracusan *thorubos* law, it would seem, could be used as a means of stopping illegal motions before they take effect. This would contrast somewhat with the Athenian practice of *graphai paranomon*: although these could be raised before a law was enacted, generally we see it come only after laws have been passed.[64] Of course, the attempt here fails, as Dionysius gets his way despite the fines *hos thorubounta*.

[63] The fine was up to 50 drachmas by the *proedroi* alone, or more with the vote of a later assembly meeting. Aeschin. 1.34–5, 3.2. See Tacon, "Ecclesiastic *Thorubos*," esp. 173–4, 179–80; Hansen, *Athenian Democracy*, 146–7. Tacon has argued persuasively that one should see the frequent *thorubos* in Athenian assemblies, to include interruptions of speakers by other speakers but, more importantly, shouting or cheering or heckling from the audience itself, as an essential means of popular self-expression.

[64] Hansen, *Athenian Democracy*, 205–12. The *graphe paranomon* also brought fines as punishment if the proposer of the illegal decree were convicted.

One aspect of Syracusan assembly meetings that has received little attention is their physical location. Diodorus 11.92.1–2 implies that on one occasion, at least, the Syracusans met in the agora, though the circumstances
were unusual (Ducetius' sudden appearance there as a suppliant, which
attracted large crowds). The precise location and extent of the agora in
classical Syracuse, presumed to be in the southern Achradina area from
perhaps the sixth century on down, is uncertain,[65] and the old assumption that, generally speaking, a *polis*'s agora served as its assembly space
in early Greece rests on precious little evidence.[66] A more attractive location for assembly meetings during the democracy is one of the theaters
of Syracuse. Plutarch attests assembly meetings held regularly in a theater
in the fourth century, in 355 and later during the time of Timoleon.[67]
The earliest-known such space in Syracuse is the so-called "Linear" theater, a rectangular rock-cut area built up against the slope of the Epipolai,
27 meters wide and rising seventeen levels, with an estimated seating capacity of 1,000 spectators. Dating to the sixth or early fifth century, this
theater was located in the Temenites section to the northwest of the city.
Arguments about the primary use of this space (theatrical shows? cult cer-
emonies?) are inconclusive, and there is no reason why political gatherings
could not have been held here as well.[68] Close by, one finds the second,
much larger theater of Syracuse. It seems to have been constructed centuries
later, in the third century BC during the reign of Hieron II (as inscriptions
of that period found in the theater attest), when it had a capacity of
14,000–17,000 people. Archaeologists have not found convincing evidence
of an earlier, Classical phase of construction for this theater, though literary
sources suggest that there could have been one: the architect Democopus
supposedly built a theater in Syracuse in the early fifth century, and sources
attest that Aeschylus performed at Syracuse in the 470s.[69] Unless the Linear
theater was Democopus', one would expect that the grand theater had a
smaller, early Classical phase. A thorough study of the site, however, shows

---

[65] H.-P. Drögemüller, *Syrakus. Zur Topographie und Geschichte einer griechischen Stadt* (Heidelberg,
1969), 50; F. Longo, "Syracuse," in L. Cerchiai, L. Jannelli, and F. Longo, *The Greek Cities of Magna
Graecia and Sicily* (Los Angeles, 2004), 202–15, at 209–10; T. Fischer-Hansen, T. H. Nielsen, and
C. Ampolo in, *Inventory*, 229. Plut. *Tim.* 22.4 seems to imply a fairly sizable space.

[66] See the excellent discussion of the location of Greek assembly meetings in Hansen and Fischer-
Hansen, "Monumental Political Architecture," 44–53.

[67] Plut. *Dion* 38.1–3; *Tim.* 34.6, 38.5–7.

[68] Drögemüller, *Syrakus*, 48–9 with Plate vi; M.-P. Loicq-Berger, *Syracuse. Histoire culturelle d'une cité
grecque* (Brussels, 1967), 95–6; Ginouvès, *Le théâtron à gradins droits*, 61–2, 76–7; T. Fischer-Hansen,
T. H. Nielsen, and C. Ampolo in *Inventory*, 229–30.

[69] For the various testimonia, see M. Trojani, "Le antichità," in L. Polacco and C. Anti, eds., *Il teatro
antico di Siracusa* (Rimini, 1981), 34–5, 41–2, 45–6.

that there is no detectable sign of this in the present remains.[70] So in the time of the fifth-century democracy the only theater that we can be sure the Syracusans would have had available for assemblies was the Linear theater, seating roughly 1,000 – a very small size for a city as populous as Syracuse – with the possibility that a slightly larger theater (seating 1,400? more?) might have existed on the site of the much grander third-century theater.

Syracusan democracy in the fourth century

Compared with the evidence for fifth-century Syracusan democracy, the case for *demokratia* in the fourth century is weak. Two periods concern us: the liberation of the city from the tyranny of Dionysius II under Dion's leadership in 357–356, and the government after Timoleon's intervention of the later 340s.[71]

The description of the events leading up to the defeat of Dionysius II and his partisans in Diodorus and in Plutarch's *Dion* does suggest a temporary revival of democratic politics in the city.[72] All through Dion's campaign in the city against the tyrant's forces in the citadel, meetings of the *ekklesia* are held and binding votes taken, including the repeated election of Dion and sometimes others as *strategous autokratoras*. Freedom (*eleutheria*) is constantly invoked, and while this word is mostly to be taken in the sense of liberation from tyranny, and thus not in itself marking democracy, the word *demokratia* also comes up: Plutarch says the Syracusans treated Dion's arrival in the city as bringing back *demokratia* after an absence of forty-eight years (*Dion* 28.4); Dionysius at one point in the fighting offers to withdraw from his tyranny and accept whatever he can get from the *demokratia* (Diod. Sic. 16.11.4). Moreover, the political interactions described in some of the assembly meetings certainly seem democratic, as factions form behind this or that leader, demagogues harangue the people (labeled *demos, polloi, ochlos*), accusations are made against officials, *parresia* (free speech) is encouraged, and meetings grow tumultuous.[73]

[70] L. Bernabo Brea, "Studi sul teatro greco di siracusa," *Palladio* 17 (1967), 97–154, at 97. Cf. Loicq-Berger, *Syracuse*, 97, who follows an older view in hypothesizing that the trapezoidal cutting visible in the orchestra is a sign of an earlier theater that could have seated perhaps 1,400. (See also Polaccio and Anti, *Il teatro*). However, this trapezoidal cutting likely occurred during a late Roman phase of construction to enable water displays. H. P. Isler, "Siracusa," in P. C. Rossetto and G. P. Sartorio, eds., *Teatri Greci e Romani*, vol. III, (Rome, 1994), 33–7; T. Fischer-Hansen, T. H. Nielsen, and C. Ampolo in *Inventory*, 229–30.

[71] See generally on these episodes, O'Neil, *Origins and Development*, 81–2; Berger, *Revolution and Society*, 45–9; T. Fischer-Hansen, T. H. Nielsen, and C. Ampolo in *Inventory*, 227; Talbert, *Timoleon*.

[72] Nepos' *Dion* is generally too abbreviated to contain useful material on Syracusan politics before Dion's final victory.

[73] E.g., Diod. Sic. 16.17.1–3; Plut. *Dion* 32.5, 33.4–35.1, 37–8, 41.1–3.

Finally, toward the end of the campaign, when victory seemed assured, the Syracusan people took the radical step of voting to reapportion land (*ges anadasmos*), elect new generals – twenty-five of them! – and expel Dion without paying his mercenaries (Plut. *Dion* 37–8).[74] In all, though conditions were naturally unsettled in the course of the war, it certainly seems that *demokratia* is the best constitutional description for the Syracusan government at the time.

However, against this picture a few things must be noted. For much of the fighting Dion was *autokrator* and seems to have run the war as he wished, in contrast to the military micromanagement displayed by the Syracusan assembly during the fifth-century democracy. Usually when Dionysius made a peace offer of some kind Dion would simply pass it on to the assembly, but sometimes he would deal with it himself without consulting the *ekklesia* (Plut. *Dion* 50). Syracusans occasionally accused him of prolonging the war so he could maintain his dominance (33.5, 49.1), suggesting that his powers as *strategos autokrator* went beyond just military affairs, and worried that he was using his extraordinary authority in a bid for tyranny himself (Diod. Sic. 16.17.3; Plut. *Dion* 31–2). The Syracusan populists were right to have their suspicions, it would seem: according to Plutarch, Dion's intentions for government after his final victory involved not *akratos demokratia*, but a Corinth-style *aristokratia*, with elements of democracy and kingship mixed in; he would be assisted in his plans by advisors and colleagues sent from Corinth. When he started to put his ideas into effect, his populist opponent Heracleides objected and was killed as a result, which settled the issue in Dion's favor. Specifics about the government that actually resulted are few – before his murder Heracleides had been invited to meetings of a *synedrion* but had declared his preference for the *ekklesia*, so perhaps we should imagine an elite council advising the principal governor or governors. Nepos describes a descent into autocratic rule during which Dion lost the support of both the elite and the ordinary citizens (*Dion* 7). Diodorus mentions the assassination of Dion and the driving out of his supporters a few years later, followed by the tyranny of a half-brother of Dionysius II (16.31.7, 16.36.5); Plutarch describes the assassination of Dion in detail and talks of Syracusan government generally in this period as amounting to a succession of tyrants (*Dion* 54–8, *Tim.* 1).

In all, we would probably come closest to the truth in viewing Syracusan affairs as having been democratically run during the year or so of Dion's

---

[74] On the remarkable program of the popular leader Hippo (*tina ton demagogon*), who proposed the land redistribution on the basis of the importance of economic equality for political liberty, see A. Fuks, *Social Conflict in Ancient Greece* (Jerusalem, 1984), 50–1, 213–23.

campaign (357–6), with the proviso that as long as Dion had the status of *autokrator* he held exceptional influence in military affairs at least. After final victory the *akratos demokratia* gave way to an oligarchic governmental structure with Dion at the center, which in turn was followed by a return to blatant tyrannies within a few years.

Syracuse under Timoleon several years later offers a similarly confused picture to Dion's time, but the end result nevertheless appears to have been demonstrably more democratic. Timoleon, a Corinthian of anti-tyrannical character,[75] led a campaign in the later 340s[76] to free Syracuse from Dionysius II once again and then defend it against the advances of Hicetas and his Carthaginian allies. He succeeded against Dionysius very quickly, occupied the city, and immediately made momentous changes: he tore down the fortress on Ortygia that had long been used as a base for autocrats, established democratic laws (*demokratikous nomous*) together with popular courts (*dikasteria*), and was especially careful, we are told, about securing equality (*isotes*).[77] All of this sounds very democratic indeed, and later events seem to confirm this conclusion. As with many other new democracies, Syracuse welcomed great numbers of new citizens into its *politeia* – tens of thousands in this case (Plut. *Tim.* 23; Diod. Sic. 16.82.3–5). Formal scrutiny of magistrates seems to have been taking place, if a vote (*psephos*) initiating the public sale of statues with accusations as if they were officials undergoing *euthunai* is any guide (Plut. *Tim.* 23.7). Plutarch further describes high-profile public indictments and trials in the *ekklesia*, sometimes accompanied by raucous behavior, and he remarks upon the presence of sycophants and demagogues in this *demokratia* as in others (*Tim.* 33.1, 34.5–6, 37.1–3). Timoleon himself supported *parresia* vigorously even when he was the target of the attacks it engendered.

Two factors complicate this otherwise democratic picture. First, Diodorus' account makes it seem that at some point Timoleon initiated a second round of legislating, for it is said at 16.82.6–7 (in an entry for a few years after the initial changes) that he revised the laws of Diocles.[78] This could suggest backsliding on the democratic reforms, since the populist

---

[75] Plut. *Tim.* 3.4. Here he is also described as *misoponeros* (anti-scoundrel? anti-riffraff?), which could have had elitist connotations. See, e.g., Dem. 21.218, where this term is used alongside *kalos k'agathos* and *sophron*.

[76] On the chronology of the events involving Timoleon and Syracuse – roughly 344 until his retirement in 337/6 – see Talbert, *Timoleon*, 44–51.

[77] Diod. Sic. 16.70.4–5; Plut. *Tim.* 22.2–3.

[78] On the complicated figure of Diocles in Syracusan history – perhaps the name of an archaic lawgiver as well as the popular leader of the late fifth century – see Manni, "Diocle di Siracusa," 220–31, and the discussion in Talbert, *Timoleon*, 134–6.

Diocles of 412 was responsible for changes that made democratic Syracuse more democratic than it had been previously. Moreover, Diodorus states that Cephalus the Corinthian was in charge of the revisions, a man reputed for *paideia* and *sunesis*: not the kind of description that suggests wild-eyed populism. (Plutarch talks of two Corinthians who assisted Timoleon as *nomothetai* for the establishment of a constitution, *Tim.* 24.3). We should also recall that Timoleon himself was a Corinthian aristocrat who was "*misoponeros*" ("scoundrel-hating," perhaps: *Tim.* 3.4), a label that could signal anti-populist sentiments. Thus, if this event truly amounted to a new round of constitutional revisions, not to be conflated with the explicit democratization discussed earlier, then one might well suspect a moderation of the democracy initially put in place.

The second caveat to keep in mind about any Timoleonic *demokratia* is the deference shown to Timoleon himself. He, like Dion, spent much time as *autokrator* in charge of military operations (often liberating other Sicilian cities from tyrannical control), which will have put him in a rather exalted position; and Plutarch notes that even after his retirement the *ekklesia* would seek his advice on the most important affairs of state (*Tim.* 38.5–7). On the other hand, we have already seen how Timoleon's position offered him no protection against accusations and suits from political rivals, and the fact that the *demos* in assembly might summon Timoleon for advice once in a while in the course of its decisive deliberations on all state business does more to confirm than undermine the case for overall democratic governance.

In sum, it is best to assume that the Syracusan democracy after Timoleon's liberation, if not as radicalized as it had once been, nonetheless merits the description of *demokratia*, at least for a few years.

Acragas

In the fifth century Acragas was one of Sicily's largest cities[79] and a frequent rival of the largest, Syracuse. In 472, several years before Syracuse's liberation, the Acragantines drove out their tyrant ruler Thrasydaeus upon his defeat in a major battle, after which Diodorus says the Acragantines "recovered their democracy" (*komisamenoi ten demokratian*, 11.53).[80] Diodorus'

---

[79] Diodorus puts the citizen population at greater than 20,000 and the total including foreigners at 200,000, 13.84.3. Cf. Diog. Laert. 8.63. T. Fischer-Hansen, T. H. Nielsen, and C. Ampolo in *Inventory*, 186–7.

[80] For an argument regarding the possibility of an even earlier, archaic Acragantine democracy based on this statement, see Robinson, *First Democracies*, 79–80.

basic reliability in his application of the term *demokratia* for this era of Sicilian history has already been discussed above under Syracuse. Apart from his statement, the main evidence for democracy at Acragas is the material collected in Diogenes Laertius' biography of the philosopher Empedocles (8.51–77). This native of Acragas lived there as an adult in the middle of the fifth century. Diogenes' information about him is compiled from a variety of sources, including Timaeus, and is heavily anecdotal. It portrays him as a man of distinction with a predilection for the populist cause (*demotikon*, 8.64; *[en] ton ta demotika phronounton*, 8.66). For example, when tyranny threatened, Empedocles is said to have "persuaded the Acragantines" to cease their *stasis* and practice political equality (*isoteta politiken*, 8.72). When a prominent citizen sought the permission of the *boule* to set up a monument for his father, Empedocles prevented it in part by speaking out concerning equality (*peri isotetos dialechtheis*, 8.65).

Two other incidents especially stand out: first, Empedocles' entrance into politics is said to have been his prosecution in the law courts of a magistrate and the host of a dinner for alleged aspirations to tyranny; he succeeded in getting them condemned and executed (8.64). The use of the *dikasterion* for launching a political career, the nature of the charge, and the severity of the punishment are all redolent of democratic political trials, as is the fact that Empedocles was considered *demotikon* (populist) for this action. Empedocles is also described as supporting the populist cause for somewhat later having overthrown (*kateluse*) the "gathering of the Thousand" (*to ton chilion athroisma*) – apparently some kind of council of wealthy aristocrats which had been created three years previously. How he managed to do this is not indicated; one imagines he had the body voted out of existence through the assembly (8.66).

David Asheri, in an important and thorough article, interprets the literary evidence as pointing not to democracy, but rather to the kind of isonomic oligarchy in which elites, free and equal among themselves, dominate the state as they strive against each other for power and offices. Once he dismisses Diodorus' use of the term *demokratia* as unreliable, he can go on to reinterpret the Empedocles material on the hypothesis that the philosopher's stand against tyranny and for equality represents not a concern for freedom and equality for all citizens, but only for the elite, of which he was indubitably a part. Asheri also points out that nowhere in these stories is a popular assembly mentioned – all we hear about are the acts and decisions of magistrates and councils of different kinds, of which Empedocles is invariably a member. If a democracy was truly in place, one would expect to hear something about the sovereign assembly of citizens.[81]

Asheri, in his attempt to explain away the testimony for a populist Empedocles, successfully underscores the indirect nature of the case for Acragantine democracy (aside from Diodorus, that is) and raises a viable oligarchic alternative. But two counter-arguments must be advanced that go beyond a defense of Diodorus' use of *demokratia*. First, to scorn the possibility of popular government because of the absence of direct references to a popular assembly in such a brief, biographical account as that of Diogenes Laertius amounts to a most unconvincing *argumentum e silentio*. Moreover, as Asheri himself notes, Diodorus refers to a *psephisma* of the Acragantine people in 406, surely implying the existence of an active assembly (13.84.5),[82] and Diodorus further describes a wartime *ekklesia* meeting at 13.87 in which *ta plethe* angrily denounced generals suspected of having been bribed by the enemy and go on to stone several to death. Clearly, Diogenes Laertius' omission of Acragantine popular assemblies in his anecdotes about Empedocles cannot be taken to mean such did not exist. Second, just as in contemporary democratic Syracuse, the new science of rhetoric seems to have played a major role at Acragas: Empedocles at times sounds like the archetypal demagogue, thundering persuasively in the law courts and other forums about the dangers of would-be tyrants and the necessity of political equality. The utility of such activity for Empedocles implies a powerful *demos*. There is also a minor Aristotelian tradition that Empedocles *invented* rhetoric (Diog. Laert. 8.57, 9.25). So while it may be possible to reinterpret our scant source material in such a way as to envision a moderately oligarchic Acragas, this is only a possibility, and it involves much explaining away of evidence that on a more straightforward reading indicates *demokratia*.

As for the practice of Acragantine democracy, in the absence of contemporary epigraphic evidence, literary and archaeological evidence offer just a few hints. The Empedocles material conjures a familiar image of *demokratia* rife with new practitioners of rhetoric impressing the people in the courts with their art, thereby advancing their own political fortunes.

---

[81] D. Asheri, "Agrigento libera: rivolgimenti interni e problemi constituzionali, ca 471–446 a.C.," *Athenaeum* 78(1990), 483–501. Hofer, *Tyrannen, Aristokraten, Demokraten*, 237–65, shares Asheri's skepticism about true democracy at Acragas in the fifth century but foregoes an attempt at institutional reconstruction in favor of analysis of Empedocles' life and thought. S. Berger thinks a democracy probably resulted, though a moderate aristocracy is possible; *Revolution and Society*, 17.

[82] Asheri's assumption that *psephisma* would not have been the contemporary term but rather *aliasma* (based on a late inscription) hardly reduces the importance of *psephisma*'s appearance in the account; "Agrigento libera," 496.

Aspirants to tyranny, real or imagined, are used to fire up public outrage and action. Diodorus' brief references depict legislation in the assembly and showcase the anger the multitudes had in the late fifth century for their generals in the war against the Carthaginian invaders, together with their willingness to exact immediate punishment. The Acragantines underwent *stasis* in 413 with an unclear result in terms of any constitutional effects (Thuc. 7.46, 7.50). But adding this event to the general picture in the Empedocles life begins to suggest that Acragas had a rather tumultuous political history from 472 to 406 with plenty of upheavals, given the sparse testimony available to us. In foreign policy we find the Acragantines willing to back an Athenian initiative of 422 to compel the Syracusans to restore the Leontine *demos* to their city (Thuc. 5.4), though one might see this as stemming more from longstanding hostility to Syracuse than any democratic fellow-feeling for the Leontines.

Excavations have revealed what appears to have been a circular *ekklesiasterion* in the city, together with a *bouleuterion*, on a small hill near the town center. Dating presents a difficulty. The *bouleuterion* seems to date to the late fourth century BC, but the *ekklesiasterion* is more complicated: de Miro would date it to the fourth or even third century, while others put it as early as the fifth century.[83] The capacity was small relative to the population of the city: the highest estimates would allow for 3,000 to be seated within it, for a citizen total in excess of 20,000.[84] How often the assembly met during the Classical democracy cannot be known, though a Hellenistic-era inscribed decree (*haliasma*) of the assembly refers to a two-month interval, which could mean that the body met every other month in that era.[85] The same late inscription refers to a Council of 110 which had obviously provided a *probouleuma* for the decree of the assembly (*halia*).

In sum, the evidence points to the existence of *demokratia* in Acragas with an active assembly and lively populist ideology for at least some portions of the fifth century, though times were tumultuous constitutionally and the evidence is open to alternative interpretations. To what degree any popular government survived the destruction by the Carthaginians, to be revived upon the resettlement of the city by Timoleon *c.* 340, is unknown.[86]

[83] E. de Miro, "L'Ecclesiasterion in contrada S. Nicola di Agrigento," *Palladio* 16 (1967), 164–8. For a fifth-century date: F. Longo, "Agrigento (Akragas)," in L. Cerchiai, L. Jannelli, and F. Longo, *The Greek Cities of Magna Graecia and Sicily* (Los Angeles, 2004), 240–55, at 251–2.

[84] Hansen and Fischer-Hansen, "Monumental Political Architecture," favor the excavator's estimate of 3,000 over the 2,050–2,750 range others give; 55 with notes 125 and 126; Diod. Sic. 13.83.3 on the citizen population.

[85] Rhodes, *Decrees*, 314, 320, 504, on *IG* 14.952.

[86] Plut. *Tim.* 35; Diod. Sic. 13.90.1–5, 13.108.2. Talbert, *Timoleon*, 146–8, 158–9.

Camarina

Camarina presents an interesting but shaky case for fifth-century Sicilian *demokratia*, for it combines limited literary evidence with some ambiguous epigraphic material. Deserted after its population was deported to Syracuse in 484 by the tyrant Gelon, the city was refounded *c.* 461 in the aftermath of battles against mercenaries and populations installed by the recently deposed tyrants (Hdt. 7.154–6; Thuc. 6.5; Diod. Sic. 11.76.5).[87] Diodorus reports (11.76) that a general agreement (*koinon dogma*) was reached at this time to settle the civil wars in Sicily by allowing *xenoi* introduced into citizen bodies by tyrants to remove themselves to "Messenia" (Messana), and by letting original populations return to their territories. The foreign political orders (*politeiai*) were thrown out of these cities, and the lands were divided up by lot for distribution to all the citizens. Camarina was refounded by people from Gela, and the land allotted. Given Diodorus' language in an earlier chapter (11.68.5) about instituting democracy generally in the cities, and the indications here of new governments and lands being freely allotted to all citizens, we might well presume that the new Camarina had a democratic constitution, like Syracuse and (probably) Gela, the city that refounded it. But the notices are vague and offer no details about the functioning of the government; discarding Diodorus' democratic terminology, one could hypothesize that a merely autonomous community resulted, perhaps with a moderate oligarchy in control instead of a democracy.

Thucydides mentions Camarina in the course of his description of the wars between Athens and Syracuse in the 420s and 410s. In 415 we find Camarina being courted by both Athens and Syracuse. At 6.75–88 Thucydides describes a *sullogos*, or public meeting, of the Camarinaeans at which ambassadors from the two great powers make their pleas. Now *sullogos* in Thucydides can mean a formal assembly such as the *ekklesia* at Athens or the *apella* at Sparta, or an informal meeting of the citizens.[88] A formal meeting is surely indicated here given the circumstances. Moreover, Thucydides implies that a decision about choosing sides was made at this same gathering: immediately following the speeches, Thucydides describes the feelings of the Camarinaeans during their deliberations (*bouleusamenoi*),

[87]   I. Fischer-Hansen, T. H. Nielsen, and C. Ampolo in *Inventory*, 203, citing F. Giudice, "La seconde e terza fondazione di Camarina alla luce dei prodotti del commercio coloniale," *Quaderni dell' Instituto di Archeologia della Facoltà de Lettere e Filosofia dell' Università di Messina* (1988), 49–57 at 56–7, notes a decline in the archaeological record consistent with a sharp decrease in habitation.

[88]   See the discussions in the commentaries of Gomme and Hornblower at Thuc. 2.21.1.

after which they provide an answer to the ambassadors, who then depart. While nothing is certain, all this is suggestive of democratic practice, with a sovereign assembly meeting to hear speeches, to deliberate, and then to come to a decision. (One might also find evidence for a tradition of strong assemblies at Camarina in the scholion to Aeschines 3.189, which describes an instance of the Camarinaeans passing a death sentence on someone via *psephisma*, i.e., through a decree in the assembly.)[89] Just as importantly, though the Camarinaeans voted for neutrality at this meeting, later in the war they changed their minds and decided to support Syracuse (Thuc. 7.33.1, 7.58.1), which means they were probably included in Thucydides' claim that it was *demokratoumenai* cities who were giving Athens so much trouble late in the war (7.55.2).[90]

According to Federica Cordano, there is something else very suggestive of democracy in Camarina in the early to mid fifth century: more than 140 inscribed lead plates discovered during excavations around the temple of Athena there in 1987.[91] Dated by letter forms to the first half of the fifth century, the small rectangular plates list a citizen's name, patronymic, and phratry number. They rather closely resemble the bronze plates discovered at Athens inscribed with name, patronymic, and deme which match Aristotle's descriptions of tickets used for the allotment of jurors there.[92] Cordano also notes parallels to the tokens in use in contemporary Mantinea (a democracy) and to those found at Styra in Euboia (constitution unknown). Cordano supposes that the Camarina plates, like the bronze Athenian ones, were probably employed for allotment of juries, and possibly also for allotted offices, for elections, or indeed for any occasion when the full public identification of citizens was called for. The accentuation of the curvature of one of the short sides of several of the plates may even indicate their use in some sort of allotment machine like the ones employed for selecting juries in Athens.[93]

[89] κατασταθεὶς ὑπὸ Γέλωνος ἐν Καμαρίνῃ καταψηφισαμένων αὐτοῦ Καμαριναίων θάνατον ἀνῃρέθη. The date for this event presumably falls at some point in the mid-480s, after which Gelon had the city destroyed (Hdt. 7.156.2; Thuc. 6.5.3). Thus the vote cannot speak specifically to the era after the city's refoundation in 461.

[90] See the discussion of Thucydides 7.55 under Gela, this chapter. Camarina is identified by a scholiast as one of the seven cities that Nicias predicts will oppose Athens (Thuc. 6.20.3) in a passage that closely resembles Thucydides' own judgments at 7.55.

[91] F. Cordano, *Le tessere pubbliche dal Tempio di Atena a Camarina* (Rome, 1992).

[92] Arist. *Ath. Pol.* 63–4; J. H. Kroll, *Athenian Bronze Allotment Plates* (Cambridge, MA, 1972).

[93] Arist. *Ath. Pol.* 63–4; P. J. Rhodes, *A Commentary on the Aristotelian* Athenaion Politeia (Oxford, 1981), 704–9. Cordano offers further remarks on democracy in Camarina in "Camarina città democratica?," *PP* 59 (2004), 283–92, where she backs off slightly from her claims: the constitution was certainly "republican" but not necessarily democratic from 461; perhaps it evolved into democracy sometime around 424.

In all, Cordano makes a reasonable case for interpreting these tokens in a democratic context. However, uncertainties remain.[94] One difficulty in assuming that the tokens were democratic sortition devices is the very material from which they are made: lead is a soft, cheap metal which is routinely used in the Greek world as a means to write a brief message and seal it by folding the tablet closed (the state in which the Camarina tablets were found, as it happens). Lead *defixiones* (curse tablets) would be inscribed, folded, deposited and left that way; lead message tablets would be subsequently opened and read, and then usually discarded or refashioned. Lead is a good medium for such activities, but it would not stand up well to the wear and tear of constant handling that would come with use in the frequent sortition procedures of *demokratiai*. It is surely no accident that the Athenian and Rhodian jury sortition tokens were fashioned of wood or bronze.[95]

A more likely solution for the use of the tablets at Camarina would involve some kind of civic archive, usable for identification of citizens, their phratry affiliation, and their status, possibly with a military purpose. We know for a fact that Greek cities sometimes used collections of lead tablets for archival purposes, as with the cavalry archive kept at Athens in which each lead token recorded information about a cavalryman and his horse. The tablets were folded after inscription and could be unfolded and consulted when needed (as when, for example, a horse died in battle and compensation was requested), but one would not expect to do this constantly to the same token; most of the time a token would be replaced once the information was checked. A lead archive at Camarina could have worked similarly, recording in individualized and updatable form the family and phratry affiliation of each citizen. The markings found on some of the tokens – including extra letters seemingly used as numbers, possibly for monetary amounts contributed by, owed by, or due to that citizen, plus in a few cases the word *tethnake*, "deceased" – would seem to prove that the archive as a whole was kept up to date. For making periodic changes of this kind a lead archive would be far more efficient than a list inscribed on stone or bronze. Musti has proposed that collectively the tokens served

---

[94] I have discussed fully the problems with Cordano's and others' association of the tablets specifically with *demokratia* in Camarina in "Lead Plates and the Case for Democracy in Fifth-Century BC Camarina," in V. Gorman and E. Robinson, eds., *Oikistes: Studies in Constitutions, Colonies, and Military Power in the Ancient World Offered in Honor of A. J. Graham* (Leiden, 2002), 61–77. The following discussion owes much to this article.

[95] The signs of curvature that Cordano notes in a small number of the lead plates are unlikely to have been caused by an allotment machine like the one used for jury selection in Athens, for it would make no sense that only 6 out of more than 140 show this wear.

as a kind of hoplite catalogue, maintained either for votive purposes or for military registration.[96] The collection, after all, was found in a temple to Athena, protectress of the city. Alternatively, Manganaro thinks that the archive marked payments made or owed to citizens for attendance in the assembly.[97]

If the lead tokens were indeed a kind of civic archive, as seems most likely, they would shed interesting light on the identification of those belonging to the *polis* of Camarina. They would not, however, necessarily prove that the constitution was democratic. Almost any kind of governing order could make use of such a citizen archive, even a tyranny, especially if the records' primary purpose was military. Given that Cordano dates the tablets by letter form to the first half of the fifth century, they could just as easily belong to the era of refoundation and domination by the tyrants Hippocrates and Gelon in 491–484 as to the later, 461 reestablishment. On the other hand, the civic archive would be perfectly consistent with *demokratia*, and some of the potential uses fit *better* with a populist order than any other. For example, if Manganaro is right about the archive's marking *ekklesiastikon* payments, a democracy would obviously be indicated.

Even if the purpose aimed at something else, though, there is something egalitarian about the equal listing of all citizens by membership in the phratries with one little tablet devoted to each person and stored together in the temple of the city's primary deity. It fits well with the allotment of land shares among all citizens that formed the basis of the refoundation of the city in 461, and the general sweeping away of oppressive constitutional orders in Sicily that took place in this era. The updating and tracking of civic status and monetary amounts suggests a significant *polis* interest in the participation of each of its citizens. It is certainly relevant to point out that wherever individualized plates at all like these have been found, the governing order has been democratic (Mantinea, Athens, Rhodes), excepting only Styra, where the constitution is simply unknown.

If we combine the literary hints with the potential uses of the lead tablets, Camarina should be considered a probable but uncertain *demokratia* for most of the fifth century after 461. It was refounded by Gela, probably a recent democracy itself (see entry in this chapter), and literary evidence hints at an active and decisive assembly. Assuming it was democratic,

---

[96] D. Musti, "Elogio di un oplita in una lamina di Camarina?," *RFIC* 122 (1994), 21–3.

[97] G. Manganaro, "Sikelika I," *QUCC* 49 (1995), 93–109. Manganaro was inspired by the *ekklesiastikon* inscription at Iasos to suggest this use, which is certainly possible, though the procedures outlined in the Iasos document do not much resemble anything we know to have taken place at Camarina. P. Gauthier, "L'inscription d'Iasos relative à l'*ekklesiastikon*," *BCH* 114.1 (1990), 417–43.

one can say little about the details of the government's operation beyond what one learns from the intriguing cache of citizen tokens. The numerically arranged phratry system evidenced by them (with perhaps eighteen phratries in total) bespeaks a certain rationality characteristic of political reforms of the era in Greece generally and may be closely tied with the land allotments.[98] Whatever the precise use of the tablets themselves, the purpose appears archival and the effect to define citizens and their public participation, whether in the assembly or lines of battle or in some other communal activity.[99]

Gela

Fifth-century Gela is never individually identified as a *demokratia* in our sources, but on two occasions it falls among groups of cities that are labeled as such. First, in Diodorus' description of the aftermath of Syracuse's 466 revolution against its tyrants and the subsequent revival of Greek Sicily, the historian notes that, (1) Syracuse liberated and reestablished *demokratiai* in the other cities that had been directly ruled or garrisoned by tyrants (11.68.5), which would certainly have included Gela, and (2) Gela resettled Camarina at this time and was among those cities that in the next few years accepted back into their cities people who had been relocated by Hieron. It no doubt participated in the *koinon dogma* (common resolution) among the cities to make peace with the mercenaries of the tyrannical era, settle them in Messana, drive out foreign (*apallotrious*) constitutions, bring back exiles and original citizens, and reapportion (*kateklerouchesan*) land to all citizens (11.76.4–6). The dating of these events, both generally and as they applied to Gela, cannot be sorted out with precision but appear from Diodorus' account to have transpired between 466 and 461. They present a picture of vigorous democratization and reestablishment of citizen bodies and landownership in the various cities including Gela after the fall of the tyrants.

The second democratic listing of which Gela must have been a part occurs in Thucydides' history. At 7.55 Thucydides describes the difficult

---

98 O. Murray, "Rationality and the Greek City: The Evidence from Camarina," in M. H. Hansen, ed., *The Polis as an Urban Centre and as a Political Community* (CPC Acts 4, Historik-filosofiske Meddelelser 75; Copenhagen, 1997), 493–504; B. Helly, "Sur les *fratrai* de Camarina," *PP* 52 (1997), 365–406.

99 Camarina minted only small-denomination coins (silver *litrai*) in the first decades after its refoundation in 461, which could have had a democratic purpose. Manganaro associates this practice with the need for assembly payments that he sees the lead tablets as marking; "Sikelika I," 101–2; U. Westermark and K. Jenkins, *The Coinage of Camarina* (London, 1980).

position in which the Athenians found themselves late in their Sicilian campaign (413 BC), noting the great similarity to themselves of the cities they were then fighting, given that these were democratic and strong in ships, cavalry, and size.[100] Context dictates that these cities (*polesi gar tautais*) to which Thucydides here refers must have been Syracuse and its allies during the campaign. The allied Sicilian cities are listed for the reader a bit farther on in this section at 7.58.1, and Gela is among them. Moreover, only a little earlier in the Sicilian narrative Thucydides mentions contributions from Gela: ships, cavalry, and other soldiers (7.33.1), closely paralleling what Thucydides had said the local democracies were able to provide in abundance.[101] There can be no doubt, then, that Gela is meant as being one of the strong, democratic communities which, together with the Syracusans, were giving the Athenians such troubles in Sicily.

If the beginning of the Geloan *demokratia* can be pinned to the mid-460s, it is likely that the end came in 405, when the Carthaginians under the command of Himilcon captured and plundered the city, resulting in little or no occupation of the city until its resettling under the protection of Timoleon many decades later.[102] That the *demokratia* lasted until the very end can be inferred from Diodorus' report of an episode from 406. Dionysius of Syracuse, responding to a Geloan request for more troops to defend the city, arrives and finds the rich (*euporotatous*) agitating against the *demos*. In response he made accusations against the wealthy in the *ekklesia*, had them condemned to death, and confiscated their property so as to pay the troops (13.93). It is rather mysterious how he gained the standing to do this (perhaps Diodorus or his source exaggerates his role), but the acts brought him great popularity with the *demos*, who had resented the elite citizens (*dunatotatous*) and called their natural superiority (*huperochen*) a kind of despotism. The events here strongly suggest the continuing operation of a *demokratia* until the elite took hostile action of some kind (*stasiazontas*) and were put down again with the help of Dionysius.

---

[100] πόλεσι γὰρ ταύταις μόναις ἤδη ὁμοιοτρόποις ἐπελθόντες, δημοκρατουμέναις τε, ὥσπερ καὶ αὐτοί, καὶ ναῦς καὶ ἵππους καὶ μεγέθη ἐχούσαις, οὐ δυνάμενοι ἐπενεγκεῖν οὔτ᾽ ἐκ πολιτείας τι μεταβολῆς τὸ διάφορον αὐτοῖς, ᾧ προσήγοντο ἄν (7.55.2). Cf. 6.20.3–4, where Thucydides gives Nicias similar things to say about the capacities of Athens' upcoming foes, and a scholion lists Gela among the seven cities mentioned in the passage.

[101] Gela also sent cavalry to Syracuse two years earlier: Thuc. 6.67.2 (with another remark on the Sicilian advantage in cavalry at 6.70.3). Gela is among the cities listed by the scholiast to Thuc. 6.20.3, a passage with clear connections to 7.55.

[102] Diod. Sic. 13.108.2–111.2; Plut. *Tim.* 35.2. Talbert, *Timoleon*, 153–7. Cf. G. Fiorentini, "L'età dionigiana a Gela e Agrigento," in N. Bonacasa, L. Braccesi, and E. De Miro, eds., *La Sicilia dei due Dionisî* (Rome, 2002), 147–67.

This episode offers the best glimpse into the operation of the Geloan *demokratia*. We see a *demos* jealous of the wealth and influence of the elite class, and, under pressure of the need to pay soldiers and the political attacks of that class, willing to use prosecutions to condemn its members and put the resulting money to public use. As often in the reporting of episodes of this type, the *demos* comes off looking petty, unstable, and unjust, though at least here the prior *stasis* of the wealthy is admitted. We cannot know whether aristocratic bias of historical writers explains the negative portrayal or if indeed the *demos* deserved its depiction here. We would need to know much more about, for example, what constituted and caused the agitation of the rich in the first place, the nature of the charges against them, and the procedures employed.

Archaeological contributions to the picture of Geloan democracy are minimal. While it has been supposed that a theater existed in the early to mid fifth century when Aeschylus reportedly spent time there, the sources are entirely indirect, and no remains have been reliably assigned to such a structure. This theater could have been used as an *ekklesiasterion*, and its date would be consistent with the era of democracy's arrival at Gela, but its existence is too uncertain to make much of it.[103]

Himera

The evidence for democracy in Himera is much like that for Gela. As with Gela, no ancient source specifies that Himera became a democracy after the fall of tyrannies in Sicily in the 460s, but it clearly was a member of the same two groups that were collectively called *demokratiai* by Diodorus and Thucydides in separate incidents. Diodorus 11.68.5 refers to cities formerly under tyrants (certainly to include Himera) having democracies established in them after the overthrow of the Syracusan tyranny in 466; and 11.76.4–6 specifies that in a few years Himera took part in the resettlement of its citizens wrongly driven out in years past by tyrants, and he notes the *koinon dogma* (common resolution) which Sicilian cities undertook to make peace with the mercenaries of the tyrannical era, drive out alien constitutions, bring back exiles and original citizens, and reapportion (*kateklerouchesan*) land to all citizens.[104] These generalized statements include Himera in the

[103] E. Borgia, "Gela," in P. C. Rossetto and G. P. Sartorio, eds., *Teatri greci e romani*, vol II (Rome, 1994), 471; T. Fischer-Hansen, T. H. Nielsen, and C. Ampolo in *Inventory*, 193–4.

[104] On the tyrannical relocations, see Diod. Sic. 11.48–9. Also claiming post-tyrannical democracy: L. Jannelli, "Himera," in L. Cerchiai, L. Jannelli, and F. Longo, *The Greek Cities of Magna Graecia and Sicily* (Los Angeles, 2004), 188–93, at 190.

ongoing democratization of Greek cities in Sicily at this time, and one further reference particular to Himera adds more detail: a Pindaric ode dating in all probability to 466 prominently associates Zeus Eleutherios and deliberative assemblies (*agorai boulaphorai*) with Himera of this time.[105] This reference should be considered together with the sudden appearance of cult for Zeus Eleutherios at Syracuse during this time just as Syracuse democratized (Diod. Sic. 11.72).

Himera must also be understood to belong to the group of *poleis* Thucydides mentions at 7.55 as being democratic, strong in cavalry and other areas, and therefore causing Athens great difficulty in its Sicilian campaign. Like Gela, Himera is mentioned at 7.58 when Thucydides lists Syracuse's local allies, and his account also notes the reinforcements, including cavalry, that Himera added when Gylippus arrived to aid Syracuse (7.1.5).[106]

In 409 the Carthaginians captured and razed Himera to the ground (Diod. Sic. 13.62), after which it was largely abandoned.[107] There is no evidence to help us understand the nature of the Himeran democracy. Recently discovered inscribed bronze plaques dating to around the turn of the fifth century probably relate to land redistribution in the pre-democratic era; they mention phratries and possibly tribes but can shed little light on later constitutional procedure.[108]

Leontini

The constitutional history of Leontini in the fifth century is slightly harder to judge than that of most of the other Greek cities in Sicily that were freed from tyrants in the 460s. On the one hand, Leontini should be included in the group of cities that Diodorus declares became democracies in the aftermath of the overthrow of the Deinomenids in Syracuse (11.68.5): it too had been tyrant-dominated in the preceding years, Hieron having shaken up their population in 476 (Diod. Sic. 11.49.2), and thus Leontini would have had every reason to join the rest of the cities in the common agreement regarding repatriation of citizens in the late 460s (11.76.4–6). On the other hand, the bookend to this familiar argument about mid–late fifth-century

---

[105] *Ol.* 12.1–5. On the ode's date and also its possible significance for Himera, see Barrett, "Pindar's Twelfth *Olympian*," 23–35.

[106] Himera is also among the cities listed by the scholiast to Thuc. 6.20.3, a passage with clear connections to 7.55.

[107] Diod. Sic. 11.49.4; Strabo 6.2.6. T. Fischer-Hansen, T. H. Nielsen, and C. Ampolo in *Inventory*, 199 for the possibility of some occupation after 405.

[108] A. Brugnone, "Legge di Himera sulla ridistribuzione della terra," *PP* 52 (1997), 262–305; *SEG* 47.1427.

Sicilian democracies – the *polesi demokratoumenais* of Thucydides 7.55 – does not apply to Leontini, for the city was no ally of Syracuse during the war with Athens. In fact, Leontini's conflict with Syracuse had brought the Athenians to Sicily in 427 (Thuc. 3.86; Diod. Sic. 12.53), and the mistreatment of the city by the Syracusans was again used as a pretext for the much larger intervention of 415 (Thuc. 6.6.1–2; 6.8.2; Diod. Sic. 12.83).

What happened to the city between the two Athenian expeditions, and what might these events tell us about Leontini's constitution? According to our accounts – most importantly Thucydides 5.4.2–4[109] – after the general peace negotiated in 424 by the Sicilian cities many new citizens came to Leontini. The enlarged *demos* desired to undertake a land redistribution, but when the local elites (*hoi dunatoi*) saw what was happening they called in the city's old enemy the Syracusans to help drive out the *demos*. Having succeeded in this, the *dunatoi* made an agreement with the Syracusans to abandon Leontini and live as citizens in Syracuse. Later, some of the *dunatoi* found themselves dissatisfied at Syracuse and returned to the old territory, to be joined by some but not all of the exiled *polloi* (masses).

Constitutionally, the assumption that makes the most sense of Thucydides' account is that Leontini was democratically governed when all this began. The ready acceptance and political involvement of new citizens and the subsequent desire for land redistribution all point this way. Moreover, the apparent impotence of the *dunatoi* to stop by internal political means such a radical move strongly indicates that some form of *demokratia* rather an oligarchic regime held sway.[110] The reaction by democratic Syracuse to help the *dunatoi* and thereby take control of the city – making the city a Syracusan *phrourion* (stronghold) according to Diodorus 12.54.7 – need not get in the way of this interpretation, as Syracuse will have viewed the offer of the Leontine aristocrats to assume control of their city primarily as an imperial opportunity, not as a democratic/oligarchic political struggle in which the Syracusans had any partisan stake.[111]

The Leontine depopulation and loss of sovereignty probably took place in the winter of 424/3.[112] Assuming that the *demokratia* present then began with the overthrow of the Sicilian tyrants in the late 460s, that would mean the government had been democratic for roughly four decades. Leontini

---

[109] Cf. Diod. Sic. 12.54, 12.83, 13.95; Xen. *Hell.* 2.3.5. On reconciling the Diodoran and Thucydidean accounts, M. Dreher, "La dissoluzione della *polis* di Leontini dopo la pace di Gela (424 a. C.)," *Annali della Scuola Normale Superiore di Pisa, Classe di Lettere e Filosofia* 16.3 (1986), 637–60, at 638–42.

[110] Dreher, "Dissoluzione," 645–7; D. Kagan, *The Peace of Nicias and the Sicilian Expedition* (Ithaca, 1981), 160–2.

[111] Dreher, "Dissoluzione," 647.   [112] Dreher, "Dissoluzione," 653–4.

was eventually repopulated (in 405 or 404, according to Diodorus 13.113–14), but nothing is known about its constitutional status in the later periods.

In the absence of further narratives or inscriptions to flesh out the popular government at Leontini, we turn to Gorgias of Leontini and the use of rhetoric there. It was Gorgias' famous mission to Athens in 427, we are told, that sparked Athenian interest in intervening militarily in Sicily in that year.[113] Plato's *Greater Hippias* claims Gorgias was judged by the Leontines to be a most effective speaker in the assembly (*en toi demoi*, 282b), and Plato has the sophist himself speak as if from long experience of addressing the common people (*ta plethe, hoi ochloi*), and specifically refers to assemblies (*ekklesiai*), popular courts (*dikasteria*), and council meetings (*en bouleuterioi*).[114] These passages imply the operation of these typically democratic institutions in Leontini, therefore, as well as the successful use of populist rhetoric by the ambitious.[115]

Selinous

The main reasons for thinking that Selinous was democratic in the fifth century match those for Gela and Himera, namely statements in Diodorus and Thucydides describing as *demokratiai* groups of cities to which Selinous surely belonged.[116] Diodorus 11.68.5 and 11.76.4–6, which assert the democratization of cities and resettlement of citizen groups in Greek Sicily, should apply to Selinous, too, as it was a Greek city previously dominated by tyrants recently overthrown. It is true, though, that unlike Gela and Himera, Selinous is not specifically mentioned by Diodorus in the discussion about resettling citizens in the aftermath of the battles with tyrants and their mercenaries. As for the Thucydides passage (7.55) regarding the *demokratoumenais* cities so troublesome to the Athenians invading Sicily, Selinous naturally belongs: it was an early and constant ally of Syracuse when Athens launched the Sicilian Expedition, an expedition sparked in fact by Selinous's war with Egesta and alliance with Syracuse (6.6.2; 6.20.3–4; 6.65.1; 7.58.1). Moreover, the Selinuntines are specifically described as having contributed the things Thucydides cites at 7.55.2 as damaging: at 7.1.5 they provide cavalry and other troops; at 8.26.1 they contribute ships

---

[113] Diod. Sic. 12.54.1; Paus. 6.17.7–9; H. Diels and W. Kranz, *Die Fragmente der Vorsokratiker* (Berlin, 1951), Gorgias testimonia 2, 3, and 14. Hereafter I will use the short form in citing fragments from Diels–Kranz, e.g., here DK 82 A2 (where testimonia are A, quotations are B).

[114] *Gorgias* 452e, 454b, 456b.

[115] For a fuller argument on Gorgias' democratic background, see E. Robinson, "The Sophists and Democracy beyond Athens," *Rhetorica* 25.1 (2007), 109–22, at 113–16.

[116] For a more full discussion of these passages, see Gela, this chapter.

to the war in the Aegean; and at 6.20.3–4 Thucydides gives to Nicias words that closely parallel his own statement at 7.55, singling out Selinous and Syracuse as having similar capabilities in war to those of the Athenians plus an advantage in cavalry. These passages make it extremely hard to imagine that Thucydides did not mean to include Selinous among the *demokratoumenais polesi* he refers to at 7.55.2.

Given the likelihood from the above evidence, then, that Selinous became democratic in the 460s and remained so (or was again) in the 410s, we must ask what more might be concluded about the government from three public inscriptions relating to Selinous and dating to the early or mid fifth century. The oldest of the three comes from Olympia and probably records an agreement regarding the reception of exiles in Selinous from Megara (either Nisaea or Hyblaea); it mentions *aisimnatai* (council members? See *Syll.*³. 642), though these could have been Megarian officials, and the dating of the document to near the turn of the fifth century would preclude learning much therefrom about Selinous post 466.[117] Next, a *lex sacra* from the first half of the fifth century describes purification procedures, some apparently to be performed on behalf of the whole city. While nothing in the document speaks to governmental type or procedures, the publishers of the text argue that its provisions probably result from the commission of sacrilegious acts during internal factional battles.[118] Finally an inscription dating to *c.* 450 records a vow to Zeus and other gods for the victory of the Selinuntines over an unknown foe, declaring in a public enactment that the many gods' names are to be written on a golden dedication which is to be set up in a temple to Apollo, and specifying how much gold is to be used.[119] The text reads somewhat like a decree but preserves no decree formula, so one cannot be certain that this was in fact an official enactment of the city, nor can one judge what civic bodies may have been involved in its promulgation.

During the fourth century Selinous was largely dominated by the Carthaginians after the city's capture in a siege by Hannibal in 409 (Diod. Sic. 13.54–9), though for brief interludes after this and into the fourth century Greeks reestablished control.[120] Constitutional information for the city in this period is unavailable.

---

[117] *IvO* 22; Jeffery, *LSAG* 271, 277; *IGDS* 28; A. J. Graham, *Colony and Mother City in Ancient Greece* (2nd edn.; Chicago, 1983), 112–13.

[118] M. Jameson, D. Jordan, and R. Kotansky, *A Lex Sacra from Selinous* (Durham, 1993). On the date, see A. J. Graham's review in *Phoenix* 49 (1995), 366–7.

[119] *IG* 14.268, *Syll.*³ 1122, Buck 98, Jeffery, *LSAG* pp. 271, 277, *IGDS* 78.

[120] Jameson, *A* Lex Sacra, 122; T. Fischer-Hansen, T. H. Nielsen, and C. Ampolo in *Inventory*, 221–2.

SOUTHERN ITALIAN CITIES

Croton (and Caulonia)

Croton's first experience with democracy probably occurred toward the end of the sixth century with the revolution of Cylon against the Pythagoreans. As discussed in *The First Democracies*, late Pythagorean sources probably deriving from Timaeus describe a popular revolt of *c.* 510 aimed at the Pythagoreans, a group of great influence or even control at Croton.[121] Corroborating evidence of democratic revolution in the city and region can be found in Polybius; however, it is likely that he refers to a *second* anti-Pythagorean disruption that took place in the mid fifth century, and this is the episode we will focus on in the present discussion.

At 2.38–9 Polybius narrates a patriotic history of Achaean political accomplishments, noting at 2.38.6 that one could not find a more pure system involving equal participation and free speech (*isegorias kai parresias*) and indeed true democracy (*demokratias alethines*) than that of the Achaeans.[122] He goes on to give examples of the early instantiation and influence of the Achaean constitution, including the time of the violent revolutionary movement targeting Pythagoreans that took place in the Greek cities of Italy.[123] Polybius claims that they embraced Achaean assistance in ending the disorder and after a time (*meta tinas chronous*) set out to copy the Achaean constitution. More specifically, Polybius claims Croton, Caulonia, and Sybaris formed a league (with some of the same institutions as that of the Achaean League) and also conducted their government (*politeia*) according to Achaean laws and principles.[124] These changes lasted until the time of Dionysius of Syracuse (2.39.7).

---

[121] Robinson, *First Democracies*, 73–8. Iambl. *VP* 257–62, with E. L. Minar, *Early Pythagorean Politics in Practice and Theory* (Baltimore, 1942), 54, n. 14 on Timaeus as the source.

[122] ἰσηγορίας καὶ παρρησίας καὶ καθόλου δημοκρατίας ἀληθινῆς σύστημα καὶ προαίρεσιν εἰλικρινεστέραν οὐκ ἂν εὕροι τις τῆς παρὰ τοῖς Ἀχαιοῖς ὑπαρχούσης (2.38.6). On what Polybius may have meant by *demokratia* – probably a looser sense than was meant in earlier authors – see Walbank, *Commentary*, 221–2. On Achaean *demokratia* see also Polybius 2.41.5, with Walbank, *Commentary*, 229–30.

[123] Strabo 8.7.1 compresses Polybius' account.

[124] οὐ μόνον δὲ κατὰ τούτους τοὺς καιροὺς ἀπεδέξαντο τὴν αἵρεσιν τῶν Ἀχαιῶν, ἀλλὰ καὶ μετά τινας χρόνους ὁλοσχερῶς ὥρμησαν ἐπὶ τὸ μιμηταὶ γενέσθαι τῆς πολιτείας αὐτῶν. παρακαλέσαντες γὰρ σφᾶς καὶ συμφρονήσαντες Κροτωνιᾶται, Συβαρῖται, Καυλωνιᾶται, πρῶτον μὲν ἀπέδειξαν Διὸς Ὁμαρίου κοινὸν ἱερὸν καὶ τόπον, ἐν ᾧ τάς τε συνόδους καὶ τὰ διαβούλια συνετέλουν, δεύτερον τοὺς ἐθισμοὺς καὶ νόμους ἐκλαβόντες τοὺς τῶν Ἀχαιῶν ἐπεβάλοντο χρῆσθαι καὶ διοικεῖν κατὰ τούτους τὴν πολιτείαν (2.39.4–6).

Though not precisely dated, Polybius' account seems to relate to the mid fifth century and thereafter,[125] bracketed by his reference to Sybaris (refounded 453) and Dionysius I's ending of the democratic institutions that were here established. One must also compare the account in Iamblichus, *Life of Pythagoras* 248–64. This famously difficult compilation of earlier sources seems regularly to merge two separate events: an early populist rising against the Pythagoreans led by Cylon of Croton in *c.* 509,[126] and a more general revolution against them in the cities of southern Italy around 450 BC corresponding to the account in Polybius.[127] Aristoxenus provides the briefer Pythagorean account of the two eras of disturbance at Iamblichus, *Life of Pythagoras* 248–50, masking the time separation with the phrase "for some time" (*mechri tinos*) before describing the burning of Milo's house in Croton, where the Pythagoreans were sitting in council[128] and the general flight of the order from cities in southern Italy. The Timaeus-sourced Iamblichan conflation of democratic revolutions is longer and a bit harder to separate. Minar assigns the crucial break to between sections 261 and 262.[129] Sections 255–61 detail the demands of the masses (*tous pollous, to plethos*) at Croton and their champions, including Cylon, for greater share in the offices and the assembly and for magistrate accountability (*euthunai*), as well as describing attacks upon the Pythagoreans (255–61). Then an omission of some kind is apparent, for the next section talks of fugitives (Pythagoreans?) and evils across the city and the land. Other cities now enter the picture too: Tarentum, Metapontum, and Caulonia, which receive decisive authority in the fugitive cases. Ultimately debts are cancelled and land redistributed (*ta te chrea apekopsan kai ten gen anadaston epoiesan*); different political leaders than those mentioned earlier are named (262–3).

---

[125] Walbank, *Commentary*, 224–6.

[126] Dated principally by its connection to Croton's conquest of Sybaris in 510; Iambl. *VP* 255.

[127] A *terminus post quem* of roughly 450 is provided by the involvement of Lysis, who later taught Epaminondas (Iambl. *VP* 249–50; K. von Fritz, *Pythagorean Politics in Southern Italy*, [New York, 1940], 78–80). There is also evidence from coins that has been taken to suggest a decline in Crotonian influence around the mid fifth century or a little after, which would suit a large-scale political crisis in southern Italy generally at that time, though conclusions from the coinage are somewhat controverial: von Fritz, *Pythagorean Politics*, 80–6, relying upon U. Kahrstedt, "Zur Geschichte Grossgriechenlands im 5ten Jahrhundert," *Hermes* 53 (1918), 180–7; Minar, *Early Pythagorean Politics*, 77; N. K. Rutter, *Greek Coinages*, 34–9, and *Historia Numorum: Italy* (London, 2001), 163–75.

[128] τέλος δὲ εἰς τοσοῦτον ἐπεβούλευσαν τοῖς ἀνδράσιν, ὥστε ἐν τῇ Μίλωνος οἰκίᾳ ἐν Κρότωνι συνεδρευόντων τῶν Πυθαγορείων καὶ βουλευομένων περὶ πολιτικῶν πραγμάτων ὑφάψαντες τὴν οἰκίαν κατέκαυσαν τοὺς ἄνδρας πλὴν δυεῖν, Ἀρχίππου τε καὶ Λύσιδος (*VP* 249).

[129] Minar, *Early Pythagorean Politics*, 57–60.

Unfortunately, in the conflation of the two eras of anti-Pythagorean agitation, most of the details for the second era have been omitted in the Pythagorean sources. While it remains clear enough from them that populist forces overthrew Pythagorean influence in the cities of southern Italy and engaged in debt cancellation and land redistribution, one has to rely on the Polybius passages described above (and Strabo's shorter version, 8.7.1) for clear indication that *demokratia* replaced the existing governments. The burning down of meeting halls (*sunedria*) of the Pythagoreans matches the Aristoxenus reference to the mid-century burning of Milo's house at Croton (*VP* 249), but Polybius makes it a regional attack and specifies that it led to a widespread constitutional revolution (*kinematos holoscherous peri tas politeias*).[130] The Greek cities in the area experienced all manner of violence and chaos (fitting *VP* 262) as the "first men" (*proton andron*) in each city were done away with in the *stasis*. Polybius then goes on to describe the Achaean arbitration and the local adoption of Achaean customs and constitutional forms, which he had just praised as *demokratia*. He says, however, that some time elapsed (*meta tinas chronous*) between the outbreak of the troubles and the adoption of Achaean institutions. Given a *terminus ante quem* of 417 for the ending of fifth-century Achaean democracy (Thuc. 5.82.1), that would mean Croton and possibly other cities adopted *demokratia c.* 450–420, probably toward the earlier end of the range.[131]

Caulonia comes up twice in prominent places in these texts: first it is mentioned at *Life of Pythagoras* 262 as one of the cities given legal authority in the cases of the Pythagorean fugitives created during the mid-century agitation, and, second, it appears in Polybius as having formed a league with Croton (and the Sybarites) and is implied to be one of the regional states that took up Achaean constitutional forms. Caulonia, a colony of Croton, has generally been assumed to have been a part of its sphere of influence during the time of Croton's great power in the first half of the fifth century and was home to a number of Pythagoreans before the disturbances.[132]

---

[130] Polyb. 2.38–9, probably based ultimately on Timaeus (Walbank, *Commentary*, 223–4). On the burning of the meeting halls cf. Justin 20.4, with von Fritz, *Pythagorean Politics*, 86–9.

[131] For Achaea, see discussion in Chapter 1. On the date of democratization, see von Fritz, *Pythagorean Politics*, 72–9; C. Riedweg, *Pythagoras*, trans. S. Rendall (Ithaca, 2005), 104–5. D. Musti, "Le rivolte antipitagoriche e la concezione pitagorica del tempo," *QUCC* 36 (1990), 35–65, would date the general political crisis to between 440 and 415 and does not see the Achaean constitutional change of 417 as a reliable *terminus ante quem*.

[132] On Caulonian Pythagoreans, Iambl. *VP* 267. On the supposed supremacy of Croton in the region in the late sixth through mid fifth centuries, see Kahrstedt, "Geschichte," Minar, *Early Pythagorean Politics*, 36–49, and T. Fischer-Hansen, T. H. Nielsen, and C. Ampolo in *Inventory*, 267. Von Fritz,

For all these reasons it makes sense to include Caulonia as one of the area states that took up democracy along with Croton as a result of the anti-Pythagorean movement in the middle of the century. Nothing more, however, can be said about the nature of this Caulonian democracy.[133]

Institutionally, little is known for sure about the Crotonian system either. No inscribed decrees survive from the city, for example. However, some extrapolations can perhaps be made from the literary material, late though it is. The first part of the Iamblichan account of the anti-Pythagorean movements – that section apparently relating to the Cylonian episode of the late sixth century – describes demands lodged by the leaders of the many (*to plethos*) that all be able to take part in office-holding and assembly meetings and that officials render account of themselves (*didonai tas euthynas*) to those chosen by lot from all.[134] These populist demands, probably met at the time (*VP* 257–8, 261), also might describe how things worked when democracy was (re)established after the mid-fifth-century revolution. One would expect in any case that *demokratia* meant access to the assembly and at least some of the offices for all citizens. That *euthunai* be conducted before allotted representatives is an interesting requirement, though also far from unusual.

The section directly pertaining to events in the middle of the century (262) specifies that the victorious faction undertook a number of actions: (1) drove out of the city those unhappy with the new political situation, together with their families; (2) cancelled debts (*kai ta chrea apekopsan*); and (3) redistributed the land (*kai ten gen anadaston epoiesan*). If this material can be trusted, the revolution was very radical, politically and economically. The oligarchic leaders initially overthrown and the wealthy driven out soon thereafter will presumably have provided the land to be distributed.

One might also potentially learn something about Crotonian institutions by examining Achaean ones that supposedly were copied. However, little information about procedures in democratic Achaea remains extant. A council and college of *damiourgoi* existed in the fourth century at (then probably oligarchic) Achaea, institutions that could have been a holdover from earlier democratic days.[135] Inscriptions from the southern Italian

---

Pythagorean Politics, 94–100, does not deny expansion by Croton but sees the Pythagorean role in "ruling" Croton and other cities as far less direct than does Minar.

[133] T. Fischer-Hansen, T. H. Nielsen, and C. Ampolo in *Inventory*, 266, notes the uncertain provenance of *SEG* 4.71 and its eponymous *damiourgos* and public organizations.

[134] ὑπὲρ τοῦ πάντας κοινωνεῖν τῶν ἀρχῶν καὶ τῆς ἐκκλησίας καὶ διδόναι τὰς εὐθύνας τοὺς ἄρχοντας ἐν τοῖς ἐκ πάντων λαχοῦσιν (*VP* 257).

[135] *SEG* 14.375.

region provide possible evidence for a Crotonian and Caulonian *damiour-gos*, conceivably confirming Achaean influence.[136]

Polybius asserts that the adoption of Achaean forms of government by Italian cities came to an end by compulsion thanks to Dionysius of Syracuse and Croton's non-Greek neighbors (2.39.7), probably in 389–388 (Dion. Hal. 20.7; cf. Diod. Sic. 14.91, 100–8, 111–12). One must assume that the democracies in both Croton and Caulonia ended at this time. No information is available for their constitutions later in the fourth century.

Rhegium (and Messana/Zancle)

The political histories of Rhegium and Messana in the Classical period are linked by the joint rule of the two by the tyrant Anaxilas and his successors early in the fifth century and by similarities in source material thereafter. They will thus be treated together here.

Both Rhegium and Messana were freed from the rule of the sons of Anaxilas[137] in the mid–late 460s BC in the general overthrow of tyrannical power sparked by the revolution in Syracuse. Diodorus 11.68.5 describes the Syracusan liberation and, indeed, democratization of cities in the region that had been ruled by tyrants.[138] Rhegium's location in Italy rather than Sicily (the unspecified but clear context of Diodorus' narrative here; see 11.72.1–2), might conceivably be taken to exempt it from Diodorus' claims of general liberation and democratization. However, both cities are specifically mentioned at 11.76.4–5, where Diodorus continues the story and notes the overthrow of the sons of Anaxilas and the liberation of the cities' lands (*eleutherosan tas patridas*). The two cities also seem to have participated in the region's *koinon dogma* (common resolution) that Diodorus goes on to describe, an agreement to make peace with the mercenaries of the tyrannical era, settle them "in Messenia" (Messana), drive out foreign (*apallotrious*) constitutions, bring back exiles and original citizens, and reapportion (*kateklerouchesan*) land to all citizens (11.76.5–6).

It is therefore tempting to assume that both Messana and Rhegium, like other cities in the region in the late 460s, became democracies of some sort: see Gela, Himera, and Selinous discussions in this chapter. However,

---

[136] *SEG* 4.71, 73–5, and 39.1045.
[137] Diod. Sic. 11.48, 11.59. On the earlier takeover of Zancle and renaming as Messana, Hdt. 6.23.2, Thuc. 6.4.6. Generally on both cities, T. Fischer-Hansen, T. H. Nielsen, and C. Ampolo in *Inventory*, 233–6, 290–3.
[138] οἱ δὲ Συρακόσιοι τοῦτον τὸν τρόπον ἐλευθερώσαντες τὴν πατρίδα τοῖς μὲν μισθοφόροις συνεχώρησαν ἀπελθεῖν ἐκ τῶν Συρακουσῶν, τὰς δὲ ἄλλας πόλεις τὰς τυραννουμένας ἢ φρουρὰς ἐχούσας ἐλευθερώσαντες ἀποκατέστησαν ταῖς πόλεσι τὰς δημοκρατίας.

whereas evidence can be found to corroborate democratic change in these other cities, the source material does not much clarify the picture for these two. Apart from an episode of *stasis* in the 420s which need not have had constitutional dimensions,[139] no further evidence emerges for government at Messana until the fourth century (see below). For Rhegium, oligarchy may have returned to the city after the removal of the tyrants. Before Anaxilas' takeover *c.* 494 a thoroughly aristocratic government had governed Rhegium, one that placed the management of affairs in the hands of 1,000 men chosen according to wealth.[140] If traditional laws were restored in the wake of the tyrants' overthrow, oligarchy surely returned to Rhegium. Another factor to consider is the Pythagorean presence at Rhegium at some point in the mid–late fifth century. Iamblichus (*VP* 251) indicates that Rhegium became a refuge for many Pythagoreans in the aftermath of the democratic disturbances that had driven them out of other Italian cities at this time.[141] The Pythagoreans were famously aristocratic politically, and according to traditions several Pythagorean Rhegians were involved in establishing constitutions (*politeiai*) in Rhegium, one of the systems being called *gumnasiarchiken*.[142]

This evidence suggests, then, that Rhegium might not have followed the general pattern of democracies taking hold after the overthrow of regional tyrants in the 460s. However, the testimony for possible oligarchy is vague and indirect, and Iamblichus is a famously unreliable (and chronologically imprecise) source. The only certainty is that by the early 420s Rhegium was undergoing serious internal disturbances, and had been for some time, as Thucydides reports at 4.1.3 (*epi polun chronon estasiaze*), with exiles agitating for outside powers to intervene. Rhegium had made an alliance with Athens in the 430s, which has led some scholars to assume that it had by this point become democratic.[143] But Athens allied with cities and peoples of all constitutional stripes when convenient, making the fact of an alliance with them hardly decisive constitutionally. In the end, the evidence for the fifth century produces a picture of violently competing

---

[139] Thuc. 5.5.1. This involved a group of Locrian settlers who were called in to Messana by one faction (giving control of the city to Locri temporarily) and then later expelled.

[140] Arist. *Pol.* 1316a34–9; more specifically, though of uncertain chronological application, Heracl. Lemb. fr. 55: πολιτείαν δὲ κατεστήσαντο ἀριστοκρατικήν. Χίλιοι γὰρ πάντα διοικοῦσιν αἱρετοὶ ἀπὸ τιμημάτων. νόμοις δὲ ἐχρῶντο τοῖς Χαρώνδου τοῦ Καταναίου.

[141] For discussion, see Minar, *Early Pythagorean Politics*, ch. 4, esp. 84–6; cf. von Fritz, *Pythagorean Politics*, 94–100. See also the treatment of Croton above.

[142] Iambl. *VP* 130, 172.

[143] F. Costabile, "Strateghi e assemblea nelle politeiai di Reggio e Messana," *Klearchos* 20 (1978), 19–57. On the alliance: ML 63, with Thuc. 4.25 and Diod. Sic. 12.54.4.

political forces in the region and the city of Rhegium (and possibly Messana as well). Probably democratic forces won through in the two cities at one or more points in the struggles, either soon after the overthrow of the sons of Anaxilas or later in the 430s or 420s, but the duration and nature of the resulting popular governments cannot be ascertained.

Better light is shed on events at both Rhegium and Messana in the early fourth century. Diodorus narrates events involving Dionysius of Syracuse that indicate rather clearly that the governments of both cities had become democratic. At 14.40 Diodorus describes a campaign that the Rhegians undertook against Dionysius in 399 after the tyrant had enslaved the Naxians and Catanians. The Rhegians marshaled forces and appointed generals for the campaign, and these crossed the straits and persuaded the generals of the Messanians to join in the campaign. The Messanian generals then joined the campaign with their forces (presumably already preparing out of worry about Dionysius?), though they did not seek approval from the Messanian *demos* (14.40.4: *aneu tes tou demou gnomes*). This quickly led to troubles (*stasis*), as one of the Messanian soldiers played the public speaker (*demegoresantos*) and argued that they should not start a war with someone who had done them no wrong. The soldiers were persuaded by the speech, having in mind that the war had not been ratified by the people (14.40.5: *ton polemon ouk epikekurokotos tou demou*),[144] and abandoned the generals to return home, effectively ending the campaign. This remarkable turn of events – collapse of an expedition due to mass desertion by citizen soldiers because proper steps to secure popular legitimation had not been followed – would seem possible only in a democratic city. One wonders what the generals were thinking in marching out at once as they did. Perhaps time was of the essence with the sudden arrival of the Rhegian forces, and they (wrongly) assumed the people, or at least those marching with them, would support their actions.[145]

In his description of events of the very next year (398), Diodorus describes an assembly meeting (*ekklesia*) in which the Rhegians met to consider a proposal from Dionysius to make a marriage alliance with him in return for territorial benefits. Many speeches were made at the meeting about the matter, after which the Rhegians decided against the marriage arrangement: *edoxe tois Rheginois me dexasthai ten epigamian*.[146] Other decisive assembly

---

[144] However, the Greek may read *epikekerukotos* – less appropriate given the context, though still possible.

[145] See Costabile, "Strateghi e assemblea," on the usurping of popular power by the generals, and relations between generals and the assemblies in fourth-century Rhegium and Messana.

[146] Cf. Diod. Sic. 14.107.3; Strabo 6.1.6.

meetings at Rhegium in this era are attested elsewhere (Ps.-Arist. *Oec.* 1349b18; Aelian, *VH* 5.20). It also appears that generals were elective and under the authority of the assembly.[147] While this evidence for the power of the Rhegian assembly is less dramatic than the episode from Messana, it nevertheless points to the high probability of a democratic regime at the time.

It would appear, then, that at some point in the later fifth century the political discord attested for Messana and Rhegium resolved itself in both cases in favor of *demokratia*, which lasted into the early years of the fourth century. It probably did not last much longer. The Carthaginians captured and destroyed "Messenia" (Messana) in 396 (Diod. Sic. 14.57–8); it was repopulated by Dionysius in the following year, but under what kind of government cannot be ascertained, even after the population drove out from the city those favoring the tyrant and declared their freedom (*eleutheria*) in 394 (Diod. Sic. 14.78, 14.88). We learn only that in *c.* 337 Timoleon freed the city from the tyrant Hippo (Plut. *Tim.* 34).

As for Rhegium, Dionysius destroyed the city in 387, selling the citizens as slaves (Diod. Sic. 14.111–12). Refounded for a time as Phoebia by the younger Dionysius (Strabo 6.1.6), the city later (351) regained its independence (*autonomia*) thanks to the rulers at Syracuse (Diod. Sic. 16.45.9).[148] The government that followed may have been a *demokratia*. Diodorus (16.68.4–6) describes an assembly meeting (*koinen ekklesian*) in *c.* 344 on the subject of a possible agreement involving Timoleon, who had recently escaped to the city after the fall of Syracuse, and the Carthaginians who pursued in force. During the ensuing assembly debate, in which the Rhegian speakers went on and on (*demegorountas makros*), Timoleon slipped away.[149] As with the other, earlier Diodoran indications of an active assembly at Rhegium, such a picture is more consistent with democracy than proof of it, but in the absence of other indications we ought probably to assume a Rhegian *demokratia* at the time. Nothing of value about

---

[147] Diod. Sic. 14.40.3, 14.87.1, 14.108.4.

[148] Costabile, "Strateghi e assemblea," 52–3, hypothesizes that a timocratic constitution of some kind followed the destruction at Rhegium based on the undated reference to aristocratic constitutions in the Heraclides Lembus reference discussed above, n. 140.

[149] ἐπικαταπλευσάντων δὲ καὶ τῶν Καρχηδονίων εἴκοσι τριήρεσι καὶ τῶν Ῥηγίνων συνεργούντων τῷ Τιμολέοντι καὶ κοινὴν ἐκκλησίαν ἐν τῇ πόλει συναγαγόντων καὶ περὶ συλλύσεως δημηγορούντων οἱ μὲν Καρχηδόνιοι διαλαβόντες τὸν Τιμολέοντα πεισθήσεσθαι τὸν εἰς Κόριν-θον ἀπόπλουν ποιήσασθαι ῥαθύμως εἶχον τὰ κατὰ τὰς φυλακάς, ὁ δὲ Τιμολέων οὐδεμίαν ἔμφασιν διδοὺς τοῦ δρασμοῦ αὐτὸς μὲν πλησίον τοῦ βήματος ἔμεινε, λάθρᾳ δὲ παρήγγειλε τὰς ἐννέα ναῦς ἀποπλεῦσαι τὴν ταχίστην. περισπωμένων δὲ τῶν Καρχηδονίων ταῖς ψυχαῖς περὶ τοὺς ἐγκαθέτως δημηγοροῦντας μακρῶς τῶν Ῥηγίνων ἔλαθεν ὁ Τιμολέων διαδρὰς ἐπὶ τὴν ὑπολελειμμένην ναῦν καὶ ταχέως ἐξέπλευσεν (16.68. 4–6).

the constitutions of Rhegium or Messana survives for later in the fourth century.

Little can be said about the nature of the democracies at Rhegium and Messana that goes beyond the episodes discussed above. An inscribed decree from Rhegium has the assembly (*halia*) deciding matters but with the curious arrangement of two probouleutic bodies, the council (*boule*) and the "*eskletos*." However, this decree dates to the second century BC and thus may not reflect Classical institutions.[150] The frequently recorded occasions of interaction between generals and assemblies in Messana and Rhegium noted above suggest the importance of the generalship in the democracies in the two cities: at times they seemed to act as key elements in maintaining the popular order and at others as competitors for power with the assemblies.[151] Another interesting feature of these democracies, especially that at Rhegium, was the amassing of naval strength. According to Diodorus 14.107.4, the Rhegians had a fleet of seventy triremes when Dionysius forced its surrender in 389. In 399 they campaigned with fifty triremes and those from Messana with thirty (Diod. Sic. 14.40). These are quite substantial numbers for non-imperial *poleis*, even if not comparable to the hundreds of triremes that larger, imperial states such as Athens and Syracuse (especially under Dionysius) could muster.

Taras (and Heraclea on Siris)

The evidence for the Tarantine democracy in the Classical period is unusually rich for a city with so little surviving continuous narrative, as several passages in multiple authors contribute useful bits of information. Aristotle in the *Politics* describes the transition from a mixed constitutional government (*politeia*) to popular government (*demokratia*) as the result of a horrific defeat in a battle with the Iapygians not long after the Persian Wars, a battle in which a great many citizens from the upper classes (*gnorimoi*) perished.[152] This event belongs in the late 470s or early 460s.[153]

---

[150] *Syll.*[3] 715: *edoxe tai haliai kathaper tai ekletoi kai tai boulai*; Rhodes, *Decrees*, 318, 321.

[151] Costabile, "Strateghi e assemblea," 34–57. Also finding the generals potentially significant for democracy in the region is F. Sartori, "The Constitutions of the Western Greek States. Cyrenaica, Magna Graecia, Greek Sicily, and the Poleis in the Massaliot Area," in G. P. Carratelli, ed., *The Western Greeks* (Milan, 1996), 215–22.

[152] 1303a3–6. For further details on the battle, see Hdt. 7.170; Diod. Sic. 11.52. Herodotus also emphasizes the catastrophic Greek casualties, but neither he nor Diodorus discusses constitutional consequences. On the coming of democracy to Taras, especially regarding the Iapygians, see M. Lombardo, "La democrazie in Magna Graecia: aspetti e problemi," in L. Canfora, ed., *Venticinque secoli dopo l'invenzione della democrazia* (Paestum, 1998), 77–106, at 87–9.

[153] Diod. Sic. 11.52 puts it in 473, though some scholars would date it a few years later: P. Wuilleumier, *Tarente des origines à la conquête romaine* (Paris, 1939), 177; F. Cordano, "*Phonos megistos hellenikos*,"

This passage comes in a section of the *Politics* in which Aristotle discusses the ways states can undergo constitutional change (*metabolai ton politeion*) through the growth of one part of the body politic with respect to another, in this case the poor (*ton aporon plethos*) versus the rich. How calmly or violently this revolution proceeded we do not know, though this portion of the *Politics* seems to assume the presence of *stasis* in revolutions unless otherwise noted, and one suspects that the remaining Tarantine *gnorimoi* will not have given up their political privileges without a contest of some kind. Strabo also refers to the Tarantine democracy, noting how the city once held great military power during the time when it was governed *demokratikos* (6.3.4). Strabo does not specify a chronology for this period, but the personalities he mentions in the succeeding lines mostly belong to the fourth century, so we can assume that the Classical Tarantine democracy endured for quite a long time, probably through most of the fifth and fourth centuries.[154]

As for the nature of the Tarentine democracy, Wuilleumier describes the constitution as "un judicieux amalgame des constitutions spartiate et athénienne."[155] That Tarantine government might have owed some institutions to its colonial founder Sparta stands to reason. It probably used ephors (they are attested for Taras's colony Heraclea and for Hellenistic Taras) and, surely before the democracy, employed a limited kingship of some kind.[156] The ephors may have been eponymous.[157] On the other hand, no evidence suggests any Athenian connections to the Tarantine government beyond the presence of offices and institutions common to many Greek cities. For example, *strategoi* existed at Taras. But so did *rhetrophulakes*,[158] unattested at Athens. Offices with different titles but potentially similar duties

---

Atti e Memorie della Società Magna Grecia 15–17 (1974–6), 203–6. It used to be thought that Tarantine coins with a seated figure first appearing *c.* 480 represented Demos and thus the new democracy, but such views were always speculative and have been generally dismissed since the nineteenth century; G. C. Brauer, *Taras: Its History and Coinage* (New York, 1986), 34–6 with n. 29.

[154] See also K. Lomas, *Rome and the Western Greeks 350 BC–AD 200* (London, 1993), 36–9, on *topoi* of radicalizing government in the region after the 350s.

[155] Wuilleumier, *Tarente*, 177 with following discussion. Brauer, *Taras*, 28, also thinks Athenian influence possible, but does not elaborate on why beyond (oddly) noting Athens' glory in the war against the Persians. Generally on the Tarantine democracy, Lombardo, "La democrazie in Magna Graecia," 87–94.

[156] *IG* 14.645; *SEG* 30.1162–70, 40.901; Hdt. 3.136. Wuilleumier, *Tarente*, 176; T. J. Dunbabin, *The Western Greeks* (Oxford, 1948), 93; Cordano, "*Phonos megistos hellenikos*"; T. Fischer-Hansen, T. H. Nielsen, and C. Ampolo in *Inventory*, 300–1.

[157] So R. K. Sherk, "The Eponymous Officials of Greek Cities: v, The Register," *ZPE* 96 (1993), 267–95, at 275.

[158] *Etym. Magn.* s.v. ῥήτρσ.

as Athenian ones existed at Taras's colony Heraclea and thus possibly at Taras too: *poluanomoi* (= *astunomoi*?) and *sitagertai* (= *sitophulakes*?). The variation in titles hardly suggests an Athenian origin.[159] The assembly was probably called the *halia* (or *haliaia*), as in other Dorian states.[160]

Generals at Taras were annually elected, and, according to a reference in Diogenes Laertius (8.79), could by law serve only one term. This latter provision, if accurately reported, put a significantly more severe (and populist) restriction on holding the generalship than existed in democracies such as Athens and Syracuse. However, the fourth-century popular leader and Pythagorean Archytas is said to have served seven terms as general. One suspects that an exception allowing multiple terms was voted him because of his enormous popularity and battlefield success, rather than any larger breakdown in the constitutional system.[161] Indeed, even he found it necessary at one point to withdraw from the generalship, which reminds one of Pericles' extraordinary run of generalships at Athens that also failed to insulate him from popular backlash.[162] Nevertheless, another anecdote about the Tarentine *strategia* (in Plut. *Quaest. Graec.* 42) depicts a different general who ignores the vote of the Tarentine citizens in a particular assembly meeting, by either threatening the use of force or asserting some kind of constitutional prerogative – the passage is ambiguous about why his will prevailed on this occasion.[163] But it is easier to believe that a power play by this particular general or *stasis* of some kind was involved on this occasion, than to think that all *strategoi* during the Tarentine democracy had veto power over all decisions of the assembled *demos*. To read the passage in such a way would seem to ruin the point of the story: the proverbial saying which Plutarch seeks to explicate (*hauta kuria*, referring to the general's dismissal of the assembly's decision) loses its force if the occasion that

[159] *IG* 14.645. Like Athens, Heraclea also had *horistai* and a *grammateus*; Wuilleumier, *Tarente*, 177–8.
[160] Heraclea's was a *halia*, *IG* 14.645. On the Tarentines calling some assemblies *grabia* or *graitia*, Hesychius s.v.
[161] *ethaumazeto de kai para tois polloïs epi pasei aretei* (Diog. Laert. 8.79); *ton de Puthagorikon Aristoxenos phesi medepote strategounta hettethenai* (Diog. Laert. 8.82). Cf. Lombardo, "La democrazie," 87–94. Aelian, *VH* 7.14 has Archytas being elected general six times, not seven.
[162] *phthonoumenon d' hapax ekchoresai tes strategias* (Diog. Laert. 8.82). Cf. Thuc. 2.65.1–5.
[163] ἀπὸ τίνος ἐρρήθη τὸ παροιμιῶδες Αὖτα κυρία; Δίνων ὁ Ταραντῖνος στρατηγῶν, ἀνὴρ δ' ὢν ἀγαθὸς ἐν τοῖς πολεμικοῖς, ἀποχειροτονησάντων αὐτοῦ τινα γνώμην τῶν πολιτῶν, ὡς ὁ κῆρυξ ἀνεῖπε τὴν νικῶσαν, αὐτὸς ἀνατείνας τὴν δεξιάν "ἄδε" εἶπε "κρείσσων"· οὕτω γὰρ ὁ Θεόφραστος ἱστόρηκε. προσιστόρηκε δὲ καὶ ὁ Ἀπολλόδωρος ἐν Ῥυτίνῳ, τοῦ κήρυκος "αὗται πλείους" εἰπόντος, "ἀλλ'" αὗταί φάναι "βελτίους" καὶ ἐπικυρῶσαι τὴν τῶν ἐλαττόνων χειροτονίαν. L. Moretti believes the passage shows the great and rather undemocratic powers of *strategoi* at Tarentum: "Problemi della storia di Taranto," in *Taranto nella civiltà della Magna Grecia* (Naples, 1971), at 47–8; T. Fischer-Hansen, T. H. Nielsen, and C. Ampolo in *Inventory*, 300, find the passage ambiguous.

supposedly launched it involved nothing more than a routine exercise of an official's constitutional authority.

Aristotle's *Politics* reveals other important and interesting features of the Tarantine *demokratia*. At 1291b17–23 one reads that among the several classes of the *demos* with livelihoods connected with the sea, the fishing class (*to halieutikon*) was especially numerous (*poluochla*) at Taras. Aristotle contrasts this with the large numbers of the naval class (*trierikon*) at Athens, underscoring the variety possible in populations even in large, coastal democracies. This highlighting of the diversity possible among democratic peoples is worth noting. Nevertheless, given the reference in Strabo to the vast fleet the Tarentines were able to amass during their *demokratia*, it would seem that the sizable fishing class at Taras could form the basis of a strong naval population at least on occasion.[164]

Aristotle mentions two more aspects of the Tarentine democracy at 1320b10–16 in a section of the *Politics* devoted to explaining how democracies may preserve themselves. He notes approvingly that the Tarentines make property (*ktemata*) common for the use of the poor, thereby gaining the goodwill of the masses,[165] and that they have two sets of offices – elective and chosen by lot – the allotted ones so that the *demos* has a share in them, the elective so that they might be governed better. The latter provision on utilizing both elected and allotted offices seems normal enough for *demokratiai* in Greece. The former institution is more intriguing, however. One wonders exactly which *ktemata* were made common for use of the poor, and how it was managed. Various solutions are possible, and it is perhaps easiest if one imagines that land was at issue, property left open to be worked or used for pasture by those needing it. However, while the word *ktemata* can certainly be used to mean real property of this kind (e.g., *Pol.* 1264a33), it is typically used more generally and often connotes movable possessions, especially in Aristotle.[166] Indeed, earlier in the *Politics* (at 1263a21–39) Aristotle discusses the viability of communal ownership practices that exist in a number of states where private ownership still obtains generally but use of possessions is freely given to fellow citizens

---

[164] *Nautikon ... megiston ton tautei* (Strabo 6.3.4).

[165] ἐκεῖνοι γὰρ κοινὰ ποιοῦντες τὰ κτήματα τοῖς ἀπόροις ἐπὶ τὴν χρῆσιν εὔνουν παρασκευάζουσι τὸ πλῆθος (1320b 10–12).

[166] Reference to the *Thesaurus Linguae Graecae* shows that (1) the term comes up in the *Politics* more often than in any other work of Aristotle's, and (2) its use there – when specific examples are given – refers to movable property (slaves, clothing, furniture, stock animals) far more often than land, which only comes up once. However, much of the time the term merely refers to wealth or possessions in a general way that could include land.

as needed. The only example Aristotle provides is Sparta – Taras's founding city – and the shared goods mentioned are slaves, horses, dogs, and agricultural produce. Xenophon in the *Constitution of the Lacedaemonians* (6.3–4) also discusses Spartan sharing of servants, hunting dogs, horses, and food. It is possible, therefore, that Taras's system of *koina ktemata* may have involved something other than giving over public land to poor people for cultivation.

However the system functioned, it has rightly been singled out for its democratic significance.[167] Inequality of wealth in a *polis* was both inevitable and a potential political battleground in a system where the poor fully participated in – and indeed sometimes dominated – political proceedings. Complaints of the poor leeching money from the rich in *demokratiai* were commonplace, even with regard to states such as Athens where huge external revenue sources (silver mines, imperial tribute) existed to fill the public coffers. Taras seems to have developed a system to mitigate the issue of wealth inequality by allowing common use of property by the very neediest. The origin or inspiration could have conceivably been Spartan, but as Aristotle makes clear, the purpose became democratic.

Taras's colony Heraclea was founded on the site of Siris in 433 or 432, probably in cooperation with Thurii.[168] No direct testimony exists for its constitutional form, but two considerations suggest that it was democratic: (1) its foundation by a *demokratia* in cooperation with another *demokratia*; and (2) the provisions of the *Tabulae Heracleenses* (*IG* 14.645) which note the actions of an assembly (*ton Herakleion diagnonton en katakletoi haliai*) and several annual magistrates (see above) and describe legal activity of magistrates (*oristai*) against individuals in connection with sacred lands. Nothing in the document requires *demokratia*, and the date is uncertain (late fourth century?), but the institutions and provisions it contains would fit best in a democratic setting, made likely in any case by the constitutions of its founding cities.[169]

Thurii

The foundation and constitutional history of Thurii is a complex matter. An initial effort in 446 to reestablish a city on the site of Sybaris soon resulted in civil strife (*stasis*) between the former Sybarites, who seem

---

[167] Cordano, "*Phonos megistos hellenikos.*"
[168] Diod. Sic. 12.36.4; Antiochus, *FGH* 555.11 (= Strabo 6.1.15). T. Fischer-Hansen, T. H. Nielsen, and C. Ampolo in *Inventory*, 259.
[169] T. Fischer-Hansen, T. H. Nielsen, and C. Ampolo in *Inventory*, 260; Rhodes, *Decrees*, 316, 21.

to have taken the lead in the effort, and settlers from elsewhere. The Sybarites reserved the most important offices (*tas axiologotatas archas*) for themselves as well as other privileges, sparking resistance from the non-Sybarite majority of the population, who ultimately slew or drove out the Sybarites (Diod. Sic. 12.10–11; cf. Strabo 6.1.13). At this point – 444 BC – the Athenians probably stepped in as (re)organizers of a Panhellenic colony, providing leaders and inviting participation from the Peloponnese and many other parts of Greece.[170]

The type of Thurian constitution is unspecified for the initial resettlement, though the reservation of privileges to one group suggests some form of oligarchy. After the overthrow of the Sybarite faction, however, the colony became democratic: Diodorus describes it unambiguously as a *politeuma demokratikon*. That a democracy resulted from the *stasis* would not be a surprising reaction against the unequal treatment meted out by the earlier regime. There was also the substantial assistance provided by democratic Athens, whose imprint may appear in the division of the citizens into ten tribes.

On the other hand, Athenian influence on the constitution at Thurii ought not be exaggerated. At the time of the city's foundation *demokratia* was already a well-established phenomenon in Magna Graecia; no reason, therefore, to assume the inspiration for such a constitution had to come from Athens.[171] Moreover, ancient accounts are full of references to different, famous non-Athenians who supposedly provided the laws for the city. Diodorus, who gives the only detailed account of Thurii's foundation, claims that Charondas devised its laws; other sources mention Zaleukos as the main figure; and Heracleides Pontikos has the sophist Protagoras responsible for writing the city's laws.[172] Though of the three Protagoras may be the most believable for reasons of chronology, the case is impossible to prove one way or another, and the traditions serve most importantly as indicators of the strong ancient belief that Thurian laws owed their character to particular lawgiving individuals, not inheritance from one of the founding cities. It was, after all, a Panhellenic foundation with participation from many regions of Greece, including Peloponnesians, Boeotians

---

[170] For this reconstruction, followed by T. Fischer-Hansen, T. H. Nielsen, and C. Ampolo in *Inventory*, 297–8, see V. Ehrenberg, "The Foundation of Thurii," *AJPh* 69 (1948), 149–70, and D. Kagan, *The Outbreak of the Peloponnesian War* (Ithaca, 1969), 155–8, 382–4. It must be noted, however, that Diodorus gives Athens a key role assisting the Sybarites from the start.

[171] See, for example, Acragas, Croton, Taras, Syracuse, this chapter.

[172] Diod. Sic. 12.11.3–4; Athenaeus 11.117, p. 508A *Suidas* s.v. Zaleukos; Diog. Laert. 9.8.50.

and others from central Greece, Ionians, and Islanders; the Athenians made up only one of the ten tribes.[173]

More concretely, one can point to important features of Thurian practice that did not fit with Athenian ones. The tribal arrangements, for example, which superficially seem to bear Athens' stamp (there being ten tribes), ended up functioning very differently. At Athens the idea of the Cleisthenic tribal reform was to mix up the population so as to break down previous associations (see Arist. *Pol.* 1319b19–27); at Thurii the tribal system did the opposite, acting to preserve old associations by grouping people into tribes on the basis of their place of origin.[174] There is also the Thurian education law that Diodorus describes (and assigns to Charondas) that has no parallel at Athens: the sons of all citizens were to be taught to read and write (*manthanein grammata*) with the *polis* paying for the teachers, in order that the poor (*tous aporous*) could participate at a higher level (Diod. Sic. 12.12.4). Finally, a law restricted the holding of the generalship to once every five years, preventing individuals from occupying the office continuously (Arist. *Pol.* 1307b6–13) – very different from Athenian practice.[175] The laws on free education for the poor and repeated generalships would seem to signal a *demokratia* willing to legislate a more radically democratic agenda than Athens was, at least in these two areas.

The duration of this Thurian democracy is not clear. Aristotle in the *Politics* lists two constitutional *metabolai*, both undated, one from aristocracy to democracy and the other from democracy (or aristocracy?) to *dunasteia*, though whether either can be reliably fixed to known events in

---

[173] N. K. Rutter, "Diodorus and the Foundation of Thurii," *Historia* 22 (1973), 155–76, at 161–7. Also seeing a less domineering Athenian role than earlier scholars is Kagan, who argues convincingly that Thurii was not part of an aggressive, expansionist western policy promoted by Pericles: *Outbreak*, 154–69. S. Berger stresses local interests in explaining subsequent Thurian behavior in "Revolution and Constitution in Thurii: Arist. *Pol.* 1307 a–b," *Eranos* 88 (1990), 9–16, though is willing to assume a larger initial role for Athens than Rutter and Kagan.

[174] This fact is highlighted by Lombardo, "La democrazie," 77–106.

[175] It must be noted that this last law could have applied to a slightly later period of Thurian history, one in which an aristocracy controlled the government rather than democracy. So assumes, for example, Berger in "Revolution and Constitution." Berger argues that the rotation of generals was an aristocratic means of preventing the rise of powerful figures popular with the people. However, it seems a bit perverse to call increased rotation of people in high offices aristocratic rather than democratic – Aristotle himself normally saw things quite the opposite way (e.g., *Pol.* 1317a40–b3, b23–5). Berger is on more solid ground when he notes the mostly aristocratic context of the section of the *Politics* surrounding 1307, which would imply that the Thuriian constitution Aristotle discusses here was an aristocracy. If so, the restrictions on repeated generalships (the law that some young turks wanted to change, ultimately destroying the constitution) could have been a holdover law from the earlier democratic era, one that the would-be dynasts naturally wished to target.

Thurii's history is not clear.[176] The latter change to *dunasteia* could have occurred in 413, for Thucydides attests *stasis* in the city during the Athenian expedition against Syracuse in which pro-Athenian Thurians won out, but then other sources tell us that after the expedition 300 pro-Athenian Thurians were ejected from the city during further *stasis* (Dion. Hal. *Lys.* 1, Plut. *Mor.* 835E). While this time of turmoil for the city seems a reasonable backdrop for constitutional change, the sources do not actually claim that such occurred, and it has already been argued that one cannot assume a close Athenian association with the Thurian democracy (and thus assume the "pro-Athenian" Thurians were democrats and their opponents oligarchs).[177] Most importantly, Aristotle describes a gradual constitutional shift at *Politics* 1307b6–19 relating to changes in the law, not a revolution based on the ejection of one political party. Thus we cannot say whether the *metabole* that Aristotle attests occurred in 413 or some other date, earlier or later.

As for the change from aristocracy to democracy mentioned at *Politics* 1307a20–33, it would seem most likely that Aristotle here refers to the establishment of *demokratia* in 444. The violent reaction he describes against elites who had fixed too-high property qualifications for office and dominated the land could match Diodorus' account of the overthrow of the Sybarites at 12.10–11, discussed above. If it does not, we are left to conclude that the Aristotle passage must refer to a return to democracy, perhaps at some point in the fourth century, after an earlier revolution resulting in oligarchy (whether in 413 or some other time).

OTHER REGIONS

Corcyra

Thucydides and Diodorus make fairly clear that Corcyra had been a *demokratia* at the time of its famously murderous civil war in the early 420s BC. The most certain indication comes in Thucydides' detailed description of events at 3.81.4 where he describes "the Corcyreans" – here to be understood as the populist contestants in the struggle – seizing an opportunity to slay or bring to trial their personal and political enemies by charging them with seeking to "overthrow the *demos*" (*tois ton demon kataluousin*).

---

[176] 1307a20–33 and a40–b19. Berger, "Revolution and Constitution," emphasizes the difficulty of matching the Aristotelian passages at 1307 with known events in Thurian history. See also Berger's *Revolution and Society*, 33–4.

[177] A point emphasized by Berger "Revolution and Constitution," 14–15.

Diodorus echoes Thucydides in his far briefer account, saying that after the opponents of the popular leaders (temporarily) took charge of events they "overthrew the democracy" (*katalusantes de ten demokratian*, 12.57.3). The language seems inescapable in its meaning, even if in the case of both authors it comes up as an aside rather than a statement intended to lay out the baseline constitutional situation on the island.

More subtle indications in these accounts seem to confirm that democratic government had been the norm. Before the violence begins we find political trials featuring prominently in the competition between the different faction leaders. One leader (Peithias) who loses a vote in the assembly finds himself sued in short order on charges of trying to enslave Corcyra to outsiders. Upon his acquittal he sues in turn his wealthy opponents on charges irrelevant to the issues of the day but designed to produce crushing fines; he succeeds in winning convictions, forcing his foes to seek sanctuary as suppliants and try to arrange special terms for payment (Thuc. 3.70.3–5). This back and forth litigation seems to employ the courtroom as an extension of a struggle for popular favor and advantage over one's foes in a wide-open political arena.[178] Moreover, the council (*boule*) then rules *against* the wealthy victims of the political trial when they try to arrange payment by installments or modify the fines in some other way (*taxamenoi apodosin*).[179] It is open to question just why the council had a say here – did it usually hear appeals of verdicts? Was it normally tasked with enforcing courtroom decisions?[180] But what is clear is that the Corcyrean *boule* was not some conservative body of the wealthy who could be counted upon to back their own class, given their actions here in rejecting what seems to have been a reasonable request to structure the payment of massive, politically motivated fines. Rather, the council, under the influence of the same leader of the *demos* (Peithias) as had been sued initially, acts like another organ of popular government. Finally, the language Diodorus uses to summarize the events reinforces the democratic impression: for him, the first victims of the struggle are "those accustomed to demagoguery and especially to leading the multitude" (*tous demagogein eiothotas kai malista tou plethous proistasthai*); Diodorus also talks about the Corcyreans

---

[178] While political trials can certainly happen in non-democracies as well – consider the famous ones that took place at Sparta – they and their results rarely seem so intimately connected to the ebb and flow of popular opinion and support as the ones here in Corcyra or in other democracies such as Athens or Syracuse. For Sparta see G. E. M. de Ste Croix, "Trials at Sparta," in M. Whitby, ed., *Sparta* (New York, 2002), 69–77 (reprinted from *The Origins of the Peloponnesian War* [London, 1972], 131–8).

[179] 3.70.5–6. Gomme, *HCT*, vol. III, 361.   [180] Gomme, *HCT*, vol. III, 361.

"regaining their freedom" (*ten eleutherian anaktesamenoi*) when the popular faction wins back control of the state. Clearly Diodorus thought Corcyra had been a democracy and interpreted his sources (probably Thucydides or deriving from Thucydides) as meaning just this.

Regarding the constitution in about 435 when the dispute with Corinth over Epidamnus broke out, no source gives any evidence; but if (as seems clear enough) Corcyra was democratic at the outset of the troubles in 427, then it is likely to have been so a few years earlier.[181] Thucydides, as focused and well-informed on Corcyrean politics throughout this period as he demonstrably was, could not have failed to mention if a constitutional revolution took place in the *polis* in the short time that elapsed between the two incidents, a revolution that would have been directly relevant both to Corcyra's decisions regarding the Athenian alliance and in setting off the civil strife of the 420s. Gehrke, however, disagrees. He argues that a moderate oligarchy ruled Corcyra before the civil war.[182] He acknowledges the important role of the popular assembly and (perhaps) popular courts, but he believes the council was strong, elective, and thus probably oligarchic. He notes the naming of oligarchic-sounding officials *probouloi* and *prodikoi* in inscriptions from Corcyra, and he finds it significant that Corcyra backed aristocrats instead of the *demos* in Epidamnus at the time. He also dismisses the constitutional significance of the words *tois ton demon katalousin* at Thucydides 3.81.4, citing Thucydides 8.64.4 by way of arguing that the phrase could be used to refer to the defeat of a faction, not only a democratic constitution.

If *probouloi* and *prodikoi* had turned up in any source showing such officials' presence in the fifth century BC. one would have to take more seriously the possibility of Corcyrean oligarchy in 435. However, the inscriptions in question run from the end of the *fourth* century down to the second century, and thus count for almost nothing concerning the fifth century, especially since we know Corcyra abandoned its democracy for oligarchy in the mid fourth century (see below).[183] The rest of Gehrke's case is equally unconvincing. That *katalusis ton demon* can on rare occasion mean the defeat of a faction rather than overthrow of a *demokratia* (as it might – or indeed might not – at 8.64.4) does not change the fact that a charge of *katalusis ton demon* before a court of law as we have at 3.81.4 must have

---

[181] So Kagan in *Outbreak*, 208–9; just as unequivocal about democracy in 427 but reserving judgment for 435 is I. A. F. Bruce, "The Corcyrean Civil War of 427 BC," *Phoenix* 25 (1971), 108–17.

[182] Gehrke, *Stasis*, 88–9, esp. n. 2, with citations of others with similar (and differing) views; likewise Kagan, *Outbreak*, 209, n. 14.

[183] *IG* 9.1.682, 685, 686, 688, 694. See Rhodes, *Decrees*, 163–5.

involved the allegation of a plot to overthrow a government, not simply a faction; Diodorus takes it that way and writes out *demokratia* in his account. The presence of the popular leader Peithias on the council at the time of the suit and counter-suit might mean members were elected rather than allotted, though Thucydides' words *etunchane gar kai boules on* could also suggest a coincidence in an allotted body. But even if the council were elective, such a body hardly need be undemocratic (see Arist. *Pol.* 1298a10–34 and 1318b27–32), nor does this council act that way, as noted above. Finally, the decision of the Corcyreans to back not the Epidamnian *demos* but its opponents, with whom the Coryreans had closer ties of kinship (1.26.3), means nothing about the constitution of Corcyra, as democracies could back aristocratic groups and vice versa in Greek politics – indeed, the oligarchic Corinthians backed the Epidamnian *demos* in this case.[184]

In sum, there is no good reason to think that the Corcyrean *demokratia* of 427 did not already exist in 435. But how long before *that* year the democracy held sway is impossible to resolve. It may have democratized many decades earlier, or not long before the troubles at Epidamnus – no evidence exists. The only piece of testimony possibly relevant to Corcyra's earlier constitutional tendencies comes from during the Cypselid tyranny, or perhaps more likely just after its end in the second quarter of the sixth century: the Menecrates cenotaph celebrating the Corcyrean *proxenos* has often been remarked upon for its repeated use of *demos* and its cognates, possibly advertising "the independence and authority of the people" of Corcyra at the time with its populist tone.[185] This need not mean actual *demokratia*, however. The evidence is too spare, and no other source offers any corroboration. But it does suggest an early popular consciousness and/or strength for the demotic assembly, whether as part of a broad oligarchy or something more progressive.

After the civil war of the 420s, in which the popular party prevailed (Thuc. 4.46–8), the Corcyrean democracy persisted for some time, though not without further rounds of civil discord. Diodorus describes an episode in 410 during which citizens wishing for an *oligarchia* tried to seize control of the state and bring in the Spartans but were thwarted with bloodshed by the populist masses (*demotikos ochlos*), who called in Athenian help. The *stasis* ended in an agreement to stop the discord and live together as one people (*koinos oikoun ten patrida*), apparently without change in the

---

[184] So Kagan, *Outbreak*, 208; see the discussion of democratic peace and alliance in Chapter 5 below.
[185] ML 4. The quotation comes from M. B. Wallace, "Early Greek 'Proxenoi,'" *Phoenix* 24.3 (1970), 189–208 at 191, who also discusses the inscription's date and political interpretation.

prevailing democratic government.[186] In 375 Xenophon reports intervention in Corcyra by the Athenians in which Timotheus took control of the island but refrained from exiling anyone or changing the laws (*oude nomous metestesen*). While it is possible to take this as hinting that Corcyra had become oligarchic, it need not – Timotheus could have found *demokratia* there already (hence no need to "change laws") and acted to secure the island against the Spartans or for the Second Athenian League.[187] The *demos* had been in control when last we heard anything definite and were still (or again) in control the next year: Diodorus describes in 374 an attempted oligarchic coup against the *demos* (*epanastantes toi demoi*) once again involving an invitation to Spartan intervention. The initial coup appears to have failed, but this time the Spartans arrived in force, and much fighting followed before the attack was defeated by the Corcyreans and Athenians in 372 (Diod. Sic. 15.46–7; Xen. *Hell.* 6.2.3–38). Finally, Aeneas Tacticus 11.15 describes an incident usually dated to 361 in which the rich and oligarchic (*ek ton plousion kai oligarchikon*) successfully plotted with the Athenian garrison commander Chares to overthrow the *demos*.[188] Since afterward things were arranged beneficially for the conspirators (*ta alla methistasan pros to sumpheron hautois*), one must assume the democracy came to an end, replaced by oligarchy. We hear little more about the constitution for the rest of the fourth century, but the epigraphic attestation and prominence of the offices of *probouloi* and *prodikoi* starting late in the fourth century suggest that it may have remained oligarchic thereafter.[189]

The nature of the Corcyrean *demokratia* is mostly to be gleaned from the testimony discussed above. Needless to say, it was relatively unstable, suffering from many an attempted revolution (at least four from 427 to 361). Inscriptions attesting an eponymous office of *prutanis* with a board of *sunarchoi* come no earlier than the fourth century, and thus cannot be certainly assumed to apply to the period of the democratic government. The assembly is called *halia* in many fourth-century and later documents,

---

[186] Diod. Sic. 13.48. Gomme considers the details of this account untrustworthy, but does not doubt that more *stasis* could have occurred on the island, *HCT*, vol. III, 497–8.

[187] Xen. *Hell.* 5.4.64; Diod. Sic. 15.36.5. C. Tuplin, "Timotheus and Corcyra," *Athenaeum* 72 (1984), 537–68; Stylianou, *Commentary*, 365; C. M. Fauber, "Was Kerkyra a Member of the Second Athenian League?," *CQ* 48 (1998), 110–16; P. J. Rhodes and R. Osborne, *Greek Historical Inscriptions, 404–323 BC* (Oxford, 2003), 111–13.

[188] On the date see Diod. Sic. 15.95.3. Whitehead, *Aineias the Tactician*, 133–4; Stylianou, *Commentary*, 550–1.

[189] See n. 183 above; also Dem. 24.202. For what it is worth, after 338 Corcyrean staters began to resemble Corinthian ones, though with Corcyrean legends (H.-J. Gehrke and E. Wirbelauer in *Inventory*, 363).

and there is no reason for this to have been different earlier.[190] Three generals command the Corcyrean fleet at Thucydides 1.47–8.

The council (*boule*) plays a prominent role in the unfolding of the *stasis* of 427, which stands in noteworthy contrast to the nearly invisible councils of many other important democracies outside Athens. This may or may not reflect a powerful role for the *boule* in the Corcyrean constitution in general, though it is suggestive. It was the arena of political struggle after the exchange of lawsuits that resulted in Peithias winning crushing fines against his oligarchic opponents: it had the power to allow the convicted men to restructure their payments but refused to do so. Then it was the site of the first violent act of the civil war, when armed oligarchs burst into the council chamber (*es ten boulen*) and murdered some sixty of their foes, including Peithias and others, both councilors and non-councilors (3.70.6). It seems clear, in all, that it was a popular organ of some importance. But caution is still in order. One must recall that the political struggle began after the prisoners back from Corinth won a (limited) victory not in the council but in the assembly (*epsephisanto Kerkuraioi*), getting a declaration of friendship with the Peloponnesians even while maintaining the Athenian alliance (3.70.2). And it was simply practical for the knife-wielding oligarchs to attack popular leaders in the council, not the *halia*: to try such a thing in open assembly with a much larger portion of the *demos* present would doubtless have been far more difficult. Better to strike the violent blow in a more controllable setting and then present a *fait accompli* to the *demos*, which is what occurred and succeeded (for a time).

The presence of Peithias and so many other popular leaders at this time on the council does not prove that it was an elective body (see above), but it does make it seem likely. Assuming it was elective, it is interesting that populists nevertheless effectively controlled it. The Greeks may have felt that the lot was more *demotikos* than election, but clearly both can function in a *demokratia* without undermining it. The Corcyrean council's size cannot be guessed, as the sixty victims of the attack included non-councilors.

J. L. O'Neil's confident discussion of the Corcyrean democracy is compromised by, among other things, his ready assumption that details from Hellenistic documents belonged in the Classical constitution. Nevertheless,

---

[190] *IG* 9.1.682, 9.1.706–10 for the earliest references to *prutanis*, the *sunarchoi*, and the *halia*. On the *prutanis* and *sunarchoi* inscription, G. Klaffenbach in H. Schleif, K. Romaios, and G. Klaffenbach, eds., *Der Artemistempel: Architektur, Dachterrakotten, Inschriften* (Berlin, 1940), 163; generally, H.-J. Gehrke and E. Wirbelauer in *Inventory* 362.

his emphasis on the differences between it and the familiar Athenian system seems appropriate.[191] The little evidence we have, especially as regards the council's membership and duties, suggests a *demokratia* with important functional variations and ultimately, as events would prove, greater fragility.

Epidamnus

The only evidence for a Classical-era Epidamnian democracy relates to its famous debacle with Corcyra and Corinth in the years leading up to the Peloponnesian War. Thucydides at 1.24 describes Epidamnus as a populous and powerful state that had become greatly weakened after "many years" of civil discord and involvement in wars with non-Greeks living in the area. Eventually, perhaps in 436, the *demos* of the city drove out the most influential citizens (*tous dunatous*), who then allied themselves with local non-Greeks and carried out a destructive war against the people in the city. We should probably assume that the *demos* in the city established a democratic government. Aristotle at *Politics* 1304a13–17 may refer to the same events when he notes that a constitutional revolution began in Epidamnus as a result of a betrothal dispute between two men that escalated when one of them, outraged, took as his allies the unenfranchised (*tous ektos tes politeias*). Within a year or two of the Epidamnian *demos*'s revolution, however, the Corcyreans – having taken the part of the exiles instead of those in the city – successfully besieged the city and forced the defenders into an agreement (Thuc. 1.29.5). While no constitutional information is available for the settlement, one can only assume that the resulting government reintegrated the aristocratic exiles (see Diod. Sic. 12.30.5) and lost some of its democratic character.

There is another passage in Aristotle's *Politics* that scholars sometimes enlist to help fill out the constitutional events of this time. At 1301b21–6 the philosopher mentions a partial (*kata morion*) change in the Epidamnian constitution involving the substitution of a council (*boule*) for tribal leaders (*ton phularchon*), while retaining the requirement that magistrates – though not others of the citizen class – come to the assembly (*heliaia*) whenever there is to be an election, and also the oligarchic feature of having one chief magistracy in the constitution. This passage is undated, and is less certainly assignable to the events described in Thucydides than the 1304a13–17 passage. Gehrke modifies some earlier scholarly treatments in

---

[191] O'Neil, *Origins and Development*, 71–3.

hypothesizing that the mixed regime of *Politics* 1301b21–6 belongs not to the government of the *demos* but to the Epidamnian constitution that followed the city's capitulation to the Corcyreans.[192] This makes good sense given the likely compromised nature of the government that replaced the surely more radical rule of the *demos*. However, it is ultimately uncertain, thanks both to the absence of any assigned date for the mixed regime in Aristotle and to the implication that its partial change was in a democratic direction (council for tribal leaders) of an oligarchic context (required attendance, single chief magistracy), which would not seem to match the circumstances of the *demos*'s losing its war and being forced to reintegrate aristocrats. The passage may refer to an entirely different set of events, of course.

The duration of the Epidamnian *demokratia* was very brief (from 436 to 433 at the outside). No details concerning the government's practices emerge in the sources. Scattered bits of evidence for various Epidamnian institutions may not have related to the short period of its democracy: Aristotle, *Politics* 1267b17 notes the presence of public slaves to work on public projects at Epidamnus, raised in the context of Phaleas' idea to have a small city population and to have public slaves to do necessary work; *Politics* 1287a5 mentions (again) that Epidamnus had one official in charge of the city's administration (*kurion tes dioikeseos*); Plutarch's *Greek Questions* 29 describes the office of Seller (*poletes*) who was to deal with local Illyrians in order to help avoid corruption and (possibly) revolution (*neoterismon*). Only the last seems to be a fair candidate for creation or maintenance during the democracy, as one can imagine that the *demos*, at war with the exiled aristocrats and some or all of the local tribes, will have been wary of too much citizen contact with their neighbors. An inscription from the late third century BC has a democratic decree formula (*edoxe tai boulai kai toi damoi*) and refers to assembly decrees (*psephismata*) but is obviously far too late to be of use in interpreting the fifth-century constitution.[193]

Cyrene

Cyrene's first experience with democratic rule probably came in the mid sixth century with the reforms of Demonax of Mantinea, as argued in *The First Democracies*.[194] This popular government did not last much longer

---

[192] Gehrke, *Stasis*, 367–8. See also J. Wilkes and T. Fischer-Hansen in *Inventory*, 330.
[193] Rhodes, *Decrees*, 185; *Syll.*³ 560.   [194] Robinson, *First Democracies*, 105–8.

than the life of Battus III, the king during whose reign the reforms of Demonax were enacted: Herodotus reports that his son Arcesilaus III struggled to restore the traditional royal powers against the new regime, suffering exile at first but eventually forcing his way back and asserting his dominance (4.162–4).

Democracy, however, returned to Cyrene in the mid fifth century with the violent overthrow of the last Battiad king, Arcesilaus IV. A scholiast to Pindar notes the murder of Arcesilaus by "the Cyreneans,"[195] while Heracleides says that, following the appearance of a dire omen for Arcesilaus, a *demokratia* came about and Arcesilaus (or his son Battus?) fled to Euesperidas and was killed.[196] The nature of this democracy, which has inspired some scholarly controversy, will be discussed below. The exact date of the overthrow of Arcesilaus and renewal of democracy is uncertain. A date in the early 450s could help to account for the aid given by Cyrene in 454 to Athenian survivors of the ill-fated Egyptian expedition (Thuc. 1.110), if, as some scholars believe, such would not have occurred under a Persian-friendly Battiad monarchy.[197] On the other hand, a date around 440 or 439 would better suit the Pindar scholiast's 200-year duration for the Battiad monarchy.[198] Neither argument is decisive, though there seems to be more in favor of a date around 440.

We hear nothing more of the Cyrenean government until the outbreak of political violence in 401. Diodorus (14.34.3–6) informs us that not long after 500 of the most influential citizens (*dunatotatoi*) had been put to death and the remaining elite had fled into exile, a man named Ariston and some associates seized control in the city. The exiles recruited 3,000 Messenian mercenaries to help them attempt to return to power. Bloody battle ensued, killing many citizens and almost all the mercenaries, after which a settlement was reached among the Cyreneans to enact an amnesty and live together in the city. Diodorus does not mention constitutional types in his narrative, but it is reasonable to conclude that either a democratic

---

[195] ὁ δὲ τελευταῖος οὗτος Ἀρκεσίλαος δολοφονηθεὶς ὑπὸ Κυρηναίων ἀπέβαλε τῶν Βαττιαδῶν τὴν ἀρχὴν ἔτη διακόσια διαμείνασαν; A. B. Drachmann, *Scholia Vetera in Pindari Carmina*, vol. II (Leipzig, 1910), 93.

[196] Ἀρκεσιλάου δὲ βασιλεύοντος λευκὸς κόραξ ἐφάνη, περὶ οὗ λόγιον ἦν χαλεπόν. δημοκρατίας δὲ γενομένης Βάττος εἰς Ἑσπερίδας ἐλθὼν ἀπέθανε, καὶ τὴν κεφαλὴν αὐτοῦ λαβόντες κατεπόντισαν (Heracl. Lemb. 17). Most scholars think the "Battus" of the second sentence is probably a mistake for Arcesilaus, both from the sense of it and Herodotus' (no doubt *post eventum*) prophecy of eight generations of ruling Battiads (4.163; cf. Drachmann, *Schol. Pind.*, vol. II, 93), though the text could be correct and describe the fate of the overthrown monarch's son; F. Chamoux, *Cyrène sous la monarchie des Battiades* (Paris, 1953), 206; B. Mitchell, "Cyrene: Typical or Atypical," in R. Brock and S. Hodkinson, eds., *Alternatives to Athens*, (Oxford, 2000), 82–102, at 96.

[197] For this view see, for example, Mitchell, "Cyrene," 95.   [198] See Chamoux, *Cyrène*, 206–9.

coup, or a democratic overreaction to a suspected oligarchic coup (such as happened at Argos *c.* 370), led to the deaths of the *dunatotatoi*, setting these events in motion. Since either is possible, we cannot know from this event whether the democracy of the mid fifth century had been overturned at some prior point or had persisted until 401. (Aid given to one side or the other in the Peloponnesian War would be no clear indicator of constitution, even if all evidence pointed to Cyreneans favoring one side, which it does not.)[199]

Scholars have sometimes seen the violence of 401 as a good period to assign an undated event referenced in Aristotle, *Politics* 1319b1–19: Aristotle, describing the most extreme form of Greek democracy, one in which even the most marginal categories of inhabitants are admitted into the citizenship, mentions the *stasis* at Cyrene as an example of what can happen when democracies go too far in this way and push a city's notables (*tous gnorimous*) past endurance.[200] Diodorus 14.34 does not report any expansion of citizenship at Cyrene before the disturbances of 401, but such an omission would not be surprising given his focus on telling the story of the Messenian mercenaries who ended up fighting and mostly dying in the factional fighting[201] rather than on explaining the origin of the political troubles in the city. His (brief) characterization of political disruption with the killing and exile of hundreds of *dunatotatoi* would seem to fit well Aristotle's talk of *stasis* in the wake of the elite class's reaction to a *demokratia* gone too far. While it is possible, of course, that Aristotle's undated passage belongs to some unknown historical event, periods after 401 do not look as promising: the context at 1319b1–19 is elaboration of Aristotle's most extreme category of democracy, which one imagines would ill suit the compromise government formed in the aftermath of the exiles' battles with the city in 401 or the oligarchic government known to exist later in the fourth century just prior to Ptolemy's *diagramma* (see below). But it could well describe the Cyrenean democracy from the mid fifth century, and if it does we should conclude that this populist government persisted until it provoked and then committed extreme violence against members of the elite, triggering constitutional crisis and civil war.

---

[199] Thuc. 7.50.2; Dem. 20.42; Mitchell, "Cyrene," 101 with n. 38.

[200] Mitchell, "Cyrene," 100 with n. 35; A. Laronde, *Cyrène et la Libye hellénistique* (Paris, 1987), 250. Aristotle goes on to describe at 1319b19–27 other techniques, such as tribal reform, that democracies use to strengthen themselves, and he gives as examples Cleisthenes at Athens and "those having established the *demos* at Cyrene": this reference to Cyrenean events, I have argued in *The First Democracies* (106–8), almost certainly belongs to the era of Demonax's reforms.

[201] On the mercenaries see also Paus. 4.26.2–3.

Our final episode of constitutional interest at Cyrene occurs in around 322. Diodorus again is the source, describing at 18.21 a *stasis* that breaks out in the city during a siege by the mercenary plunderer Thibron. The *demotikoi* win the internal struggle, forcing out exiles who then seek the aid of Ptolemy in Egypt. The populist victory is temporary: Ptolemy's intervention soon thereafter results in his control of the city and issuance of a new constitution, the terms of which survive in a remarkable document, the so-called *diagramma* of Ptolemy.[202] It can be deduced with fair confidence that Cyrene had been ruled by an oligarchy before this *stasis*, both from Diodorus' reporting of events (lack of food causing the *demotikoi* to rise against the rich implies that the elite classes were in control of the city's distribution of supplies during the siege) and because of the provision of the *diagramma* that changed the primary ruling body from the Thousand to the Ten Thousand. A ruling body of 1,000 in such a large city must have meant oligarchy.[203] Therefore, it would seem that the amnesty and joint government agreed upon by the citizens in the aftermath of the crisis of 401 – perhaps a moderated democracy or a polity – eventually gave way to outright oligarchic rule by the 320s. The constitution laid forth in the *diagramma* itself also looks oligarchic, if a slightly more inclusive one than that which immediately preceded it.[204]

The nature of Cyrenean democracy
There is more evidence to go on in assessing the nature of the Cyrenean *demokratia* than for many other Greek *poleis*, though scholars nevertheless have disagreed about how democratic the city truly was.

The first point one should recognize is that Aristotle's discussion at *Politics* 1319b1–19 clearly implies that at *some* point in Cyrene's history its democratic government was sufficiently radical to have served as an

---

[202] *SEG* 9.1.
[203] *SEG* 9.1.35–6. M. Cary, "A Constitutional Inscription from Cyrene," *JHS* 48 (1928), 222–38, at 234; Laronde, *Cyrène*, 251; Mitchell, "Cyrene," 101.
[204] Cary, "Constitutional Inscription," sees greater democracy in the *diagramma* than the document warrants. While it is true that the increase in primary assembly numbers from 1,000 to 10,000 represents a significant and meaningful expansion, the imposition of a 20-minae property qualification on members of that very body severely undermines its potential as vehicle for popular participation in the government (it being just a guess of Cary's that such would cost only a third or a quarter of the potential citizens a role – severe enough if so, and the fraction could easily be much higher). Combine this fact with the parallel existence of (1) a body of 101 *gerontes*, (2) an allotted *boule* of 500 men over the age of fifty, and (3) the permanent occupation of the office of *strategos* by Ptolemy himself, and the constitution seems too restrictive to speak of democracy, mixed or not. Cf. A. A. Kwapong, "Citizenship and Democracy in Fourth Century Cyrene," in L. A. Thompson and J. Ferguson, eds., *Africa in Classical Antiquity* (Ibadan, Nigeria, 1969), 99–109; Laronde, "*Cyrène*," 249–56.

example for Aristotle of the most extreme kind of *demokratia*. Let us look at his discussion:

The last kind of democracy, because all the population share in the government, it is not within the power of every state to endure, and it is not easy for it to persist if it is not well constituted in its laws and customs . . . With a view to setting up this kind of democracy and making the people powerful their leaders [*proestotes*] usually acquire as many supporters as possible and admit to citizenship not only the legitimate children of citizens but also the base-born and those of citizen-birth on one side, I mean those whose father or mother is a citizen; for all this element is specially congenial to democracy of this sort. Popular leaders [*demagogoi*] therefore regularly introduce such institutions; they ought however only to go on adding citizens up to the point where the multitude outnumbers the notables and the middle class and not to go beyond that point; for if they exceed it they make the government more disorderly, and also provoke the notables further in the direction of being reluctant to endure the democracy, which actually took place and caused the revolution at Cyrene; for a small base element is overlooked, but when it grows numerous it is more in evidence.[205]

"Demagogues" in this type of democracy, then, act to expand their power base and strengthen the *demos* by adding to it those who would never qualify for citizenship under more restrictive regimes (even democratic ones). They do this at their peril, for adding too many upsets the order of the state and provokes the elite to react – as happened at Cyrene. Popular leaders there must have had sufficient power in the city to enact controversial legislation that brought about a radically broad citizenship. They will surely have been able to control proceedings in other areas, too, presumably through an increasingly inclusive popular assembly to which the demagogues could make their appeals.

As argued above, it makes the most sense of the literary evidence to associate Aristotle's words here with Cyrene of the late fifth century. There is further evidence for a strong and vital democracy at this time as well. Archaeological investigation shows that a building campaign in the second

---

[205] *Pol.* 1319b 1–19, trans. Rackham. τὴν δὲ τελευταίαν, διὰ τὸ πάντας κοινωνεῖν, οὔτε πάσης ἐστὶ πόλεως φέρειν, οὔτε ῥᾴδιον διαμένειν μὴ τοῖς νόμοις καὶ τοῖς ἔθεσιν εὖ συγκειμένην ἃ δὲ φθείρειν συμβαίνει καὶ ταύτην καὶ τὰς ἄλλας πολιτείας . . . πρὸς δὲ τὸ καθιστάναι ταύτην τὴν δημοκρατίαν καὶ τὸν δῆμον ποιεῖν ἰσχυρὸν εἰώθασιν οἱ προεστῶτες προσλαμβάνειν ὡς πλείστους καὶ ποιεῖν πολίτας μὴ μόνον τοὺς γνησίους ἀλλὰ καὶ τοὺς νόθους καὶ τοὺς ἐξ ὁποτερουοῦν πολίτου, λέγω δὲ οἷον πατρὸς ἢ μητρός· ἅπαν γὰρ οἰκεῖον τοῦτο τῷ τοιούτῳ δήμῳ μᾶλλον. εἰώθασι μὲν οὖν οἱ δημαγωγοὶ κατασκευάζειν οὕτω, δεῖ μέντοι προσλαμβάνειν μέχρι ἂν ὑπερτείνῃ τὸ πλῆθος τῶν γνωρίμων καὶ τῶν μέσων, καὶ τούτου μὴ πέρα προβαίνειν· ὑπερβάλλοντες γὰρ ἀτακτοτέραν τε ποιοῦσι τὴν πολιτείαν, καὶ τοὺς γνωρίμους πρὸς τὸ χαλεπῶς ὑπομένειν τὴν δημοκρατίαν παροξύνουσι μᾶλλον, ὅπερ συνέβη τῆς στάσεως αἴτιον γενέσθαι περὶ Κυρήνην· ὀλίγον μὲν γὰρ πονηρὸν παρορᾶται, πολὺ δὲ γινόμενον ἐν ὀφθαλμοῖς μᾶλλόν ἐστιν.

half of the fifth century produced the city's first public assembly space, near the agora, as well as a stoa-like building that could have been used for courts.[206] Furthermore, the series of inscribed stelai of the *demiourgoi* at Cyrene begins in this period, in which we find these public officials meticulously overseeing accounts of revenues and expenditures (probably from temple lands, to be spent on public festivals and sacrifices). The *demiourgoi* do this in a very transparent way, suggesting a new emphasis on public accountability.[207] Finally, ostraka dated by letter forms to the second half of the fifth century (and some perhaps to the fourth) suggest the use of ostracism at this time, an institution strongly associated with democratic practice.[208]

Nevertheless, some scholars have questioned how democratic the Cyrenean government was. Laronde prefers the word "republic" to democracy for the government appearing after the overthrow of the Battiads, and he highlights the prominent role of the aristocracy in the military, in athletics, and in making dedications.[209] However, most of the evidence he relies upon to come to this conclusion dates to the fourth century, while it is for the fifth century that the case is clearest for strongly democratic government. More importantly, there is no reason why a Greek *polis* cannot have both a prominent aristocratic class *and* democracy at the same time: Athens in the mid fifth century certainly exemplifies this, with men from leading families dominating political and especially military positions, while at the same time the *demos* retained and even expanded its primacy. At Cyrene the direct literary testimony for *demokratia* – indeed, the most radical form of *demokratia* according to Aristotle – combined with material evidence for ostracism and a building campaign aimed at expanding public political

---

[206] L. Bacchielli, "Modelli politici e modelli architettonici a Cirene durante il regime democratico," in G. Barker, J. Lloyd, and J. M. Reynolds, eds., *Cyrenaica in Antiquity* (Oxford, 1985), 1–14. Bacchielli ties these buildings and the democracy generally in Cyrene to greater influence from Athens in this period. The stoa-like building, for example, is unusually shaped and seems to mimic the design of the Stoa of Zeus Eleutherios at Athens. The evidence for influence from Athens in this period is sparse and unnecessary to explain Cyrene's turn to democracy, though the connections may have been real. Ptolemy's *diagramma* mentions a *prutaneion* (*SEG* 9.45; listed in Hansen and Fischer-Hansen, "Monumental Political Architecture," 32).

[207] *SEG* 9.11–44, with the interpretation of S. Applebaum, *Jews and Greeks in Ancient Cyrene* (Leiden, 1979), 33, 87–90.

[208] *SEG* 44.1540; L. Bacchielli, "L'ostracismo a Cirene," *RFIC* 122.3 (1994) 257–70.

[209] Laronde, *Cyrène*, 27, 129–36, 146–7, 251–2. Also with doubts about the level of democracy is Mitchell, "Cyrene," 96, 100–02. Her concerns, however, are based primarily on her speculation about the existence of a weak hoplite class, and she sees a difference in kind from the Athenian democracy more than an absence of democracy at Cyrene. Applebaum, curiously, thinks it more likely that the "completely democratic" regime begins after 401 (*Jews and Greeks*, 33).

structures should place beyond doubt that democracy existed there. At best, Laronde's evidence suggests that aristocrats managed to continue to play leading roles in the state during its democracy. It also, perhaps, traces an increasing aristocratic influence in the fourth century, peaking in the third quarter of the fourth century, around the time when the evidence from Diodorus and the *diagramma* of Ptolemy suggest that oligarchy replaced whatever government preceded it.

As for the institutions of democratic Cyrene, sources tell us a fair amount, but it is often uncertain in which eras they existed, especially for the fifth century. For example, scholars have often looked to the *diagramma* of Ptolemy to supply answers. There we find many offices and public bodies listed, including a public assembly of 10,000, a council, a *gerousia*, a *strategia* (generalship), an ephorate of five, and more.[210] Unfortunately, we do not know for sure if all of these persisted from earlier eras or if some were introduced by Ptolemy. The ephors and *gerousia*, for example, might be thought of as traditional Cyrenean institutions remaining from early in the city's history; but a *gerousia* does not seem well matched to radical democratic government, and either or both could have been newly "brought back" by Ptolemy – or the immediately preceding oligarchy – in a nod to perceived Cyrenean tradition.[211] The *diagramma*'s body of the Ten Thousand replacing the Thousand of the oligarchy was probably a new formulation. Certainly, the property qualification of 20 minae for membership in the Ptolemaic citizen body was an innovation. Previously the assembly was called simply the *demos* and was active in legislation, as we know from the fourth-century decree of the Oath of the Founders.[212] *Demiourgoi* also existed in the prior constitution, as early as the fifth century, as inscriptions attest;[213] documents also show generals making dedications in the fourth century.[214] A council (*boule*) may be signaled by Herodotus 4.165 for the time of the Battiads, and it seems probable that such a body existed during the fifth-century democracy, with or without a *gerousia* alongside.

A complete history of Cyrenean democracy in the Classical period is hard to construct, and chronological precision is unobtainable.

---

[210] *SEG* 9.1; M. Austin in *Inventory*, 1245.
[211] The ephors, however, certainly existed at some earlier point in Cyrenean history: Heracl. Lemb. 18, with Chamoux, *Cyrène*, 214–16. For ephors and a *gerousia* proposing a measure to the council at neighboring Euhesperides in 350–320 BC, see *SEG* 18.772.
[212] *dedochthai toi damo[i]*: ML 5, at line 11.   [213] *SEG* 9.11–44 (*demiourgoi*, a board of three);
[214] *SEG* 9.76 (tithing to Apollo); see also Laronde, *Cyrène*, 129–36.

Nevertheless, that a *demokratia* featuring such radical features as ostracism, a broadly defined and numerous citizen body, and demagogues who provoked violence against the wealthiest citizens certainly existed at some time in the Classical period, probably in the second half of the fifth century and perhaps during portions of the fourth century. The functioning of this democracy did not prevent aristocrats from playing leading roles in the state, especially in the fourth century, and may have incorporated such unusual offices as ephors or even a *gerousia*.

CHAPTER 3

Classical demokratiai *in eastern Greece*

This chapter discusses (in roughly alphabetical order) democracies located on the coasts and islands of the Aegean, as well as on Rhodes and the Black Sea coasts, from 480 to 323 BC. Of the city-states considered below, all either *certainly* or *probably* experienced at least one period of democratic government during this era. While it is always possible that further examples of *demokratia* cropped up on occasion in these or other communities of the eastern Greek world, the following represent the cases for which we have the strongest evidence.

Briefer summary treatments follow the main entries at the chapter's end.

PROLOGUE: THE ATHENIAN EMPIRE AND EVIDENCE FOR DEMOCRACY

Before we look at the case studies, however, we must raise the issue of the use of membership in the Delian League/Athenian Empire as evidence for a democratic constitution. Scholars have sometimes suggested that all member states of Athens' fifth-century empire became democracies, thanks largely to an aggressive Athenian policy of enforced democratization among its allies. If this assumption were correct, my task in this chapter would have been considerably easier: finding Classical democracies in eastern Greece would simply be a matter of identifying those states – 329 by a recent count[1] – which became league members. However, the truth is that the association of *demokratia* with membership in the Athenian Empire is more complex than this, and one cannot assume that the latter inevitably led to the former. We will discuss Athens' alleged policy of democratic promotion within its empire (as well as other possible causes of democratization in eastern Greece and beyond) in Chapter 4; here we will consider the evidence for the notion that the empire consisted mostly or entirely of democratic

[1] M. H. Hansen and T. H. Nielsen in *Inventory*, 111–14, 1356–60.

states, and the use that can be made of this in our investigation of specific Classical democracies in eastern Greece.

In a brief 1927 contribution to the *Cambridge Ancient History*, E. M. Walker made the case for the universality of democracy in subject states of the Athenian Empire.[2] He based his argument largely on passages from literary sources that stated or implied that all members of the empire had been democratic, or passages that attested an Athenian policy of democratic promotion within the empire. Decades later the authors of *The Athenian Tribute Lists* refuted Walker's argument point by point, and scholars since have generally been cautious about assuming a direct correspondence between the empire and *demokratia* among its member states.[3]

The clearest statements in ancient sources claiming or implying universal democracy in the Athenian Empire come from authors of the fourth century or later. Aristotle states in the *Constitution of the Athenians* that Athens permitted Chios, Lesbos, and Samos, allies of special status, to retain their constitutions (*eontes tas te politeias par' autois*, 24.2), suggesting that all other league members potentially might have, or in fact did have, their governments tampered with by the Athenians. Xenophon in the *Hellenica* speaks of the Greek cities of the Ionian region in the mid 390s as no longer being democratic "like they were in the time of the Athenians" (*oute demokratias eti ouses, hosper ep' Athenaion*, 3.4.7). Isocrates on two occasions paints glowing pictures of widespread democracy under Athenian sponsorship in the days of its empire. At 4.103–6 he talks of the Athenians having justly favored the many (*to plethos, tous pollous*) over the few among the allies and having established the same constitution among them as at Athens; at 12.68 he claims the allies paid their tribute not to benefit Athens but to preserve their own democracy and freedom (*huper tes demokratias kai tes eleutherias tes auton*) and to prevent having to suffer oligarchy.

But Aristotle, Xenophon, and Isocrates are all obviously generalizing in these too-brief passages, and they speak so vaguely that one cannot be sure if some or all members of the empire are meant. Enough specific examples of Athenian constitutional interventions within the empire are on record to know that Aristotle is right that the Athenians had been

[2] E. M. Walker, "Democracy in the Empire," *CAH*, vol. v, edited by J. B. Bury, S. A. Cook, and F. E. Adcock (Cambridge, 1927), 471–2.
[3] B. D. Meritt, H. T. Wade-Gery, and M. F. McGregor, *The Athenian Tribute Lists*, vol. iii (Cambridge, MA, 1950), 149–54. Gomme, *Commentary on Thucydides*, vol. i, 380–5; R. Meiggs, *The Athenian Empire* (Oxford, 1972), 208–11; T. J. Quinn, *Athens and Samos, Lesbos, and Chios, 478–404 BC* (Manchester, 1981), 55; P. J. Rhodes, *Commentary*, 299, and *The Athenian Empire* (Oxford, 1985), 39; J. K. Davies, *Democracy and Classical Greece* (2nd edn.; Cambridge, MA, 1993), 74–5.

perfectly willing to use constitutional imposition to help control Athens' subjects, but whether this was done *universally* across the empire is not indicated in this passage. One might also note the failure of Thucydides at 1.19.1 to mention Athenian imposition of *demokratia* in dealing with its allies – exaction of tribute is referred to instead – when he had just contrasted Sparta's method of control of subjects by the favoring of *oligarchia*.[4]

Xenophon's passage, part of a report on events involving Agesilaus and Lysander at Ephesus in 396, contrasts the constitutional confusion in the region at this time with earlier eras of Athenian rule and with decarchy under Lysander. To infer from this statement that *all* cities throughout the Athenian Empire had been democratic would make far too much of it. Isocrates' exaggerated rhetorical encomiums of Athens' glorious past defy credibility in general and cannot be taken verbatim as evidence for universal democratization any more than they can for an accurate representation of other aspects of Athens' imperial administration.

Nevertheless, these passages do have a certain cumulative weight, and they also fit with statements in earlier authors suggesting that at least by the last decade or two of the Athenian Empire democratic government among the allies was very common and indeed the norm. Thucydides at 8.64–5 reports that Peisander and his associates, on the eve of the oligarchic revolution at Athens, abolished democracies and established oligarchies in the allied cities they came upon on their way back to Athens from Samos, and other envoys did the same across the rest of the empire. The narrative does not claim that *demokratia* was universal throughout the empire, but the obvious implication is that it was typical, since the conspirators with Peisander would inevitably touch upon multiple democracies on the way from Samos back to Athens, and that many more democracies could be found in all directions. Moreover, Thucydides elsewhere makes clear that pro-democratic partisanship by Athens during the Peloponnesian War had wide-ranging impact, and Pseudo-Xenophon discusses the Athenian promotion of the *demos* in cities throughout the empire as if it were an efficacious policy.[5]

The likeliest conclusion, then, is that *demokratia* became very common indeed throughout the Athenian Empire, at least by its later stages. On

[4] On this passage see S. Bolmarcich, "Thucydides 1.19.1 and the Peloponnesian League," *GRBS* 45.1 (2005), 5–34. Bolmarcich is not concerned with Athens and democracy here, but her interpretation paves the way for the point.
[5] Thuc. 3.87.1; Ps.-Xen. *Ath. Pol.* 1.14, 1.16, 3.10, though cf. 3.11. See also Diod. Sic. 13.47.8, which talks of an Athenian general in 410 discovering Paros had had an oligarchic revolution, and putting the *demos* back in charge.

the other hand, this does not mean that for any given Aegean *polis* under Athenian influence one can simply assume it to have been democratic from 478 (or 454) to 404 – the testimony for widespread democratization within the empire is far too weak for this. For the purposes of this chapter, therefore, membership in the Delian League/Athenian Empire will only be used to help corroborate a case for *demokratia* that other evidence suggests; it cannot on its own constitute proof of popular government.

ABDERA AND TEOS[6]

We begin with this pair of cities, a colony and mother-city with an unusually close relationship. Teians founded Abdera *c.* 545 when abandoning their own city to escape Cyrus and the Persians. Later, either in the years immediately following this foundation, or perhaps immediately following the Ionian Revolt *c.* 493, Abderites in turn refounded their mother-city.[7] Such an extraordinary event probably explains the extremely close relationship of the two cities in the Classical period and later, a relationship that blurred the usual distinctions between independent *poleis* to the point that scholars can reasonably talk of *sumpoliteia* between the two.[8] A similar or identical constitutional type is overwhelmingly likely in this case, and thus the two cities will be discussed together here.

Indirect evidence from literary and epigraphic sources point to democratic government at Abdera and Teos in the fifth century. The most specific institutional evidence comes from the famous public imprecations decrees of Teos, which, among other things, list curses against wrongdoers that officials of both Abdera and Teos were to read aloud at three annual festivals. The first decree (ML 30) is dated to *c.* 470; the second, more recently discovered one (*SEG* 31.985) dates to the same general period, between 480 and 450. In the inscriptions the office of *aisumnetes* (elected monarch) comes in for negative treatment, which, together with signs of prior injustice and hints of a more stable, community-oriented, majority-driven government in the present and future, suggest to the publisher of the

---

[6] Portions of this treatment draw on Robinson, "Democracy Beyond Athens," 109–22.

[7] The evidence for this event consists of passages from Pindar's *Second Paean* and the second, more recently discovered, Teian public imprecations decree (*SEG* 31.984). See A. J. Graham, "Adopted Teians: A Passage in the New Inscription of Public Imprecations from Teos," *JHS* 111 (1991), 176–8 (= Graham, *Collected Papers on Greek Colonization* [Leiden, 2001], 263–8).

[8] See A. J. Graham, "Abdera and Teos," *JHS* 112 (1992), 42–73 (= *Collected Papers*, 269–314); P. Herrmann, "Teos und Abdera im 5. Jahrhundert v. Chr.," *Chiron* 11 (1981), 1–30. Generally on Abdera see L. Loukopoulou in *Inventory*, 872–5, and B. Isaac, *The Greek Settlements in Thrace* (Leiden, 1986), 73–108, though the latter largely ignores issues of internal politics.

more recent document that in the era of the decrees Abdera and Teos were possibly building democracy in opposition to earlier tyranny or oligarchy.[9] In particular, at one point the latest document mentions that a quorum of 500 men is needed at Abdera, and 200 at smaller Teos, before a magistrate can sentence anyone to death. Setting a quorum like this makes for a very democratic provision. D. M. Lewis concludes from it that Abdera was indeed a democracy at the time.[10]

There is also more general evidence than the imprecations decrees. Teos, located in Ionia, would have been subject to the twice-over change from tyrannical regimes to democratic ones in the region Herodotus reports for the period during and after the Ionian Revolt. At 5.37–8 Herodotus describes the actions of Aristagoras in 499 as he launched the Ionian Revolt: after seemingly (*logoi*) giving up his own tyranny over Miletus, he installs *isonomia* there in order to encourage enthusiastic support from the populace. He then did the same thing in the rest of Ionia, driving out the cities' tyannical rulers himself in some cases and in others turning the tyrants over to the cities to deal with as they wished. This ended the tyrannies in the cities.[11] Elsewhere in his history Herodotus uses *isonomia* as a near-synonym for *demokratia* (3.80.3 with 6.43.3), which strongly suggests that the historian means to indicate that popular governments of one kind or other came to be established in a number of Ionian cities at the start of the Ionian Revolt.[12]

After the suppression of the rebellion by the Persians and the (apparent) return of tyrannies, Herodotus reports at 6.43.3 another general constitutional change, this one due to the Persian general Mardonius: upon reaching Ionia, the general removed all the tyrannies in the cities and established democracies in their place (*tous gar turannous ton Ionon katapausas pantas ho Mardonios demokratias katista es tas polias*). Herodotus calls this action a

---

[9] Herrmann, "Teos und Abdera," 24. [10] "On the New Text of Teos'" *ZPE* 47 (1982): 71–2.

[11] καὶ πρῶτα μὲν λόγῳ μετεὶς τὴν τυραννίδα ἰσονομίην ἐποίεε τῇ Μιλήτῳ, ὡς ἂν ἑκόντες αὐτῷ οἱ Μιλήσιοι συναπισταίατο· μετὰ δὲ καὶ ἐν τῇ ἄλλῃ Ἰωνίῃ τὠυτὸ τοῦτο ἐποίεε, τοὺς μὲν ἐξελαύνων τῶν τυράννων, τοὺς δ' ἔλαβε τυράννους ἀπὸ τῶν νεῶν τῶν συμπλωσασέων ἐπὶ Νάξον, τούτους δὲ φίλα βουλόμενος ποιέεσθαι τῇσι πόλισι ἐξεδίδου, ἄλλον ἐς ἄλλην πόλιν παραδιδούς, ὅθεν εἴη ἕκαστος . . . τυράννων μέν νυν κατάπαυσις ἐγίνετο ἀνὰ τὰς πόλις· (5.37–8).

[12] For Herodotus' use of the term *isonomia* and his definition of democracy, see my discussion in *The First Democracies*, 47–50, and M. Ostwald, *Nomos and the Beginnings of the Athenian Democracy* (Oxford, 1969), 107–13, who finds *isonomia* in Herodotus to be closely associated, though not coterminous, with *demokratia*. Gregory Vlastos in two articles effectively counters the arguments of some scholars that *isonomia* meant merely a non-tyrannical state of affairs, as opposed to a populist one: "Isonomia," *AJPh* 74 (1953), 337–66 and "ISONOMIA POLITIKH," in J. Mau and E. G. Schmidt, eds., *Isonomia. Studien zur Gleichheitsvorstellung im griechischen Denken* (Berlin, 1964), 1–35. On what happened at Miletus in 499, see the discussion below under that state's heading.

great wonder (*megiston thauma*) for those who disbelieve his earlier claim that Otanes the Persian argued in favor of democracy in the Persian Debate (3.80). It is worth noting that Herodotus apparently wants to use the Ionian democratization under Mardonius as evidence for the more dubious claim about Otanes. This only stands to reason, of course, as many in Herodotus' audience could be presumed to have known something about the constitutions of Ionian cities earlier in the fifth century, whereas the elaborate debate imputed to Persian conspirators on the eve of Darius' accession in *c.* 522 will have seemed far-fetched. Scholars are nevertheless divided about how much to believe Herodotus' claim that Mardonius established democracies in Ionia at this time, despite the historian's unequivocal language. Some accept the statement,[13] others have had doubts and suggest that it was an exaggeration of some kind.[14] The fact that we discover one or two Ionian cities soon afterward tyrannically governed (still? again?) is the main reason for caution.[15] However, such tyrannies would at most imply that Herodotus' generalized claim for the region did not apply universally, or not for long; it is *not* good evidence for the notion that Herodotus uses *demokratia* here as a kind of shorthand for "autonomy" or "constitutional government." Such a meaning hardly squares with his use of the term in the rest of his history and would also fail to account for the one or two tyrannies mentioned in the area soon afterward.

For the purposes of this study, Herodotus' claim at 6.43.3 for mass democratization in Ionia is too vague to use as a basis for asserting the definite existence of *demokratia* in every *polis* in the region at the time. But it does offer circumstantial corroboration for cases such as Teos, where we have other reasons for believing democracy took hold early in the century. In this way Herodotus 6.43.3 acts with respect to Ionian states around 492 much as membership in the Delian League does for Aegean states later in

---

[13] E.g., Graham, "Abdera and Teos," in *Collected Papers*, 266; L. Scott, "Appendix 11, Deposition of Tyrants, 43.3," *Historical Commentary on Herodotus Book 6* (Leiden, 2005), 542–5. Scott offers the best discussion of the issue to date, and while he accepts that the tyrants were removed and governments describable by Herodotus as *demokratia* installed, he considers the real nature of these governments to be a matter of "speculation."

[14] P. Briant, *From Cyrus to Alexander: A History of the Persian Empire*, trans. P. T. Daniels (Winona Lake, IN, 2002), 496–7; P. J. Rhodes, "Oligarchs in Athens," in R. Brock and S. Hodkinson, eds., *Alternatives to Athens* (Oxford, 2000), 119–36 at 124–5; O. Murray, *Early Greece* (2nd edn.; Cambridge, MA, 1993), 260; M. M. Austin, "Greek Tyrants and the Persians, 546–479 B.C.," *CQ* 40 (1990) 289–306.

[15] Discussed by How and Wells, *A Commentary on Herodotus*, 2.80. The examples are Strattis at Chios (Hdt. 4.138 with 8.132) and Aeaces in Samos (Hdt. 6.25), plus some other Greek cities outside Ionia in the Aegean region. (It is not always clear whether Herodotus refers to Ionia proper or to the eastern Aegean seaboard generally when he uses that term.)

the century: on its own it is insufficient to count as proof of *demokratia*, but in combination with other evidence it adds useful weight. The case for Teian and Abderite democracy in the fifth century is therefore strengthened – both from the Herodotus passage with respect to Teos, and, as it happens, from the fact that Teos and Abdera were members of the Delian League.

It is also probably no accident that Abdera in the fifth century was home to two very famous thinkers known for their populist beliefs. Protagoras and Democritus both came from Abdera, and both seem to have been supporters of *demokratia*. Cynthia Farrar's claim that Protagoras was a democratic political theorist pushes the evidence a bit: the Platonic dialogue and other fragments of his teachings do not specify a clear constitutional affiliation, though it is certainly true that Protagoras' faith in an individual's ability to judge matters and his ideas about the participation of ordinary citizens in the *polis* contrast sharply with Plato's and at least imply a democratic orientation.[16] Democritus has left a surer record, declaring a preference for democracy by claiming that poverty in democracy is to be chosen over so-called prosperity among tyrants just as freedom is to slavery.[17] There are also possible verbal echoes of the public imprecations decrees in some of Democritus' sayings[18] and evidence that he served as a magistrate in Abdera.[19]

In all, it would seem to be too much of a coincidence for these two populist thinkers – an extremely rare type among known sophists and philosophers – to have come from Abdera without the city's having provided some sort of democratic context. Together with the other evidence discussed above, the case for *demokratia* becomes very strong.[20] That evidence will not allow precise dating for the democratic regimes in Teos and Abdera, but the likely range spans most of the fifth century, from as early as the 490s – or with more certainty, the second quarter of the century – until the dissolution of the Athenian Empire. About the fourth century nothing

---

[16] C. Farrar, *The Origins of Democratic Thinking: The Invention of Politics in Classical Athens* (Cambridge, 1988), 44–98, quotation at p. 77. See also E. Schiappa, *Protagoras and Logos* (Columbia, 1991), 168–71; R. Müller, "Sophistique et Democratie," in B. Cassin, ed., *Positions de la sophistique* (Paris, 1986), 179–93.

[17] DK 68 B251: ἡ ἐν δημοκρατίῃ πενίη τῆς παρὰ τοῖς δυνάστῃσι καλεομένης εὐδαιμονίης τοσοῦτόν ἐστι αἱρετωτέρη, ὁκόσον ἐλευθερίη δουλείης.

[18] D. M. Lewis, "The Political Background of Democritus," in E. M. Craik, ed., *Owls to Athens: Essays on Classical Subjects Presented to Sir Kenneth Dover* (Oxford, 1990), 151–4.

[19] DK 68 A2, with the numismatic evidence noted in C. C. W. Taylor, *The Atomists: Leucippus and Democritus* (Toronto, 1999), 231, n. 63.

[20] J. Mejer also concludes that there was a democratic context for Democritus in Abdera in "Democritus and Democracy," *Apeiron* 37 (2004), 1–9.

definitive can be said. An inscription from the early second century directly attests *demokratia* at that time.[21]

Since the literary evidence for Classical democracy in the two cities is so vague and indirect, information about the nature of their government must be gleaned from the Teian imprecations decrees of the fifth century and, to a lesser extent, from numerous decrees on record from the late fourth century and thereafter. The fifth-century documents refer to a number of officials. Apart from the presumably outlawed *aisumnetes*, the most important magistracy mentioned appears to be a board of *timouchoi*, who in these decrees are to read out the curses, or be subject to them themselves if they fail to do so (ML 30, ll. 29–35). In one of the two decrees an office of treasurer (*tamias*) is mentioned, with someone acting as *tamias* also being liable to punishment if the curses are not read out. A secretary (*phoinikographeus*) is further liable if he fails to read them under orders from a *timouchos*. In much later documents the *timouchoi* are listed together with the generals (*strategoi*) as proposers of decrees and thus appear to be (or certainly to have later become) leading officials.[22] Aeneas Tacticus 18.16 attests a *strategos* at Teos in the fourth century or earlier.[23]

The fifth-century documents from Teos thus show a strong emphasis on magistrates properly carrying out their functions or facing punishment. We see in the more recently found decree a further check on public authority with the oath presumably to be taken by all citizens, declaring that one will not engage in prosecution, arrests, property confiscation or execution without (at Teos) the vote of at least 200 and conviction by a law of the city and (at Abdera) without the vote of 500 or more.[24] This would, of course, apply to magistrates as well as ordinary members of the *demos*, and simultaneously signals the primacy of the larger community and the limitations it was thought best to place upon the exercise of public authority. The other imprecations decree also contains a very early version of an entrenchment clause designed to protect the decree from later meddling.[25]

---

[21] *SEG* 41.1004. See Rhodes, *Decrees*, 533, n. 15.

[22] Rhodes, *Decrees*, 393–4, 494; G. Gottlieb, *Timuchen: Ein Beitrag zum griechischen Staatsrecht* (Heidelberg, 1967), 18–24, asserts the Teian *timouchoi* "nahmen zweifellos einen hohen Rang im Staate ein" (22) and can perhaps be compared to the early Athenian archons and the Chian *basileus*.

[23] On the date of the event described in Aeneas see discussion in Whitehead, *Aeneias the Tactician*, 150.

[24] *SEG* 31.985, with Graham, "Abdera and Teos," in *Collected Papers*, 284–6.

[25] ML 30, ll. 35–41, pronouncing death upon those who would damage the stele or its letters. See Rhodes, *Decrees*, 524.

Decrees from Teos dating from the end of the fourth century down to the second century describe some other interesting constitutional features, including explicit provisions for the proposing of new laws and the initiating of public and private suits by whoever wishes (*ho boulomenos*).[26] The applicability of such provisions to the earlier, Classical era cannot be established.

AMPHIPOLIS

Amphipolis was founded by Athens in 437 BC in a strategic region of the northern Aegean. Scholars generally make the (reasonable) assumption that Athens founded the city as a *demokratia*, and while no texts directly confirm this, corroboration seems to be at hand in Thucydides' description of events in 424 when the Spartan general Brasidas persuaded the Amphipolitans to abandon the Athenian alliance and accept him and his troops into the city. Thucydides 4.104.4 notes that, upon Brasidas' first appearance, those in the city opposed to him had control over the mass of citizens (*kratountes toi plethei*) and thus kept the gates closed to him; and Thucydides 105.1 describes Brasidas' fear that the mass of citizens (*to plethos*) would never yield the city (*ten polin... ouketi proschoroio*) if he failed to get them to do so before help arrived, resulting in his offering very moderate terms to them, which ultimately they accepted. Both of these passages imply that the *plethos*, the majority of ordinary citizens, held political power, and they thus support the natural assumption that Athens had founded a democratic city.[27]

Although Brasidas later on introduced a Spartan governor into the city, this need not signify that he changed the city's constitution.[28] On the other hand, it was one possible occasion for the city to have become oligarchic, as we know it probably was at some point in the first half of the fourth century. The fall of this oligarchy may have led to renewal of democracy. Aristotle in the *Politics* at 1306a2–4 adds to his list of examples of oligarchies succumbing to revolution an event at Amphipolis: Cleotimus used some newly arrived Chalcidian settlers (*epoikoi*) to foment *stasis* against

---

[26] *Syll.*³ 344, 578; Rhodes, *Decrees*, 391–4.

[27] Graham, *Colony and Mother City*, 37 with n. 11 on Thucydides. Also assuming an Amphipolitan democracy at the time: P. Flensted-Jensen in *Inventory*, 820; Hornblower, *Commentary*, vol. II, 336; Isaac, *Greek Settlements*, 42; de Ste Croix, *Peloponnesian War*, 37; J. Papastavru, *Amphipolis, Geschichte und Prosopographie* (Leipzig, 1936), 47–8.

[28] Thuc. 4.132.3. P. Flensted-Jensen in *Inventory*, 820. For discussion of Thucydides' language and Brasidas' possible betrayal here of his promise to keep the liberated cities autonomous (e.g., 4.86), see Gomme, *HCT*, vol. III, 623–4.

the wealthy (*tous euporous*). Probably connected to this event is the notice earlier in the *Politics* (1303b1–2) in which new settlers (*epoikoi*)[29] caused most of the Amphipolitans to end up banished, an example of settlers bringing factional strife. Some scholars would connect these events with a notice in Demosthenes (23.150) that "the Olynthians" came to control Amphipolis, probably in the mid-360s.[30] In truth, the Chalcidian settlers of Aristotle's anti-oligarchic revolution may or may not have been these "Olynthians," but it is reasonable enough to date the *stasis* to this era. The upheaval seems to have resulted in *demokratia*: an inscribed decree dating to soon after Philip II of Macedon captured the city in 357 carries a prescript typical of formal democracy, "decreed by the people" (*edoxe toi demoi*).[31] The document also contains an entrenchment clause to punish those who would violate the duly voted decree (*psephisma*). To what extent Philip allowed the Amphipolitans control over their own affairs is unknown, though the content of this decree (which banishes citizens known to have worked against Philip) suggests the assembly would act as Philip wished.

BYZANTIUM (AND CALCHEDON)

The only direct evidence for a Calchedonian democracy relates to its neighbor Byzantium, and thus the two cities will be discussed together here.

About neither city are we well informed constitutionally for the fifth century. At the time of Darius' Scythian expedition in the late sixth century Byzantium was ruled by a tyrant, Ariston, according to Herodotus (4.138).[32] After this notice we have no information until the Peloponnesian War's later stages (411–408), when we find a Spartan governor (*harmostes*) had been installed (Xen. *Hell.* 1.3.15), followed after the war by more harmosts and a likely oligarchic regime given the general Spartan practice at the time.[33] For the intervening decades, both Byzantium and Calchedon had been members of the Delian League, but that is an insufficient marker of popular government without corroborating evidence. Gehrke speculates that democracy began with Byzantium's entry into the league, though

---

[29] The text actually reads *apoikoi*, but editors have usually adopted the more sensible *epoikoi* after Spengel, given the context here and at 1306a3.
[30] M. Zahrnt, *Olynth und die Chalcidier* (Munich, 1971), 101 with n. 37.
[31] So M. N. Tod at Tod 150 (= *Syll.*[3] 194). See also Diod. Sic. 16.8.2; Dem. 1.8.
[32] 513 BC, though this date is uncertain: Briant, *From Cyrus to Alexander*, 142.
[33] Xen. *Anab.* 6.2.13, 6.4.18, 7.1.38–9, 7.2.5–13 for the harmosts. On the probability of oligarchy or decarchy, see Gehrke, *Stasis*, 36.

there is no direct evidence for this.[34] Byzantium rebelled from the league more than once; on no occasion, however, do our sources discuss the city's motives for doing so or its constitutional status before or after changing sides.[35] In the end, therefore, one finds insufficient evidence to prove the common (and not unreasonable) assumption that Byzantium had been democratic for most of the fifth century under the Delian League.[36]

The picture becomes clearer at the end of the fifth century and in the early fourth. Xenophon and Diodorus attest *stasis* at Byzantium in 403, resulting in renewed Spartan intervention, a brutal tyrannical regime under the Spartan commander Clearchus, followed by his removal by a Spartan army.[37] The subsequent constitutional form is not mentioned by our sources, though one would assume oligarchy given the continuing Spartan influence,[38] as well as what happened next. In 390 Byzantine leaders admitted into the city the forces of the Athenian general Thrasybulus, who then changed the government from oligarchy to democracy (*ex oligarchias eis to demokrateisthai*).[39] This government seems to have been of long duration. Decades later, in the 350s, Byzantium took control of Calchedon and established a democratic government there, probably replacing an oligarchy: Theopompus compares the democracies in the two cities and says that Byzantium had long been democratic (*polun ede chronon*), while the Calchedonians had lived better and more prudently before being corrupted by *demokratia*.[40] Theopompus' choice of words for the earlier, superior state of affairs at Calchedon (*bioi beltioni, ek sophronestaton kai metriotaton*) matches typical descriptions of oligarchies by their supporters.[41] In the absence of evidence to the contrary, one assumes that the democracies now in both cities persisted for the remainder of the Classical period.

---

[34] *Stasis*, 35 with n. 5, extrapolating on the implication in Theopompus F62 (see below) that the Byzantine *demokratia* known to exist in the fourth century was of long duration.

[35] See the recapitulation of events in Isaac, *Greek Settlements*, 224–8; L. Loukopoulou and A. Laitar in *Inventory*, 916.

[36] See, for example, Gehrke, *Stasis*, above and V. P. Nevskaia, *Byzantion in the Classical and Hellenistic Periods* (thanks to A. Zaikov for his translation of relevant portions of this Russian work into English; a German translation is available as W. P. Newskaja, *Byzanz in der klassischen und hellenistischen Epoche*, trans. H. Bruschwitz, ed. W. Hering [Leipzig, 1955]). Cf. my treatment in "Democracy Beyond Athens," 109–22, at 118–19.

[37] Diod. Sic 14.12.2–7; Xen. *Anab.* 7.2.5–13.

[38] Xen. *Anab.* 6.2.13, 6.4.18, 7.1.38–9, 7.2.5–13; Gehrke, *Stasis*, 37.

[39] Xen. *Hell.* 4.8.27. Dem. 20.60 gives the names of those who delivered up (*paradontes*) the city to Thrasybulus.

[40] Dem. 15.26 for the conquest; Theopomp. *FGH* 115 F62 = Athenaeus 12.32, p. 526 D–F on the constitutions. See below for analysis and quotation of the Theopompus fragment.

[41] On Theopompus' attitude toward different constitutions (moralizing in approach rather than advocating one type or another), see M. Flower, *Theopompus of Chios* (Oxford, 1994): 78–81.

The nature of democracy in Byzantium

We possess some interesting descriptive tidbits about democracy in Classical Byzantium, as well as documentary evidence from later periods about the governmental procedures.

Aristotle, in a section of the *Politics* devoted to explaining how different types of *demos* illustrate different kinds of democracies, describes the Byzantine *demos* as especially full (*poluochla*) of fishermen (*halieis*), like the *demos* at Taras, but in contrast with other sea-related groups such as the naval one at Athens and the commercial or ferrying classes dominant elsewhere.[42] This close association of the Byzantine population – and popular government – with the sea recalls the passage from Theopompus already noted above: in it the historian criticizes Byzantium's long-running *demokratia* because, the city being a trading port, the people tended to hang around the market and the harbor and in taverns drinking and behaving dissolutely; this luxurious and democratic way of life soon corrupted the people of Calchedon after that city's democratization, even though previously the citizens had behaved well.[43] At the heart of the critique is an equation stating that when *demokratia* and a port city go together, corruption and luxury tends to follow. Aristotle is not concerned with moral laxity in his passage but, like Theopompus, implies that a close connection existed between the nature of the Byzantine democracy and the large component of the *demos* that gained its livelihood from the sea. Aristotle's specification of fishermen as the key component, whereas Theopompus focuses on commercial aspects more generally (*ep' emporiou*), need not detract from their more general agreement on the significance of the relationship at Byzantium and (for Theopompus) Calchedon. The result was *demokratia* that functioned, at least at the level of the daily life of the ordinary citizens, in distinctly different ways from other democracies, including, apparently, the more navally oriented Athenian democracy.

---

[42] 1291b16–28, with 1317a22–9 on the importance of such differences for explaining why democracies are of multiple kinds.

[43] περὶ δὲ Βυζαντίων καὶ Καλχηδονίων ὁ αὐτός φησι Θεόπομπος τάδε· ἦσαν δὲ οἱ Βυζάντιοι καὶ διὰ τὸ δημοκρατεῖσθαι πολὺν ἤδη χρόνον καὶ τὴν πόλιν ἐπ' ἐμπορίου κειμένην ἔχειν καὶ τὸν δῆμον ἅπαντα περὶ τὴν ἀγορὰν καὶ τὸν λιμένα διατρίβειν ἀκόλαστοι καὶ συνουσιάζειν καὶ πίνειν εἰθισμένοι ἐπὶ τῶν καπηλείων. Καλχηδόνιοι δὲ πρὶν μὲν μετασχεῖν αὐτοῖς τῆς πολιτείας ἅπαντες ἐν ἐπιτηδεύμασι καὶ βίωι βελτίονι διετέλουν ὄντες· ἐπεὶ δὲ τῆς δημοκρατίας τῶν Βυζαντίων ἐγεύσαντο, διεφθάρησαν εἰς τρυφὴν καὶ τὸν καθ' ἡμέραν βίον ἐκ σωφρονεστάτων καὶ μετριωτάτων φιλοπόται καὶ πολυτελεῖς γενόμενοι (Theopomp. *FGH* 115 F62 = Athenaeus 12.32, p. 526 D-F. There may be a problem with the Greek in the last sentence with the awkward phrase διεφθάρησαν εἰς τρυφήν. See Flower, *Theopompus*, 79, n. 40.

We learn further details from the Aristotelian *Oeconomica*, at 1346b. At some unspecified point in Byzantine history – but probably during its democracy, given the action taken – the city desperately needed funds and adopted a variety of measures. One of them was to invite new citizens from those inhabitants who had only one native parent and would pay 30 minas. The law normally required two native parents (*ex aston*) to attain citizenship. The relative strictness or looseness of citizenship requirements is one of the ways to distinguish different types of *demokratia* from each other, according to Aristotle's *Politics*; by this criterion the Byzantine state would have appeared rather conservative (like Athens after the Periclean law), at least until the financial crisis forced a change, which may or may not have been temporary.[44]

Inscribed state decrees survive at Byzantium from only the Hellenistic and later periods,[45] making it difficult to draw firm conclusions about democratic procedures in the fourth and (possibly) fifth centuries. These late attestations include a typical democratic decree formula, *edoxe tei boulei kai toi demoi* ("decreed by the council and the people"), an eponymous magistrate called a *hieromnamon*, a council or subset of a council known as the Fifteen (*pentakaideka*), and powerful generals (*strategoi*) who had a role in proposing decrees.[46] More certainly going back to earlier epochs were the civic subdivisions known as *hekatostues* ("hundreds"), since these are attested not only at Byzantium but also at its founder Megara and other Megarian colonies.

TAURIC CHERSONESUS

The Tauric Chersonesus is the *polis* named *Chersonesos* located on the north coast of the Black Sea in the area of the native *Tauroi*, not to be confused with the cities of the Thracian Chersonesus. *Demokratia* at the Tauric Chersonesus is confirmed for just after the Classical period by an inscribed citizens' oath of *c.* 300–280 in which one was to swear, among other things, "I will not overthrow the democracy" (*oude kataluso tan damokratian*).[47]

But scholars have long supposed that democracy also characterized the government of Chersonesus in the preceding Classical era. Until recent decades the only evidence for this proposition came from very poor and indirect sources. Heraclea Pontica, together with the Delians, founded the

---

[44] *Pol.* 1292a1–6, 1319b6–11.   [45] Dem. 18.89, however, refers to a Byzantine *psephisma* from *c.* 341.
[46] Isaac, *Greek Settlements*, 234–6; Rhodes, *Decrees*, 197; L. Loukopoulou and A. Laitar in *Inventory*, 917.
[47] *Syll.*[3] 360.

city, something we know from Pseudo-Scymnus, lines 826–31. The date for the foundation, though not directly attested anywhere, has long been supposed to be *c.* 424–422 because of a confluence of events concerning the Delians and the Heracliots: both had hostile engagements with the Athenians in this time frame (Thuc. 4.75, 5.1, 5.32) and thus were presumed to have a motive to jointly found the colony. Scholars have seen democracy coming into the pictu because Justin's brief summary of Heraclean history in this era mentions frequent internal strife and because one could read pro-Athenian democrats into Justin's curious story that the Heracleans helped Lamachus' Athenian force when his ships were ruined in a storm, despite his prior ravaging of Heraclean lands (16.3.8–16.4.3). The supposition that party politics explains the behavior is not a bad one, and, combined with Heraclea's early history of democracy,[48] could well imply a democratic constitution at Chersonesus' founding.[49] Still, the indirectness of the evidence makes for a weak case.

The evidentiary base for a claim of Classical-era *demokratia* at Chersonesus improved dramatically with the discovery in recent decades of forty-five ostraka dating to the fifth century. J. G. Vinogradov has argued persuasively that these were used for ostracism, indicating a vigorous democracy at the colony,[50] a procedure that could have come to Chersonesus through its connection to Megara, founder of Heraclea Pontica, or (less likely) Miletus, both alleged practitioners of ostracism.[51] The inscribed potsherds look very much like ones found at Athens and used there in ostracism: for example, besides the names themselves, sometimes there appear on the ostraka insults or exclamations, including (both at Athens and Chersonesus) *ito* and *katapugon*.[52] These and other telling similarities add much weight to

---

[48] See Robinson, *First Democracies*, 111–13.

[49] S. Y. Saprykin, "The Foundation of Tauric Chersonesus," 227–48, and J. Hind, "Megarian Colonisation in the Western Half of the Black Sea," 131–52, both in G. R. Tsetskhladze, ed., *The Greek Colonization of the Black Sea Area* (Stuttgart, 1998); Saprykin, *Heracleia Pontica*, 50–6; Hornblower, *Commentary*, vol. 11, 246–7; S. M. Burstein, *Outpost of Hellenism: The Emergence of Heraclea on the Black Sea* (Berkeley, 1976), 33–5.

[50] Y. G. Vinogradov, "Ostrakismos als strenges Kampfmittel für Demokratie im Lichte des neuen Funde aus Chersonesos Taurika," in D. Papenfuss and V. M. Stroka, eds., *Gab es das griechische Wunder?* (Mainz, 2001), 379–86; *Bulletin épigraphique* in *REG* 113 (2000), no. 487; Y. G. Vinogradov and M. I. Zolotarev, "L'ostracismo e la storia della fondazione di Chersonesos Taurica," *Minima Epigraphica et Papyrologica* 2 (1999), 111–31.

[51] See Megara entry in Chapter 1, and Miletus, this chapter. Forsdyke, *Exile, Ostracism, and Democracy*, 287–8, agrees with Vinogradov ("Ostrakismos," 385) that ostracism at Chersonesus quite possibly represents the parallel development of a practice similar to the Athenian one rather than direct borrowing from Athens.

[52] Vinogradov and Zolotarev, "L'ostracismo," 113, 118. The Chersonesus ostraka require some restoration for these terms: ιτ[ω] and κ]αταπυ[γων.

the argument that the potsherds at Chersonesus indeed signal the existence of ostracism or a similar popular procedure for exiling troublesome individuals.

Caution may be in order, however, with regard to the chronology of the democracy. In order to make sense of ostraka dating from all across the fifth century, Vinogradov needs an earlier date for the colony than the last quarter of the fifth century and proposes *c.* 528, a time that could fit both Delian and Heraclean expulsions of citizens and thus the jointly founded colony at Chersonesus referred to by Pseudo-Scymnus. A colony established by exiled democrats from Heraclea in the last third of the sixth century would allow for ostracism throughout the fifth century.[53] The difficulty here is not so much with the speculative foundation proposal itself – it seems as reasonable as the speculations behind the 424–422 date favored by others – but with the overall picture of the colony provided by archaeological discoveries. There are indeed some remains at Chersonesus from the early to mid fifth century and perhaps the late sixth, but material starts to accumulate in significant amounts only in the late fifth and the fourth centuries. Further, sepulchral material and building foundations first appear from the late fifth century and after. These facts have led some scholars to reject the idea that a true *polis* with elaborate governmental procedures (such as ostracism) could have existed before the late fifth century and either endorse the old solution of a Heraclean colony in the late 420s or propose new ideas for one establishing itself sometime from 425 to 375.[54]

One wonders how securely we can date the forty-five ostraka. If they indeed date from all across the fifth century, it is hard to square their democratic implications with the relative lack of other archaeological evidence for a settled colony before the later portions of the century. (Could a prior makeshift *emporion* of Greek traders have carried out multiple ostracisms? It is possible, one may suppose.) Perhaps future archaeological discoveries will fill out the picture of an earlier fifth-century city – it is dubious, after all, to argue conclusively from silence in archaeological matters and declare that no earlier city could have existed because not enough remains for it have (yet?) turned up. It is also possible that the ostraka in fact derive from the late fifth century or after, which would better harmonize with the bulk of the archaeological material discovered. Vinogradov, while insisting on fifth-century dates based on pottery styles and letter forms, admits that

---

[53] Thuc. 1.8, 3.104; Hdt. 1.64.2; Arist. *Pol.* 1304b31–4. Vinogradov, "Ostrakismos," 382–5.
[54] Saprykin, "Foundation"; Hind, "Megarian Colonisation."

others date them to the fourth.[55] However this may be, the onus of the argument must lie with those who would reject the existence of an earlier fifth-century Chersonesus to explain how the remains of ostracisms got there. Whatever date one assigns the ostraka, their presence makes a *demokratia* in Chersonesus at some point in the Classical era (either fifth or late fifth and fourth centuries) hard to dispute.

As for the kind of democracy practiced in Chersonesus, we can only rely on the ostraka and perhaps the early Hellenistic oath for indications. Ostracism bespeaks an active and powerful *demos* that kept city leaders firmly under its control. The inscription of *c.* 300–280 implies that *damiourgoi* were the highest officials of the city.[56] The document also suggests with its oaths that ordinary citizens had the frequent responsibility to serve as officials, deliberate on public matters, make public charges against wrongdoers, and vote as jurors in court.[57]

COS

About the democracy that existed in Hellenistic Cos inscribed decrees of the *polis* keep us exceptionally well informed. Two third-century decrees, one from early in the century and one from toward the end, refer explicitly to the *damokratia* of the state.[58] Numerous other decrees from the late fourth century through the third show democratic enactment and motion formulae, and the substance of many of these documents demonstrates an active and powerful assembly of the *damos* at work.[59]

For the Classical period, however, uncertainty remains about the establishment and chronology of a Coan democracy. A passage from Aristotle's *Politics* (1304b20–7) makes clear that at some point Cos had been democratic: it says that *demokratia* fell through when the notable citizens (*gnorimoi*) worked together against it, provoked by the emergence of wicked demagogues, who did things such as use the courts to strip wealthy individuals of their property (*sukophantountes*) and incite the masses (*to plethos*)

---

[55] Vinogradov, "Ostrakismos," 380.   [56] *Syll.*³ 360.16.

[57] *kai damiorgeso kai bouleuso ta arista kai dikaiotata polei kai politais . . . eisangel[o] kai krino psa[pho] kata tous nomous, Syll.*³ 360.24–5, 35. Rhodes, *Decrees*, 206, 208.

[58] *Syll.*³ 398; *Tituli Calymnii*, ed. M. Segre (Bergamo, 1952 [1944–5]), 64. Rhodes, *Decrees*, 222. The later decree explicitly contrasts the *damokratia* of the *polis* with oligarchy and tyranny.

[59] For detailed treatments of the Hellenistic democracy of Cos as revealed by the inscriptions, see S. S. M. Sherwin-White, *Ancient Cos* (Göttingen, 1978), 175–223; V. Grieb, *Hellenistische Demokratie* (Stuttgart, 2008), 139–98; Carlsson, *Hellenistic Democracies*, 202–43.

against them generally.[60] When did this democracy at Cos arise? Aristotle gives no chronological indications in his passage, leaving scholars to speculate. I have argued previously that the attested *demokratia* might have begun with the late Archaic episode (*c.* 490 BC) described at Herodotus 7.164, in which the tyrant Cadmus voluntarily put aside the ruling power he had inherited from his father and gave it to the people (*es meson Kooisi*).[61] Such an association is possible but not required by the evidence.

Other scholars have nominated the time around 366/5 BC, when sources discuss the establishment of a new *polis* capital and, possibly, the political unification of the island for the first time. Diodorus and Strabo describe the event, in which the Coans decided to move (*metoikizein*) to the city still occupied in the time of the two authors. Diodorus emphasizes that many people moved and that impressive construction of walls and harbor took place, while Strabo adds that the move took place due to factional disputes (*stasis*) and the Coans changed the name of the city to match that of the island, Cos.[62] Whether or not the move to a new capital city meant unification of the island for the first time remains controversial;[63] more important for our purposes is whether the democracy attested by Aristotle belongs in this era. S. M. Sherwin-White argues that it does, but her argument depends to a great extent on the *metoikesis* having involved unification of the island for the first time, an event which she believes would have harmed aristocratic interests and thus implies the prior existence of *demokratia*. She also claims that the revolution Aristotle describes must have happened after 366/5 since the island had not before been unified.[64] Both of these contentions are dubious, especially the latter: even if one grants that full unification only occurred in 366/5 – an idea certainly open to challenge[65] – such need not have prevented Aristotle from discussing this or that change to democracy on Cos before that year. Various sources refer to Cos or the Coans as one entity prior to 366/5, including fifth-century coins, the Athenian tribute lists, and Herodotus.[66] Aristotle might easily

---

[60] αἱ μὲν οὖν δημοκρατίαι μάλιστα μεταβάλλουσι διὰ τὴν τῶν δημαγωγῶν ἀσέλγειαν: τὰ μὲν γὰρ ἰδίᾳ συκοφαντοῦντες τοὺς τὰς οὐσίας ἔχοντας συστρέφουσιν αὐτούς... τὰ δὲ κοινῇ τὸ πλῆθος ἐπάγοντες. καὶ τοῦτο ἐπὶ πολλῶν ἄν τις ἴδοι γιγνόμενον οὕτω. καὶ γὰρ ἐν Κῷ ἡ δημοκρατία μετέβαλε πονηρῶν ἐγγενομένων δημαγωγῶν, οἱ γὰρ γνώριμοι συνέστησαν (1304b20–7).

[61] *Robinson, First Democracies*, 103–4.   [62] Diod. Sic. 15.76.2; Strabo 14.2.19.

[63] See, e.g., Sherwin-White, *Ancient Cos*, 43–64; N. Demand, *Urban Relocation in Archaic and Classical Greece* (Norman, 1990), 127–32; Stylianou, *Commentary*, 484–5; G. Reger in *Inventory*, 753; Carlsson, *Hellenistic Democracies*, 216–18.

[64] *Ancient Cos*, 64–8. Grieb follows Sherwin-White (*Hellenistiche Demokratie*, 177).

[65] See especially Stylianou, *Commentary*, 484–5 and Carlsson, *Hellenistic Democracies*, 217–18.

[66] Hdt. 1.144, 2.178.

have done the same, whatever the precise nature of city relationships on the island, as he collected examples to fortify his point about demagogues and democracy.

More persuasive is Gehrke's cautiously advanced argument that *demokratia* probably preceded the events of 366/5 and that the *stasis* to which Strabo refers should be taken to be Aristotle's overthrow of the democracy by wealthy Coans who were angered by the misbehavior of demagogues.[67] The sources complement each other more smoothly with this reading. Even here, however, one must acknowledge that scholarly desperation plays a great role in the association: we know of so few internal political events on the island in the Archaic and Classical periods that the temptation to assign the attested *demokratia* of *Politics* 1304b with the events of 366/5 – or, for that matter, Cadmus' actions of 490 – becomes overwhelming. Nevertheless, democracy on Cos in the mid-to-late fourth century seems a likely proposition given the vital Hellenistic democracy that followed immediately after; and, if Gehrke is right, democracy also held sway earlier in the fourth century before oligarchs temporarily derailed it.

Whatever the date of the events noted in Aristotle's passage, they throw a useful light on the style of the Coan democracy. The presence of demagogues harrying the rich is, of course, a commonly voiced criticism of democracies; here, though, the reference to *sukophantountes* emphasizes the extent to which the power and aggression of the popular courts in particular characterized the Classical Coan democracy for Aristotle. This is especially useful information given the picture that emerges from the Hellenistic inscriptions about the central role of the assembly at Cos, with very little on the courts. If we can trust that the procedures testified in these later documents (mostly from the late fourth and third centuries) also applied in the time of the Classical democracy – an uncertain proposition – we can learn quite a bit more about the practice of Coan *demokratia*, which included some unusual features.[68] The eponymous magistrate was, uniquely, the *monarchos*, and this office is indirectly attested for the fifth century;[69] the chief officials were a board of five *prostatai*, who had executive, administrative, financial, and religious duties. They also proposed many of the decrees we have on record, signaling in effect an additional layer of *probouleusis* before the council considered the proposals made by the board (individuals proposed the rest of the decrees). The *prostatai*,

[67] Gehrke, *Stasis*, 97–9.
[68] On the Hellenistic democracy, Sherwin-White, *Ancient Cos*, 175–223; V. Grieb, *Hellenistische Demokratie*, 139–98; Carlsson, *Hellenistic Democracies*, 202–43.
[69] Sherwin-White, *Ancient Cos*, 189–92; Carlsson, *Hellenistic Democracies*, 223–4.

furthermore, served six-month terms – a very democratic feature for such an important office – not year-long ones like the *monarchos*.[70]

Finally, Sherwin-White argues that at Cos one could sometimes propose matters directly to the *damos*, without prior consultation of the council, which would be a striking practice (and illegal in Athens, for example). She uses as evidence the fact that in some of the surviving decrees the usual enactment formula, "decreed by the council and the people" (*edoxe tai boulai kai toi damoi*), is missing, and only the motion formula, "to be decreed by the people" (*dedochthai toi damoi*) remains, seemingly cutting the council out of the picture.[71] If the usual enactment formula had been replaced by a different one including the *damos* and excluding the council, Sherwin-White's argument would be more persuasive. However, as both Rhodes and Carlsson point out, the explanation for the missing enactment formulae could easily involve incomplete publication of these inscriptions rather than an absence of *probouleusis*, since the council is never mentioned in the motion formula in any of the decrees.[72] Thus, as intriguing as they would be, Sherwin-White's radically democratic-seeming "*damos*-decrees" may never have been an actual practice.

But even without "*damos*-decrees," the Hellenistic Coan *demokratia* presents unusual offices and features to go along with the typical traits of popular government, suggesting, among other things, that the constitution was "an individual blend," clearly not "adopted wholesale from another state."[73]

CYME (IN AEOLIS)

Aristotle's *Politics* at 1304b39–1305a1 adds the example of Cyme to a list of cases meant to illustrate Aristotle's point in this section that revolutions in *demokratiai* typically are brought on by the outrageous behavior of dem-agogues. Men of property would band together to protect themselves and their property; or, after suffering exile, elites (*gnorimoi*) returned in force and replaced the democracy with oligarchy. The latter happened at Megara (1304b34–9), and the next lines read: "And the same thing happened also at Cyme during the time of the *demokratia* that Thrasymachus overthrew."[74]

---

[70] Six-month terms: Sherwin-White, *Ancient Cos*, 186, 205; Grieb, *Hellenistische Demokratie*, 160–1; Carlsson, *Hellenistic Democracies*, 226.
[71] Sherwin-White, *Ancient Cos*, 176–80.
[72] Rhodes, *Decrees*, 237; Carlsson, *Hellenistic Democracies*, 231–3.
[73] Sherwin-White, *Ancient Cos*, 223.
[74] συνέβη δὲ ταὐτὸν καὶ περὶ Κύμην ἐπὶ τῆς δημοκρατίας ἣν κατέλυσε Θρασύμαχος (1304b40).

Stephen White has argued persuasively that the Cyme Aristotle mentions here is probably the Aeolian city and not the Cyme of the Italian coast.[75] White also asserts that this Thrasymachus is not some unknown person of that name, as is usually maintained, but the famous sophist from Calchedon. If White is right, we could assign a range of dates for the replacement of democracy at Cyme based on the sophist Thrasymachus' presumed adult lifetime: perhaps *c.* 410 to 370 following White's reasoning about the sophist's activities.[76] However, White's arguments for the identity of Aristotle's Thrasymachus and the sophist are not especially convincing: even if White is correct in his (questionable) assumption that Aristotle would have indicated which other Thrasymachus he meant if he had *not* meant the famous sophist, that is a rather thin reed, particularly since it in no way explains how the sophist from Calchedon and occasional visitor at Athens could have ended up leading an oligarchic revolution in Cyme.

The uncertainties about the identity of Aristotle's Thrasymachus, therefore, are too great to enable us to date when the attested Cymaean democracy existed and when it was replaced by (one presumes from the context) oligarchy. Other information provides a bit more help. By the late fourth century democracy seems to have returned to Cyme, for an honorary decree from between 319 and 306 BC begins "Decreed by the people" (*edoxe toi damoi*).[77] This might imply that the Aristotelian democracy occurred later rather than earlier in the Classical period. In fact, however, it could have been both: in the fifth century Cyme was a member of the Athenian Empire, appearing on the tribute lists from 452/1 to 421/0; and even before this, Herodotus refers to the overthrow and driving out of Cyme's tyrant Aristagoras in the opening stages of the Ionian Revolt and implies that tyranny there was replaced by *isonomia*, a word that probably connotes *demokratia* in this context.[78] Thus Cyme may well have been democratic for most of the fifth century and returned to democracy before the fourth century's end. Aristotle's oligarchic revolution (whenever it occurred) could have lasted for decades, but it seems more likely to have been temporary.

---

[75] Stephen A. White, "Thrasymachus the Diplomat," *CPh* 90.4 (1995), 307–27, Appendix 2. See also Aubonnet, *Aristote Politique*, vol. II.2, 171, n. 2. White's arguments from geography and Aristotle's known interests make good sense; the chronological deductions carry less weight and surely get wrong the date of the events at Heraclea.

[76] White, "Thrasymachus," Appendices 1 and 2, drawing upon Ian Storey, "Thrasymachus at Athens: Aristophanes fr. 205 *(Daitales)*," *Phoenix* 42 (1988), 212–18.

[77] C. Michel, *Recueil d'inscriptions grecques* (Brussels, 1900–27), no. 510.

[78] Hdt. 5.37–8. On the democratic force of *isonomia* in Herodotus, see 3.80 and 6.43.3, with Robinson, *First Democracies*, 47–50.

We learn the most about the nature of Cymaean *demokratia* from the *Politics* passage, though its points are intended to be generic. Demagogues, it would seem, ran wild there before triggering the democracy's overthrow. Aristotle indicates that at Megara and Cyme, as in other democracies, the *demagogoi* drove out many of the wealthy in order to have money or property to distribute publicly.[79] A little later Aristotle elaborates on how this sort of thing could happen, from slandering (*diaballontes*) the wealthy, which presumably would result in their conviction in court and enable confiscation of their property, to excessive exactions in the form of liturgies, to outright division of estates (*tas ousias anadastous poiountes*).[80] We cannot say exactly which of these took place in Cyme, if indeed any of them did – the description is too generalized to know or be sure. The significance of the passages is rather in Aristotle's grouping of Cyme with other *demokratiai* – Cos, Rhodes, Heraclea, Megara – which, in terms of behavior that critics of democracy like, he would say "went too far" in their exercise of popular sovereignty in the courts and/or the assemblies at the expense of the wealthier classes, and ultimately at the expense of the democracy itself.[81]

HERACLEA PONTICA

Heraclea Pontica was founded as a democratic colony in the mid sixth century but lost its democratic government (at least for a time) early in its history.[82] That it returned to democracy at some point in the Classical period is apparent from Aeneas Tacticus' reference to Heraclean democracy at 11.10.2, describing an event usually dated to 370 or a little later,[83] and from Aristotle's *Politics* 1305b22–39, where the philosopher describes one way by which oligarchies collapse – when the oligarchs engage in demagogy among the masses to the point of causing constitutional change – and names Heraclea as an example.[84] The difficulty comes in deciding when this turn to democracy took place and how long it lasted.

---

[79] οἱ γὰρ δημαγωγοί, ἵνα χρήματα ἔχωσι δημεύειν, ἐξέβαλον πολλοὺς τῶν γνωρίμων (1304b36–7).

[80] *Pol.* 1305a3–7.

[81] Plutarch mentions a *boule* sometimes using a secret ballot, *basileis*, and an official in charge of the *desmoterion* (prison), but it is unclear whether these existed during the democracy; *Mor.* 291E–292A; L. Rubinstein in *Inventory*, 1044.

[82] Robinson, *First Democracies*, 111–13, based largely on Arist. *Pol.* 1304b31–4.

[83] Burstein, *Outpost of Hellenism*, 125, n. 62; Whitehead, *Aineias the Tactician*, 128, 132.

[84] δημαγωγοῦντες γὰρ πρὸς τὰς κρίσεις μεταβάλλουσι τὴν πολιτείαν, ὅπερ καὶ ἐν Ἡρακλείᾳ ἐγένετο τῇ ἐν τῷ Πόντῳ (1305b35–7).

S. M. Burstein holds that Heraclea remained oligarchic through most of the Archaic and early Classical periods until 424 BC, when a democratic revolution took place.[85] The evidence for a revolution in 424 is scant and indirect, but the events of the time at least offer a fair context for a change to democracy. In 425 Athens dramatically raised the tribute in its empire, and tribute lists soon began to include cities of the Pontic region for the first time, suggesting Athens was expanding the scope of its imperial tribute collection to the cities of the Black Sea.[86] Heraclea, however, resisted its inclusion; as a result, the Athenian general Lamachus was soon (in 424) laying waste to Heraclean territory, before a sudden flood destroyed his ships and forced a desperate retreat to Calchedon – curiously, with the aid and escort of the Heracleans, according to Justin's epitome of Trogus.[87] Burstein and others believe this seemingly strange act of the Heracleans does not suggest honorable kindness or calculation of favor as Justin proposes but rather signals an internal democratic revolution that suddenly rendered the Heracleans willing not only to help Lamachus but then to ally with the Athenians, an alliance indirectly suggested by bits of evidence from the last quarter of the fifth century.[88]

Aristotle's passage at *Politics* 1305b34–6 implying a transition from oligarchy to democracy at Heraclea could be applied to this period. However, it should be noted that the *Politics* reference says the oligarchy collapsed because of demagoguery before the masses to help with "judgments" (*kriseis*, surely meaning trials). Such an internal explanation picks up on none of the circumstances of 424 discussed above. Burstein connects 1305b34–6 with another passage from the *Politics*, 1306a38–b3, which notes the rise of stasis within an oligarchy at Heraclea after a cruel trial judgment against one Eurytion. This association of the two passages is possible, and the second one suits the context of 424 no better than the first.[89]

In the end, the reconstruction of Heraclea's constitutional history that assigns renewed democracy to 424 and has it last until the 360s fits the available evidence but is not required by it.[90] That there was a Heraclean *demokratia* at some point in the Classical period, however, is beyond a

---

[85] Burstein, *Outpost of Hellenism*, 33–4.
[86] Burstein, *Outpost of Hellenism*, 33; Meiggs, *Athenian Empire*, 328–9.
[87] Justin 16.3.9–12; Thuc. 4.75.2; Diod. Sic. 12.72.4.
[88] The evidence includes a proxeny decree that may be dated to 423 and possible tribute payments in the 420s; Burstein, *Outpost of Hellenism*, 34, 37–8, Sapiykin, *Heracleia Pontica*, 50–4 (with references to Russian language studies proposing various democratic scenarios). On the tribute, Meiggs, *Athenian Empire*, 328–9.
[89] Burstein, *Outpost of Hellenism*, 37; cf. Gehrke, *Stasis*, 71.
[90] See also the cautious discussion by A. Avram, J. Hind, and G. R. Tsetskhladze in *Inventory*, 956.

doubt. Aeneas Tacticus 11.10b–11 describes the foiling of a plot against the *demokratia* in Heraclea, and the events mentioned surely belong to the first half of the fourth century, probably c. 370.[91] According to Aeneas, with the rich on the point of launching an attack on the *demos*, the popular leaders (*prostatai tou demou*) responded by persuading the people (*to plethos*) to reorganize the civic bodies by dividing up the populace into sixty centuries (*hekastues*) instead of just four centuries and three tribes. The effect of this was to disperse the wealthy class throughout the whole citizen body as they performed their duties, including military service, keeping them outnumbered.[92] This plot was foiled, it would seem, but in the 360s another seems to have succeeded, for when Clearchus took over as tyrant in 364 it was an oligarchic council whose authority he overcame.[93]

The Aeneas Tacticus passage paints a typical picture of *demokratia*, with popular leaders accomplishing goals by persuasion of the popular assembly. The Aristotle passages at *Politics* 1305b–1306b suggest a lively court system with the *demos* engaged in trials of their leaders even in the last days of the oligarchy. One can only assume that a popularly dominated court system continued under the democracy, and magisterial power was kept in check thereby. The absence of public decrees from Heraclea before the Roman imperial period[94] makes it difficult to learn much about the offices and procedures of the Heraclean democracy. Burstein, drawing heavily on commonalities with mother-city Megara, other Megarian colonies, and colony Chersonesus, hypothesizes the existence from early on of a probouleutic council with a prytany-like body of *aisumnetai*, and a board of *damiourgoi* holding the highest executive authority.[95]

IASUS

Iasus is usually judged to have been a *demokratia* in the fourth century on the strength of two inscriptions. If the revised dating on one of them is correct, there can be no doubt about it.

---

[91] Burstein, *Outpost of Hellenism*, 125, n. 62; Whitehead, *Aineias the Tactician*, 128, 132.

[92] παραπλησίως δὲ ἐν Ἡρακλείᾳ τῇ ἐν τῷ Πόντῳ, οὔσης δημοκρατίας καὶ ἐπιβουλευόντων τῶν πλουσίων τῷ δήμῳ καὶ μελλόντων ἐπιτίθεσθαι, προγνόντες οἱ προστάται τοῦ δήμου τὸ μέλλον, οὐσῶν αὐτοῖς τριῶν φυλῶν καὶ τεσσάρων ἑκατοστύων, ἔπεισαν τὸ πλῆθος ἑξήκοντα εἶναι ἑκατοστύας, ἵνα ἐν ταύταις καὶ εἰς τὰς φυλακὰς καὶ εἰς τὰς ἄλλας λειτουργίας φοιτῶσιν οἱ πλούσιοι. συνέβαινεν καὶ ἐνταῦθα διεσκεδασμένους εἶναι τοὺς πλουσίους καὶ ἐν ταῖς ἑκατοστύσιν ὀλίγους ἑκάστοθι παραγίγνεσθαι ἐν πολλοῖς δημόταις (11.10b–11).

[93] Burstein, *Outpost of Hellenism*, 19, 47–54; Gehrke, *Stasis*, 71–2; Saprykin, *Heracleia Pontica*, 131–4.

[94] For the inscriptions, as well as an explanation for their paucity and lateness, W. Ameling, *The Inscriptions of Heraclea Pontica* (Bonn, 1994), esp. at 1–2.

[95] Burstein, *Outpost of Hellenism*, 19–20.

Iasus, with the rest of Caria, came under the control of the Hekatomnid family ruling as Persian satraps in the 390s.[96] An inscribed decree of the mid fourth century punishing conspirators in a plot against Mausolus opens with a typically (but not necessarily) democratic decree formula, "decreed by the council and the people" (*edoxe tei boulei kai toi demoi*).[97] The document lists a great many state officials and describes in exacting detail the selling off of the property of the banished conspirators. Simon Hornblower judges mainly on the basis of this document that Iasus must have been an exception to the general pattern under Mausolus of the promotion of oligarchy among the Greek cities of Caria.[98]

Another decree regulates the practice at Iasus of public payments for assembly attendance (the *ekklesiastikon*). The text and interpretation of this extraordinary document was thoroughly reevaluated by Philippe Gauthier in 1990.[99] Whereas before commentators had dated it anywhere from the fourth to the second centuries BC, Gauthier convincingly demonstrates that it must have been produced between about 330 and 300 BC, based on an improved reading of the name of an official whom we know to have been active in that range of years and also based on the carving and letter forms. With less certainty, Gauthier favors the first five years or so within this span, in the aftermath of Alexander's conquest, based on the inscription's content; if it does not belong here, then probably it dates to around 300, he argues.

Accepting Gauthier's preferred dating places the document at the very end of the Classical period. The thrust of the regulation leaves no doubt about the democratic nature of the state that passed such a law. Payment for public service is listed by Aristotle in the *Politics* as one of the signature institutions of *demokratia*, especially the latest and most extreme forms of it, and payment for assembly attendance in particular comes up prominently among the venues for democratic pay.[100] While rarely attested outside Athens, it is mentioned on occasion in reference to other cities, including Rhodes and, through this document, Iasos. Moreover, Aristotle discusses the practice as if it were a generic institution, not unique to Athens or

[96] P. Flensted-Jensen in *Inventory*, 1108, 1117–18; S. Hornblower, *Mausolus* (Oxford 1982), 31–8, 112–14.

[97] *Syll.*[3] 169 = W. Blümel, ed., *Die Inschriften von Iasos*, vol. 1 (Bonn, 1985), 1. Another decree from slightly later (352–344 BC) also uses the formula [*edoxe tei bou*]*lei kai toi demoi*; Blümel, ed., *Inschriften*, 52. Cf. *SEG* 36.983.

[98] Hornblower, *Mausolus*, 52–3, 107, 114; cf. 77–8.

[99] *Inschriften von Iasos*, 20 = Rhodes and Osborne 99; Gauthier, "L'inscription d'Iasos," 417–43.

[100] 1292b41–93a9; 1294a37–b41; 1297a35–8; 1304b26–7; 1317b35–8. Cf. Cicero, *Rep.* 3.35, 48. Note, however, that the moderately oligarchic Boeotian federal constitution allowed for payment for council members (*Hell. Oxy.* 19.4 [Chambers]). Travel expenses may explain the exceptional practice.

deriving from it – and in the case of Iasos there's no reason to think Athens had anything to do with its establishment, as Caria generally lay outside Athenian influence during the Hekatomnid period.[101] Therefore we must consider that the reason we find so few references to it in literary or documentary sources relates more to the impoverished state of our evidence for the details of non-Athenian political practice than any great rarity in its use.[102] In any case, the clear attestation of its practice in Iasus in the last third of the fourth century confirms the presumption from the earlier decree that Iasos was democratic in this era.

The two documents in question tell us useful things about the administration of affairs in Iasus. For one thing, we learn that the assembly regularly met at least once per month, which is often enough for a small *polis* of limited influence with a population only of the order of 800 citizens.[103] Furthermore, the city seemed very concerned to regulate and publish political matters in exacting detail. The exhaustive nature of the listing of officials and conspirators and the disposition of the conspirators' property in the mid-fourth-century decree has already been noted. The officials we learn about include the eponymous magistrate the *stephanephoros*, as well as archons (four of them), treasurers (four), *astunomoi* (two), *sunegoroi* (four), and *prutaneis* (six). *Prostatai* are noted in the decree establishing the *ekklesiastikon* procedures. Given the small population and the probouleutic council, the number of these officials alone is impressive.

Earlier editors had read the *ekklesiastikon* decree to attest public payment for certain officials as well as assembly-goers, but Gauthier's thoroughly revised, superior text no longer implies this (which does not mean officials were not paid, of course, only that this decree – focused as it is on the *ekklesiastikon* – does not state it). But the decree further exemplifies the precision at Iasus where public officials and public funds are concerned: it not only describes the amount of money to be disbursed each month on what day, which officials disburse the money (probably the *tamiai*, word restored), and which officials receive the money and control its distribution (the *neopoiai*) – all of which might perhaps be expected in such a document – but also lays out the exact method by which the money should be distributed, even down to the length and width of the narrow aperture in the wooden boxes (one per tribe) the *neopoiai* are to have with them to receive the tokens (*pessa*) of the citizens as they file in to the meeting. It

---

[101] Hornblower, *Mausolus*, 52.
[102] G. E. M. de Ste Croix, "Political Pay outside Athens," *CQ* 25 (1975), 48–52; O'Neil, *Origins and Development*, appendix 2, 175–9.
[103] Diod. Sic. 13.104.7.

would seem the citizen lawmakers at Iasus wanted to leave no room for error in how this system was to be implemented and to minimize any chance for corruption or inequitable distribution by officials or participants.

As for the fifth century, relatively recently discovered documents show the typically (but not necessarily) democratic decree formula (*edoxe tei boulei kai toi demoi*) on two decrees.[104] Iasus was a member of the Athenian Empire, with tribute recorded from 450. It may thus have been democratically governed for a time in this century as well, though the case is less certain and any democratic continuity into the fourth century is likely to have been disrupted by the Spartan capture of the city in 412 and Lysander's later reconquest and depopulation of it in 405.[105]

Iasus almost certainly remained a *demokratia* in the Hellenistic period, as attested by inscribed documents.[106] Though we cannot be sure, some of the later characteristics one discerns might have applied in the Classical period as well: an enormous number of officials, with nearly forty different titles on record; a prominent board of *prutaneis* that served six-month terms ensuring rapid turnover; frequent decrees in the early Hellenistic period decrees individual proposers the rule; high levels of participation in assembly and a relatively large council.[107]

OLBIA

The evidence for a Classical *demokratia* in Olbia (also known to the Greeks as Borysthenes) is indirect but fairly convincing for the period after 400 BC. A fourth-century legislative inscription, probably from the century's first half,[108] offers two reasons to suppose a *demokratia* existed at the time. First, the enactment formula declares in a typically (though not necessarily) democratic fashion that the council and the people issued the decree (*edoxe boulei [kai de]moi*). Such a formula also appears in later Olbian inscriptions but is unattested earlier. Secondly, in the course of describing the substance of the law, the inscription states that the buying and selling of coined gold and silver must take place "on the stone in the *ekklesiasterion* [assembly hall]" (*epi] tou lithou tou en toi ekklesias[terioi*). References to ancient *ekklesiasteria* – a roofed or unroofed construction devoted to meetings of an *ekklesia*[109] – are extremely rare. The existence of such a building

---

[104] *SEG* 36.982.   [105] Thuc. 8.28–9; Diod. Sic. 13.104.7. P. Flensted Jensen in *Inventory*, 1117–18.
[106] Rhodes, *Decrees*, 340; Carlsson, *Hellenistic Democracies*, 183–4.
[107] Carlsson, *Hellenistic Democracies*, 171–84.
[108] *Syll.*[3] 218; L. Dubois, *Inscriptions grecque dialectales d'Olbia du Pont* (Geneva, 1996), 28–35.
[109] See Hansen and Fischer-Hansen, "Monumental Political Architecture," 53–75.

would seem to bespeak the importance of the *ekklesia* to the community. The constitution of the time apparently became more radically inclusive in 331, when, as attested by Macrobius, the city came under attack by Zopyron. The Olbians in response turned to radical measures, including freeing slaves, giving citizenship to resident foreigners, and canceling debts; it worked, as they thereby managed to fend off the enemy.[110]

These indications suffice to make probable an Olbian *demokratia* in the fourth century. Could it have begun earlier? Y. G. Vinogradov, who for decades has published on Olbia and its history, would deny this, and adduces a number of indications for an early fourth-century adoption of democracy that followed a late fifth-century tyranny. Of primary importance is the apparent establishment of a cult of Zeus Eleutherios (the Liberator) at this time based on the appearance of the name on three dedications.[111] This cult accompanied the democratic liberation of Syracuse in the 460s (see previous chapter), and for Vinogradov its appearance marks the end of Scythian-sponsored royal or tyrannical control of Olbia and the beginning of the democracy. Vinogradov also points to a contemporary votive epigram from a statue that offers praise for a citizen, possibly for overthrowing a tyrant, in language reminiscent of that used to commemorate the celebrated Athenian liberators Harmodius and Aristogeiton – though the epigram requires substantial restoration to be read this way.[112] Finally, Vinogradov notes an Olbian decree of the third quarter of the fifth century for which he reconstructs a very fragmentary opening formula as "Decision of the Olbiopolitans" ([*dogm*]a [*Olbio*]*polite*[*on*]), which, if correctly restored, would contrast strikingly with the more democratic formula of the fourth-century monetary legislation mentioned above.[113]

Vinogradov's insistence that the democracy only began in about 400 is not beyond question, however. Problems begin with the fifth-century

---

[110] Macrob. *Sat.* 1.11.33 (Borysthenitae obpugnante Zopyrione servis liberatis dataque civitate peregrinis et factis tabulis novis hostem sustinere potuerunt); *SEG* 32.794.

[111] Y. G. Vinogradov, "Zur politischen Verfassung von Sinope und Olbia im fünften Jahrhundert v.u.Z.," in Y. G. Vinogradov, ed., *Pontische Studien: Kleine Schriften zur Geschichte und Epigraphik des Schwarzmeerraumea* (Mainz, 1997), 165–229.

[112] *SEG* 31.702; Dubois, *Inscriptions d'Olbia*, 20–4. Vinogradov, "Zur politischen Verfassung," 217–21; Y. G. Vinogradov and S. D. Kryžickij, *Olbia: Eine altgriechische Stadt im nordwestlichen Schwarzmeerraum* (Leiden, 1995), 134–5; Y. G. Vinogradov, *Olbia: Geschichte einer altgriechischen Stadt am Schwarzen Meer* (Konstanz, 1981). Cf. K. A. Raaflaub, "Zeus Eleutherios, Dionysius the Liberator, and the Athenian Tyrannicides: Anachronistic Uses of Fifth-Century Political Concepts," in P. Flensted-Jensen, T. H. Nielson, and L. Rubinstein, eds., *Polis & Politics: Studies in Ancient Greek History* (Copenhagen, 2000), 249–75 at 262–5. For skepticism about the early dating of this inscription and the restoration of the word for tyrant, see the review by A. J. Graham of Y. G. Vinogradov, *Olbia, Gnomon* 55 (1983), 462.

[113] *SEG* 31.701; Dubois, *Inscriptions d'Olbia*, 15–16.

"Decision of the Olbiopolitans": only one letter of *dogma* is at all legible, making for a very adventurous restoration. Moreover, this line may not even be the opening one of the text.[114] Vinogradov's assumption that only a tyranny would allow a deposed tyrant from Sinope to settle in Olbia is also questionable.[115] Furthermore, the dating of other key documents that Vinogradov uses to support a changeover to democracy soon after 400 (Zeus Eleutherios inscriptions, honorary epigram, noted above) is rather uncertain, with other epigraphers preferring substantially later, Hellenistic dates for them.[116] Therefore, one must admit the possibility that the democracy indirectly attested for the first half of the fourth century might have begun in the fifth. A good time for it might have been the 430s, in the context of Olbia's joining the Athenian Empire.[117]

About the nature of the Olbian democracy not much can be said beyond matters of detail. That it radicalized under pressure of external attack in the last third of the fourth century, erasing debts and granting citizenship to foreigners, tells us nothing very useful about its normal function. It passed proxeny decrees with fair frequency in the fourth century and thereafter.[118] Decrees from this time sometimes show individuals making the proposals, and at other times officials.[119] This could indicate a relatively broad participation in the legislative process, though such a conclusion is speculative. Officials attested from the fifth and the fourth centuries include *archontes*, the Seven, an *aisumnetes* of the Molpoi (borrowed from mother-city Miletus and apparently the eponymous official during the fifth century), *agoranomoi* and a board of five *teichopoiai*.[120]

PAROS

The island *polis* of Paros was certainly democratic by the late fifth century. Diodorus 13.47.8 notes that in 410 an Athenian general discovered that the city had undergone an oligarchic revolution and, taking action, succeeded

---

[114] Graham, Review, 461–2; Rhodes, *Decrees*, 203.   [115] Vinogradov, *Olbia*, 24.
[116] Graham, Review, 462, after assessing some of Vinogradov's dates and restorations on these inscriptions, declares his theory "a house of cards."
[117] Hdt. 4.76–80 and Thucy. 2.97.6 may imply a Scythian protectorate of some kind over Olbia during the fifth century, as has been alleged, but this need not mean tyrannical government. Cf. Vinogradov and Kryžickij, *Olbia*, 132–4. Olbia did become a member of the Athenian Empire, probably around the time of Pericles' Pontic expedition of 43/(?) (Plut. *Per.* 20; *IG* 1³ 1453 r) Dubois, *Inscriptions d'Olbia*, 17–19). One might imagine that the *demokratia* arose at this time.
[118] Dubois, *Inscriptions d'Olbia*, 39–47; *SEG* 32.704–7.
[119] Rhodes, *Decrees*, 207–8; Dubois, *Inscriptions d'Olbia*, 7, 47–8.
[120] A. Avram, J. Hind, and G. R. Tsetskhladze in *Inventory*, 938–9.

in putting the *demos back* in charge.[121] Thus the island must have been democratic beforehand and may well have been so for some time until the aftermath of Athens' Sicilian disaster in 412–410 (including the brief oligarchic revolution at Athens), in which many of Athens' imperial subjects revolted and/or changed constitutions. But we have no information about when democracy first came to Paros, or exactly how long before 410 the oligarchy took over (probably not long).[122] The island was under Persian control during the reign of Darius;[123] it probably joined the Delian League soon after the league's founding;[124] it shows up on the tribute lists from 450/49 to 416/15.[125] Thus the democracy implicit from before 410 may have first emerged under Athenian imperial influence, or it could have done so even earlier (but see below).

In the fourth century Paros probably also employed democratic government, though the evidence – both literary and epigraphic – is more indirect. Early in the century an otherwise unknown man named Pasinus took over the island and established a tyranny (or an oligarchy?) to the shock of Athenians who had thought the place secure.[126] This Athenian presumption of stability with respect to their interests may imply a preceding democracy.[127] Athenian intervention on behalf of the island and against the Spartans is attested *c.* 393; the result may have restored the preexisting *demokratia*.[128] Two inscriptions from the beginning of the fourth century show potentially democratic decree formulae (*edoxe tei boulei kai toi demoi*) as well as other references to council and people; another from the second half of the century prominently mentions the *demos* of the Parians.[129] An Athenian decree of 373/2 also refers to an authoritative *demos* and council (*boule*) of the Parians, though this comes in the aftermath of a factional crisis of some kind, one that required the arbitration of the Second Athenian League.[130]

---

[121] *kai katalabon oligarchian en tei polei, toi men demoi ten eleutherian apokatestese.*

[122] D. Berranger-Auserve, *Paros ii* (Clermont-Ferrand, 2000), 92–4. Gehrke, *Stasis*, 125.

[123] Aesch. *Persians*, 864–82; Hdt. 6.133.

[124] Hdt. 8.112; Meritt, Wade-Gery, and McGregor, *The Athenian Tribute Lists*, vol. III, 189–90, 198.

[125] G. Reger in *Inventory*, 765.

[126] Isoc. 19.18: *oiometha gar malista tauten ten neson asphalos echein.*

[127] Berranger-Auserve, *Paros ii*, 95.

[128] Plato, *Menex.* 245b (possibly to be taken with Xen. *Hell.* 4.8.1–7: Berranger-Auserve, *Paros ii*, 95).

[129] *IG* 12.5.110, III, 114. Michel dates the first two (*Inscriptions grecques*, nos. 407 and 408) to the beginning of the fourth century (followed by Rhodes, *Decrees*, 261).

[130] Rhodes and Osborne 29 = *SEG* 31.67, with M. Dreher, *Hegemon und Symmachoi: Untersuchungen zum Zweiten Athenischen Seebund* (Berlin, 1995), 109–54. Dreher interprets the decree anew and argues that the document attests the league arbitration of an internal Parian dispute, not Paros's rejoining of the Second Athenian League after a pro-Spartan revolution. He rejects the interpretation of Gehrke, *Stasis*, 125–6.

The few passing literary references to Parian events noted above tell us nothing about the function of the Parian democracy. Public documents from the fourth century (and later) help only slightly more: they refer to some of the important officials, including an eponymous archon, a treasurer (*tamias*), and *prutaneis* and a *grammateus* who publish decrees. The close correspondence between Athenian and Parian magistracy titles is probably not accidental. It is matched by very similar formulation of language in Athenian and Parian decrees.[131] Moreover, archaeologists have recently found pieces of an Athenian-style *kleroterion* (lottery device) on Paros, though no associated material provides a chronology for them, leaving one to guess at a date sometime between the fourth and second centuries BC.[132] Put all this together with the frequent Athenian alliances and interventions in the fifth and fourth centuries noted above and the Parian *demokratia* emerges as a prime candidate for having been directly established or at least influenced in its character by the Athenians.

RHODES

The Rhodian democracy had its beginnings in the fifth century but seems to have developed further in the fourth and continued as a democracy well into the Hellenistic period. Our sources describe repeated episodes of struggle between supporters of democracy and oligarchy at Rhodes, often with an interstate dimension, and though *demokratia* seemed to prevail more often than not, it is not until the late fourth century that it takes more permanent root.

For most of the fifth century the three great *poleis* of Rhodes were Camirus, Ialysus, and Lindus. In 408 a synoecism took place, and the three cities gave up part of their populations to form a new *polis* called Rhodes (*Rhodos*, the same name as the island). Rhodes the city and island henceforth acted as a single *polis*, at least in terms of international affairs, with Camirus, Ialysus, and Lindus acting as constituent tribes (*phylai*) of Rhodes, though retaining autonomy for local matters.[133]

The constitutions of the *poleis* Camirus, Ialysus, and Lindus before the synoecism seem to have been democratic prior to 411. In that year a group of powerful Rhodians (*dunatotatoi*) contacted the Spartans inviting them to aid the island in rebelling from the Athenian cause. In this they

---

[131] Rhodes, *Decrees*, 263.
[132] K. Müller, "Zwei Kleroterion-Fragmente auf Paros," *AA* (1) 1998, 167–72; G. Reger in *Inventory*, 765.
[133] T. H. Nielsen and V. Gabrielsen in *Inventory*, 1196–7.

succeeded, and the Rhodians were intimidated and ultimately persuaded to join the Peloponnesians. It is hard to imagine such a change without newly oligarchic government coming as well, given who sparked the change (the *dunatotatoi*) and who enforced it (the Spartan forces led by Dorieus the Rhodian, a member of the Diagorean family which is seen to rule the island in the 390s, on which see below).[134] One might add that as members of the Athenian Empire this late in its history, *demokratia* seems likely *prima facie*; and two fifth-century decrees from Lindus carry typically (but not necessarily) democratic decree formulae (*edoxe tai boulai kai toi demoi*), contrasting with a decree issued after 411 (*edoxe tai boulai*).[135] In all, the cities of the Rhodians were probably democratic before 411, though we do not know for how long before that year.[136]

In 408 the island synoecized and the new city of Rhodes was created, though this need not have had constitutional consequences, nor do our sources indicate that there were any.[137] Oligarchy seems to have remained, for in 395 a democratic revolution overthrew a Rhodian government led by the Diagorean family. This revolution ought not be confused with a switch in alliance from the Spartan to the Athenian one sometime earlier, perhaps a year or two or three, as I. A. F. Bruce has convincingly shown.[138] The Diagoreans must have supported the change in alliance, which was instigated by the Athenian Conon at the head of a Persian fleet. Conon was also present for the democratic revolution in 395, but this time played a more hesitant role – while his troops were paraded and stationed in such a way as to indirectly support the conspirators (all Rhodians), they did not take any direct part, and Conon himself made sure to leave the scene, perhaps because of fears of what the Diagorean government would think if the revolution failed.[139] But it succeeded. The *Hellenica Oxyrhynchia* describes how the revolutionaries came together in the agora carrying daggers, declared their intention to attack the "tyrants" (*tous tyrannous*),

[134] Thuc. 8.44, with Gomme, *Commentary on Thucydides*, 5.91–2; Diod. Sic. 13.38, 13.45. T. H. Nielsen and V. Gabrielsen in *Inventory*, 1199, 1201, 1202–3.
[135] Rhodes, *Decrees*, 265, 269; Gomme, *Commentary on Thucydides*, 5.92.
[136] That the Rhodian cities were probably members of the Delian League from its beginning (*ATL* 3.207–13; Meiggs, *Athenian Empire*, 55–6) does not tell us anything constitutionally.
[137] Diod. Sic. 13.75.1; Strabo 14.2.9–10. R. M. Berthold, *Rhodes in the Hellenistic Age* (Ithaca, 1984), 20–2.
[138] "The Democratic Revolution at Rhodes," *CQ* n.s. 55 (1961), 166–70. The significant testimony for the alliance shift is Diod. Sic. 14.79.6 and Paus. 6.7.6; the *Hellenica Oxyrhynchia* makes clear that the democratic revolution was a different event (below).
[139] Bruce, "Democratic Revolution," 168–70. Exactly what the Athenians were doing with the parading of their soldiers cannot be certainly determined, however, owing to the need for restoration of the *Hellenica Oxyrhynchia* text at 15(10).1.

killed the Diagoreans with eleven other citizens meeting as magistrates, and immediately called the masses of the Rhodians to an assembly (*sunegon to plethos to ton Rhodion [ei]s ekklesian*). Ending the previous regime, they established a democracy (*demokratia*).[140]

The new popular government did not have long to conduct its affairs unmolested. As the Corinthian War continued in Greece, friends of the Spartans in Rhodes rose in revolution *c.* 391 against the *demos* and succeeded in driving out those sympathetic to the Athenians, at least for a time. The Spartans, persuaded to intervene on behalf of the faction of the "wealthier" citizens (*plousioteroi*) who were attacking the *demos*, sent aid, and the strife continued, with the Athenians aiming to help the popular faction.[141] Two passages in Aristotle's *Politics* describing an (undated) oligarchic revolution against a Rhodian democracy probably refer to this event.[142] They inform us that elites at Rhodes (*gnoromoi* and, more specifically, *trierarchoi*, warship captains) united to overthrow the *demos* in response to lawsuits being directed at the elites and because of demagogic excesses: the provision of public pay and the cutting off of payments owed to the ship captains.[143] After the fighting breaks out, Diodorus and Xenophon describe in vague terms how the factions fare at this or that point in this civil war but

---

[140] 15(10).2–3: οἱ συνειδότες τὴν π̣[ρᾶξιν, ὡ]ς ὑπέλαβον [κ]αιρὸν ἐγχειρεῖν εἶναι τοῖς ἔργ[οις, συ]νελέγοντο [σὺ]ν ἐγχειριδίοις εἰς τὴν ἀγοράν, καὶ Δωρίμαχος [μ]ὲν αὐτῶν ἀναβὰς ἐπὶ τὸν λίθον οὗπερ εἰώθει κη[ρύ]ττειν ὁ κῆρυξ, ἀνακραγὼν ὡς ἠδύνατο μέγιστον "[ἴ]ωμεν, ὦ ἄνδρες" ἔφη "πολῖται, ἐπὶ τοὺς τυράννους [τὴ]ν ταχίστην." οἱ δὲ λοιποὶ βοήσαντος ἐκείνου τὴν [βο]ήθειαν εἰσπηδήσαντες μετ' ἐγχειριδίων εἰς τὰ συν[έ]δρια τῶν ἀρχόντων ἀποκτείνουσι τούς τε Διαγο[ρε]ίους καὶ τῶν ἄλλων πολιτῶν ἕνδεκα, διαπραξά[μ]ενοι δὲ ταῦτα συνῆγον τὸ πλῆθος τὸ τῶν Ῥοδίων [εἰ]ς ἐκκλησίαν. ἄρτι δὲ συνειλεγομένων αὐτῶν Κόνων ἧκε πάλιν ἐκ Καύνου μετὰ τῶν τριήρων· οἱ δὲ τὴν σφαγὴν ἐξεργασάμενοι καταλύσαντες τὴν παροῦσαν πολιτείαν κατέστησαν δημοκρατίαν, καὶ τῶν πολιτῶν τινας ὀλίγους φυγάδας ἐποίησαν. ἡ μὲν οὖν ἐπανάστασις ἡ περὶ τὴν Ῥόδον τοῦτο τὸ τέλος ἔλαβεν.

[141] Diod. Sic. 14.97, 99; Xen. *Hell.* 4.8.20–5, 4.8.30. Diodorus and Xenophon conflict in some important details. See the judicious solutions of H. D. Westlake, "Rival Traditions on a Rhodian Stasis," *MH* 40 (1983), 239–50. Westlake tends to favor Diodorus' account, and for sensible reasons.

[142] 1304b27–31 and 1302b21–33. Unlike most scholars, Hornblower, *Mausolus*, 127 (followed by Berthold, *Rhodes*, 31, n. 41) takes the Aristotle passages to refer to a later revolution involving Mausolus (see below). However, the testimony for that event suggests external factors (Mausolus especially, but also the context of the Social War) sparked the rebellion, not the internal, class-based rising that our sources for 391 imply and that the Aristotle passages require. See the argument in Westlake, "Rival Traditions," 246–7.

[143] The identical phrase *dia tas epipheromenas dikas* ("on account of lawsuits being directed at them") appears at both 1302b21–33 and 1304b27–31, tying together the two passages on the causes of Rhodian stasis and strongly implying the same episode of oligarchic revolution against democracy is being described. However, it is possible to read the passage at 1302b differently, in such a way that the second reference to Rhodian *stasis* could be to a separate episode, one in which contempt (*kataphronesis*) led the *demos* to attack oligarchs, not oligarchs the *demos*; N. Luraghi, "Crollo della democrazia o sollevazione anti-oligarchica? Syracusa e Rodi in Aristotle, *Politica* 5 1302 b15–33," *Hermes* 126 (1998), 117–23.

do not tell us who ultimately prevailed. It has often been guessed that the popular faction won and the *demokratia* was restored, mostly on the strength of Demosthenes' "On the Liberty of the Rhodians," for the speech implies a fairly longstanding democracy at Rhodes prior to its overthrow by Mausolus.[144]

Demosthenes' oration also attests the next case of revolution at Rhodes: around 355, while the Rhodians fought the Athenians in the Social War, the Carian Mausolus replaced a Rhodian democracy with an oligarchy.[145] This oligarchy presumably continued until the island surrendered to Alexander in 332. What happened then constitutionally is not known. A Macedonian garrison was established on the island, which remained until the Rhodians drove it out upon Alexander's death in 323.[146] Alexander had made a habit of establishing democracies in Greek states liberated from Persian control,[147] and scholars have usually supposed *demokratia*, perhaps a moderated one, assumed control of Rhodes in 332 and remained in power into the Hellenistic period.[148]

Aristotle's passages in the *Politics* at 1302b and 1304b describing the democratic conditions at Rhodes that drove the oligarchs to revolution provide the most striking information we have about the nature of the fourth-century Rhodian *demokratia*. We read that the demagogues provided *misthophora*, a word used to mean, especially by Aristotle, city payments offered for public service, such as on citizen law courts.[149] Public pay was typical of democracy according to Aristotle and could extend to juries, magistracies, council, and assembly.[150] We do not know to how many institutions public pay extended at Rhodes – all of the above? Just one or two? However, it probably amounted to a serious level of expenditure, since the "demagogues" who brought about its establishment also felt the need to restrict payments to warship captains. We can also guess that

---

[144] Hornblower, *Mausolus*, 125–6, considers democracy likely from such factors as a possible backlash against Sparta and Persia after the King's Peace, growing Athenian power in the era, and Rhodes' joining of the Second Athenian League right from the start – none of which is decisive, however. See also Berthold, *Rhodes*, 26–9; Gehrke, *Stasis*, 139; T. H. Nielsen and V. Gabrielsen in *Inventory*, 1206.

[145] Dem. 15.3 and *passim*. Theopompus fr. 121 probably belongs to the same period. Hornblower, *Mausolus*, 127–30; Berthold, *Rhodes*, 30–2.

[146] Arr. *Anab.* 2.20.1–3; Curt. 4.5.9, 4.8.12–13; Diod. Sic. 18.8.1.

[147] Arr. *Anab.* 1.17.10–18.2; *Syll.*³ 283 = Rhodes and Osborne 84. See A. B. Bosworth, *Conquest and Empire: The Reign of Alexander the Great* (Cambridge, 1988), 192–4.

[148] Berthold, *Rhodes*, 34–7. On the Hellenistic democracy, see below.

[149] *Ath. Pol.* 27.4. Also *ta dikasteria misthophora* at *Pol.* 1274a9.

[150] *Pol.* 1294a37–41, 1297a35–8, 1317b35–8. However, as noted above (under Iasus), the moderately oligarchic Boeotian constitution allowed for payment of council members (*Hell. Oxy.* 19.4 [Chambers]).

the public pay had probably only recently been established by 391 (if we have applied the *Politics* passages to the correct event), as its introduction helped to inspire the oligarchic revolution that followed. One assumes that the popular leaders persuaded the *demos* gathered in assembly to pass the various measures.

The Aristotle passages also note one more populist practice the elites at Rhodes found oppressive: lawsuits aimed at them. We do not know if sycophants or the like brought the cases simply to strip money from the wealthy, or if they represent aggressive prosecutions for alleged malfeasance by officials – both are certainly well attested in democracies, especially in hostile sources – and when Aristotle joins these complaints to those about the measures successfully promoted by the "demagogues," one gets the impression of a radically populist government in early fourth-century Rhodes, even if it is understood that the perspective given surely derives from hostile elites victimized (or sympathetic to those victimized) by the circumstances.

We might glean more details about the Classical *demokratia* in Rhodes by reference to the institutions of the Hellenistic period, though (as always) such inferences must remain uncertain. That Rhodes was democratically governed in the Hellenistic period is maintained by most scholars, and with good reason, for the majority of literary references point this way and contemporary inscriptions claim it to have been so, though room exists for disagreement thanks especially to a discordant reference in Strabo and the influence of the naval class.[151]

An obvious democratic feature that could have had its origins in the Classical period is the system of jury allotment. A number of individual bronze "jury tickets" have been found that date from perhaps the end of the third century and later, probably made for insertion into some kind of randomization device similar to the Athenian *kleroterion*.[152] Moreover, assemblies appear to have had decisive authority on all major issues, worked with an allotted, probouleutic council, and had the power to initiate legislation; no evidence exists for any property qualifications for either body.[153]

---

[151] The Strabo passage in question is 14.2.5. J. L. O'Neil, "How Democratic was Hellenistic Rhodes?," *Athenaeum* 59 (1981), 468–73; Berthold, *Rhodes*, 34–54; L. Migeotte, "Démocratie et entretien du peuple à Rhodes," *REG* 102 (1989), 515–28, at 525–8; V. Gabrielsen, *The Naval Aristocracy of Hellenistic Rhodes* (Aarhus, 1997), 24–36; Rhodes, *Decrees*, 535–6; Grieb, *Hellenistische Demokratie*, 263–353, esp. 316–20 and 344–53.

[152] P. M. Fraser, "Notes on Two Rhodian Institutions," *ABSA* 67 (1972), 119–24, with J. Bingen, "Epigraphica (Thrace, Rhodes)," *ZPE* 46 (1982), 183–4, and G. Touchais "Chronique des fouilles et découvertes archéologiques en Grèce en 1980: Rhodes," *BCH* 105 (1981), 862–3.

[153] Gabrielsen, *Naval Aristocracy*, 24–31.

Finally, if Migeotte is correct, the Rhodians had an unusual system in place for support of the poorer classes by the wealthy. Strabo 14.2.5 has often been mistranslated in this regard: Strabo is describing a system not of public grain distribution but of rich provision for a wage, which allows the working poor to subsist even as they row in the fleet or do the city other useful service. The liturgies that allowed this system probably functioned more like an *eisphora* (a special tax). Thus the Rhodians crafted a remarkable device to avoid stasis by creating a kind of social pact between rich and poor.[154] Strabo explicitly identifies the practice as existing by an old custom (*ethei tini patrioi*), thus raising the likelihood that it operated as early as the fourth century.

SUMMARY TREATMENTS

Aphytis

Aristotle in the *Politics* cites the case of Aphytis in the course of his detailed discussion of the four types of *demokratia*.[155] Aristotle prefers democratic cities with an agricultural citizen body (*georgikon demon*) and cites the example of Aphytis for their law that promotes this characteristic: by regulation there, property assessments are made according to divisions so small that even the poor have no trouble in surpassing the requirements.[156] The clear implication, both from the context of Aristotle's discussion and the inclusiveness of the law, is that Aphytis was a *demokratia* and an admirably (to Aristotle) moderate one thanks to its *georgikon demon*.

Unfortunately, we have very little evidence for the date of this democracy. Aristotle says that in the present day (*nun*) one could profitably apply this law of the Aphytaeans. This may imply that he was describing a law currently in force. Beyond this, there is not much. Aphytis was a member of the Delian League in the fifth century, and during the Peloponnesian War it proved to be a very loyal ally on more than one occasion, which could be suggestive of a democratic constitution at the time.[157]

---

[154] Migeotte, "Démocratie et entretien," 515–25. Even if Migeotte is wrong about seeing payments rather than grain provision, the social support system developed is unusual for a Greek *polis*.

[155] *Pol.* 1319a14–19.

[156] τιμῶνται γὰρ οὐχ ὅλας τὰς κτήσεις, ἀλλὰ κατὰ τηλικαῦτα μόρια διαιροῦντες ὥστ᾽ ἔχειν ὑπερβάλλειν ταῖς τιμήσεσι καὶ τοὺς πένητας (*Pol.* 1319a17–19). The precise way in which the law achieved the results Aristotle claims is somewhat obscure. For a possible explanation, see Aubonnet, *Aristote Politique*, 262.

[157] See events and sources in P. Flensted-Jensen in *Inventory*, 825.

Cnidus

In the *Politics* Aristotle twice attests revolution in Cnidus that resulted in the overthrow of an oligarchy; neither passage specifies what kind of government followed its fall, but since one of the passages has the *demos* doing the toppling, we might well presume *demokratia* resulted.[158] Scholars have been divided about whether these passages refer to one event or two, though their proximity and degree of concordance suggests that they refer to one event.[159]

The greater problem concerns the date of the event, for Aristotle provides no chronological indications. Possibly, this revolution took place in the Archaic period. Plutarch's description of the nature of the Cnidian oligarchy (that might be taken to be the one preceding the democracy at issue) can be taken to hint at an earlier rather than a later date.[160] However, the late fourth century in the context of Alexander's conquests and democratizations also makes a suitable setting. Three factors together make it probable that Cnidus was democratic under Alexander, whatever the date Aristotle had in mind for the revolution he describes: first is the general statement that Alexander ordered that oligarchies be replaced with democracies during his sweep down the coast of Asia Minor;[161] second, the decree formula for Cnidus changes from what could have been an oligarchic one (*edoxe Knidiois*) to a more democratic one (*Knidion ho damos*) later in the century;[162] finally, by the end of the fourth century democracy of some kind in the city was a certainty, given the coins of Cnidus from *c*. 300 with the legend *DEMOKRATIA*.[163] None of these factors alone would suffice, but together they strongly suggest that Cnidus democratized in the time of Alexander's conquests.

Ephesus

The little evidence we possess for Ephesian constitutional history in the fifth century points to democracy. On the basis of stories about the life and sayings of the philosopher Heraclitus and the exile of his friend Hermodorus, it would seem that a populist order took control of the city, perhaps in connection with Mardonius' establishment of *demokratiai* along

---

[158] *Pol.* 1305b12–18, 1306b3–5.
[159] See discussion and references in Robinson, *First Democracies*, 101–3.
[160] *Quaest. Graec.* 4. Discussed in Robinson, *First Democracies*, 102.   [161] Arr. *Anab.* 1.18.2.
[162] So argues Hornblower, *Mausolus*, 116. See also Rhodes, *Decrees*, 328–9.
[163] P. Flensted-Jensen in *Inventory*, 1124.

the coast of Ionia in 492 BC.[164] Ephesus later joined the Delian League, and a passage in Xenophon's *Hellenica* (3.4.7) refers in general terms to Ephesus and other cities in the region as *demokratiai* in the time of Athenian control.

No source reports a change in the Ephesian popular constitution during the fifth century, though a possible occasion for revolution was its revolt from Athens in *c.* 412 and subsequent control by the Persians.[165] In the fourth century there is no precise information until 334, when we find Alexander overthrowing an oligarchy, restoring exiles, and reestablishing democracy.[166] A multitude of inscribed decrees from the later fourth century show a democratic opening formula (*edoxe tei boulei kai toi demoi*), and the numerous proposers of single decrees from the fourth and early third centuries suggest a broadly active citizen body.[167] The formulaic clauses used in the decrees vary strikingly from the Athenian style.[168]

Eretria

Eretrian democracy may have had its start with the revolution of Diagoras against Eretrian oligarchs in the late sixth century, though the nature of the resulting government cannot be certainly determined from the evidence.[169] Euboea joined the Delian League, rebelled in 446, and was soon reduced again by the Athenians, an occasion for possible democratization or redemocratization in Eretria. However, no direct evidence for constitutional imposition exists: the Chalcis Decree of 446/5 (or 424/3), which a decree for Eretria mimics to some extent, does not provide a good analogy for Eretrian democratization since the Chalcis Decree itself does not show democratization.[170] In 411 Euboea once again revolted from the Athenian Empire, and seems to be oligarchically governed, based on an inscription with the opening formula "Decreed by the Council"

---

[164] Heraclitus fr. 121 DK; Diog. Laert. 9.2–3; Hdt. 6.43; Gehrke, *Stasis*, 57–8; L. Rubinstein in *Inventory*, 1071–2.

[165] Thuc. 8.19 and 109; Xen. *Hell.*, 1.2.6. H. D. Westlake, "Athens and Amorges," *Phoenix* 31 (1977), 319–29, at 323–4; M. Piérart, "Chios entre Athènes et Sparte," *BCH* 119 (1995), 253–82, at 257–8, for Ephesian Revolt and the new fragment of the Spartan War contributions stone.

[166] Arr. *Anab.* 1.17.10–12. This passage suggests a back-and-forth striving between democratic and oligarchic factions in previous years; Gehrke, *Stasis*, 59–60.

[167] Rhodes, *Decrees*, 364, 496–7.   [168] Rhodes, *Decrees* 364.

[169] Arist. *Pol.* 1306a31–6, with 1289b33–40. *IG* 12 Suppl. 549 lists a heavily restored proxeny decree dated to early fifth century beginning with [*edochsen . . . tei bo*] / [*le*]*i . . . kai toi* [*demoi*]. Rhodes, *Decrees*, 246, 248.

[170] *IG* I^3 39 and 40. M. Ostwald, "Athens and Chalkis: A Study in Imperial Control," *JHS* 122 (2002), 134–43; K. Reber, M. H. Hansen, and P. Ducrey in *Inventory*, 653.

(*edoxe tei boulei*), which contrasts with a later, perhaps early fourth-century decree showing the more democratic "Decreed by the Council and the People."[171]

In the early fourth century any democracy hinted at by the decree formulae gave way to a succession of tyrants.[172] However, democracy returned to Eretria briefly around 342 when the *demos* drove out Plutarchus,[173] and more lastingly in 341 when an Athenian expedition overthrew the last tyrant and established an autonomous regime with the *demos* in charge.[174] A recently published fragment of an inscribed decree from this new government details the measures taken by the Eretrian democracy designed to prevent the return of tyranny or oligarchy.[175] Probably dating to soon after the new government's 341 arrival, it is the most thorough anti-tyrannical (and anti-oligarchic) legislation on record from ancient Greece. Athenian influence seems likely in much of it, both because of Athens' military role in bringing about the overthrow of the Eretrian tyrants, and the correspondence to certain Athenian laws[176] of provisions in the first part of the law, such as punishments for those attempting or succeeding in overthrowing the *demos*, protections and rewards for killers of tyrants, and public prayers or imprecations against malefactors. But much of the new fragment of the Eretrian law is unique: it goes into detail about what are acceptable government institutions (*boule* and *prutaneie* chosen by lot from all Eretrians) and what to do if violence is used to establish a tyrannical or oligarchic constitution, including if the loyal citizens are driven out of the walls by fighting. The law thus looks like a mixture of original measures with ones earlier used by the Athenians and adapted to local conditions, all designed to use every available measure to keep the *demos* of the Eretrians in control of their city.[177]

---

[171] *IG* 12.187A, B. Rhodes, *Decrees*, 248–9; K. Reber, M. H. Hansen, and P. Ducrey in *Inventory*, 653.

[172] On possible democracy in the 390s, followed by the tyrants and perhaps intermediate democratic regimes, see D. Knoepfler, "Loi d'Érétrie contre la tyrannie et l'oligarchie," *BCH* 126 (2002), 149–204, at 157, 194–8.

[173] Dem. 9.57, schol. Dem. 5.5.

[174] Philoch. fr. 160: τ]ότε δὲ ἐκπολιορκήσαντες αὐτὸν Ἀθηναῖοι τῷ δή/[μῳ] τὴν πόλιν ἀπέδωκαν (*IG* 12.189). Gehrke, *Stasis*, 65–6; K. Reber, M. H. Hansen, and P. Ducrey in *Inventory*, 653–4.

[175] Knoepfler, "Loi d'Érétrie," *BCH* 125 (2001), 195–238 and *BCH* 126 (2002), 149–204. The newly published fragment appears to supplement *IG* 12.9.190.

[176] E.g., the law of Demophantos of 410/9 (Andoc. 1.96–8), the fourth century *nomos eisangeltikos* (Hyp. 4.7–8), and the Areopagus law of 337/6 (Rhodes and Osborne 79). Knoepfler, "Loi d'Érétrie," *BCH* 126, 198–9.

[177] Knoepfler also stresses the originality of many components of the Eretrian law: "Loi d'Érétrie," *BCH* 126, 199–202.

Erythrae

Erythrae may have first experienced *demokratia* at some point in the Archaic or early Classical period when the oligarchy of the Basilidae was overthrown by a *demos* unhappy at being ruled by a few.[178] But the resulting government is not described, and it may not have been democratic, since an Erythraean inscribed decree, possibly from the first half of the fifth century, calls for juries of only nine men from each tribe and requires a property minimum from them as well.[179] In *c.* 453/2, however, Athens imposed regulations on Erythrae that almost certainly meant *demokratia*: a decree describes the establishment of a council (*boule*) whose membership was to be allotted.[180] The new establishment of so fundamental a body as a *boule* must mean the Erythraean constitution was significantly modified or a new one imposed, and an allotted council strongly implies *demokratia*.

The fourth century apparently begins with a democracy, judging from two inscriptions,[181] but in about 387 civil strife erupted with oligarchs holding the city and the *demos* the countryside.[182] By the middle of the century, under Mausolus' influence, an oligarchy controlled the city, as seems to be attested by two inscriptions in which the *boule* made the decisions without reference to the *demos*.[183] A democratic decree formula returns only in the 330s after Alexander's liberation and presumed redemocratization of the city.[184]

Hestiaea/Oreus

Aristotle attests an oligarchy in the period following the Persian Wars, followed by a revolution of unstated result between the wealthy (*euporous*) and the popular faction (*demotikous*) at *Politics* 1303b31–7. Democracy seems probable given the context of the Aristotle passage.[185] An Athenian

---

[178] Arist. *Pol.* 1305b18–23. The only indication of date Aristotle gives for the event is "*en tois archaiois chronois.*"

[179] *I. Erythrae* 2B. Rhodes, *Decrees*, 530; L. Rubinstein in *Inventory*, 1074.

[180] *IG* i³ 14. The date is uncertain, with a speculative restoration of the Athenian archon of 453/2 but is likely to have been decreed around this time. If the lacunose text has been interpreted correctly, one could not hold a council seat repeatedly within a four-year period, a further democratic feature. See *Athenian Tribute Lists*, vol. II, D10. O'Neil, *Origins and Development*, 47–8.

[181] *SEG* 36.1039 (c. 400); Tod 106 = *I. Erythrae* 6 (early fourth century). Both contain democratic decree formulae and the first mentions the *demos* in assembly.

[182] *SEG* 26.1282. Gehrke, *Stasis*, 68; L. Rubinstein in *Inventory*, 1075.

[183] *I. Erythrae* 8; *SEG* 31.969. Hornblower, *Mausolus*, 109–10.

[184] *I. Erythrae* 21. Gehrke, *Stasis*, 69.   [185] Gehrke, *Stasis*, 73–4.

colony was established on the site in 446 (or in the 420s) that appears to have been democratic.[186]

A second Aristotle *Politics* passage attests certain *demokratia* at Hestiaea/Oreus: 1303a16–20 describes the fall of an oligarchy and its replacement by democracy[187] when someone unfriendly to the existing government was allowed to gain powerful office. This event is usually dated to the first half of the fourth century, possibly *c.* 395, though Aristotle gives no indication.[188] A tyrant ruled Hestiaea/Oreus in *c.* 382–79; at some point after his overthrow, a democracy with a very active assembly took charge.[189] Factional infighting gripped the city in 357 and again in the 340s, until in 341 an Athenian expedition took control of the city and restored its *demokratia*.[190]

Istrus

Aristotle in the *Politics* (1305b1–12) refers to an undated political revolution at Istrus in which an oligarchy that restricted office-holding to too few suffered revolution and became a democracy (*eis demon apeteleutesen*). This could have taken place at any point in the Classical period, or possibly the late Archaic. Out of desperation some have supposed that the change might have been sparked by Pericles' mid-fifth-century Black Sea expedition (Plut. *Per.* 20), though nothing in the Aristotle or Plutarch passages suggest any connection between the two.[191]

Miletus

The constitutional history of Miletus in the fifth century is a confused and contentious one, and scholars have disagreed often on its proper reconstruction, as the available evidence is scanty and often chronologically imprecise.[192]

---

[186] *IG* I³ 41. K. Reber, M. H. Hansen, and P. Ducrey in *Inventory*, 657.

[187] *hos ex oligarchias politeian kai demokratian kateskeuasen* (1303a20).

[188] Gehrke, *Stasis*, 74; K. Reber, M. H. Hansen, and P. Ducrey in *Inventory*, 657.

[189] Tyranny and its overthrow: Diod. Sic. 15.30.3–4 (Stylianou, *Commentary*, 279 on the date). Democracy: Aeschin. 3.103–5 (*demokratoumenon ton Oreiton kai panta prattonton meta psephismatos*).

[190] Schol. Aeschin. 3.85; Dem. 18.87. Gehrke, *Stasis*, 74; K. Reber, M. H. Hansen, and P. Ducrey in *Inventory*, 657.

[191] A. Avram, J. Hind, and G. R. Tsetskhladze in *Inventory*, 933.

[192] For useful treatments see L. Rubinstein in *Inventory*, 1084–6; V. Gorman, *Miletos the Ornament of Ionia* (Ann Arbor, 2001), 135–6, 215–36; N. Robertson, "Government and Society at Miletus, 525–442 B.C.," *Phoenix* 41 (1987), 356–98; H.-J. Gehrke, "Zur Geschichte Milets in der Mitte des 5. Jahrhunderts v. Chr.," *Historia* 29 (1980) 17–31, *Jenseits von Athen und Sparta* (Munich, 1986), 133–6, and *Stasis*, 114–16; Meiggs, *Athenian Empire*, 115–16, 562–5.

Herodotus tells us that at the beginning of the century the tyrant Aristagoras, attempting to build support for his rebellion against the Persians, made a grand gesture of withdrawing from office and establishing *isonomia* in the city.[193] Although scholars have been uncertain about what to make of the new government, especially since Aristagoras clearly left himself a leading role whatever its exact constitutional structure, Herodotus' use of the term *isonomia* elsewhere in his history[194] strongly implies that democracy was established here, or at least announced.[195] The failure of the Ionian Revolt brought destruction to the city, which was reestablished soon after the defeat of the Persians in 479. Scholars usually judge that an oligarchy ruled Miletus from this point until sometime in the middle of the century. The city had joined the Delian League early on and maintained its oligarchic government down through the 450s, with Athens helping the government remain in power at one point at least.[196] But a rebellion from the empire followed sometime soon after, probably between 446 and 443, as a result of which it is likely that Athens established a democratic government. That democracy followed the revolt is not explicitly stated anywhere, but it is the implication of Pseudo-Xenophon 3.11, and a Milesian decree from the 430s includes a reference to the authority of the people to decide matters (*en doxei toi demoi*).[197]

The Milesian democracy continued through most of the Peloponnesian War, even after the city's revolt from Athens in 412, until in 405 Lysander aided Milesian oligarchs in overthrowing the *demos*.[198] But around 402 Tissaphernes intervened in the city, banishing members of the pro-Spartan faction, and probably restored democracy, given a later inscription's democratic decree formula.[199] The constitution may have remained democratic during the early fourth century, but this cannot be known for sure. Carian

---

[193] 5.37: καὶ πρῶτα μὲν λόγῳ μετεὶς τὴν τυραννίδα ἰσονομίην ἐποίεε τῇ Μιλήτῳ, ὡς ἂν ἑκόντες αὐτῷ οἱ Μιλήσιοι συναπισταίατο. (Quoted at greater length in note 11.)

[194] See especially Hdt. 3.80.3 with 6.43.3, and the discussion and references provided in the Abdera and Teos section, above.

[195] Gehrke, *Jenseits*, concurs about democracy being established; Gorman, *Miletos*, 136, is more skeptical.

[196] Ps.-Xen. *Ath. pol.* 3.11; *IG* I³ 21. The dating of the latter is uncertain, and the Ps.-Xenophon passage offers no chronological context. Gorman, *Miletos*, 225–36; Robertson, "Government and Society," 384–9.

[197] Rhodes, *Decrees*, 374, 379 (on *Klio* 52 [1970], 165–73), noting the resemblance to Athenian procedures; L. Rubinstein in *Inventory*, 1085–6; Gorman, *Miletos*, 227–9, 236.

[198] Diod. Sic. 13.104.5–6; Plut. *Lys.* 8. See Xen. *Hell.* 1.6.7–12 for the assembly (*ekklesian*) during the democracy in 406; Thuc. 8.17.1–4 for the rebellion in 412. Gehrke, *Stasis*, 114–15.

[199] Xen. *Anab.* 1.1.7, with no. 45 (from 380/79) in F. Sokolowski, *Lois sacrées de l'Asie Mineure* (Paris, 1955). Rhodes, *Decrees*, 374, 379. Gehrke, *Stasis*, 115–16.

rulers probably controlled it mid-century, as indicated by coins and a Milesian dedication to them at Delphi, which could have meant an oligarchic constitution.[200] If it was oligarchic before Alexander captured the city, he surely returned it to *demokratia*.[201] A decree apparently belonging to the late 330s promotes concord while proclaiming that the citizens should live in democracy for all time.[202] Miletus remained democratic into the Hellenistic period.[203]

Mytilene

The evidence for the Mytilenian constitution in the fifth century is very sparse. Like Miletus and other cities in the region, the Ionian Revolt of the early 490s brought an end to local tyrannies and put in their place (for a time, at least) *isonomia*, which in Herodotus' usage seems to mean democracy.[204] However, passages in Thucydides concerning the Mytilenean Revolt of 428–7 imply that the government had come into the hands of oligarchs at some point prior to the rebellion against Athens.[205] As for the period after the revolt, whether or not *demokratia* followed is unknown, though it is usually assumed that the *demos*, whose action triggered the collapse of the oligarchic rebellion, took up power in the city.[206]

A Sparta-dominated oligarchy controlled Mytilene after 405, but by 390 no longer ruled the city (Xen. *Hell.* 2.2.5, 4.8.28). By the second half of the fourth century Mytilene certainly had democratized, as a number of decrees show, including one from the 330s actually referring to *damokratia*.[207] A passage in Pseudo-Demosthenes 13.8 from roughly the middle of the century refers to the overthrow of the *demos* at Mytilene, so democracy apparently had returned at some point in the first half of the century before losing out to an oligarchy, to be followed by two tyrants, before the epigraphically attested democracy returned, probably in 332.[208]

---

[200] Hornblower, *Mausolus*, 107, 111–12; Gehrke, *Stasis*, 116–17.

[201] Arr. *Anab.* 1.18–19.6. Carlsson, *Hellenistic Democracies*, 248–9, 276.

[202] *en damokrasiai ton panton krono(n)*; A. J. Heisserer and R. Hodot, "The Mytilenean Decree on Concord," *ZPE* 63 (1986), 109–28.

[203] Rhodes, *Decrees*, 379–80; more comprehensively, Grieb, *Hellenistische Demokratie*, 199–261; Carlsson, *Hellenistic Democracies*, 248–76.

[204] Hdt. 5.37–8, plus 3.80.3 with 6.43.3. See Miletus discussion above.

[205] Thuc. 3.27.3, 3.39.6, 3.50.1.

[206] Gehrke, *Stasis*, 120, 369–70. Treated obliquely in Legon, "Megara and Mytilene," 200–25, and D. Gillis, "The Revolt at Mytilene," *AJPh* 92 (1971), 38–47.

[207] *IG* 12.2.4 and 5, *SEG* 36.750 (*damokratia*), 752. Rhodes, *Decrees*, 256–8.

[208] Dem. 15.19; Isoc. *Ep.* 8; Arr. *Anab.* 2.1.5 and 3.2.6. M. H. Hansen and T. H. Nielsen in *Inventory*, 1028; Gehrke, *Stasis*, 121–2.

The democratic decrees from Mytilene show an unusual enactment formula, reading *egno bolla kai damos* rather than the more typical *edoxe tai bolai kai toi damoi.*

Samos

As with other Ionian cities, Samos may have had an early fifth-century experience with *isonomia* (probably meaning a form of democracy) with the ouster of its tyrant in the outbreak of the Ionian Revolt, and then *demokratia c.* 492 with Mardonius' actions in the region.[209] However, corroborating evidence is lacking – indeed, Herodotus notes a Persian-installed tyrant ruling Samos during the Persian Wars (8.85.3, 9.90) – and after the Persian Wars Samos probably became aristocratically governed.[210] In 441 BC Pericles overthrew an oligarchy in Samos and replaced it with *demokratia.* A revolution against Athenian rule soon followed and was suppressed the next year – and while Diodorus tells us that Pericles restored *demokratia* there, Thucydides does not, which has led to much scholarly disagreement about the constitution put in place afterward.[211] Whatever the case, Samos must have been oligarchic again in 412 when the *demos* rose up against the powerful class (*tois dunatois*), killed them or drove them out, and ran the city thenceforth.[212] This democracy remained loyal to Athens until the end of the war when Lysander put an oligarchy in charge again, a decarchy with a harmost.[213] Oligarchy probably remained in Samos down to the establishment of an Athenian cleruchy on the island in 365, though a period of *demokratia* is possible.[214]

The nature of the Samian constitution from 439 to 412, despite our ignorance, is particularly instructive from the perspective of Athenian democratic policy. Either Athens left the island oligarchically governed after suppressing the revolt, or Athens installed democracy in 439 but allowed it

---

[209] Hdt. 6.13.2, 6.43.3. See discussions above, especially Ephesus and Miletus.

[210] G. Shipley, *A History of Samos, 800–188 B.C.* (Oxford, 1987), 108–9. Cf. J. P. Barron, *The Silver Coins of Samos* (London, 1966), 89–91; Quinn, *Athens and Samos, Lesbos and Chios*, 10–23; Gehrke, *Stasis*, 140, n. 3.

[211] Thuc. 1.115–17; Diod. Sic. 12.28.4; *IG* I³ 48. Hornblower, *Commentary*, vol. I, 192–3; Shipley, *History of Samos*, 113–22; Gehrke, *Stasis*, 141–2; W. Schuller, "Die Einführung der Demokratie auf Samos im 5. Jahrhundert v. Chr.'" *Klio* 64 (1981), 281–8.

[212] Thuc. 8.21, 63.3, 73.2. The case is persuasively made in full detail by M. Ostwald, "*Stasis* and *autonomia* in Samos: A Comment on an Ideological Fallacy," *SCI* 12 (1993), 51–66. Hornblower, *Commentary*, vol. I, 193 and vol. III, 808–9 takes Andrewes' ideas (in Gomme, *Commentary on Thucydides* 5.45) too far in doubting an oligarchy ruled before this revolution. Gehrke, *Stasis*, 142–4.

[213] Xen. *Hell.* 2.3.6–7; Diod. Sic. 14.3.5; Plut. *Lys.* 14.2.

[214] Diod. Sic. 14.97.3. Gehrke, *Stasis*, 144–5; L. Rubinstein in *Inventory*, 1096.

to lapse at some point between those dates without attempting to reverse it (until playing the secondary role it did in 412). Either way, the case represents further evidence that Athens did not have a consistent doctrine of enforcing *demokratiai* throughout the empire, even after war with the Peloponnesians broke out in 431.[215]

Thasos

Mardonius forced the surrender of Thasos to the Persians in 492; nothing is known of its constitution before or after, though it is at least possible that Mardonius' policy in that year of establishing democratic governments among some conquered Greek states extended to this island.[216] After the overthrow of Persian power in the Aegean, Thasos joined the Delian League as an ally but was reduced to tributary status after its unsuccessful revolt from Athens in the 460s. The Thasians capitulated by agreement, and Thucydides (1.100–1) describes multiple consequences but does not mention constitutional change.[217] Whether introduced at this point or earlier or later, Thasos was a *demokratia* in 411, when the Athenian general and oligarchic conspirator Dieitrephes overthrew the democracy there (*ton demon katelusen*) in favor of oligarchy.[218] The next few years brought further civil discord and constitutional tumult to Thasos, and scholars have not reached agreement on all the dates, documents, and reversals, but *demokratia* certainly returned by 407 at the hands of the Athenian general Thrasybulus.[219] Thasos came under Spartan control and probably oligarchy after the battle of Aegospotami.[220]

Democracy eventually returned to Thasos in the fourth century, as one inscription would seem to attest,[221] and various reversals from Spartan to Athenian alliances and back again provide possible occasions for constitutional change: the Athenians regained control of the island in 389, then their party lost out and suffered exile a few years later, then Thasos joined

---

[215] Hornblower, *Commentary*, vol. III, 808, agrees that Athens was only really concerned with ally loyalty, not constitutional form, despite his different take on Samian events in 412 (above n. 212).

[216] Hdt. 6.43–4. Pouilloux (*Recherches sur l'histoire et les cultes de Thasos*, vol. I [Paris, 1954], 43) supposes an oligarchy preceded the Persian takeover: G. Reger in *Inventory*, 779.

[217] Nor do other sources: Diod. Sic. 11.70.1; Plut. *Cim.* 14.2.   [218] Thuc. 8.64.2–5.

[219] Xen. *Hell.* 1.4.9; Diod. Sic. 13.72.1; *SEG* 38.851A. G. Reger in *Inventory*, 779; *SEG* 51.1096; A. J. Graham, "An Ellipse in the Thasian Decree about Delation (ML 83)?," *AJPh* 110 (1989), 405–17; Y. Grandjean and F. Salviat, "Decret d'Athènes, restaurant la démocratie à Thasos en 407 av. J.-C.: *IG* XII 8, 262 complété," *BCH* 112 (1988), 249–78; Gehrke, *Stasis*, 159–62; ML 83.

[220] Xen. *Hell.* 2.2.5; Nep. *Lysander.* 2. Gehrke, *Stasis*, 162–3.

[221] *IG* 2² 1441, dated to 354/3. Gehrke, *Stasis*, 164.

the Second Athenian League around 375.[222] But in fact little can be gleaned about Thasos' constitution in these years, except perhaps to note that from the fourth century onward one finds many entrenchment clauses in the decrees from Thasos.[223]

[222] Dem. 20.59, 61; *IG* 2² 17, 24, 33, 43. G. Reger in *Inventory*, 779; Gehrke, *Stasis*, 163–4.
[223] Rhodes, *Decrees*, 294–6.

CHAPTER 4

The spread of democracy in the Classical period

As we have seen in the foregoing chapters, a great many communities in Greece were governed democratically during the Classical period. Some had relatively brief democratic interludes (e.g., Corinth and Thessaly), but most others went for decades at a time under democratic government, and several were democratic for most of the period from 480 to 323 BC. As became clear from the individual studies, certainty about the length of this or that constitutional regime is rarely attainable, since we lack anything like a continuous political narrative for the vast majority of these *poleis*, and only a few have even intermittent descriptions of any length. But there is enough information about enough *poleis* to judge that by the fifth and fourth centuries *demokratia* had become a widespread and persistent phenomenon in the Greek world, with examples to be found in every region of Greece from early in the fifth century to late in the fourth.

To see the truth of this at a glance, look at Figure 4.1, which illustrates the establishment and duration of *demokratia* in individual states grouped by region.[1] Dark gray lines represent periods in which we can be fairly certain that democracy obtained in that city; light gray ones indicate less certainty, either about the dates or whether actual democracy existed there. (Leucas and Istrus, for example, definitely democratized at some point in the Classical period, but we do not know when, hence the long, light gray lines; Sicyon's lines are light gray because it is uncertain whether its government at the indicated times was a *demokratia* or not). Naturally, a chart like this loses nuance and elides ambiguities in presenting results; the individual treatments in the previous chapters, which are the basis for the results of the figures, should be sought for details regarding the basis of judgment in each case. Nevertheless, we can learn from Figure 4.1 a great deal about the general picture of democracy in Classical Greece.

---

[1] My thanks to Xin Fan, Chris Molnar, and Heather Roberts for assisting in assembling various versions of this figure.

To start with the most obvious, the chart demonstrates a remarkable numerical growth from democracy's earlier beginnings. In the sixth century *demokratia* had made appearances in only a few city-states. In my book *The First Democracies* I discussed nineteen possible episodes of early (*c.* 700–480 BC) popular governments, out of which, I argued, some smaller number probably represented actual early democracies. To go from this mere handful of cases to the fifty-four we can register with a high degree of confidence for the Classical period represents a major expansion. Of course, these two numbers (<19 and 54) may exaggerate to some extent the degree of expansion, given that the amount of overall constitutional testimony increases for the Classical period over the Archaic. But the proportion of claims for democracies with respect to non-democracies appears to go up in the later period as well as the total number, so there is no reason to believe the growth that one discerns in moving from the sixth to the fifth and fourth centuries is somehow illusory.[2]

Some might also worry that these results (and the results from my study of the Archaic period before) necessarily leave out of the story the majority of the Greek city-states, thanks to the simple fact that we are informed about the politics of relatively few out of many – compare the number of cities discussed here with the more than one thousand *poleis* which are attested and earn entries in Hansen and Nielsen's *Inventory of Archaic and Classical Poleis*. Naturally, one wishes the viable sample size were larger. But it is a fact of the Greek historian's life that useful political testimony, whether from literary and historical treatments or substantial collections of epigraphical material, is limited to a small subset of the total number of Greek *poleis* that once existed. As it happens, the collection of fifty-four city-states treated in the previous chapters of this book and listed on Figure 4.1 represents a large proportion of the best-known and most famous Greek communities beyond Athens and Sparta. Trends that played out among them will no doubt contribute meaningfully to our picture of democracy in Greece generally. In any case, fifty-four is a much larger and more useful sample size than the database of one – Athens – on which the vast majority of scholarly work about democracy in Greece has focused thus far.

Figure 4.1 also highlights *demokratia*'s remarkable geographic breadth: every region, from the colonies in the west to the Greek mainland to the eastern Greek world and the Black Sea, shows the appearance of not just one but several *demokratiai* in the course of the Classical period. While some

---

[2] Given the skepticism in some quarters about the existence of even a handful of democracies in Archaic Greece, I do not expect many will challenge the idea that fifty-four evident Classical cases represents substantial real growth in *demokratia* from the Archaic age.

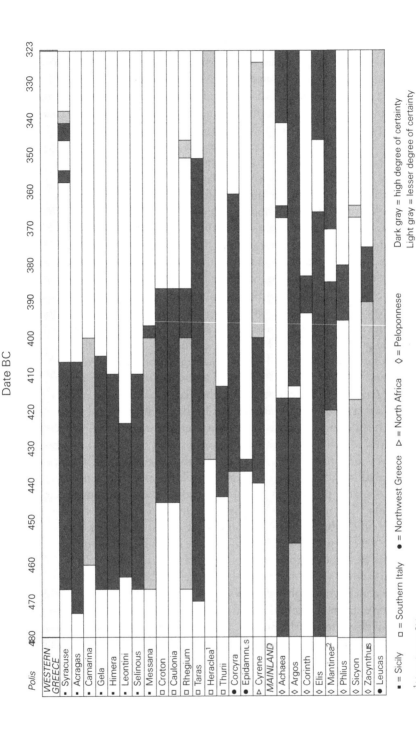

Figure 4.1 The establishment and duration of democracies in Greek city-states

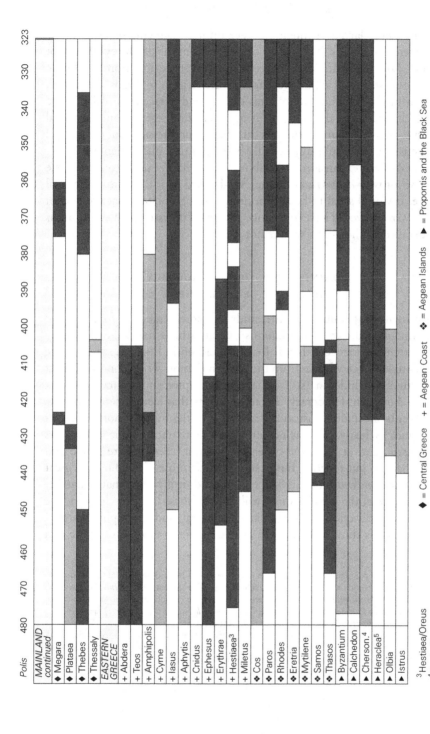

Figure 4.1 (*cont.*)

◆ = Central Greece   + = Aegean Coast   ❖ = Aegean Islands   ▲ = Propontis and the Black Sea

[3] Hestiaea/Oreus
[4] Tauric Chersonesus
[5] Heraclea Pontica

cities had popular government for very limited segments of time, many more were democratic (as far as we can glean from the patchy evidence) for decades. Long-lived democracies are found in every region, from the Tauric Chersonese in the Black Sea to Paros in the Aegean to Argos, Mantinea, and Elis in the Peloponnese to Taras in Italy and Syracuse in Sicily. To be sure, a closer look at the chart turns up interesting regional and temporal patterns – we will return to these as this chapter progresses – but the general picture is of a geographically broadly based political phenomenon.

How did this expansion come about? This chapter seeks to answer the question of why *demokratia* became established as it did across Classical Greece. It would seem to be an important enough matter that scholars of ancient Greece would have long since addressed the issue with voluminous and detailed studies – but such is not the case.

EXPLAINING CLASSICAL DEMOCRACY'S
EXPANSION – EARLIER VIEWS

The primary impediment to the study of the emergence of democratic governments apart from the famous one at Athens has been the scanty and scattered evidence at hand. Jochen Bleicken in his 1994 study of the Athenian democracy broke from the pattern of most writers on the subject and actually included a (still quite brief) chapter and source appendix on non-Athenian democracy. There he insists that lack of source material prevents substantial historical treatment of the topic of non-Athenian democracy.[3] Clearly, this has not proved to be correct, as this volume, its predecessor, and at least one other study attest.[4] Sources are scarce and can be hard to put together but exist in sufficient quantity to learn a great deal about *demokratia* outside Athens. Indeed, it is hoped that, whatever readers make of the conclusions I will draw in these last two chapters, the case-by-case collection of literary, archaeological, and epigraphic material in the previous three chapters will enable others to more easily pose and

---

[3] "Eine Geschichte der Demokratien außerhalb Athens gibt es nicht, und sie wird auf Grund der desolaten Quellenlage auch wohl kaum jemals geschrieben werden können"; *Die athenische Demokratie* (2nd edn.; Paderborn, 1994), 579. E. Will offered three pages on the subject of non-Athenian democracy in his study *Le monde grec et l'orient*, vol. 1: *Le Ve siècle (510–403)* (Paris, 1972), 461–4, with a similarly dismissive attitude toward all cases except Argos and Syracuse.

[4] O'Neil's *Origins and Development* presents a broad survey of democracy as it existed in the Greek world from the Archaic through Roman times, devoting much space to non-Athenian examples and thus attempting an unusually comprehensive view. However, the book only occasionally comments upon, and offers little in-depth analysis of, how and why democracy expanded as it did beyond Athens (e.g., pp. 37, 55–6). Some of the book's contentions will be discussed below.

answer large questions about democracy across the Greek world. There is potentially more material to consider as well: I limited myself in this volume to discussing *poleis* that I believe represent the strongest cases and best information for Classical popular government – there are other possibilities that one might investigate.[5]

Besides the scarcity of evidence there has been another impediment to full investigation and understanding of the phenomenon of democracy's expansion in Greece, and that is the towering example of Athens itself. The enormous quantity of literary and epigraphical source material pertaining to Athenian politics and society, as compared with that for any other state in Greece, has often led scholars to present the history of Athenian democracy as if it were the history of Greek democracy. This sleight of hand becomes obvious upon examining just about any textbook of Greek history or Western civilization: as soon as the narrative turns to the development of democracy, writers describe Solon and Cleisthenes, Ephialtes and Pericles – Athenian politicians all – as if that were the whole story. Even specialized studies tend to conflate Athenian and Greek democracy. For example, the recent volume entitled *Origins of Democracy in Ancient Greece* devotes almost the entire book to the Athenian case. No other example of Greek democracy receives any individual attention, and only in the introductory and background chapters are democracies beyond Athens considered at all. The quality of the book is not the issue – it offers, in fact, a first-rate study of the rise of democracy in Athens, including its background and social and political context, from different scholarly perspectives – it is just that you would never know from the title the severe limitations of its reach.[6]

In other specialized studies the shadow of Athens looms just as large, though in a somewhat different way. Scholars often see Athenian influence at every turn when accounting for the appearance of democracy anywhere else in Greece. Wolfgang Schuller has argued that the main cause of the emergence of *demokratia* outside Athens was Athens itself, especially through its powerful fifth-century sea league. Schuller focuses his attention on a handful of cases where Athens directly intervened to support or establish other democracies, and he concludes that democracy outside Athens was so fragile it usually required Athenian support. But his survey of non-Athenian democracies is far too limited in number, too brief, and

---

[5] For example, many more possibilities are potentially derivable from membership in the Delian League toward the end of the Peloponnesian War or democratic-seeming decree formulae – I have been cautious in using either to establish a presumption of *demokratia*.

[6] Kurt A. Raaflaub, Josiah Ober, and Robert W. Wallace, *Origins of Democracy in Ancient Greece* (Berkeley, 2007).

too conveniently selected to be convincing.[7] Schlomo Berger, in studying democracy in Greek cities in Sicily and Southern Italy, asserts that from early on Athens was the pattern for democracy there, one which other states merely imitated. Berger offers no proof for this claim but simply argues by assertion. Since Athens was "the foremost example of democracy," and the best attested historiographically, it must have provided the example that others followed.[8] Even J. L. O'Neil, whose study on the origins and development of democracy in Greece includes discussions of many non-Athenian cases – more than in Schuller or Berger, though many fewer than those discussed in the previous chapters here – frequently ties the rise and fall of classical democracy's fortunes to what is going on at any given time in Athens.[9]

There is abundant reason to question this orthodoxy. The vast majority of democratic examples discussed in the previous chapters did not, as best we can tell from the evidence, arise thanks to Athenian influence or intervention; other causes can be advanced with more support from the available sources. But before we consider these causes or alternative theories about what triggered the expansion of democracy in the Classical period generally, I will first present what seems to be the case for Athenian leadership, especially as concerns the fifth century, when Athens' power was at its height and democracy was expanding dramatically in Greece.

ATHENS AS DRIVER OF DEMOCRATIC GROWTH

There is, naturally, something to be said for the idea that the most famous and powerful *demokratia* in antiquity played a role in promoting governments like its own. For one thing, within its fifth-century Aegean empire, instances of Athenian encouragement of democracy can be documented in several cases. We know, for example, that Athens established democratic governments in fifth-century Erythrae, Miletus, Samos, and Paros after

---

[7] W. Schuller, "Zur Entstehung der griechischen Demokratie außerhalb Athens," in H. Sund and M. Timmermann, eds., *Auf den Weg gebracht, Idee und Wirklichkeit der Grundung der Universität Konstanz* (Konstanz, 1979), 433–47. Schuller bases his view in part on the assumption that Athens only became a true democracy itself thanks to external entanglements (the Persian Wars, the Delian League), and thus it makes sense to him that other democracies needed external impulses to democratize as well. See "Wirkungen des ersten attischen Seebunds auf die Herausbildung der athenischen Demokratie," in J. M. Balcer, ed., *Studien zum attischen Seebund* (Konstanz, 1984), 87–101.

[8] "Democracy in the Greek West," 303–14, quotation at 303. Similar assumptions about the effect of the Athenian example can be found in Caven, *Dionysius I*, 25–6, and A. Lintott, "Aristotle and Democracy," *CQ* 42 (1992), 114–28, at 124. On western Greek democracies, cf. Lombardo, "La democrazie," 77–106.

[9] *Origins and Development*, 47, 54–5, 76–8.

rebellions or revolutions in these cities. Not so well documented, but nevertheless likely, is early Athenian constitutional involvement in Amphipolis, Eretria, Hestiaea/Oreus, Mytilene, and Thasos.[10]

Moreover, there are numerous general statements in ancient authors indicating a pro-democratic stance by Athens, especially when dealing with its imperial subject states. Pseudo-Xenophon, writing in the last third of the fifth century, says more than once that, abroad, the Athenians tend to support the masses and attack the respectable (i.e., the elite classes likely to favor oligarchy); and they do so because it helps them preserve the empire, by making friends with that class of people corresponding to the one in charge at Athens (1.14, 1.16, 3.10–11). In the Aristotelian *Constitution of the Athenians*, we are told that the Athenians were very domineering in their empire, except for the few allies (Chios, Lesbos, Samos) which helped to guard the empire and were allowed to keep their existing constitutions – implying that all the others were fair game for "regime change" given the opportunity (24.2). Other authors make similar statements regarding Athens' tendency to promote democracies or democratic factions, especially when competing for influence with its great rival Sparta, which encouraged oligarchy among its allies. Thucydides testifies to this during the Peloponnesian War (3.82.1)[11] and Diodorus does so for the 370s or 360s (15.45.1). Aristotle echoes this general perception, stating in the *Politics* that the Athenians used to put down oligarchies and the Spartans democracies (1307b22–4). More vaguely, Lysias boasts in his funeral oration that during their period of naval domination the Athenians compelled their allies to live in equality (*to ison echein*) and kept the many from being enslaved to the few (2.55–6). Finally, Isocrates (4.103–6) makes the hyperbolic claim that Athens established its style of government in *all* cities of its empire – a demonstrably incorrect statement which echoes the more vague claims in the Lysian funeral oration (55–6); but both are evidence at least for the later perception among Athenians that their empire in its heyday had adopted an effective, pro-democratic policy.[12]

---

[10] See individual treatments in Chapter 3. Chalcis and Colophon also offer possibilities for Athenian constitutional intervention based on epigraphic documents, but the evidence is far from clear. See especially M. Ostwald, "Athens and Chalkis: A Study in Imperial Control," *JHS* 122 (2002) 134–43.

[11] Cases where the Athenians could be found supporting democratic factions (successfully or not) during the war include episodes involving Corcyra, Megara, and Boeotia. See discussions in Chapter 1, and below.

[12] See the discussion at the beginning of Chapter 3 for the alleged prevalence of democracy in the Athenian Empire. Assumptions by modern scholars that Athens aggressively pressed *demokratia* upon its allies go back a long way, at least as far as L. Whibley, *Greek Oligarchies, Their Character and Organisation* (London, 1896), 54–7.

There may also have been more subtle kinds of Athenian influence. As Greece's leading state in the fifth century – not just a military power, but a cultural and economic one as well – Athens certainly attracted attention, and political leaders elsewhere might have looked to it as an example, much as scholars like Berger have assumed. Athenian speakers occasionally boast of their city's prominence and political influence. Demosthenes at 24.210 claims that many Greeks were voting to adopt Athenian laws (*nomois*). More famously, and, with respect to the issue at hand, potentially of more importance given its earlier date, the funeral oration of Pericles would seem to attest a broad and specifically constitutional influence.[13] Thucydides at 2.37.1 reports that the Athenian leader said "Our constitution (*politeia*) does not copy the laws (*nomois*) of our neighbors; we ourselves are more a model (*paradeigma)* to some than an imitator of others."

One can point to occasional cases even beyond the empire where Athenian institutions seem to have been replicated and can surmise that the influence the orators spoke of might have been at work. As seen in Chapter 2, Diodorus claims that the Syracusans patterned their new law on petalism in the 450s after Athenian ostracism (11.86–7); and we know that Athens was a leader in the foundation of the Panhellenic colony at Thurii in southern Italy in the 440s, and that this colony's constitution had a democratic bent.[14] Byzantium in 390 makes for a clear example of fourth-century Athenian intervention and replication.[15] Closer to Attica, Athenians assisted indirectly in the democratic revolution in Thebes early in the fourth century; it may have done the same in the fifth century after Oenophyta, though this is far from clear.[16]

Even in the Peloponnese, the sphere of greatest influence of Athens' longtime rival Sparta, scholars have sometimes seen the hands of Athenians at work. The Argive democracy of the fifth century, like the one in Athens, used ostracism,[17] and some have thought that this and other similarities in the Argive and Athenian constitutions show Athenian influence. J. L. O'Neil sees suspicious commonalities in Argive *strategoi* as chief executive officials and the listing of the council before the magistrates (like Athens, unlike Elis and Mantinea) in an alliance document from 420 BC.[18]

---

[13] Discussed by Schuller, "Zur Entstehung," 441–2. P. J. Rhodes highlights the passage at the beginning of "The Impact of Athenian Democracy," in D. M. Lewis *et al.*, *CAH²*, vol. v (Cambridge, 1992), 87–95.
[14] Diod. Sic. 12.11.3.   [15] Xen. *Hell*. 4.8.27; Dem. 20.60. See Chapter 3.
[16] See discussion under Thebes and Boeotia in Chapter 1.
[17] Arist. *Pol*. 1302b18–19; scholion to Aristophanes, *Knights*, 855. See discussion in Chapter 1 under Argos, with the discovery of an Argive *ostrakon* possibly used in the procedure.
[18] Thuc. 5.59.5, 5.47.11. O'Neil, "Origins and Development," 41.

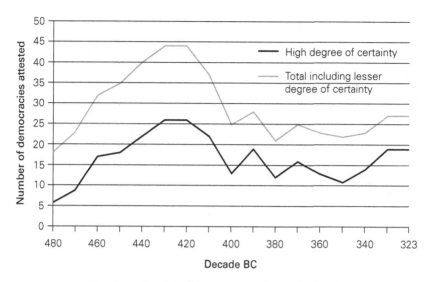

Figure 4.2 Number of democracies in Greece, by decade

Perhaps these should be connected with the time spent in Argos *c.* 470 by the famous Athenian politician Themistocles after his ostracism from Athens – he could have acted as a democratic agitator in the region, especially since Sparta seemed eager to see him off.[19] Later, democratic exiles from the Peloponnese sometimes fled to Athens: we know from an inscription that some Mantinean refugees from the Spartan invasion of 385 ended up in Athens,[20] which is not entirely surprising, since the Mantineans had appealed for Athenian help when Sparta first attacked. Though Athens did not, in fact, lend a hand in this case, or when the Arcadians sought their help in 370, it did so around 375 in Zacynthus, an island just off the west coast of the Peloponnese, helping to establish an opposition faction of democrats there.[21]

Finally, data from this very study could be seen as supporting the idea of an Athens-driven expansion of *demokratia*. Figure 4.2 shows the number of democracies in Greece decade by decade over the whole Classical era. One immediately notices a steep, sustained increase from the 470s to the 430s BC – a period precisely matching the rise and acme of the Athenian

[19] Thuc. 1.135.2–3; Plut. *Them.* 23. Andrewes, "Sparta and Arcadia," 1–5; W. G. Forrest, "Themistocles and Argos," 221–9.
[20] *IG* 2² 33.
[21] Diod. Sic. 15.45–6; Xen. *Hell.* 6.2.2. See discussion of Zacynthus in Chapter 1.

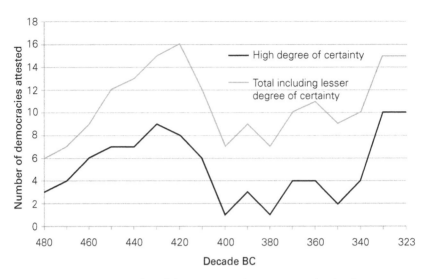

Figure 4.3 Number of democracies in the Aegean area, by decade

Empire. If Athenian force and prosperity truly did propel democracy's increase, one would expect the figure to look much like this, with peaking Athenian fortunes tracking closely with increasing Greek democratization. Figure 4.2, then, could be taken as statistical confirmation for Athens' influence over the process. (We will return to this figure presently.)

Adding up all these various events, statements, and data, from the examples of direct Athenian constitutional interventions to the various avenues for/indications of indirect Athenian influence, one can see why it is that people might assume a leading role for Athens in spreading democracy in the fifth and fourth centuries. But, in truth, the evidence listed above is far from conclusive. Not all of it can be accepted at face value; and even if it could, it need not lead to the conclusion that Athens served as the prime mover in the spread of *demokratia* in Greece.

Let us start by looking again at the evidence that went into Figure 4.2. To see whether one can conclude from it that Athens' Aegean empire was behind the spread of democracy, we need to break things down by region, comparing trends in numbers of democracies in the Aegean (the zone of Athens' imperial power and greatest influence) with the other regions of Greece (where Athenian reach was obviously more limited). Figures 4.3 and 4.4 do this. Figure 4.3 shows the changing numbers of democracies in the Aegean; 4.4 charts the numbers elsewhere in Greece. Even a quick glance

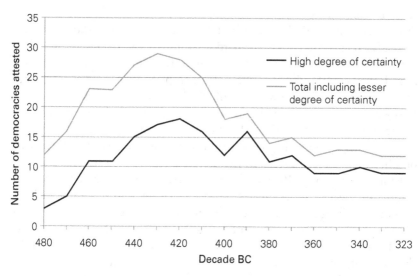

Figure 4.4 Number of democracies outside the Aegean area, by decade

reveals the problem with thinking that the combined data demonstrates Athenian influence over the process: *both* tables show similar bubbles of increasing numbers of democracies in the early and middle fifth century, which means that the Aegean region did not lead the way. If Athenian power and influence had truly been the key factor, we would have expected Aegean democracies to multiply earlier and more dramatically than elsewhere in Greece. But this was clearly not the case. In fact, looking more closely at the data, it is apparent that the rate of increase for non-Aegean Greece was slightly *steeper* than the Aegean, and the total number peaks around the same time or even earlier. Something that did not involve Athenian dominion had to be acting broadly across the rest of Greece to cause the dramatic rise in *demokratiai* outside Athens' Aegean power base.[22]

As for the literary testimony for Athenian influence, it is important to note first that in none of the passages cited above does any ancient author assert that Athens was attempting to spread democracy throughout the Aegean or Greece. No one makes this claim.[23] What our sources tell us,

---

[22] What this something (or things) was is discussed below. For the data that went into Figures 4.1–4, see the appendix. The spike in Aegean democratization at the end of the Classical period (absent elsewhere in Greece) relates to Alexander's efforts, also discussed below. My thanks to Heather Roberts for her work on these figures.

[23] The closest any text comes is, perhaps, the Lysian funeral oration at 55–6, where the speaker claims that Athens in the heyday of its naval supremacy made its allies free of faction (*astasiastous*), thought

at least when they provide explanations for the events they record, is that when Athens supported populist factions or governments it did so for military advantage or to better safeguard its empire. Pseudo-Xenophon claims that the Athenian *demos* tends to promote the worst (lower classes) and punish the best (the elites) in cities of the empire as the most effective way of preserving its own power.[24] Similarly, Aristophanes refers to Athenian mistreatment of the upper classes in allied states under the excuse of punishment for rebellious activity during the Peloponnesian War.[25] Any goal of promoting democratic government broadly in Greece or for the benefit of others beyond the Athenians themselves is nowhere indicated.

Moreover, even as Pseudo-Xenophon argues that this self-interested favoritism toward the poorer classes and factions is the natural inclination of the ruling *demos* at Athens, he notes that there are cases on record of the opposite taking place, mentioning Boeotia and Miletus.[26] As we saw in Chapter 1, it makes the best sense of the available sources to conclude that a weak Theban democracy collapsed after the battle of Oenophyta in 457, with the victorious Athenians choosing to support oligarchs. And Athens seems certain to have backed a ruling oligarchy at Miletus for years in the mid fifth century (Chapter 3). To these examples we should add the various Carian autocratic rulers whom Athens seemed happy to leave alone as they collected tribute from them over the years,[27] and also the case of Samos, where Athens either allowed an oligarchy to reassume control in 439, or allowed a democracy it helped to install at the time to be overthrown and replaced by an oligarchy at some point between 439 and 412 (Chapter 3).

The picture that emerges, then, is of a defensively motivated and, at best, inconsistently applied Athenian preference for democratic factions and governments, arising most often in the context of helping to keep hold of allied cities.[28] One might expect such practice to increase in time of threat to the empire, and, according to Thucydides, this is what happened in the era of the Peloponnesian War. After having described the initial stages of the bloody civil war between democratic and oligarchic factions

---

it wrong for the many to be enslaved to the few, and instead compelled that they live on equal terms (*to ison echein*). Whatever was meant by this claim, the biased point of view, blatant exaggerations, and many historical errors of the speech as a whole render it hard to credit.

[24] Ps.-Xen. *Ath. pol.* 1.14, 1.16, 3.10.   [25] *Peace*, 639–40.

[26] Ps.-Xen. *Ath. pol.* 3.10–11.   [27] R. Meiggs, *The Athenian Empire* (Oxford 1972), 54 5.

[28] Meiggs, *Athenian Empire*, 54–5, 208–13, also perceives something less than a consistently pro-democratic Athenian doctrine, particularly in the early decades of the empire. So too, on different grounds, K.-W. Welwei "'Demos' und 'Plethos' in athenischen Volksbeschlussen um 450 v. Chr.," *Historia* 35 (1986), 177–91.

in Corcyra, in which the Athenians played a role in supporting the populist faction, Thucydides states (3.82.1):

[The revolution] seemed the more [savage], because it was among the first that occurred; for afterwards practically the whole Hellenic world was convulsed, since in each state the leaders of the democratic faction (*hoi ton demon prostatai*) were at variance with the oligarchs (*hoi oligoi*), the former seeking to bring in the Athenians, the latter the Spartans. And while in time of peace they would have had no pretext for asking their intervention, nor any inclination to do so, yet now that these two states were at war, either faction in the various cities, if it desired a revolution, found it easy to bring in allies also, for the distress at one stroke of its opponents and the strengthening of its own cause.[29]

Thus only *after* the outbreak of war in 431 did the pattern form, says Thucydides; it was during the following twenty-seven years of conflict, with the survival of the Athenian Empire at stake, that opportunities arose for Athenian democratic favoritism to emerge more clearly.[30] Two of the most securely attested installations of *demokratia* by Athens (in Paros and Thasos, mentioned above and discussed in Chapter 3), and two unsuccessful attempts (in Megara and Boeotia, Chapter 1) take place during the war. Even during the war, however, there is reason for caution in assuming too much[31] about Athenian eagerness to intervene: in this passage Thucydides clearly places the initiative for the interventions in the hands of the local populist factions, not of Athens.[32] And at 1.19, where the historian compares Athenian and Spartan resources on the eve of war, he points to Spartan use of oligarchy to control its allies but says nothing about a corresponding Athenian policy of insisting upon democracy among

---

[29] C. F. Smith translation (*Thucydides*, Cambridge, MA, 1920), slightly modified. καὶ ἔδοξε μᾶλλον, διότι ἐν τοῖς πρώτη ἐγένετο, ἐπεὶ ὕστερόν γε καὶ πᾶν ὡς εἰπεῖν τὸ Ἑλληνικὸν ἐκινήθη, διαφορῶν οὐσῶν ἑκασταχοῦ τοῖς τε τῶν δήμων προστάταις τοὺς Ἀθηναίους ἐπάγεσθαι καὶ τοῖς ὀλίγοις τοὺς Λακεδαιμονίους. καὶ ἐν μὲν εἰρήνῃ οὐκ ἂν ἐχόντων πρόφασιν οὐδ' ἑτοίμως παρακαλεῖν αὐτούς, πολεμουμένων δὲ καὶ ξυμμαχίας ἅμα ἑκατέροις τῇ τῶν ἐναντίων κακώσει καὶ σφίσιν αὐτοῖς ἐκ τοῦ αὐτοῦ προσποιήσει ῥᾳδίως αἱ ἐπαγωγαὶ τοῖς νεωτερίζειν τι βουλομένοις ἐπορίζοντο. There are grammatical difficulties with the second sentence, especially regarding the phrase οὐδ' ἑτοίμων – there may be a manuscript error here, rendering the text uncertain. See Gomme, *Commentary on Thucydides*, vol. II, 372–3 and Hornblower, *Commentary*, vol. I, 480–1.

[30] M. Ostwald also argues that Athenian interest in establishing democracies among its allies did not predate the Peloponnesian War, though on slightly different grounds: "*Stasis* and *autonomia* in Samos," 51–66.

[31] Victor Hanson certainly assumes too much by occasionally claiming (with little supporting argument) that Athens sought to spread democracy – even to Sparta – and that the Peloponnesian War was in large measure about democracy. *A War Like No Other: How the Athenians and Spartans Fought the Peloponnesian War* (New York, 2005), 13–14, 104–5, 301–3. Stewart Flory has drawn attention to this mistake in his review of Hanson's book, *BMCRev* 2006.03.40.

[32] Such also was the case at Megara in 424 (Thuc. 4.64.3) and Boeotia in the same year (Thuc. 4.76).

its allies, instead talking only of Athenian acquisition of ships and tribute money.[33]

In all, then, even within the context of its own empire, we have many reasons to doubt that Athens followed a consistent policy of promoting democracy, judging both from general descriptions of Athenian practice and from particular cases of toleration or support for non-democratic regimes. Outside the Athenian sphere of influence, the case for such promotion as a tenet of state policy only becomes weaker. Inconsistency marked the Peloponnesian cases mentioned above: Athens was willing around 375 to assist democrats in Zacynthus, an island state and thus a perfect addition to their budding Second Sea League; but factions struggling for *demokratia* in the heart of the Peloponnese (Mantinea in 385, Arcadia in 370) had to look elsewhere. Clearly attested cases of Athenian constitutional interventions from the fifth or fourth centuries are rare, and suspected cases often have little to support them beyond guesses based ultimately on the (dubious) assumption that this was the sort of thing the Athenians did.[34]

How about the notion that the Argive democracy and institutions – and perhaps those of Elis and Mantinea as well – were spurred or influenced by Themistocles during that politician's sojourn in Argos sometime in the late 470s or early 460s?[35] In truth, there is no evidence whatsoever that the ostracized Athenian engaged in any political agitation at this time, democratic or otherwise.[36] Moreover, the chronology of events is

---

[33] καὶ οἱ μὲν Λακεδαιμόνιοι οὐχ ὑποτελεῖς ἔχοντες φόρου τοὺς ξυμμάχους ἡγοῦντο, κατ᾽ ὀλιγαρ-χίαν δὲ σφίσιν αὐτοῖς μόνον ἐπιτηδείως ὅπως πολιτεύσουσι θεραπεύοντες, Ἀθηναῖοι δὲ ναῦς τε τῶν πόλεων τῷ χρόνῳ παραλαβόντες πλὴν Χίων καὶ Λεσβίων, καὶ χρήματα τοῖς πᾶσι τάξαντες φέρειν. καὶ ἐγένετο αὐτοῖς ἐς τόνδε τὸν πόλεμον ἡ ἰδία παρασκευὴ μείζων ἢ ὡς τὰ κράτιστά ποτε μετὰ ἀκραιφνοῦς τῆς ξυμμαχίας ἤνθησαν (1.19). Bolmarcich, "Thucydides 1.19.1 and the Peloponnesian League," 5–34, does not argue the point made above, but her reading of the passage invites it.

[34] Thus with Athenian influence in: (1) the Black Sea, occasionally speculated upon with no direct support in the sources (see Chapter 3, under Olbia, Istrus, Tauric Chersonese, Heraclea), and (2) Greek Italy and Sicily, as put forward by Berger, "Democracy in the Greek West." In fact, only at Thurii is Athenian constitutional influence in the west certainly ascribable, and even there it is mitigated by the fact of being a joint venture with other cities and its influence on the result easily overestimated (see discussion in Chapter 2).

[35] Andrewes, "Sparta and Arcadia," 1–5; Forrest, "Themistocles and Argos," 221–9, as above. Skeptical is O'Neil, "Exile of Themistocles," 335–46; S. Brenne, "Thukydides 1, 135, 2–3 (ca. 431–395 v. Chr.): Die Ostrakisierung des Themistokles (470 v. Chr.)," in P. Siewert, ed., *Ostrakismos Testimonien I* (Stuttgart, 2002), 247–57. The Themistocles hypothesis is not helped by Cartledge's assumption that the Athenian must have had something to do with the Argive honorary decree for the *perioikos* Gnosstas *c*. 470, in *Sparta and Lakonia*, (2nd edn., London, 2002), 185–6. See discussions under the respective city-state headings in Chapter 1.

[36] The more general notion of Themistocles as a strong populist in his actions at Athens has also sometimes been attacked: J. Wolski, "Thémistocle était-il promoteur de la démocratie athénienne?," *Acta Antiqua Academiae Scientiarum Hungaricae* 32 (1989), 43–9.

not supportive of a Themistoclean wave of new *demokratiai*. Argos first democratized in the 490s (or possibly even earlier), in the aftermath of its defeat at the battle of Sepeia – not the late 470s or early 460s. And it is simply unknown when Mantinea and Elis turned to popular government. The former may have done so in the late sixth century; the case for neither is certain before the 420s; the year 471 comes up as a possibility only because Strabo (8.3.2) alleges that Elis synoecized around this time, which hardly need involve democratization, let alone democratization thanks to Themistocles.

Nor do Argive institutions themselves seem to reveal Athenian stimulus. Take the allegation of influence because both democracies featured power-ful boards of generals, a prominent council, and the use of ostracism.[37] This claim is most unconvincing, especially with respect to the first two. Elected generals are found in practically every democracy about which we know anything concerning officials, and they often played strong political roles; and councils were an essential component in almost every constitution to be found in Greece. The only Athenian institution, in fact, which one might reasonably speculate had been copied is ostracism: unlike generals or councils, this was a peculiar sort of institution, one that is harder to ima-gine developing independently. But three considerations suggest caution before we assume that Argos took the idea from Themistocles and Athens. First, chronology makes the priority of the Athenian practice uncertain. Allegedly an innovation of Cleisthenes, the Athenians first used ostracism only in 488/7.[38] Argos, as already noted, democratized in the 490s, or pos-sibly even in the late sixth century. That it used ostracism is claimed in two literary sources[39] and is supported by the discovery by excavators at Argos in 1985 of an ostrakon inscribed with a person's name. The sherd is fairly early, with the pot dating to the first quarter of the fifth century and the letter forms of the inscription suggesting the second.[40] Second, it seems highly unlikely that while in Argos Themistocles – a victim of ostracism himself at the time – would have agitated for its use there or anywhere else; if there was transmission, we must surely imagine some other mechanism.

---

[37] O'Neil, *Origins and Development*, 41, noted above.
[38] Arist. *Ath. Pol.* 22.3–4; Androtion, *FGH* 324 F6. See Rhodes, *Commentary*, 1993), 267–9, H. Taeuber, "Androtion *FgrHist* 324 F 6 (ca. 340 v.Chr): Die Einführung und erste Anwendung des Ostrakismos (488/7 v.Chr)," in P. Siewert, ed., *Ostrakismos Testimonien I* (Stuttgart, 2002), 401–12, and Forsdyke, *Exile, Ostracism, and Democracy*, 281–4, for discussion of the sources and, in particular, whether the Athenian law on ostracism was actually only instituted when it was first used in the early 480s, as Harpocration's text claims.
[39] Arist. *Pol.* 1302b18; scholiast to Aristophanes, *Knights* 855.
[40] Pariente, Piérart, and Thalmann, "Rapports . . . 1985," 764–5.

And, third, literary or archaeological evidence attests the use of ostracism or a similar practice in six different Greek states outside Athens (Argos, Cyrene, Megara, Miletus, Syracuse, and Tauric Chersonesus), and in only one case is the origin traced to Athenian influence (the problematic claim of Diodorus 11.86–7 regarding Syracusan petalism).[41] This raises the very real possibility that what came to be known as ostracism derived not from the Athenian model (or, for that matter, from any one of the other places where it is attested) but from an older Greek practice.[42]

Furthermore, other aspects of Argive institutions suggest that its democracy failed to mimic the Athenian one. Argive institutions are laid out in Chapter 1 and will be considered further in the next chapter, but it is worth pointing out some contrasts here: *artunai* instead of archons are the officials referred to most routinely in documents; there were five generals instead of ten; the assembly met and announced its decrees as the *aliaia* or the *aliaia teleia* or the *aliaia ton hieron*, not the *ekklesia* or *ekklesia kuria* or *ekklesia synkletos*; the formulae for inscribing state decrees differed; the Eighty had no direct parallel at Athens – if it was not a subset of the main council, one is hard pressed to discover any counterpart at all (a group designated by its number of members could hardly be composed of ex-magistrates like the Athenian Areopagus, for example); and the bronze financial documents that have recently come out of the ground at Argos confirm what had been suspected before: that councilors and most other officials served not one-year terms, as at Athens, but for only six months before being replaced.

In all these fundamental and highly visible ways, the Argive democracy does not bear any institutional resemblance to the Athenian one. Nor need we assume Argos's ostracism derived from Athenian practice. Together with the complete absence of direct evidence for Athenian stimulus (Themistoclean or otherwise), one can readily see the problem with attempts to explain the Argive *demokratia* by way of Athens.

Finally, with respect to orators' occasional remarks about Athenian constitutional influence abroad, one naturally must take such patriotic, self-congratulatory claims with a grain of salt. Demosthenes 24.210 (on the copying of Athenian laws by others) is vague in meaning and extent, and surely unreliable. Potentially weightier is the earlier statement Thucydides gives Pericles in the funeral oration about the Athenian democratic

---

[41] See discussion in Forsdyke, *Exile, Ostracism, and Democracy*, 285–7.

[42] Argued by Forsdyke, *Exile, Ostracism, and Democracy*, 283–8. "In general, consideration of the evidence from outside Athens suggests that Athenian ostracism was simply one elaboration of a more generalized Greek practice of using written ballots – whether leaves or potsherd – as a means of determining a penalty (removal from public office or exile)" (285).

paradeigma. But if we examine the passage carefully, we see that his claim is of more limited scope than is sometimes imagined. All Pericles actually says at Thucydides 2.37.1 is that, constitutionally, Athens did not copy its neighbors' laws and was a model for some rather than (or more than) an imitator of others: χρώμεθα γὰρ πολιτείᾳ οὐ ζηλούσῃ τοὺς τῶν πέλας νόμους, παράδειγμα δὲ μᾶλλον αὐτοὶ ὄντες τισὶν ἢ μιμούμενοι ἑτέρους. This boils down to a rather narrow statement, hardly a declaration of the Athenians' success (even less, of intent) in the projection of their constitution across Greece. And this comes in a speech that was an exercise in civic self-glorification intended to stir the patriotic feelings of Athenians assembled to commemorate those fallen in battle. One would expect, if anything, an exaggerated picture of Athenian stature and appeal.

Overall, then, the hypothesis that Athens drove the expansion of democracy throughout Classical Greece turns out to be extremely shaky. Even within the Athenian Empire, known cases of intervention in favor of *demokratia* are limited in number and must be considered alongside counter-examples where non-democracies were backed or tolerated for long periods of time; outside the realm of Athenian subjects, evidence is lacking to an even greater degree. Demonstrating an Athenian desire (let alone an established doctrine) to promote democracy generally in the Aegean or in Greece founders for absence of testimony. It is only with the coming of the Peloponnesian War in the last third of the century that evidence begins to accumulate for Athenian interventions – and yet between twenty-eight and forty-three of the fifty-four democracies charted on Figure 4.1 seem to have had their beginnings *before* 431. And as we have seen, the rapid democratization of the early to mid fifth century happens more urgently outside the Aegean than in it, which is not what one would expect if Athenian power drove the process.

The point here is not to deny that Athens played any role in expanding the reach of *demokratia* in Greece (it surely did; we will return to this later), but merely to show the inadequacy of the assumption that Athens acted as the prime mover in spreading Classical democracy. So what further or better explanations might there be for *demokratia*'s obvious growth during this period? I would propose two. The first is that in various regions of Greece, states other than Athens played vital roles in instigating democratic revolutions in their locales. With respect to the Peloponnese, Argos stands out, and it had help in the fourth century from the Thebans and Arcadians. In Sicily, one must look to Syracuse. And even in the Aegean, the home of what would become Athens' naval empire, one can point to the role Miletus played – and perhaps even the Persians – in encouraging a trend toward popular government before the Athenian Empire ever came to be. Let us examine the role of these regional leaders in promoting democratic governments, before turning to another, more generalized mechanism for classical democracy's growth.

SICILY

If one looks toward the western Greece portions of Figure 4.1, one immediately notices a pattern. In Sicily (and, to a lesser extent, neighboring southern Italy – Taras's long-running democracy is exceptional) the democracies are grouped overwhelmingly in the fifth century. That this coincides with the longest period of Syracuse's democracy is no accident. In book 11 of his history, Diodorus writes that after the inhabitants of Syracuse overthrew their tyrant ruler,[43] the victors did an extraordinary thing:

> The Syracusans, after having freed their country in this fashion, made an agreement allowing the [tyrant's] mercenaries to withdraw from Syracuse, and, having freed the other cities that had been ruled by tyranny or had garrisons, established democracies in the cities.[44]

As most Greek cities of Sicily had in recent years been controlled by tyrants, particularly those from Syracuse, this is a statement of wide application. As we saw in Chapter 2, the Syracuse-championed democratization will have included at a minimum the cities of Gela, Himera, and Selinous, and probably extended to Camarina, Leontini, and Messana as well (and to Rhegium in southern Italy). Acragas alone seems not to have owed its popular government to Syracusan intervention, as it threw out its tyrant and democratized a few years before Syracuse did. Diodorus goes on to state that Syracuse prospered after these efforts and maintained its own *demokratia* for almost sixty years. He also talks of the general prosperity that Greek Sicily enjoyed thanks to the liberation of the cities. Altogether, these passages would seem to establish clearly a leading role for Syracuse in spreading democracy in mid-fifth-century Sicily.

Scholars have not always accepted at face value Diodorus' claims about *demokratia*, however. David Asheri's *Cambridge Ancient History* article illustrates this line of argument in its assertion that it was not a question of

---

[43] Thrasyboulus (c. 466 BC). On the date see W. S. Barrett, "Pindar's Twelfth *Olympian* and the Fall of the Deinomenidai," *JHS* 93 (1973), 23–35.

[44] οἱ δὲ Συρακόσιοι τοῦτον τὸν τρόπον ἐλευθερώσαντες τὴν πατρίδα τοῖς μὲν μισθοφόροις συνεχώρησαν ἀπελθεῖν ἐκ τῶν Συρακουσῶν, τὰς δὲ ἄλλας πόλεις τὰς τυραννουμένας ἢ φρουρὰς ἐχούσας ἐλευθερώσαντες ἀποκατέστησαν ταῖς πόλεσι τὰς δημοκρατίας (11.68.5). See also 11.72 and 11.76.

actual democracy springing up in Syracuse and other area cities, but rather autonomous republics, perhaps with moderately oligarchic systems. These places were "liberated" primarily in the sense of being freed from tyranny and need not have been democratic internally.[45] We must consider this view before accepting Syracusan democratic leadership in the region.

Asheri's opinion stems in large part from his distrust of the term *demokratia* as used by Diodorus (who wrote centuries after the events), a term which in later times could stand for any kind of autonomous constitutional entity.[46] Caution is indeed called for. However, that the term might be applied to non-democracies in later Greek history does not mean that actual democracies were not involved here. Furthermore, Diodorus' chief sources for the period, Timaeus (350–260) and Ephorus (405–330), wrote much closer to the time in question than he did: Ephorus wrote in the late Classical period, and drew much from the still earlier Philistus, while Timaeus wrote not too long after Ephorus at the beginning of the Hellenistic period.[47] Since Diodorus is well known to have been more of an epitomator than a contributor of original material, there is no reason to believe that his use of constitutional terminology here does not stem directly from these earlier sources.[48]

Moreover, as was shown in the discussions in Chapter 2, corroborating evidence can be found in almost all of the individual cases of Sicilian democracy, including the most crucial one of all – Syracuse itself. There we can test Diodorus' use of the term *demokratia* and see that other ancient authors, most importantly Thucydides (who lived at the time and clearly knew much about Sicily and its history), described Syracuse as democratic and implies that its allied cities were too. Other, more indirect evidence strongly supports the constitutional testimony, especially regarding Syracuse.[49] We can therefore probably trust Diodorus when he applies the same term to the cities of Sicily undergoing Syracuse-inspired popular revolutions.

Finally, in the fourth century, after Syracuse succumbed once again to tyranny, evidence for democracy in other cities of Sicily declines to nil. Grey lines are replaced by blank whiteness in that section of Figure 4.1. Carthaginian wars destroyed some cities, and autocratic

---

[45] Asheri, "Sicily, 478–431 B.C.," 147–70.
[46] See also N. K. Rutter on Diodorus in "Syracusan Democracy," 137–51.
[47] On Diodorus' sources see Stylianou, "The Sources," in *Commentary*, 50–84.
[48] See Chapter 2, note 8.
[49] See also Robinson, "Democracy in Syracuse, 466–412 BC," 189–205, from which much of the argument of Chapter 2 has been adapted.

Syracusan belligerence probably ruined others. It is not impossible that *demokratia* persisted in some places, and by the middle of the century it does make a fitful comeback in Syracuse and, conceivably, elsewhere (see Chapter 2), but on the whole the sudden absence of testimony for popular government in Syracuse's period of Dionysian tyranny underscores the significant role that city played in encouraging or discouraging Sicilian popular government.

THE PELOPONNESE

Figure 4.1 tells a somewhat different story regarding democracy in the Peloponnese. The states that had democracies in that part of Greece generally retained them for long periods of time in the fifth century and, to a lesser degree, in the fourth as well. Argos maintained its popular government as long as and more consistently than any *polis* in the region. Elis and Mantinea also remained democratic for most of the Classical period, undergoing comparatively brief interludes of oligarchy in the fourth century. Achaea, too, seems to have been more consistently democratic in the fifth than the fourth century. But Peloponnesian states with shorter known periods of democracy generally experienced these periods in the fourth rather than the fifth century: Corinth, Phlius, and Zacynthus. The trend lines that emerge in the Peloponnese are therefore more complex than those from Sicily but nevertheless align to a large degree with the fortunes and practices of certain leading states, particularly Argos and Sparta.

Argos had the longest running *demokratia* in the region: it began with a revolution in about 494 (or somewhat earlier), and by the 460s had matured into the system most familiar from our sources. From that point onward we hear of only one change in Argos's constitution down to 322 BC: a Spartan-inspired oligarchic coup in 417 BC that did not survive the year. Traditions hold that Argos had contested with the Spartans for dominance in the Peloponnese for centuries. By the Classical period Sparta had become ascendant, and through most of this period maintained a fairly consistent policy of promoting oligarchies among its allies and others as well.[50] But Argos did not give up trying to assert its will or undermine Spartan control in the region. Democracy became a facet of this longstanding struggle, a new avenue through which Argos could seek to achieve its ends.

[50] Thucydides (1.19), Aristotle (1307b22–4) and Diodorus (15.45.1) inform us this was Sparta's general policy, and plentiful episodes in Thucydides, Diodorus, and Xenophon's *Hellenica* offer specific examples. Indeed, examples of Spartan intervention resulting in the imposition of oligarchic regimes (including decarchies) are far more numerous in the sources than Athenian ones installing *demokratia*.

Thucydides tells us that in 421 Argos aimed at achieving leadership over the Peloponnese for itself (*elpisantes tes Peloponnesou hegesesthai*, 5.28.2). The Argives proceeded to plot with the Corinthians to establish an alternative Peloponnesian alliance to that of the Spartans. The first state to sign up was Mantinea, and among the reasons given for their decision was that the Argives were "democratically governed like themselves" (29.1). Elis, almost certainly a democracy at this time, also joined (31.1). Other states wavered, including Boeotia and Megara. Why? According to Thucydides (31.6), it was because of the Argive democracy, which the oligarchic Boeotians and Megarians worried would suit them less well in an ally than the Spartan order. Eventually Corinth pulled out, and Argos's Peloponnesian power play suffered defeat at the battle of Mantinea in 418 – which was immediately followed by Sparta's fomenting of the oligarchic coup at Argos mentioned above. The non-democratic government failed to last, but the attempt itself further illustrates the degree to which Argos's identity as a democracy had become bound up in its struggle for power with the Spartans.

Other incidents from the fifth and fourth centuries demonstrate Argos's promotion of democratic elements in the Peloponnese. Argos is said to have been behind Mantinea's synoecism, or coalescing as a *polis* from smaller communities (Strabo 8.3.2), probably sometime after the Persian Wars, which may or may not have had constitutional implications. In the 390s, when Argos and Corinth found themselves working together against Sparta once again, far from pulling away from the Argive democracy, Corinth succumbed to it, and for a few years Corinth joined Argos in a kind of democratic *sumpoliteia*, or shared political community (see discussion in Chapter 1). When in 385 Sparta invaded Mantinea and overthrew the democracy there, we are told that they exiled sixty popular leaders and "Argolizers" (*ton Argolizonton kai ton tou demou prostaton*), directly associating Argive sympathizers with leaders of Mantinea's democracy. Sparta also reversed the (Argive-assisted) synoecism and split the *polis* of Mantinea into four or five villages.[51] What were these "Argolizers" doing to earn this label from Xenophon? We do not know. They were obviously closely associated with the most radical leaders of the city. They could have been accused of taking bribes from the Argives or otherwise trying to steer Mantinean policy in a pro-Argos and anti-Sparta direction. They also could have been agitating for a more populist form of *demokratia*: Mantinea, unlike Argos, was known for its unusually conservative style of democracy. Aristotle in

---

[51] Xen. *Hell.* 5.2.1–7; Diod. Sic. 15.5, 15.12; Paus. 8.8.7–10; Isoc. 4.126, 8.100; Polyb. 4.27.6, 38.2.11–12.

the *Politics* remarks upon it, calling it an example of the oldest (and, for him, the best) kind of democracy.[52] Perhaps the "Argolizers" were trying to open things up and remake the *politeia* more along the Argive model. Either way, Xenophon hints at illicit connections between Mantineans and Argives: before invading, since the Spartans accused the Mantineans of disloyalty to their alliance, and, specifically, of having sold grain to the Argives while Sparta was at war with them.[53]

After the Battle of Leuctra in 371, Sparta's domination of the Peloponnese was shattered by the Thebans, who then joined with Argos in supporting budding democracies in the region. The Arcadian League stands out here, for this new federal democracy worked closely with Argos and the Thebans in efforts to fight Sparta and support democratic regimes or factions in the Peloponnese. Examples include Phlius in 369, Sicyon in 368–7, Elis in *c.* 365 and possibly Pellene around the same time.[54]

In all, Argos's inspiration or sponsorship of democratic causes and alliances in the Peloponnese leaves no doubt that it made use of *demokratia* in its foreign policy, sometimes alone and sometimes in cooperation with other democratic states.[55] In doing so, Argos played a powerful role in the creation or maintenance of democracies in the region.

THE AEGEAN

It would go too far to claim that Athenian support for democratic factions and governments during its fifth-century empire, even if applied inconsistently and relatively late in its reign, did not over the years help to increase the number of democracies in the Aegean. Figure 4.1 shows that most of the democracies in the Aegean and Propontis certainly or probably had their beginnings in the fifth century rather than the fourth, and Athenian efforts to expand and keep control over its empire no doubt contributed to this result. Athens would not have had to intervene directly in every case: once favoritism toward democratic factions and government had become fairly well established (by the time of the Peloponnesian War), pressures will have mounted internally within the subject states to conform to the preferences of the regional hegemon.[56]

---

[52] 1318b6–27. See discussion in Chapter 1.

[53] Xen. *Hell.*, 5.2.2, with 4.7.2–7 for the Spartan invasion of Argos in 388.

[54] See entries in Chapter 1 for details. On Pellene, Xen. *Hell.* 7.2.11–14, 7.4.17–18.

[55] R. A. Tomlinson acknowledges a place for democratic politics as part of Argos's anti-Spartan foreign policy but only emphasizes it for the period 404–370 and makes unwarranted assumptions about the "moderate" nature of the government; *Argos and the Argolid*, chs. 9–13, 19.

[56] As the authors of the *ATL* put it, "We believe that the cities of the Empire were, for the most part, under democratic constitutions; some had had these constitutions imposed by Athens, others

However, it must be pointed out that the early momentum in the region toward popular government indicated by the figure did not come from imperial Athens alone. In fact, before the Delian League was even formed in 478, we have multiple indications that *demokratia* was spreading in the area. First of all, several examples from the sixth century show that the idea of popular government was not new to the region by the turn of the century.[57] Next, in 499 BC, the ruler of Miletus is said to have given up his tyranny, at least in word, and granted the Milesians "*isonomia*" – and then did the same for the rest of Ionia, driving out tyrants and establishing "*isonomia*" in cities generally, all in an attempt to get the populace of Ionia behind his cause, a rebellion from Persia (Herodotus 5.37–8). Now the Greek term *isonomia* has different possible connotations, but, as was discussed in Chapter 3, Herodotus uses the word as a virtual synonym for *demokratia* in parts of his history,[58] and in the context of 5.37–8 it seems clear that a constitutional descriptor is intended. At the very least, we can say that at this time several Ionian states overthrew their tyrants and introduced more egalitarian governments.

Moreover, this experiment did not end with the rebellion's defeat by the Persians. Herodotus (6.43) tells us that after the reconquest, the Persian general Mardonius himself deposed tyrants and established democracies – and Herodotus uses the word *demokratia* this time.[59] Thus, on the one hand, we find Miletus exercising its influence to spread popular government in the region at the very beginning of the fifth century, and then their Persian foes doing the same thing a few years later (perhaps acknowledging their mistake in having earlier relied on repressive tyrannies, and now experimenting with popular government as a way to try to diffuse future confrontations). Outside evidence to confirm this new impetus toward *demokratia* in particular cases is largely unavailable, though Cos could well be one.[60] Whatever the breadth of these twin sponsorships, there can be no doubt that when the Athenian Empire assumed control of the region decades later, democracy was already a presence.

(probably a great many) had adopted that form of polity without pressure from Athens... But during the Empire democracy was not only the fashion, it was no doubt expedient"; Meritt *et al.*, *The Athenian Tribute Lists*, vol. III, 154. R. Legon well illustrates the politics involved in democracies attempting to hold out within the Spartan sphere of influence and oligarchies in the Athenian during time of war in "Megara and Mytilene," 200–25, esp. p. 222.

[57] See the possible cases of early *demokratia* in Chalcis, Chios, Cnidus, Naxos, and Samos described in Chapter 3 of Robinson, *First Democracies*.

[58] See discussions of Abdera/Teos and Miletus in Chapter 3. The passages in Herodotus showing the near-synonymous use are 3.80 and 6.43.3.

[59] See the entry for Abdera/Teos in Chapter 3 for discussion of this passage.

[60] Robinson, *First Democracies*, 103–4.

Finally, when it comes to the fourth century, another non-Athenian agent proved to be a major force for democratization: Alexander of Macedon. As Figure 4.1 shows, there occurs a noticeable surge of new or renewed democracies in the late 330s, coinciding with the time Alexander liberated many Greek states in the course of his invasion of Persian-dominated Asia Minor. The key passage attesting this process overall is Arrian, *Anabasis* 1.18.1–2. It describes Alexander sending out forces across Aeolia and Ionia in the aftermath of his capture of Ephesus in 334: "And he ordered the oligarchies everywhere to be overthrown, and democracies (*demokratias*) to be set up."[61] While corroboration of this policy is only to be gained piecemeal (see treatments of Ephesus, Erythrae, Miletus, and Rhodes in Chapter 3), there is no reason to doubt Alexander authored such a policy, and the resulting trend cannot be missed.

So we see that there were a significant number of state actors involved in spreading democracy during the Classical period in various regions across Greece. Athens surely was important in the context of its Aegean empire, but it had a late start even there, and elsewhere (and in the fourth century generally) other states collectively played a more powerful role. That multiple states contributed to such a large-scale process only stands to reason, and the evidence, once collected toward this purpose, is rather overwhelming. One suspects that, even more than the power of its fifth-century empire, Athens' massive overrepresentation in the available literary and epigraphic sources is the main reason why this single city has stood so far above the rest in the scholarly imagination as instigator of *demokratia*.

But the growth of democracy in Greece almost certainly involved more than just direct sponsorship by regional powers. Such a hegemonic explanation seems insufficient to account for all of the populist movements and governments shown to have arisen in the previous chapters. For one thing, *demokratia* did not arise in Greece in the sixth century thanks to a great patron; rather, it had shown itself to be a self-propagating phenomenon, appearing in widely separated parts of the Greek world thanks to independent developments within city-states across Greece.[62] Thus there is no *a priori* reason to think hegemonic intervention from an Argos, Syracuse,

---

[61] καὶ τὰς μὲν ὀλιγαρχίας πανταχοῦ καταλύειν ἐκέλευεν, δημοκρατίας δὲ [τε] ἐγκαθιστάναι (1.18.2).

[62] This is the main conclusion of Robinson, *First Democracies*, ch. 4. For an interesting modern comparison, see S. P. Huntington's discussion of how countries across the world tended to adopt democracy in the late twentieth century without foreign imposition or decolonization in "How Countries Democratize," in Xiaobo Lü, ed., *Promise and Problems of Old and New Democracies* (New York, 2000), 81–118.

Athens, or Alexander would have been required to explain democracy's continuing expansion in the fifth and fourth centuries. With respect to those Classical *demokratiai* that appeared without any attested outside instigation – perhaps twenty-three of the cases explored in previous chapters[63] – one must ask, then, how it was that these cities came to popular government. Given the breadth of democracy's eventual reach across Greece, extending through and beyond areas of hegemonic influence by democratic powers, surely something subtle and generalized must have been happening alongside the direct interventions to make democracy seem an increasingly familiar and viable governing option – a constitutional form that ordinary citizens or would-be leaders of a Greek *polis* might hear about, aspire to, or indeed fight for, with or without outside assistance, if the opportunity arose.

PEER POLITY INTERACTION AND THE EXPANSION OF CLASSICAL *DEMOKRATIA*

The most promising framework for illustrating how a process of increasing democratic awareness and normalization could have unfolded in Greece is peer polity interaction, a concept that historians developed to explain large-scale changes over time among the Greek city-states. John Cherry, Colin Renfrew, and Anthony Snodgrass pioneered this theory to explain how it was that peer polities – autonomous political communities of roughly equivalent size – might interact to develop along very similar lines politically, culturally, and technologically, *without* undergoing conquest by more advanced entities. The experience of Archaic Greece in particular required explanation: how did the Greek *poleis* develop in parallel as they did while retaining their autonomy?[64] Peer polity interaction answers the question by pointing to such processes as warfare, competitive emulation, symbolic entrainment (i.e., the adoption of advanced symbolic systems by peer communities), transmission of innovation, and increased flow of exchange of

---

[63] A list of states probably or certainly turning to democracy at least once in the Classical period without attestation of direct intervention by a regional power could include: Argos, Achaea, Elis, Leucas, Megara, Phlius, Sicyon, Thebes, Plataea, Syracuse, Acragas, Croton, Tarentum, Corcyra, Epidamnus, Cyrene, Cos, Heraclea Pontica, Iasus, Rhodes, Hestiaea/Oreus, Istrus, and Miletus. This grouping must be considered tentative, however: it excludes some cases where there is no attested outside intervention but such seems probable, and it includes some cases where such interventions were certainly possible and the silence of our scanty sources cannot carry great weight. See Chapters 1 through 3 for discussions of the individual cases.

[64] C. Renfrew and J. F. Cherry, eds., *Peer Polity Interaction and Socio-Political Change* (Cambridge, 1986). See especially Renfrew and Cherry's "Introduction: Peer Polity Interaction and Socio-Political Change," 1–18, and A. Snodgrass, "Interaction by Design: The Greek City State," 47–58.

goods. As a result of such processes, it is asserted, one finds dramatic commonalities in Greek city-state developments down through the Archaic period, including: strikingly similar artistic monuments, like the kouroi, being found across Greece; the practice of hoplite warfare, in all its peculiarity in the Mediterranean context; the development of the Greek alphabet; parallel *polis* institutions being replicated by means of colonial initiatives from many different cities; codified law appearing in many *poleis* together with traditions about the travels of great lawgivers; monumental temples built along similar lines being constructed all over Greece; collective changes in pottery art styles; and the growth of Delphi and Olympia as central spaces for communication and competitive display.

John Ma has developed the idea of peer polity interaction further by applying it to the cities of the Hellenistic world.[65] The purpose differs in this period: rather than seeking to explain parallel change over time, Ma uses the theory to emphasize and reconceptualize the lively ongoing *polis* networks operating in the period – a period in which "superpowers" (the great Hellenistic kingdoms, regional leagues, and eventually Rome) played strong, even dominating roles, and yet did not inhibit a constant, ongoing and vital interaction between city-states. He highlights such political and cultural practices as invitations of panels of judges or arbitrators from other cities, the production of matching honorific decrees (i.e., one city's honor for an outstanding citizen is repeated in a corresponding decree from another city),[66] negotiations of *asulia* (inviolability) between cities, the diplomacy of asserted kinship to connect cities, the settling of regional conflicts by complex multi-city brokered treaties, and visits from city to city by *theoroi* with various ensuing entertainments, exchanges, gestures, and honors. A network of peer interaction can be illustrated in the artistic realm as well, as with the building of monumental altars *c.* 200 BC and thereafter in various cities of Asia Minor and the islands, which seems not to have imitated one royal model but to have arisen as an independent, interconnected phenomenon.[67] In all, the various means and languages of networking Ma explicates as part of Hellenistic peer polity interaction can

[65] J. Ma, "Peer Polity Interaction in the Hellenistic Age," *P&P* 180 (2003), 9–39, inspired by Renfrew and Cherry's book, but also A. H. M. Jones' "The Hellenistic Age," *P&P* 27 (1964), 3–22 and the work on Hellenistic cities by Philippe Gauthier (see Ma, "Peer Polity Interaction," 13, n. 4).
[66] The example Ma traces in detail (at "Peer Polity Interaction," pp. 15–16) is Priene and Iasos in 196, citing Blümel, ed., *Inschriften von Iasos*, 73, and C. V. Crowther, "Iasos in the Second Century BC, III: Foreign Judges from Priene," *BICS* 40 (1995).
[67] Ma, "Peer Polity Interaction," 25, drawing upon A. Linfert, "Prunkaltäre," in M. Wörrle and P. Zanker, eds., *Stadtbild und Bürgerbild im Hellenismus* (Munich, 1995).

be seen to have vitally connected the cities while it conferred a kind of parity upon them.

Ma believes that similar networks existed in the preceding Classical period, even though the evidence for their operation is not as rich.[68] He is surely correct in this judgment. Indeed, it would be extremely surprising if peer interactions that helped to shape the nature of the *polis* in the Archaic period, and later sustained city-state vigor in the Hellenistic period, somehow disappeared in the intervening two hundred years. And, of course, we know that many of the specific practices highlighted in the studies by the scholars noted above continued in the Classical era (see below).

How, then, might we trace the impact of peer polity interaction upon the spread of *demokratia*? The potential explanatory power of the model is obvious, and the fact of democracy's growth has been established here already. What remains to be discussed is which strands of city-state inter-action seem most likely to have facilitated an expanding awareness of *demokratia* and conduced to its normalization as a constitutional type within the networked world of the Greek *poleis*.

A number of Greek practices and behaviors, some noted in earlier stud-ies, others not, stand out as likely conduits of political exchange in the Classical era, exchange that, as democratic states and their citizens par-ticipated in it, will have inevitably broadened the understanding (though not necessarily the immediate approval) of democracy and its ideals. The major Panhellenic religious centers and festivals certainly provided con-stant opportunities for exchanges of political views and experiences, pos-itive and negative. Anthony Snodgrass places great emphasis on the role Delphi and Olympia played in the Archaic period (which continued into the Classical era too) both as central clearing houses for information on a variety of matters, including political ones, and as premier sites for *polis* self-glorification and competition through dedications, as the many rich treasuries demonstrate.[69]

Snodgrass also emphasized the highly conventional, almost ritualized elements of hoplite combat as a result of peer polity interaction; but hoplite warfare and warfare in Greece more generally should also be noted as a rich source of shared knowledge and experiences which, at times, had strongly

---

[68] Ma, "Peer Polity Interaction," 34–5. Ma also notes the countervailing, dominant models of hege-mony by Athens, Sparta, and Thebes that may have interfered to some degree in the workings of peer polity interaction in the Classical period, 35–6. It seems unlikely, however, that the influence of these relatively small-scale hegemonies inhibited *polis* interactions to a greater degree than the vast Macedonian monarchies or the Roman Empire did in the Hellenistic era.

[69] Snodgrass, "Interaction by Design."

political dimensions. Warfare between *poleis* was endemic in Greek history, and typically involved a great deal of political exchange before, during, and after the actual combat, from back-and-forth diplomatic missions over cause, to the intermingling of leaders and troop detachments from different *poleis* as cities lined up in groups in many major battles, to the post-combat negotiations over the return of bodies, to the exchanges or ransoming of prisoners after hostilities ceased.[70]

One might also point to Greek social conventions facilitating contact between different *poleis* – *proxenia* institutionally, and, in a more general sense, guest-friendship (*xenia*), to include the welcoming of political exiles from other cities for years at a time – ubiquitous and ever-present means for experiences of different political orders to be shared. The elite classes will be overrepresented in these and other means of inter-*polis* contact, which only magnifies the potential impact of the knowledge transferred since they represent the most active classes politically in democracies and, even more, in non-democracies.

Such well-understood religious, military, social, and political channels of exchange across *polis* boundaries formed major parts of the network of peer polity interaction that existed in Greece. In all, they will have contributed to an expanding consciousness of what democratic government looked like institutionally and ideologically across the Greek world, which, over time, helped to normalize a constitutional order that was relatively rare at the beginning of the Classical period. They also will have opened conduits for political actors in cities governed by non-democratic constitutions to learn enough about *demokratia* to envision its potential implementation locally should opportunities arise. Operating alongside the more direct action of hegemonic democratic powers, peer polity interaction will thus have made indirect yet broadly based contributions to the spread of democracies.

To illustrate in greater detail an example of how peer polity interaction could have assisted in democracy's expansion, let us consider another medium, one that other scholars have not discussed with respect to these issues: the activities of the sophists in the fifth century.[71] The sophists, those widely traveled teachers and intellectuals so despised by Plato, may in fact

---

[70] The Corinthians' use of captured Corcyrans to foment political revolution in Corcyra upon their return home (Thuc. 3.70.1, noted in the Corcyra entry in Chapter 1) is perhaps the most striking exploitation on record of the political possibilities of prisoner holding and exchange, even if the example here involves an oligarchy's attempting to undermine democracy, not the reverse. Less extreme political contacts and interactions between prisoners and victors as a result of wars will have been routine, which ultimately may have had greater impact over time than specific, short-term plotting.

[71] The following draws heavily on my article "The Sophists and Democracy Beyond Athens," 109–22.

have been agents in spreading democratic thinking in Greece, not because this was their purpose, but because of their backgrounds, the connections they utilized, and the information and techniques they shared.

The idea that the older sophists and Greek democracy were in some way connected is not entirely new, of course. Scholars have often seen links between the two. The most common approaches, however, have been either to sift through what little we know about the opinions of the sophists to see how well they accord with a democratic ideology, or to discuss the conditions in fifth-century Athens (where many of them spent time) to gauge what effect the democratic constitution there had in attracting them to the city or in nourishing their practice once they arrived. In general, the conclusions have been positive about a connection on both counts. Edward Schiappa in his study of *Protagoras and* Logos, for example, concludes that the older sophists in general and Protagoras in particular advanced the cause of democracy in terms of theory.[72] Reimar Müller concurs, arguing that the political positions of the sophists showed support for the concept.[73] As for the Athenian democracy, G. B. Kerferd states that Athens "was the real centre of the sophistic movement."[74] Without Athens, he doubts the movement would have existed at all, and he credits both the democratic constitution and Pericles for making it so. Jacqueline de Romilly agrees, stating that only Periclean Athens could provide the necessary catalyst, and claiming that its "uncharted path" of democracy would have been irresistible to those "frustrated by the oppression of tyranny or the rigidity of oligarchy in their own homelands."[75]

However, in concentrating solely on trying to recover the ill-attested political positions of the sophists, or on Athens' role in providing a congenial setting for them, we pass over a potentially more fundamental democratic connection. That is, we should ask in what kind of political context did the older sophists first develop their ideas and practices? As is well known, most of the early sophists came from outside Athens and developed reputations as thinkers, speakers, and teachers before ever reaching Attica. Robert Wallace underscores this point in his article "The Sophists in Athens": he notes that, despite the Athenocentrism of our sources, they make it quite clear that most of the famous sophists came from outside Athens, which for many of them was just one stop on the lecture circuit, as it were. Furthermore, the intellectualism the sophists represented had

---

[72] Schiappa, *Protagoras and* Logos, 168–71.

[73] R. Müller, "Sophistique et Démocratie," 179–93.

[74] G. B. Kerferd, *The Sophistic Movement* (Cambridge, 1981), 15.

[75] J. de Romilly, *The Great Sophists in Periclean Athens*, trans. J. Lloyd (Oxford, 1992), 18, 19–22.

precursors from all over the Greek world. We ought not, therefore, simply assume a formative role for Athens and its democracy.[76]

Indeed, taking Wallace's article as a cue, we can see that focusing on Athens as the birthplace of the sophists makes little sense. What can be said about their true originating environments? Is it right to talk of the sophists, as Romilly does, as having to escape to Athens to avoid "the oppression of tyranny or the rigidity of oligarchy"? In fact, not at all. When we consider the cases of the older sophists, of whom any canonical list would include Protagoras, Gorgias, Prodicus, Hippias, Thrasymachus, and perhaps Antiphon, we immediately notice that all of these men came from states which certainly or probably practiced *demokratia* during the time of their early careers. Antiphon, as an Athenian, needs no further discussion. But let us take a quick look at the background of the others.

Protagoras is often thought of as the first sophist, though given the difficulties in deciding which early intellectuals deserve the label "sophist" and which do not – another of Wallace's points of emphasis – one should perhaps not insist on that honor for Protagoras. He is thought to have lived roughly from 490 to 420 BC, and he came from the *polis* Abdera, also the home of Democritus.[77] As we have seen (Chapter 3), Abdera presents a very strong case for democracy from the 490s, or at least by the second quarter of the fifth century, until the end of the Athenian Empire. That we have some reason to think Protagoras probably supported *demokratia* (as Democritus more certainly did) is unusual among the sophists. Farrar goes so far as to call him "the first democratic political theorist in the history of the world."[78] While this may be true, it is not essential to the issue at hand – a sophist could benefit and learn from a democratic system, with its popular courts, assemblies, widely distributed offices, *parrhesia* (free speech), and suchlike, without necessarily approving of it, and indeed Protagoras is one of the very few sophists that we *can* surmise was a supporter.[79]

Gorgias of Leontini was of the same generation as Protagoras, born sometime around 485. The testimonia we have associate him with a number of other Sicilian thinkers. He was supposedly a student of Empedocles of

[76] R. W. Wallace, "The Sophists in Athens," in D. Boedeker and K. A. Raaflaub, eds., *Democracy, Empire, and the Arts in Fifth-Century Athens* (Cambridge, MA: Harvard University Press, 1998), 203–22.

[77] Mejer, "Democritus and Democracy," 1–9.

[78] Farrar, *Origins of Democratic Thinking*, 77. See also Schiappa, *Protagoras and Logos*, 168–71; R. Müller, "Sophistique et democratie."

[79] Some have argued for Gorgias being a liberal thinker and thus perhaps pro-democratic, though skepticism is probably in order; S. Consigny, *Gorgias, Sophist and Artist* (Columbia, SC: University of South Carolina Press, 2001), 117–18.

Acragas.[80] He also is said to have taught another Acragantine, Polus.[81] He is further alleged to have interacted with rhetorical pioneers Tisias and Corax of Syracuse. One of the traditions associating him with them has Gorgias and Tisias together going on the famous diplomatic mission to Athens in 427; another has Gorgias bringing Corax's rhetorical manual with him on that trip.[82] Gorgias became a great traveler and moneymaker, enough for Isocrates to snipe at him by saying he never stayed anywhere long enough to pay taxes on his enormous income.[83] But before his broader travels in Greece we must assume that the community he knew best was Greek Sicily, in particular the cities Leontini, Acragas, and Syracuse given his origin and associations. The evidence indicates that all three of these communities had democratic governments by the 460s (see treatments in Chapter 2), and thus Gorgias will have developed his career in democratic settings. That he was well known in political circles at Leontini, where his citizenship would have allowed him full political participation, is suggested by the fact that he was chosen for the diplomatic mission to Athens in 427, allegedly for his effectiveness as an assembly speaker.[84] This background nicely matches the words put in his mouth by Plato in the *Gorgias*, on those occasions when the great sophist is made to describe the utility of his art. Repeatedly Gorgias describes the rhetoric he teaches as useful in courtrooms, in meetings of popular assemblies, in council sessions – anywhere that *ta plethe* (the masses), or *oi ochloi* (the mobs), are present to be persuaded.[85] In the *demokratiai* of his Sicilian homeland he would have had plenty of opportunity to practice his craft, and see it practiced by others.

Hippias, Prodicus, and Thrasymachus, as far as we can tell, were born and reached their acme slightly later than Protagoras and Gorgias, but they were all active in the mid-to-late fifth century and are counted among the most influential early sophists. There is no particular reason to believe they supported democracy, but that is irrelevant to the argument being made here.

Hippias, the polymath and mnemonic specialist, came from Elis, a state he is said to have represented on diplomatic missions all over Greece,

---

[80] DK 82 A2, A3, A14.   [81] DK 82 A2; Plato's *Gorgias*.

[82] DK 82 A2; Paus. 6.17.7–9. Cosigny, *Gorgias*, 111. Some scholars have come to doubt whether Tisias and Corax actually authored the seminal works attributed to them or even whether they were two separate people. See Cole, *Origins of Rhetoric*, 22–9, 53–4, 82–3 and "Who was Corax?," 65–84; Schiappa, *Beginnings of Rhetorical Theory*. What exactly they wrote or even whether they were one or two men is not important for my purpose here, which is simply to note Gorgias' connections to them and thus to Syracuse according to the traditions about him.

[83] 15.15.   [84] Plato, *Hippias maior* 282b–c. Cosigny, *Gorgias*, 111.   [85] 452e, 454b, 456b.

suggesting a degree of involvement in city politics.[86] Elis probably adopted democracy in the late sixth or the early-to-mid fifth century and was still popularly governed in the later fifth century down into the fourth, as is discussed in Chapter 1.

Prodicus' homeland, the island of Ceos off the Attic coast, affords less constitutional information than those of the other sophists for the fifth century and is not treated in earlier chapters of this book. All we know for sure is that the four cities of the island, either singly or together, were members of Athens' Delian League. It is also possible that there was a federation of some kind uniting the four cities. Inscriptions from the late fifth and fourth centuries throw a little more light on the subject. For a time there was a confederation; more importantly, the decree formula for all the cities (individually and collectively) is a democratic one and copies the form of Athenian decrees: *edoxe tei boulei kai toi demoi*, "resolved by the council and the people." One of these dates back to the late fifth century.[87] Also worth noting about the decrees is the evident servility toward Athens – one document records approval of an Athenian demand to be the sole recipient of Ceos' ruddle export (ruddle is a red ochre used as a dye); another settles affairs on the island after an abortive revolt against the second Athenian naval league. One would expect Ceos to have been at least as vulnerable to Athens' commands during the openly imperial Delian League of the fifth century, and thus also liable to the democratic influence on its government; but nothing can be proved.[88] For Prodicus' part, the sophist is recorded as having served on multiple missions representing the Ceans in Athens and speaking before the council there. As with most of the others, this bespeaks a certain degree of political involvement in his native land.

Finally, Thrasymachus of Calchedon, according to the traditions, was an expert rhetorician who wrote on the subject as well as taught it. The testimonia specify his familiarity with all three categories of rhetoric – epideictic, dikanic, and symbouleutic – implying some personal experience in each setting. Strong evidence for Calchedonian *demokratia* exists only for the fourth century, but it is commonly (and not unreasonably) assumed to have been democratic during Athens' Empire in the fifth century (see discussion in Chapter 3).

In sum, an obvious pattern emerges from this discussion of the background of the older sophists: *demokratia* was the likely governmental form

---

[86] DK 82 A2.   [87] *Syll.*[3] 1218.

[88] On the Cean state, see G. Reger in *Inventory*, 747–51; Rhodes and Osborne, *Greek Historical Inscriptions*, 196–209; Rhodes, *Decrees*, 223–8; Ch. Papageorgiadou-Banis, "Koinon of the Keians? The Numismatic Evidence," *Revue Belge de Numismatique* 139 (1993): 9–16.

in the home state of every one of them in the period in their lives when they will have been embarking on their careers and establishing their reputations. The evidence is weaker for Prodicus and Thrasymachus than for Protagoras, Gorgias, Hippias, and Antiphon, but the overall picture is impossible to miss. Romilly, therefore, was almost certainly wrong to suggest that sophists flocked to Athens "frustrated by the oppression of tyranny or the rigidity of oligarchy in their own homelands." On the contrary, while Athens may have formed a congenial environment, it was also a relatively familiar environment, politically speaking.

But if Romilly is wrong to have assumed a uniquely attractive constitutional setting in Athens for the sophists, the above results also show that she and other scholars have been right to stress the importance of democracy itself in encouraging sophistic discourse.[89] The reasons for this encouragement follow naturally. Popular government in Greece meant large-scale public involvement in judicial proceedings, in debates over policy, and in magisterial boards, whether elective or chosen by lottery (see next chapter). Institutions such as these naturally create a need for the kinds of skills most sophists are said to have taught. These included rhetorical techniques tailored for different settings, such as the courtroom, in case one is sued or is suing someone else, or the council chamber or assembly hall, whether one makes a speech or wishes to evaluate the speeches of others. More broadly, one can see how interest would arise in other, more abstract issues associated with the sophists, including the truth or falsity of language, or ethical standards, or the nature of the human community, when so many more citizens are involved in the process of politics and arguing about the public welfare than would be the case in oligarchies or tyrannies. Sophistic questions and interests could arise in non-democracies too, of course, and no doubt did (we know sophists visited oligarchies as well as democracies);[90] but democracies, with their vastly enlarged pool of politically engaged citizens, not to mention their litigiousness, their sycophants, and their demagogues, provided an ideal venue for them.

But we can go a step farther than this: the sophists did not merely learn from the democratic conditions they found themselves in early in their careers but surely played a role in continuing to spread those conditions.

---

[89] Plato, at *Republic* 492–3, articulates in a hostile way the close association between the sophists and the popular "teachings" of the democratic *polis*. See comments by J. Ober in "The Athenian Debate over Civic Education," in J. Ober, ed., *Athenian Legacies* (Princeton, 2005), 128–56, at 144–6.

[90] Gorgias, for example, is said to have impressed the leading Thessalians when he was there (Plato, *Meno* 70 b–c; see also Aristotle, *Pol.* 1275b26–30). It would be speculative in the extreme to make a connection between his activity and later populist movements there (see entry on Thessaly in Chapter 1).

They supply a further example of peer polity interaction at work in the political sphere. The sophists were a group of itinerant intellectuals who learned and taught techniques of popular political power. It does not matter for our purposes if they thought this was what they were doing, or even if they were supporters of democracy themselves. Nor do we have to cast them in the role of law-code designers for colonies (though Protagoras allegedly was, for democratic Thurii – see Chapter 2). Nothing so formal is required. Simply by traveling all around Greece, awing large crowds, and instructing smaller groups of well-to-do students in techniques useful for getting ahead in open political arenas, they maximized Greece's exposure to ideas and practices born in and suited to democratic milieux. The sophists' early immersion in popular government made them veritable ambassadors of democratic perspectives wherever they went, not because they proclaimed the virtues of *demokratia*, but because of the democracy-honed techniques for success that they taught. Thus, wittingly or not, they will not only have normalized democratic ideas and practices, but probably also helped to plant the seeds for new democracies where the constitutional form had not yet reached and for a more radical practice of it where *demokratia* already existed.

CONCLUSION

The activities of the older sophists in the fifth century exemplify, as one strand of a much larger network, how peer polity interaction can provide a generalized explanation for the spread of democracy in Classical Greece. Working as a background force, the operation of peer polity interaction will have helped to lay the groundwork for democracy's growth through the promotion of awareness of its ideals and practices all across Greece, especially among the classes of *polis* citizens most likely to involve themselves in political matters. When combined with the inherent turbulence of the internal politics of city-states in Greece, and the manifest acts of democratic support by local hegemons in different regions of Greece, one arrives at a suitably broad description of processes to account for the large-scale phenomenon that the expansion of Classical *demokratia* represents. Athens played a prominent role in these processes, both as one of the regional hegemons and as a participant in peer polity interaction, but it would be a mistake to see it in itself as the chief cause of the democratic transformations remaking much of the Greek political world in the fifth and fourth centuries.

CHAPTER 5

The nature of Classical democracy outside Athens

In the previous chapter we examined the big picture of Greek democratic expansion in the fifth and fourth centuries, recognizing its extent and assessing its causes. This final chapter will tackle another large issue: how might we describe the functioning of democracy outside Athens in the Classical period? While other scholars have occasionally touched upon this issue in broad studies of Greek politics or democracy, none have addressed it in detail.[1] The fifty-four cases of *demokratia* examined in Chapters 1 through 3 provide a greater variety and quantity of material to work with than previous scholars had available, and they will enable us to attain a better understanding of the nature of democracy as it applied across the Greek world than earlier studies.

The task is complicated by the nature of the material. Not without reason have scholars mostly avoided comparison of different Classical democracies: beyond Athens, the source material declines alarmingly in quantity. But it is not just an issue of quantity. The bits and pieces of testimony that survive vary in type from place to place. Syracuse, for example, has a fair amount of ancient historical narrative concerning major political events, but no inscriptions to help us understand its day-to-day institutional procedures. Meanwhile, at Iasus and similar places, inscriptions detail valuable information about the routine function of the democratic government there, but we lack any narrative accounts concerning political attitudes or political change over time. And for no city other than Athens do we have a wealth of material from genres of literature such as forensic oratory or comedy. Nevertheless, as we shall see, by putting what we have all together

---

[1] See, for example, Busolt and Swoboda, *Griechische Staatskunde*, vol. 1, 436–42; Will, *Le monde grec et l'orient*, 461–4; Bleicken, *Die athenische Demokratie*, ch. 13; O'Neil, *Origins and Development*; Ruzé, *Délibération et pouvoir*; R. Brock and S. Hodkinson, eds., *Alternatives to Athens: Varieties of Political Organization and Community in Ancient Greece* (Oxford, 2000), chs. 1, 5, 8, 9, 18; Raaflaub, Ober, and Wallace, *Origins of Democracy*, chs. 1–3.

one can arrive at some useful conclusions about the commonalities and variations in Greek democratic practice. Many democratic institutions, especially those attested epigraphically, can be broadly compared. And we can glean much about political attitudes too, as we have already seen in a number of cases from Chapters 1–3. One must remain realistic about what we can know about any given case: we make the most progress in the overall picture.

It would be convenient to be able to put the results together in a neat taxonomy, perhaps something like Figure 4.1 from the last chapter, this time with gradations according to degree of democracy. We might imagine having one category for the most "radical" democracies, one for the most "moderate" ones, and others for those in between. This, however, will not work, for three reasons. First, the spotty nature of the evidence would make such fine judgments a matter of guesswork in too many cases for the chart to have much value. Second, the categories themselves are arbitrary. Barry Strauss has argued against using such terms as "radical" and "moderate" with respect to the Athenian democracy, asserting (with good reason) that the terms are tendentious and unsupported in the ancient source material.[2] These same criticisms might apply to non-Athenian democracy as well. At the very least, more neutral terms of comparison indicating degrees of *demokratia* should be chosen. Some have fallen back on Aristotle's categories in the *Politics* and talk of Type 1 through Type 4 democracies. But these rubrics are oddly and inconsistently constructed by Aristotle,[3] and they defy accurate application since the criteria that Aristotle employs for differentiating between types – often citizenship rules – are matters about which we are ignorant in most cases; thus, attempts to use these categories for non-Athenian democracies are not usually very productive.[4] Finally, such a chart would limit democratic variation to a one-dimensional axis of "more" or "less" democracy, when multiple dimensions are identifiable. Ideally, one would track institutional progressiveness along one axis, breadth of participation along another, and international democratic activism along a third. (More on democratic multi-dimensionality later.)

So we will do without tabulated results. The following assessment of the nature of Classical democracy outside Athens, its common threads and its deviations, may thus seem more impressionistic, but such an approach

---

[2] B. S. Strauss, "Athenian Democracy: Neither Radical, Extreme, Nor Moderate," *AHB* 1.6 (1987), 127–9.
[3] Arist. *Pol.* 1291b30–1293a12 and 1318b6–33, cf. 1298a10–34. Discussed in Robinson, *First Democracies*, 37–9.
[4] E.g., O'Neil's rather loose application of the Aristotelian types in *Origins and Development*.

is more faithful to the source material and still produces an informative collective picture.

ONE "TRUE" DEMOCRACY?

But before we begin drawing conclusions about extra-Athenian democratic practice in Greece, we must confront a preliminary issue relating to definitions. Some would contend that, whatever scattered Greek texts might mention briefly about *demokratiai* here or there, only at Athens could you find *true* democracy. For only at Athens did the conditions enabling the development of such an extreme style of politics exist, and only there is a fully democratic practice revealed in the sources. Claims for the other candidates rest on such gossamer testimony (which often comes from later sources) that they amount at best to pale shadows of an Athenian original. The level of popular participation in these other claimed democracies will not have matched that at Athens, and most were so unstable that they depended upon Athens for their continued existence.

So the thesis seems to run. While the foregoing is a composite argument that no one scholar has urged in these exact terms, some commentators come close (see below), and the perspective it reflects turns up widely. This perspective, I believe, is a natural result of scholarly attentions for so long being focused fiercely and exclusively on Athenian political history, thanks to the very real deficits in source material relating to cases elsewhere. We must consider its merits before proceeding with an analysis that, to the contrary, would suppose that many "true" democracies existed in Greece.

One finds the most cogent arguments along these lines in scholarly works by Kurt Raaflaub. For the most part Raaflaub in his relevant writings is concerned with the Athenian democracy: when it began, under what circumstances it matured, and why it functioned in the remarkable ways that it did. His references to non-Athenian democracy, therefore, come in passing, but are worth noting. Raaflaub maintains that Athens invented "fully realized" democracy (in the mid fifth century, from 462 to 450) because only at Athens did the peculiar conditions exist for its creation – among them, the Athenian naval empire, which in numerous ways encouraged the integration of poorer citizens into the political process. While Raaflaub allows that other types of *demokratiai* existed, he denies that the same level of democratic equality would have adhered, and he emphasizes the uniqueness of the situation at Athens that resulted in the breakthrough to true democracy there.[5]

[5] See K. A. Raaflaub, "Equalities and Inequalities in Athenian Democracy," in J. Ober and C. Hedrick, eds., *Demokratia: A Conversation on Democracies, Ancient and Modern* (Princeton, 1996), 139–74,

Raaflaub takes note of the earlier work of Wolfgang Schuller regarding the establishment of democracy outside Athens. Schuller also associates a unique and pioneering Athenian development of *demokratia* with its post-Persian War fleet and empire. Greater opportunities for and rising prosperity among the poorer classes enhanced their political participation and power; and the demands of empire led to a more intensive practice of democracy in the city with more and more business coming before the *demos*. Schuller also raises specific cases of alleged non-Athenian democracy and generally rejects them: among the few that one might judge to have actually been democratic, most were either closely connected to the Athenian original, and thus dismissable as secondary developments, or they were politically unstable. Cities in either category in no way measured up to the uniquely robust and fully democratic system inaugurated by the Athenians, he suggests.[6]

One might point to a number of weaknesses in these contentions. First of all, it must be emphasized that the argument for a uniquely "true" democracy at Athens lacks support from ancient authors. Classical sources, Athenian or otherwise, never claim that Athens was the sole true democracy in Greece, or even that it was the most radical one.[7] Rather, what writers do assert – historians, philosophers, and orators – is that *demokratia* could be found in many places. Aristotle in particular shows in the *Politics* that he was very well aware of the existence of democracies of various types, moderate, middling, and extreme, all across the Greek world; he never creates a special category for the Athenian case.[8] Other authors of the fifth and fourth centuries, while not making as fine distinctions as Aristotle elaborates in the *Politics*, nevertheless attest a similar dispersion. Herodotus and Thucydides both refer to democratic governments near and far across Greece, despite their frequent narrative focus on Athenian politics and history. Demosthenes, being naturally even more focused on Athens in his

---

esp. at 149, and more recently, "The Breakthrough of *Demokratia* in Mid-Fifth-Century Athens," in *Origins of Democracy*, 105–54, esp. 141.

[6] Schuller, "Zur Entstehung," 433–47, and "Wirkungen des ersten attischen Seebunds," 87–101.

[7] Plato in the *Laws* comes close. At 693d Plato claims that monarchy and democracy are the two more or less mother forms (*hoion meteres*) of constitutions, and the height (*akron*) of monarchy is the Persian form and the height of democracy is "ours" (i.e., the Athenian). Most other constitutions are variations (*diapepoikilmenai*) from these. He then goes on to explain how the excessive freedom of the Athenian system declined from the more moderate earlier Athenian constitution (698a–701d). Clearly Plato is not literally claiming that other democracies derived from the Athenian one, and it was perhaps inevitable that Plato would use the Athenian democracy (the only one he seemed to know well) to work through his theorizing about excessive democratic freedom.

[8] Nor can it be convincingly argued that Aristotle interprets Greek democracy generally through the lens of Athens – his discussions and use of examples suggests a decided lack of Athenocentrism, as Mogens Hansen has shown in *Polis and City-State* (Copenhagen, 1998), 104–5.

speeches to Athenian audiences, repeatedly mentions that *demokratiai* exist elsewhere. Aeneas Tacticus does too. Xenophon tends to avoid constitutional labels but makes abundantly clear that popular governments were to be found in many places. Diodorus, relying on Classical-era historians such as Ephorus and Philistus, describes democratic *poleis* all over Greece. Thus, as far as we can tell from the contemporary sources, it did not occur to the ancient Greeks that "true" democracy only resided at Athens.

Second, there is an element of circularity involved in the arguments summarized above for a solely Athenian "full" democracy. If we base our understanding of *demokratia* – what it looks like, what might spark its appearance, its egalitarian potential – on the particulars of the Athenian case, we cannot in fairness then declare other cases to have been deficient because they did not follow the Athenian pattern. While it is surely correct to emphasize the uniqueness of the circumstances at Athens and the relationship of these circumstances to the particular government that developed there (Raaflaub does this well), doing so does not actually tell us anything generalizable about *demokratia* in Greece. Why must we assume that the *only* path to democratic equality was the one the Athenians took? It may well be that at Athens, where there was an extraordinarily large population and a vast territory needing effective integration, plus a long tradition of prestige and authority for the conservative Areopagus council, only a series of events as dramatic as the ones that actually transpired from about 508 to the 450s, involving revolution, war, destruction of the city, a new empire, massive naval service, and opportunities for major reform and rebuilding, could have resulted in the democracy that emerged. But to assert this hardly precludes that in other *poleis*, including ones that may have had fewer initial obstacles, *demokratia* might have evolved along a different path and yet still be "fully realized."

Finally, if one means to assert the unique or uniquely extreme nature of Athenian democracy in Greece, one should carefully consider a broad swath of examples of *demokratia* beyond Athens and make comparisons from there. Raaflaub does not do so because his main concern is Athenian history and politics; the few comparative judgments he makes are incidental to his chief purpose, which is to contribute to the debate about how and when Athens achieved its own democracy and the nature of that democracy. Schuller, on the other hand, aims more squarely at comparison and does consider other cases. The problem is his brevity, selectiveness and tendentiousness. All early cases of potential *demokratia* are dismissed (in less than one page) as being too uncertain; attention is then focused on the second half of the fifth century, especially on a few democracies with which we know Athens was involved. Internal problems and outside inter-ventions are highlighted, fragility and dependence on Athens is asserted, and counter-examples ignored or only briefly noted. The whole survey takes four pages.[9] One can do better, as I hope the earlier chapters of this study have already shown.

COMMONALITIES

Let us reject, then, the ill-attested and demonstrably problematic notion that Athens created the lone "true" or "fully realized" democracy and accept instead the view expressed in contemporary ancient sources that numerous *demokratiai* existed in Classical Greece. What characteristics defined their shared constitutional identity? We will start with the theoretical discussion of Aristotle and then move to examples drawn from the explorations of the first three chapters to judge the nature of the commonalities.

The constitutional analysis in Aristotle's *Politics* is unmatched among Classical sources for its depth and comprehensiveness. Nevertheless, with respect to democracy's definition and features, most of Aristotle's remarks echo those to be found in earlier works of the fifth and fourth centuries.[10] Whether this was a consequence of Aristotle's awareness and use of earlier writings on the subject or resulted from universal notions among educated Greeks of the era cannot be known with certainty; but, in any case, Aristotle was no outlier in his expressed ideas on this subject, and we will thus use his analysis as a convenient starting point for a discussion of general democratic characteristics.

For Aristotle, *demokratia* exists in a city-state when the people (*demos*) control the governing structure (*politeuma, politeia*).[11] Typically this means the poor (*aporoi*) in their great numbers will hold the upper hand, not the wealthy.[12] The *demos*'s control is expressed by its domination of public assembly meetings which all citizens can attend; juries also have broad

---

[9] Schuller, "Zur Entstehung," at 436–40.

[10] For an extended discussion of the shared conclusions of Aristotle and fifth-century authors (Aeschylus, Herodotus, Ps.-Xenophon, Euripides, Thucydides) who discuss *demokratia* and its definition, see Robinson, *First Democracies*, ch. 2. Comments on *demokratia*'s definition from important fourth-century political writers including Plato, Demosthenes, and Aeschines also generally parallel the ideas expressed in Aristotle's *Politics* and are indicated in notes appended to the Aristotle citations below.

[11] *Pol.* 1278b9–14. Cf. Dem. 20.107–8. On the terms *politeia* and *politeuma* here, see M H Hansen, "Polis, Politeuma, and Politeia: A Note on Arist. *Pol.* 1278b6–14," in D. Whitehead, ed., *From Political Architecture to Stephanus Byzantinus* (Stuttgart, 1994), 91–8.

[12] *Pol.* 1279b18. Cf. Dem. 21.208–12. On reconciling the *demos* vs. the *aporoi* as *kyrioi* in democracy according to Aristotle, see Robinson, *First Democracies*, 37–8.

authority and are in the hands of the people.[13] Further typical characteristics include the allotment, and sometimes election, of magistrates from and by all citizens,[14] with relatively small property qualifications – or none at all – for most of the positions.[15] Offices have short terms and are not to be filled repeatedly by the same person, the idea being that the people should rule themselves in turn.[16] Magistrates are held accountable to the people by various means including the *euthuna*, or scrutiny, when their term of office is complete.[17] Ostracism is typical,[18] as is pay for attending jury courts and assemblies.[19] In general, the principles of freedom and equality guide a democracy.[20] In the more extreme forms of democracy, one can find so much popular participation that the multitude (the *plethos*) could be said to rule rather than the law: that is, decrees of the assembly override the law and eclipse all authority of the magistrates.[21] Demagogues flourish, especially in this last type of democracy.[22]

[13] 1273b36–1274a3; 1317b25–8. Cf. Aeschin. 3.6–8.
[14] 1291b38–1292a4; 1294b7–13; 1300a31; 1305a30–4; 1317b18–21; cf. *Rhet.* 1.8.4 [1365b]. Cf. Plato, *Resp.* 557e.
[15] 1291b38–41; 1305a30–2; 1306b6–16; 1317b22–3.
[16] 1308a13–15; 1317b23–6. See also 1261a30; 1317b19–20. Cf. Plato, *Resp.* 557e. There were cases of non-repeating officials in other kinds of governments, such as with the ephors at Sparta. Perhaps not coincidentally Aristotle criticizes the ephorate as the most democratic element in the Spartan constitution (*Pol.* 1270b6–35; cf. 1266a33–41).
[17] 1274a15–18; 1281b32–4; 1318b21–31. Cf. Aeschin. 3.15.
[18] 1284a17–22, 1284b20–5; 1288a19–26; 1302b15–19.
[19] 1294a37–41; 1297a35–8; 1304b26–7; 1317b35–8.
[20] 1291b30–7; 1301a26–b4; 1301b29–1302a1; 1308a11–13; 1317a40–b17; 1318a3–9. Cf. Plato, *Resp.* 557b, 558c, 564a; Aeschin. 3.6, 3.220.
[21] 1292a1–37; 1293a9–10. Interestingly, this is one area where Aristotle's views are not echoed in other treatments of *demokratia*, at least not the more charitably inclined ones (though Plato's *Republic* 557e–558c is congruent with Aristotle in a generalized way). For fifth- and fourth-century proponents of democracy, one of its great virtues was precisely adherence to the law, especially as compared with the sometimes arbitrary ways of monarchs and oligarchs: Hdt. 3.80; Eur. *Suppl.* 403–50; Dem. 22.51; Aeschin. 1.4–5, 3.6. These contrasting views of law and democracy reflect not so much a fundamental disagreement on constitutional characteristics as polemically driven emphases on different aspects of government, with Aristotle choosing to highlight the (for him excessive) purview of the *demos* in assembly, proponents preferring to focus on matters of due process. On the importance of due process in the legal arguments that democrats at Athens made regarding judicial review, see A. Lanni, "Judicial Review and the Athenian 'Constitution,'" in M. H. Hansen, A.-C. Hernández, and P. Pasquino, eds., *Démocratie athénienne – démocratie moderne: tradition et influences* (Vandœuvres, 2009).
[22] 1292a4–30. The term demagogue (*demagogos*) is not always used with such negative force by other writers (e.g., Hyperides 5.17); and speakers who routinely address the *demos* in democracies, whether referred to in this way or others, occasionally are mentioned in more neutral or even positive terms (e.g., Aristoph. *Knights* 191–3; Thuc. 2.65.9; Aeschin. 3.220; Hyperides 5.28; Dinarchus 1.72). However, suspicion of rhetoric-wielding democratic politicians was rampant, as is reflected even in the passages cited here – Pericles was so superior to the ordinary run of popular leaders, Thucydides hyperbolically claims, that with him *demokratia* existed in name only. This widespread suspicion makes the contrast between Aristotle and other writers concerning demagogues far less stark than the lawful/lawless divide discussed in the previous note. On Aristotle's discussion of demagogues, see

This list of defining features covers both institutions and what we might call ideological characteristics. Institutions include governmental bodies such as assemblies and courts that wield decisive authority, or, alternatively, laws and practices such as ostracism or *euthunai*. Ideological characteristics are rather more nebulous. Aristotle mentions a few: prevalence of freedom and equality; popular participation so dominating that law itself is overthrown; and overactive demagogues.

The multitudinous ancient texts bearing on Athenian history and culture show that Athenian practices generally accorded with Aristotle's defining features during the period of its democracy.[23] But did non-Athenian democracies fit them? It seems that they did, as can be illustrated with many examples from the democracies explored in the first three chapters. Naturally, given the state of the evidence, we can only expect that some *poleis* will show some characteristics and others will show others; only the best-attested cases such as Argos and Syracuse could exemplify all or almost all of the features that Aristotle discusses (and they do). On the whole we find striking confirmation that what Aristotle and other Classical authors considered characteristic of *demokratia* indeed occurred in democracies all across Greece.[24]

First and most fundamentally, the *demos* was indeed supreme. Ancient authors describing events involving *demokratiai* make the primacy of the *demos* obvious, especially as seen in popular assemblies: all important matters seem to be referred to the *demos*, debated publicly, and resolved with finality – no council or magistrate countermands the decision of the assembly. A dominating assembled *demos* is specifically attested in many

---

R. Zoepffel, "Aristoteles und die Demagogen," *Chiron* 4 (1974), 69–90. On demagogues as political leaders in the Athenian context, see M. Ostwald, *From Popular Sovereignty to the Sovereignty of Law* (Berkeley, 1986), 199–202; Ober, *Mass and Elite*, 105–8, 166–70.

[23] This needs no demonstration. For a brief comparison of Aristotle's typology with the Athenian case, see Robinson, *First Democracies*, 39–42.

[24] I should note that there is a degree of circularity in some of the source material, since Aristotle's *Politics* provides both the theoretical framework here and many of the specific examples used to illustrate that framework. But this presents no real problem: first of all, even if the illustrative material given below came predominantly from Aristotle (which it does not), it would be worthwhile to show that Aristotle's theoretical analysis was in fact broadly based and not just extrapolation from the situation he witnessed at Athens, as has occasionally been suspected (see Hansen, *Polis and City-State*, 104–5). Secondly, as we have seen, most Classical authors who treat the subject define *demokratia* in much the same terms as Aristotle; and the evidence for the nature of the democratic governments in the states discussed in the first three chapters of this book comes from many sources, not just Aristotle's *Politics*. The only potentially dangerous circularity comes when a characteristic attested for a given state has been essential in establishing that the state's constitution was indeed democratic – it would then be problematic to turn around and use that state in this discussion as an example of how non-Athenian democracies showed that very characteristic. I will mark such cases with an asterisk.

non-Athenian democracies, including those at Argos, Corinth, Elis, Mantinea, Arcadia, Phlius, Thebes, Syracuse, Iasus, *Plataea and *Messana. Limitations placed on the purview of the *demos* were rare and prove the rule. When the Corinthians, for example, colluded with Argos in 421 BC to help to create a new Peloponnesian alliance in opposition to the Spartan one, they worked to persuade the Argive *demos* to vote power to a committee to negotiate with and approve potential partners rather than to bring matters back to the *demos* for public discussion in every individual case – which was obviously the normal procedure. The *demos* agreed, but conditionally: if Athens and Sparta came up as potential allies, the matter had to be referred back to the *demos* again.[25]

The courts were another venue for the supremacy of the *demos* in non-Athenian as well as Athenian democracy. Popular juries could wield enormous, typically irreversible authority, with many cases involving politicians or otherwise having political dimensions. From the designated space for trying military offenses outside the walls at Argos where an outraged *demos* stoned Thrasylus,[26] to the many *kriseis* lodged against the rich at Heraclea Pontica,[27] to the "unjust" treatment of former exiles by the *demos* in the Phliasian courts,[28] the use of the judiciary to establish popular dominance is widely attested, with references to it arising with respect to the above democracies as well as to those in Sicyon, Gela, Cyme, Corcyra, and *Rhodes.

Often related to the power of the *demos* in the courts is the accusation that democracy amounted to the rule of the poor over the rich. Such a phrasing may or may not accurately reflect the nature of the government, but there's no doubt that wealth disparity often arose as an issue and the *demos* and its leaders acted with it in mind. Just as the elite exiles at Phlius objected to their loss of property and rough handling in the courts there, the wealthy at Mantinea and also at Cos deeply resented the actions taken against them by popular leaders.[29] At Gela Dionysius convinced the *demos* to condemn trouble-making wealthy citizens and seize their property,[30] while at Thebes Pelopidas used his wealth to benefit the poor and brought down an opposing politician with a verdict involving a crushing fine.[31] Land redistribution and debt cancellation were the order of the day when

---

[25] Thuc. 5.27–8. See discussion in Chapter 1 under Argos.
[26] Thuc. 5.60. See also *IG* 4.554, implying that lawsuits often arose after magistrates' terms of office. Both in Chapter 1 under Argos.
[27] Arist. *Pol.* 1305b–1306a, with the Heraclea Pontica entry in Chapter 3.
[28] Xen. *Hell.* 5.3.10–11. See Chapter 1, under Phlius.
[29] *Hell.* 5.2.7, with entry for Mantinea in Chapter 1, and Arist. *Pol.* 1304b20–7 with Cos in Chapter 2.
[30] Diod. Sic. 13.93.   [31] Plut. *Pel.* 3.1–3, 25.4, 25.7.

democracy won through at Croton.[32] Other democratic communities that are said to have acted upon wealth divisions include Taras, Cyme, Heraclea Pontica, and Rhodes.

Also connected to judicial power in *demokratiai* was the tendency to aggressively scrutinize and punish office-holders and other leaders. The *euthuna*, while not a uniquely democratic feature, was especially associated with democracy,[33] and it is directly attested in several non-Athenian cases.[34] Ostracism, too, reflected a fundamental desire to put power in the hands of the *demos* to control elite leaders and could be found outside Athens at Argos, Megara, Syracuse, Cyrene, and Tauric Chersonesus. Even when institutional measures such as *euthunai* and ostracism are not attested, an abiding concern for keeping officials in line can be detected in other ways. The imprecations decrees from Teos show a conspicuous insistence on the punishment of magistrates who do not carry out their duties.[35] Cases of generals and other leaders being punished, possibly recklessly, by a *demos* looking to safeguard its power litter the narratives regarding Syracuse and Argos during their democracies. And, at Thebes, the great Epaminondas found himself charged with treason and removed from command when suspected of having pressed the Spartans insufficiently in a battle, and on another occasion both he and Pelopidas, despite a successful venture, were tried for holding on to their offices beyond the legal time limit.[36]

One can point out, of course, that democracies were hardly the only governments to punish leaders for misconduct. Multiple examples can be produced from the histories of Sparta and Rome, the most prominent ancient oligarchic states, of commanders being penalized for illegal or misguided actions. Nevertheless, there seem to be many more cases among democracies. One also can sometimes detect a hesitation in oligarchies to mete out the kinds of severe penalties that our accounts show angry democratic assemblies eagerly embraced when its leaders were suspected of misbehavior. We see a perfect illustration of the contrast in the case of the confrontation on the Argive plain in 418 BC described by Thucydides, when a last-minute truce negotiated by the Spartan king Agis and two (of five) Argive generals prevented a huge battle from being fought.[37] Outrage

[32] Iambl. *VP* 262–3.
[33] Hdt. 3.80.6. *Pace* Rhodes, "Nothing to Do with Democracy," 104–19 at 116.
[34] See Argos, Mantinea, and Arcadia in Chapter 1, and Croton in Chapter 2.
[35] ML 30; *SEG* 31.985. See Chapter 3 under Abdera and Teos.
[36] Diod. Sic. 15.72.1–2; Plut. *Pel.* 25. For these episodes see Thebes, Chapter 1.
[37] Thuc. 5.59–60, 63, with discussion in Argos, Chapter 1. See Hornblower, *Commentary*, ad loc. for the opinion that Thucydides is deliberately highlighting the contrast between democracy and oligarchy in his reporting here.

greeted both leaders when they returned home, the citizens in each city thinking that a great opportunity to smash their rival had been thrown away. Thucydides' description of the military circumstances suggests that it was the Spartan king who truly let a golden moment slip by, while the Argive generals probably saved their army from catastrophe. Nevertheless, in democratic Argos the enraged people stoned the lead general and confiscated his property; meanwhile, the furious Spartans threatened Agis with a fine and the razing of his house but never did either. In the end they simply required the king to gain the approval of an advisory board the next time he led the soldiers out on campaign. The contrasting treatment of the offending leaders is instructive.

Characteristically democratic features in office-holding are also found among non-Athenian examples. Offices seem to be of brief duration, typically held for only one year before replacements are elected or chosen by lot; in some cases offices were occupied for only six months at a time (discussed below). Use of the lot in choosing officials was probably commonplace, though it is directly attested only occasionally, such as Croton (Chapter 2), Syracuse after Diocles (Chapter 2), and in fourth-century Eretria (Chapter 3). Occasionally one finds evidence of public payments awarded for magistracies or for attendance at assemblies or on juries – there were definite cases at Iasus and Rhodes (Chapter 3), and a possible case of Camarina (Chapter 2), to go along with the Athenian example. It is unclear whether the relatively few attestations of public pay signals rarity of the practice or merely the accident of epigraphic survival; Aristotle, in any case, talks of it as if it were fairly normal in democracies.[38]

Demagogues in democracies come in for much criticism by Aristotle and other writers, and their exploits (and those of popular leaders given other labels) fill the slender narratives that we have for non-Athenian democracies. *Demagogoi* at Cyrene brought in too many illegitimate citizens and thus provoked a violent reaction from the elites;[39] at Syracuse they multiplied, making assembly meetings tumultuous and radicalizing the laws;[40] they introduced public pay at Rhodes which, with their other misdeeds, sparked a counter-revolution;[41] and at Argos they caused the *skutalismos*, resulting in the slaughter of hundreds of wealthy citizens before they fell

---

[38] Arist. *Pol.* 1294a37–41; 1297a35–8; 1304b26–7; 1317b35–8. De Ste Croix, "Political Pay outside Athens," 48–52; O'Neil, *Origins and Development*, appendix 2, 175–9. For the efficacy of the practice in the one place we can measure it – Athens – see M. M. Markle, "Jury Pay and Assembly Pay at Athens," repr. in P. J. Rhodes, ed., *Athenian Democracy* (Oxford, 2004), 95–131.

[39] Arist. *Pol.* 1319b1–19, discussed under Cyrene, Chapter 2.

[40] Diod. Sic. 11.87, 11.92, 13.33–4; Plut. *Nic.* 28. See Syracuse, Chapter 2.

[41] Arist. *Pol.* 1302b and 1304b; Rhodes, Chapter 3.

themselves before the wrath of the *demos*.[42] Leaders labeled *prostatai tou demou* whipped up fears of oligarchic revolution at Syracuse[43] and Argos;[44] at Elis one rallied the *demos* after an attempt to assassinate him failed, enabling him to triumph over internal enemies and negotiate a truce with external ones.[45] Other examples of powerful demagogues and *prostatai* can be found in the accounts for democratic Thebes, Mantinea, Corcyra, Cos, and Cyme.

Unusual attachment to the spirit of freedom and equality is detectable in source references in a number of non-Athenian cases. At Syracuse, worship of Zeus Eleutherios (the Liberator) begins with the coming of democracy in the 460s BC, and at Himera around the same time this deity could be found and is associated with deliberative assemblies (*agorai boulaphorai*) there.[46] The Sicyonian democracy moved by Euphron was allegedly founded on the basis of equality,[47] and a concept much talked about at Acragas during its popular government was *isotes*.[48] Achaean democracy had long exemplified the principles of *isegoria* and *parrhesia* (equal/free speech), claims Polybius.[49] Of course, to a critic of democracy like Aristotle, undue devotion to the ideals of freedom and equality could lead to a state of lawlessness, where participation is too broad and the masses rule, not the law. As with the accusations of demagoguery, or poor domination of the rich, the fairness or unfairness of such a characterization is not relevant at the moment; that non-Athenian *demokratiai* were accused of it is. So at Corinth during the brief span of its democracy excessive participation (by "metics") resulted in "tyrannical" rule, according to the hostile Xenophon.[50] Chaos and disorder supposedly characterized the hapless Theban democracy of the fifth century before its overthrow by a disgusted elite.[51] And fifth-century Syracuse frequently appears in our accounts as a home to tumultuous assembly meetings and mob rule.[52]

---

[42] Diod. Sic. 15.57–8, with Isoc. 5.52; Dion. Hal. 7.66.5; Plut. *Mor.* 814B, Aristides, *Panath.* 273. See discussion under Argos, Chapter 1.

[43] Thuc. 6.35–40. See Syracuse, Chapter 2.   [44] Aen. Tact. 11.7–10, Argos, Chapter 1.

[45] Xen. *Hell.* 3.2.21–31. Elis, Chapter 1.

[46] Diod. Sic. 11.72.2; Pind. *Ol.* 12.1–5. See entries for Syracuse and Himera, Chapter 2.

[47] Xen. *Hell.* 7.1.44–5. Sicyon, Chapter 1.

[48] Diog. Laert. 8.65. Acragas, Chapter 2. We risk circularity here, however, given the importance of the egalitarian language for confirming Diodorus' application of the label *demokratia* to Acragas during Empedocles' time.

[49] 2.38.6, 2.38.10. Achaea, Chapter 1   [50] *Hell.* 4.4.1–8. Corinth, Chapter 1.

[51] Arist. *Pol.* 1302b25. Thebes, Chapter 1.

[52] Diod. Sic. 13.19, 13.91–2; Plut. *Nic.* 28; Thuc. 6.17, 6.63. Syracuse, Chapter 2. See also the treatments of *Thessaly (Chapter 1) and Hestiaea/Oreus (Chapter 3).

In all, it is safe to say that, collectively at least, non-Athenian democracies richly demonstrate the characteristics of *demokratia* that Aristotle and other writers describe. But our results from the first three chapters allow us to go further still in identifying and evaluating features that Classical democracies shared or allegedly shared.

One interesting commonality emerges regarding the size of assembly spaces. Consider the well-known situation at Athens: there, the *demos* met in the Pnyx, an open space on the slope of a hill not far from the Acropolis. Archaeological inspection suggests that the capacity of the Pnyx was roughly 6,000–8,000 people for most of the Classical period, and literary evidence suggests that normal attendance was around 6,000.[53] This has posed an interesting problem: we know that the citizen population of the state was in the order of 50,000–60,000 in the fifth century and perhaps 30,000 in the fourth century, so only a small fraction of the "ruling" citizen body could ever attend any given meeting to rule. What does this say about the Athenian democracy? One might attribute this situation to the unusual geographical extent of the Athenian *polis*, controlling as it did the vast territory of Attica, from parts of which it was a long trek indeed to the Pnyx in Athens. Alternatively, one might suppose the reason for the too small assembly space was related to Athenian values. L. J. Samons, for example, acknowledges the geographical factor but moves beyond it to tie the low participation to something else: the ultimate unimportance of *demokratia* to Athenian society, at least compared with more fundamental practices such as religion.[54]

But it turns out that there is no need to recover a uniquely Athenian answer, whether geographical or cultural. If we consider the assembly spaces at democratic Argos, Acragas, Mantinea, Megalopolis, and Syracuse, the same phenomenon emerges: very small areas for the assembly relative to the estimated citizen population. At Argos the seating capacity of the theater with straight tiers just west of the agora was roughly 2,500, serving a citizen population of perhaps 10,000–20,000; the *ekklesiasterion* at Acragas seated perhaps 3,000 of a citizen population in excess of 20,000, while the similarly sized theater at Mantinea was matched with a population that could have approached 18,000. The only known Syracusan assembly space contemporary with the fifth-century democracy was very small indeed – perhaps 1,000 people could be seated in it – for a population well in excess

---

[53] Hansen, *Athenian Democracy*, 128–32.
[54] L. J. Samons, *What's Wrong with Democracy?* (Berkeley, 2004), 168–71. For a critique of Samons' thesis, see M. H. Hansen's review in *BMCR ev* 2006.01.32.

of 20,000. Finally, at Megalopolis the presumed remains of the Thersilion might have had a capacity of 6,000, serving a body nominally of "Ten Thousand" (the *Murioi*) but potentially far larger assuming the whole citizen population of Arcadia was entitled to attend.[55]

The pattern of undersized assembly spaces stands out clearly and leads to some important conclusions. First, in Greek democracies generally there was no expectation that anything like the full citizen population would turn out for any one assembly meeting. Whether in Athens or Argos or Acragas, merely having the opportunity to attend meetings once in a while was deemed quite sufficient for ordinary citizen participants; and a strong degree of either apathy or occupation with private affairs by the *demos* was in fact counted upon in planning the size of assembly spaces. Second, the elevated participation levels that *demokratiai* were famous for (and criticized for by foes) consisted not in the size of any one gathering, but even more in large attendance numbers *over time*, with frequency of assembly meetings (plus other avenues for participation such as councils, juries, etc.) being just as important as the peak numbers attending any one meeting. Thus, we need not try to find some peculiarly Athenian explanation for the diminutive capacity of the Pnyx relative to the Athenian population, nor ought we consider only the Athenian example when wrestling with theoretical or practical issues of participation in ancient democratic *poleis*.

FALSE COMMONALITIES – FOREIGN AND MILITARY POLICIES

There are other common characteristics that seem to apply to democracies generally across Greece that either do not stand up to close scrutiny or do not, in the end, appear to have been a function of the democratic constitutions themselves. These false commonalities relate to naval forces, foreign interventions, and war with other democracies.

Naval power

It has been thought that, historically speaking, democracy and naval power go hand in hand. Famous examples include modern Britain and the contemporary United States. In the ancient world an obvious example is Athens

[55] See assembly space discussions of Argos and Mantinea in Chapter 1, and Acragas and Syracuse in Chapter 2.

of the fifth and fourth centuries. That historical cases should show such a relationship makes a certain intuitive sense, especially in an ancient context: the outfitting and rowing of large fleets demands great manpower, typically from the lower classes, which could have the effect of enhancing the status of these men politically. Plato thought it inevitable that states relying on naval power would honor the basest citizens (*Laws* 707a–b). The correspondence at Athens between the growth of naval power and democracy in the fifth century seems fairly clear.[56] One political scientist examining democracies in the era of the Peloponnesian War goes so far as to assert that "most democracies were naval powers" and that "the democratic states were primarily sea-faring states."[57]

But are such assumptions truly generalizable? Based on the earlier chapters of this study and a survey of known naval powers in the ancient Greek world, the answer is no. Democratic sea powers did exist, but so did many non-democratic ones, and the vast majority of democracies were not naval powers.

First, let us define "naval power." Starting in the fifth century BC, Greek historians used the term *thalassokratein* or equivalent terms to describe the exercise of dominant naval strength. We need not quibble over how dominant a state must become to be considered a "naval power" – a reputation for prowess and the ability to produce large numbers of warships will suffice. The earliest such power mentioned repeatedly in Greek sources[58] is that of King Minos of Crete. Herodotus brushes aside the stories about him and other legendary figures, but Thucydides takes Minos more seriously, considering his early naval mastery to have been historical. The possibilities for an actual Bronze Age Cretan thalassocracy have been debated by

---

[56] See the works of Raaflaub and Schuller discussed at the beginning of this chapter. On the other hand, Paola Ceccarelli has challenged the idea that the two were necessarily connected at Athens: "Sans thalassocratie, pas de démocratie?," *Historia* 42 (1993), 444–70. Additionally, evidence shows that many others rowed the triremes at Athens alongside the citizen thetes, including metics and slaves, a point which might be taken to undermine arguments for a powerful relationship between democratic empowerment and rowing the fleet at Athens: V. Gabrielsen, "Socio-economic Classes and Ancient Greek Warfare," in K. Ascani, ed., *Ancient History Matters. Studies Presented to Jens Erik Skydsgaard on His Seventieth Birthday* (Rome, 2002), 203–20; A. J. Graham, "Thuc. 7.13.2 and the Crews of Athenian Triremes," *TAPhA* 122 (1992), 257–70.

[57] B. Russett and W. Antholis, "The Imperfect Democratic Peace of Ancient Greece," *Grasping the Democratic Peace* (Princeton, 1993), 58–9.

[58] De Souza argues that Greek sources are anachronistic in their application of the term thalassocracy to states much before the fifth century, and contends that true naval powers in Greece were only beginning to develop in the late sixth century. Even if this was the case, a survey of earlier alleged naval powers will deepen the basis of this investigation. P. de Souza, "Towards Thalassocracy? Archaic Greek Naval Developments," in N. Fischer and H. van Wees, eds., *Archaic Greece: New Approaches and New Evidence* (London, 1998), 271–93.

historians and archaeologists; the various arguments need not be rehearsed here.[59] To whatever extent Minoan Crete may have exercised supremacy over the sea, no credible evidence exists to claim that its government was democratic.

Other supposed early thalassocracies have come down to us in the form of the "List of the Thalassocracies" contained in Eusebius' *Chronicon*, but there are good reasons to dismiss this list as unreliable.[60] States whose naval power of the Archaic or Classical periods rests on firmer evidentiary ground include Corinth, Samos, Phocaea, and Aegina. Thucydides singles out Corinth as the first Greek state to conduct naval affairs in the manner of his own day, the first to build triremes, and the first (along with their colonists the Corcyraeans) to fight a sea battle (*naumachia*). He also credits them with using their fleet to suppress piracy at a time when the Greeks were starting to make greater use of the sea. Thucydides puts all this in the context of early Corinth's wealth and commercial success, about which there need be no doubt, given Corinth's leading role in colonization and the production and trade of pottery and other goods. In terms of its government, Corinth went from the Bacchiad oligarchy to Cypselid tyranny to constitutional oligarchy in the Archaic period. In the fifth century Corinth remained oligarchic and navally powerful, actually selling ships to the Athenians at one point (before the Themistoclean building program). The Corinthians sent forty ships to fight at Salamis in 479, where they especially distinguished themselves (according to most Greeks, we are told), and manned fully ninety warships of their own at the battle of Sybota

---

[59] Hdt. 3.122, cf. 1.171; Thuc. 1.4, 1.8.2. See, e.g., the opposing views of Starr and Buck: C. G. Starr, "The Myth of the Minoan Thalassocracy," *Historia* 3 (1954), 282–91; R. J. Buck, "The Minoan Thalassocracy Re-examined," *Historia* 11 (1962) 129–37. Thucydides also credits Agamemnon with having developed great naval power, though he voices some discomfort with using Homer as his source (1.9).

[60] Excerpted from Diodorus' lost seventh book (fr. 11), and perhaps ultimately deriving from a treatise on thalassocracies by Diodorus' near contemporary Castor of Rhodes, the Eusebian text lists seventeen peoples alleged to have maintained thalassocracies before fifth-century Athens, including the Lydians, Pelasgians, Thracians, Rhodians, and, for later periods, Phrygians, Carians, Milesians, and others. The list's lateness, lack of elaboration, and highly schematic character, not to mention the absence of any corroboration for many of the names listed, cast doubt on its utility for reconstructing Archaic history. Myres, though admitting that there are problems with the list, argues for its credibility by placing its ultimate origins in the fifth century and defending the possible historicity of many of the thalassocracies listed. If the list does go back to a fifth-century source it might merit greater consideration, but Myres' arguments for this proposition are not strong; J. L. Myres, "On the 'List of Thalassocracies' in Eusebius," *JHS* 26 (1906) 84–130; J. K. Fotheringham, "On the 'List of Thalassocracies' in Eusebius (continued)," *JHS* 27 (1907) 75–89, esp. 88–9; J. L. Myres, "The 'List of Thalassocracies' in Eusebius: A Reply," *JHS* 27 (1907), 123–30; A. Momigliano, "Sea Power in Greek Thought," *CR* 58 (1944), 1–7 at 1–2; T. J. Figueira, *Excursions in Epichoric History* (Lanham, MD, 1993), 48–9; de Souza, "Towards Thalassocracy?"

in 433. There are no references to Corinthian naval strength in the time of its brief turn to democracy.[61]

Samos, which may have flirted with popular government on two occasions in the Archaic period,[62] also gained notoriety for its naval power. Thucydides tells us that the Samians received triremes from Corinth very early in their history (1.13.3), and much later at the time of the battle of Lade in 494 the Samians contributed sixty ships (Hdt. 6.8). Reports of a Samian "thalassocracy," however, coincide only with the reign of the tyrant Polycrates (c. 540–523). Herodotus declares that Polycrates was the first Greek (putting aside stories about Minos and the like) to seek thalassocracy, and that he had high expectations of winning an empire over Ionia and the islands.[63] In the Classical period Samos never achieved the level of dominance it enjoyed under Polycrates, but it remained navally strong, as it was one of the few members of the Delian League to continue to supply ships instead of tribute before its failed rebellion against Athens in 440. As we have seen in Chapter 3, Samos's government for most of the fifth century was oligarchic. Popular government may have broken through intermittently in the 490s, though it did not last; a democracy was imposed by the Athenians in 441 and possibly reimposed in 439, but an oligarchy was back (or still) in charge two or three decades later. A democratic revolution against this oligarchy, aided by Athens, came in 412.[64]

Phocaea also receives notice for its early prowess at sea. Herodotus and Thucydides both remark on its victorious naval battles against western powers in the mid sixth century. With sixty ships it managed to defeat

[61] Thuc. 1.13, 1.46; Hdt. 6.89, 8.1, 8.43, 8.94; C. J. Haas, "Athenian Naval Power before Themistocles," *Historia* 34 (1985), 29–46, at 36–7; J. B. Salmon, *Wealthy Corinth* (Oxford, 1984), 81–158, 223–4, 231–9. See Corinth section in Chapter 1.

[62] See Robinson, *First Democracies*, 118–20; J. Roisman "Maiandrios of Samos," *Historia* 34 (1985), 257–77, at 264–7.

[63] Hdt. 3.122; cf. Thuc. 1.13.6. Polycrates was at least partly successful: Herodotus reports many victories in battle, including one at sea against the combined forces of the Milesians and Lesbians, and the conquest of numerous cities and islands. Early in his reign Polycrates could boast of having one hundred penteconters; later he sent off undesirable exiles in forty triremes with a request not to return, implying possession of a substantial fleet of these warships. Samos was also known at this time for its impressive harbor works, which surely assisted in the maintenance of a large fleet. Herodotus further notes the numerous mercenaries Polycrates hired to help him wage his wars (Hdt. 3.39, 3.44–9, 3.54, 3.60). Samos also appears on the Eusebian list of thalassocracies, with dates roughly in accord with the Polycratean era (534–517 according to Myres, "List of Thalassocracies" [1906]). Haas, "Athenian Naval Power," 37–9, believes that Polycrates' naval power, as impressive as it was, amounted more to piracy than true military strength, until the Persian threat forced the tyrant to make greater preparations. See Shipley, *History of Samos*, 81–99, 106, on Samian wealth and Polycrates' piratical naval power; H. T. Wallinga, *Ships and Sea-Power before the Great Persian War* (Leiden, 1993), 84–102, on the importance of finances and the Egyptian connection.

[64] Samos, Chapter 3.

twice that number of opposing Carthaginian and Etruscan vessels at the battle of Alalia (Hdt. 1.166; Thuc. 1.13.6). The Phocaeans' tactical skills are still evident at Lade in 494, but by this time they have been reduced to contributing only three warships (Hdt. 6.8, 11–12). H. T. Wallinga believes that the Phocaeans had a fleet of 120 penteconters in the mid sixth century and in general argues that the Phocaeans, thanks in part to the profitable commercial relations they had established with wealthy Tartessos, became for a time an unusually potent naval power.[65] There is no evidence for Phocaean democracy (or any other particular constitutional type) in the sixth century at the height of its strength; during the Ionian Revolt, when it provided only three ships at Lade, we might guess that like many of its allies some form of *demokratia* had made an appearance, based on Herodotus' vague reference to Ionian *isonomia* at 5.37–8, though there is nothing to corroborate it in the case of Phocaea.[66]

Aegina, an island state that managed to produce substantial fleets, also figures among Archaic and Classical naval powers, but its case is more problematic. Herodotus refers to a victorious sea battle against Samian forces in 519, successes at sea against the Athenians prior to Xerxes' invasion (to the point that Themistocles could justify having 100–200 triremes built to oppose its power), and the superior performance of the Aeginetan contingent at the battle of Salamis.[67] Aegina is also named on the Eusebian thalassocracy list for the years 490–480.[68] The wealth of the island is not uncommonly linked to its successes at sea.[69] However, Thucydides discounts early Aeginetan (and Athenian) fleets as having been small and composed mostly of penteconters instead of the more advanced triremes (1.14.3). The state's totals of eighteen and thirty ships contributed at Artemisium and Salamis do not particularly impress (though fleets of seventy ships or more are reported for other clashes).[70] Haas attributes mere "piratical" power to Aegina, and Figueira is also skeptical of accounts of early

---

[65] Hdt. 1.163–7; Paus. 10.8.6; Wallinga, *Ships and Sea-Power*, 66–83; de Souza, "Towards Thalassocracy?" Phocaea appears on the Eusebian list for the years *c*. 577–533, and Myres, "List of Thalassocracies," expresses great confidence in the reality of this entry.

[66] See the discussion under Abdera and Teos in Chapter 3.

[67] Hdt. 3.59, 5.81–9, 6.88–93, 7.144, 7.179–82, 8.93. Cf. Strabo 8.6.16; Plut. *Them.* 4, with F. J. Frost, *Plutarch's Themistocles: A Historical Commentary* (Princeton, 1980), 80–7. At Hdt. 5.81.2 the actions against Athens are associated specifically with the great prosperity of Aegina.

[68] Myres, "List of Thalassocracies." J. B. Bury and R. Meiggs, *A History of Greece to the Death of Alexander the Great* (London, 1975), 162, call Aegina the "strongest naval power in the Aegean" around the turn of the century.

[69] Hdt. 5.81.2; Paus. 2.29.5; Ael. *VH* 12.10. T. J. Figueira, *Aegina, Society and Politics* (New York, 1981), 166–70.

[70] Hdt. 6.92, 8.1, 8.46; Thuc. 1.105.2.

Aeginetan mastery at sea, though there can be no doubt about the association of the island with seaborne commerce and warfare in the Archaic
and Classical periods.[71] Perhaps it is most prudent to think of Aegina as a
second-tier thalassocrat, one showing great prowess at sea for a small state
yet rarely if ever dominating. The constitution of Aegina, for which the
evidence is mostly indirect, appears to have been consistently oligarchic in
the Archaic and Classical periods.[72]

Though mentioned less prominently in our sources, Classical naval
powers did exist which had democratic governments for at least a portion
of their history. Corcyra mustered the second largest fleet in Greece (after
Athens) on the eve of the Peloponnesian War and was a democracy at
the time (see Chapter 2). However, the wealthy island state had a long
history of sea power before this and we do not know when it became
democratic – surely not as far back as the seventh-century naval battle
with Corinth reported in Thucydides, and the earliest date for which
there is convincing evidence is the third quarter of the fifth century.[73] The
probability, therefore, is that its prowess at sea long preceded its popular
government.

Syracuse could also produce numerous warships. The tyrant Gelon
reportedly offered to make available 200 triremes for the Greek cause
in the Persian Wars (Hdt. 7.158; cf. Thuc. 1.14.2). No fleet of that size
is mentioned during the period of Syracusan democracy of 466–406, but
warships in significant numbers did make appearances and, most famously,
overcame the Athenian expeditionary force during the siege of Syracuse.
After the return of tyranny in the fourth century, Syracuse continued naval
operations and in fact became a leader in the building and use of the new,
larger warships that would replace triremes as the pride of late Classical
and Hellenistic fleets.[74]

Strabo alleges that Taras during the period of its democracy amassed
the greatest naval force in its region. However, this was part of a more
general military flourishing in the city at that time: Strabo extols Taras's
large land forces as well, both infantry and cavalry.[75] Moreover, Aristotle

---

[71] Haas, "Athenian Naval Power"; Figueira, *Epichoric History*, 46–51, 325–61; Figueira, *Aegina*, 166–214.

[72] Figueira, *Aegina*, 299–343; T. J. Figueira in *Inventory*, 621.

[73] Naval power: Thuc. 1.13.4, with Thuc. 1.25, 1.33, 1.36 and Hdt. 3.48–53. Democracy: Corcyra,
Chapter 2.

[74] During the democracy: Diod. Sic. 11.88.4–5, 12.30.1 (builds 100 triremes); Thuc. 3.115.1–5, 4.1,
4.24–5.Versus the Athenian expedition: Thuc. 7.7, 7.12, 7.50–72; Diod. Sic. 13.7–13. Large warship
construction under Dionysius: L. Casson, *Ships and Seamanship in the Ancient World* (Baltimore,
1995), 97–9, 449; J. S. Morrison, J. F. Coates, and N. B. Rankov, *The Athenian Trireme* (Cambridge,
2000), 46–7.

[75] Strabo 6.3.4.

makes a point of contrasting the naval class (*trierikon*) that predominated at Athens with the fishing class (*to halieutikon*) that existed in large numbers at Taras.[76] These references make it harder to assert a particular relationship between democracy and naval power at Taras, though the two undoubtedly coexisted.

Only Rhodes stands out as an indisputable example beyond Athens of great naval power consistently coinciding with democratic government. The island state first became a democracy in 395 (see Chapter 3). Oligarchic revolutions and periods of foreign domination suggest constitutional instability during much of the fourth century, but the evidence for a stable and moderate democracy for most of the Hellenistic period is strong, and this was also the time of Rhodes' greatest wealth and naval influence.[77]

The results of this brief survey suggest two main conclusions about naval power and democracy outside Athens in the Archaic and Classical periods. First, it is clear that democratic thalassocracies were not the norm. We have found a mix of government types attested, from tyranny to oligarchy to democracy. Furthermore, those sea powers that did have democratic regimes did not always have them throughout the time of their high naval reputation: Corcyra had been a force at sea long before democracy is attested in the 430s and 420s, while Syracuse and especially Samos seem to have had their most potent fleets in the days of their tyrants. It would be dubious, therefore, to maintain even in these cases that democratic government was an essential enabling or facilitating factor in a state's sea power.[78] The same might be said of Taras thanks to what our sources say about the nature of the *demos* there and its generally waxing military strength, though sea power and democracy at least did coincide. Only Rhodes presents a clear example of a special relationship between the two.[79] If we place this handful

---

[76] *Pol.* 1291b17–23. See Taras in Chapter 2.

[77] Rhodes, Chapter 3. Berthold, *Rhodes*, 19–58; Gabrielsen, *Naval Aristocracy*, 24–36, 85–111; O'Neil, *Origins and Development*, 86, 109–20; Casson, *Ships and Seamanship*, 127–31; C. Starr, *The Influence of Sea Power on Ancient History* (Oxford, 1989), 54, 59–60.

[78] We might add Chios to this list: it brought 100 warships to the battle of Lade and contributed ships instead of tribute to the Delian League, and it thus qualifies as a naval power. That it was democratic during these times, however, is highly questionable. Hdt. 6.8; Strabo 821a, 955c. O'Neil, *Origins and Development*, 39–40; Quinn, *Athens and Samos, Lesbos and Chios*, 39–49; Meiggs, *Athenian Empire*, 208, 361–2; L. Rubinstein in *Inventory*, 1067–8. Other potential sea powers for which the testimony is thinner include Miletus (Hdt. 3.39, 6.8), Lesbos (Hdt. 3.39, 5.26, 6.8; Thuc. 1.19, 3.11), and Ionia generally (Thuc. 1.13.6).

[79] Even here, however, it is perhaps worth pointing out that the powerful aristocratic classes of Rhodes became so closely involved with the navy that they had at least as much at stake as the lower classes in its continued effective operation – suggesting that a less close relationship between *demos* and naval strength obtained at Rhodes than at Athens. Polyb. 4.47.1, 7.27.7; Diod. Sic. 20.93.6–7; Cic. *Rep.* 1.31.47; cf. Strabo 14.2.5. Berthold, *Rhodes*, 38–45; Gabrielsen, *Naval Aristocracy*. Cf. Figueira, *Aegina*, 307–8, 341–3 for aristocrats and the Aeginetan navy.

of mostly suspect cases (plus that of Athens, of course) in the context of the forty-eight other democracies studied in previous chapters that were not naval powers, the supposed relationship seems increasingly specious.

Second, our survey suggests that other factors are more prominent than constitutional type in promoting thalassocracy. Geography played a role, naturally, given the predominance of islands and coastal states. But Starr has argued that the key elements for prospective ancient sea powers were wealth and size.[80] As it happens, all of the most prominent powers discussed above were remarked upon for their extraordinary wealth, either generally or during their period of naval ascendancy. This correlation stands to reason, of course, because building, manning, and maintaining substantial fleets of warships was very expensive.[81] On the other hand, the size of a political community emerges less clearly as a determining factor. This might have to do in part with definitions. Starr considers the only true sea powers of the ancient world to have been Carthage, Athens, and Rome (with some discussion of Corinth, Persia, and others) and thus clearly had in mind a grander definition of thalassocracy than the loose one employed here.[82] Setting the bar a little lower, we have found that smaller states – if sufficiently wealthy – could also exercise disproportionate naval strength (e.g., Samos, Phocaea, Aegina, Corcyra). Money enabled communities of moderate size to hire the mercenary crews and soldiers needed to fill out their fleets, diminishing the natural advantage larger states had with their greater citizen populations. Wealth, therefore, would seem to have been a universal requirement for thalassocracy, and having a large *polis* did not hurt. Democracy appears to have been almost a non-factor.

"Democratic peace" and democratic interventions

In recent decades a number of political scientists have advanced the thesis that democracies rarely, if ever, go to war with one another. Termed "democratic peace" (or sometimes "liberal peace"), this theory has received substantial support from analyses of the last two hundred years or so of warfare: during this time, as the results show convincingly, there has been no shortage of major interstate conflicts, and no shortage of conflicts involving democracies, but very few actually involving one democracy going to

---

[80] Starr, *Sea Power*, 24–7. Wallinga, *Ships and Sea-Power*, also stresses the necessity of wealth.

[81] See the useful discussion of financial requirements for the projection of naval power in the Greek cities, especially in the cases of Athens and Rhodes, in V. Gabrielsen, "Naval Warfare: Its Economic and Social Impact on Greek Cities," in T. Bekker-Nielsen and L. Hannestad, eds., *War as a Cultural and Social Force* (Copenhagen, 2001), 72–98.

[82] Starr, *Sea Power*, 24–8, 83–4. Cf. de Souza, "Towards Thalassocracy?"

war against another democracy.[83] The pattern is quite striking and has convinced a great many that a powerful relationship must exist between having democratic government and an absence of war with other democratic states. Some scholars have extended their study of democratic peace to the ancient world, hoping thereby to further bolster their arguments for the existence of a strong historical connection between democracy and peace with other democracies.[84] In response, ancient historians (including the present author) have begun to address the issue.[85] So as not to duplicate work already published elsewhere, the following treatment will summarize the conclusions scholars have already reached and supplement them based on the investigations of the earlier chapters of this study.

The predominant view of ancient historians writing on the subject thus far has been extreme skepticism about the existence of a democratic peace in ancient Greece. All too easily can one find examples of wars fought between *demokratiai* in the Classical period. The most famous, no doubt, was the Athenian decision to attack Syracuse with the Sicilian Expedition of 415–413 BC. The attempt by proponents of democratic peace to dismiss the resulting war as not counting because of the supposedly questionable nature of Syracuse's democracy fails to convince.[86] A partial listing of other democratic wars of the era would include Acragas versus Syracuse in 445 BC, Taras versus Thurii probably in the late 440s, Thebes versus Plataea in 373, Athens versus Amphipolis in the 360s, and Athens versus Byzantium, Cos, and Rhodes during the Social War of 357–355. In addition, democratic allies of democratic combatants were often drawn into combat with each

[83] The bibliography on the subject is vast. See the survey and discussion in D. Kinsella, "No Rest for the Democratic Peace," in *American Political Science Review* 99.3 (2005), 453–7.

[84] B. Russett and W. Antholis, "Do Democracies Fight Each Other? Evidence from the Peloponnesian War," *Journal of Peace Research* 29.4 (1992), 415–34; Russett and Antholis, "Imperfect Democratic Peace," 43–71; T. Bachteler, "Explaining the Democratic Peace: The Evidence from Ancient Greece Reviewed," in *Journal of Peace Research* 34.3 (1997), 315–23; S. Weart, *Never at War*, and "Remarks on the Ancient Evidence for Democratic Peace," in *Journal of Peace Research* 38.5 (2001), 609–13.

[85] E. W. Robinson, "Reading and Misreading the Evidence for Democratic Peace," in *Journal of Peace Research* 38.5 (2001), 593–608, and "Response to Spencer Weart," in *Journal of Peace Research* 38.5 (2001), 615–17; M. H. Hansen and T. H. Nielsen, eds., *An Inventory of Archaic and Classical Poleis* (Oxford, 2004), 84–5; E. W. Robinson, "Thucydides and Democratic Peace," *Journal of Military Ethics* 5 (2006), 243–53, and "Greek Democracies and the Debate over Democratic Peace," in M. H. Hansen, A.-C. Hernández, and P. Pasquino, eds., *Démocratie athénienne – démocratie moderne: tradition et influences* (Geneva, 2010), 277–306. D. Pritchard raises the theory as part of a more general discussion in "How Do Democracy and War Affect Each Other? The Case Study of Ancient Athens," *Polis* 24 (2007), 328–52, at 337 8.

[86] Weart, *Never at War*, 31–4. See Robinson, "Reading and Misreading," 595–9, with responses by Weart and Robinson again, plus Hansen and Nielsen, eds., *Inventory*, 84–5. Also unconvinced is L. Asmonti: "On Syracuse and Democracy. Diod. Sic. XIII.20–32," delivered at the University of Reading Classics Seminar, 31st October 2007 (thanks to the author for providing a copy).

other in the larger wars noted above: for example, various democratic Sicilian *poleis* participated in the wars raging on and off among the major democratic powers fighting on the island from 455 to 406; and Argos and other democratic allies of Athens engaged against democratic allies of Sparta and Syracuse at various points during the Peloponnesian War.[87]

Indeed, the conclusion seems inescapable that Classical Greek democracies do not show the same striking pattern of forbearance from violent conflict against one another that modern democracies tend to. Nevertheless, there are occasional signs of constitution-based cooperation between democracies.[88] Thucydides notes on more than one occasion how, after the outbreak of the Peloponnesian War, democracies (and democratic factions) would often look to each other for help against oligarchies, while oligarchies (and oligarchic factions) tended to work together and were suspicious of democracies.[89] This phenomenon clearly continued after the war and well into the fourth century, as Sparta persisted in favoring oligarchies at the expense of democracies and Athens and certain democracies did the reverse. Demosthenes presumes a common bond between democracies (and common antipathy toward oligarchy) at 15.17–20. Indeed, a trait shared by some of the non-Athenian democracies surveyed in the first three chapters of the present study was a tendency to intervene on behalf of democratic causes: Argos, Arcadia, Thebes, and Syracuse could all be found over the years to have expended substantial effort intervening abroad toward this end.[90] Might we assert as a general rule that, even if no "democratic peace" existed in Classical Greece, ancient democracies did share a predisposition to intervene militarily on each other's behalf?

A broader view of the evidence suggests that the answer here is mixed at best: a pattern of democratic intervention is frequently detectable but it is not consistent, nor does the interventionism necessarily have to do with the constitution itself. Much as Athens did not always attempt to

---

[87] Robinson, "Reading and Misreading," 603–4; Hansen and Nielsen, eds., *Inventory*, 85. Simply noting the mainland democracies discussed in Chapter 1 that were members of Sparta's Peloponnesian League, the Aegean democracies of Chapter 3 that were members of the Delian League, and the Sicilian democracies of Chapter 2 that fought against either Syracuse or Athens in the second half of the fifth century, one rapidly realizes how many democracies found themselves on opposing sides during major wars of the Classical period.

[88] I have explored these affinities in greater detail than what follows here in "Thucydides and Democratic Peace" and "Greek Democracies and the Debate over Democratic Peace."

[89] E.g., 1.19, 1.126, 3.82.1, 5.28–31, 5.44, 8.64–5. More tendentiously, 3.47.2.

[90] Democratic interventions: by Argos (Chapter 1), in Corinth, Mantinea, Sicyon, Arcadia, and Phlius; by Mantinea and Arcadia (Chapter 1), in Tegea, Sicyon, Elis, and Pellene; by Thebes (Chapter 1), in Plataea, Thespiae, and Boeotia generally, plus Achaea; by Syracuse (Chapter 2), in numerous Sicilian cities.

install democracies whenever and wherever it could (see discussion in Chapter 4), non-Athenian *demokratiai* also failed to act consistently.[91] Moreover, it should be noticed that the states providing all the examples of democratic interventions here happen to be states that showed aggressive behavior throughout their history, under *any* type of regime: Argos, Thebes, and Syracuse were regional powers that all through the Archaic and Classical periods behaved intrusively toward other *poleis* as they strove to establish local areas of influence; that they also did so in the time of their democratic regimes ultimately tells us little or nothing about democracy as a driver of foreign intervention. As for Arcadia, its federal state was born into direct conflict with Sparta in the aftermath of Thebes' victory at Leuctra, a conflict long since polarized along democratic/oligarchic lines; that Arcadia turned to other democracies (Argos, Thebes) and sought to solidify and create further democratic allies (Tegea, Sicyon, Elis, Pellene) only stands to reason under the circumstances. Beyond Argos, Arcadia, Thebes, and Syracuse, we do not detect analogous patterns of behavior among the numerous non-Athenian *demokratiai* discussed in the foregoing chapters.

Thus we would do best to avoid making a generalized claim about any shared democratic tendency to intervene on behalf of other democracies, even though more evidence can be garnered for such activity than for the non-existent ancient "democratic peace."

VARIATIONS

So far the bulk of this chapter has explored commonalities (real and perceived) among Classical democracies. Overall, we have found that ancient Greek notions about what characterized *demokratia* are amply demonstrated in the testimony about non-Athenian examples of the constitution. Numerous "true" democracies existed in the Greek world sharing fundamental features, both institutional and ideological. But to assert this much is not to deny that variations in democratic practice existed, or that particular examples of *demokratia* might show distinguishing characteristics. Let us, then, consider some of the interesting ways (beyond foreign and military policies) in which Classical democracies might differ from each other and from the familiar case at Athens.

First, one must point out the apparent variety of *types* of democracy one could encounter in the Classical period. As Aristotle repeatedly notes in

---

[91] E.g., Thebes in the fourth century with respect to Thessaly, Epaminondas' expedition to Achaea, and probably Messenia (Thebes, Chapter 1); Syracuse with respect to Leontini (Leontini, Chapter 2); Corcyra with respect to Epidamnus (Corcyra and Epidamnus, Chapter 2).

the *Politics*, there were different varieties with greater and lesser levels of democracy. He classifies his democratic types (*demokratias eide*) according to multiple criteria: citizen birth (legitimate or not, one or two citizen parents); property qualifications for office-holding; predominant occupation of the *demos* (farming, pasturing, fishing, menial, etc.); frequency of active participation by the *demos*; and whether the law (*nomos*) rules or the masses (*plethos*) do. He usually groups the results into four types, though he is not entirely consistent about them, and different discussions highlight different characteristics. Nevertheless, one always finds a general progression from a more restricted (and, for Aristotle, responsible) style of democratic practice to the more extreme and "lawless" type.[92]

The evidence from the various states discussed in the first three chapters of this study would seem to bear out the general notion that some states carried out a more populist democratic practice than others. Argos and Syracuse, on balance, illustrate a fairly unconstrained form. The records portray each as having had a dominating, even domineering *demos* that jealously guarded its power and occasionally acted capriciously against its elite leaders. Generals were often tried or summarily punished for malfeasance, proven or unproven; ostracism in one form or another awaited some who had committed no crime at all; and plots against the *demos* were often suspected and could be uprooted with ferocity. There were many officials, such as the fifteen generals at Syracuse who suffered operational micromanagement by the *demos* in assembly, or the myriad boards attested in the new Argive financial documents, boards that served very short terms of office. In both *poleis* councils took a back seat to the assemblies, if the surviving narrative accounts are any indication.[93]

On the other hand, Mantinea would seem to show a more restrained style of *demokratia*.[94] Here some responsibilities of the *demos* were delegated to a smaller body of electors who chose all the most important magistrates in the state. The people are said to have been happy to spend less time hassling with the details of governance, retaining their sense of control in the state through assembly deliberations – which took place less often than elsewhere – and in watching out for official wrongdoing through *euthunai*.[95]

However, such contrasting cases oversimplify the situation. Surely Aristotle's ranging of types along a line from least to most responsible, even

[92] *Pol.* 1291b30–1292a38; 1292b24–1293a12; 1318b6–1319b33. See Robinson, *First Democracies*, 37–9.
[93] See Argos, Chapter 1, and Syracuse, Chapter 2.
[94] Aristotle, of course, mentions Mantinea as just that at *Pol.* 1318b6–27.
[95] See Mantinea, Chapter 1.

if loosely based on observable phenomena, unnecessarily collapses a wide range of practice into a one-dimensional progression. Consider citizenship. For Aristotle, degree of inclusiveness is one of the cardinal methods of separating prudent, limited democracies from the extreme forms. Thus relatively moderate, "Type 2" democracy limits citizenship to those "beyond any challenge," while only the radical "Type 4" cases allow those with only one citizen parent to count fully.[96] But we know for a fact that setting a high bar for full citizenship did not always track with popular radicalism in actual democracies. Athens in the second half of the fifth century – in most respects matching Aristotle's description of "Type 4" democracy – operated under the Periclean citizenship law, which restricted full membership to those with two Athenian parents. One can easily imagine cases where great participatory prerogatives might be granted to relatively restricted citizen bodies, and conversely limited access to power dispersed widely among a population.

As it turns out, defining actual local citizenship rules is an area where we are not well informed when it comes to cases of non-Athenian democracy.[97] But we may at least posit that this is something about which rules and traditions probably varied from place to place without necessarily corresponding to, say, the degree of demotic domination in the assembly and the courts. Thus, we can see the outlines of a multidimensional typology of *demokratia* emerging. On one axis could be the level of citizen inclusion; on another, the degree of governing assertiveness by the participating *demos*. Another axis might track the degree of foreign activism on behalf of democratic causes, following the discussion above. Other axes are imaginable. Scholars sometimes speculate about the relative power of councils versus the *demos* in democracies: one might construct an axis with the apparently strong Corcyran council at one extreme and the weaker (or at least less visibly potent) ones at Argos, Syracuse, and Thebes toward the other end.[98] However one might choose to build a multidimensional typology, having three or four (or more) axes rather than just one would avoid reducing matters to a simplistic linear progression.

Other areas of variation present themselves as well. One finds vast differences locally with respect to the titles of officials and other institutions.

---

[96] *Pol.* 1292a1–6, 1319b6–11.
[97] A few exceptions: Cyrene (Chapter 2), Byzantium (Chapter 3), and Olbia (Chapter 3).
[98] See individual discussions of these cases in Chapters 1 and 2. I have been skeptical in each of these cases that a weak council can truly be inferred from the available evidence. The claims all suffer from dependence on a very poor argument from silence given our exiguous source material. Nevertheless, collectively, the relative obscurity of democratic councils in Argos, Syracuse, and Thebes may be worth noting.

Names and boards familiar from the famous Athenian example do crop up, but not especially often (which is only what one would expect given the results from Chapter 4 regarding the limited Athenian role in spreading *demokratia*). At Mantinea the most important offices, to judge from references in an extant treaty, were the *demiourgoi, polemarchoi*, and *theoroi*, not the Athenian *archontes* or *prutaneis* or *strategoi*.[99] At Argos, higher magistrates are called *artunai*; an especially important body was the Eighty, which had multiple responsibilities and no clear parallel at Athens or anywhere else; and then there were completely unique boards such as the *anelateres*, who may have been collectors of fines.[100] The eponymous magistrate in Byzantium was the *hieromnamon*; at Cos, interestingly, the *monarchos*.[101]

Most variations in office titles, numbers and other details do not in themselves signify much about the nature of the democratic practice in the cities. Sometimes, however, they do. The Arcadians chose only one *strategos* to command the forces of their confederacy. This would naturally put much greater political and military power in the hands of one individual than was normal for *demokratiai*; the federal nature of the state, not to mention its fight for survival against Sparta from the beginning, probably explains the practice.[102] The unique Coan *monarchos* may also have been unusually influential as well – he seems to have come from the upper classes and served alone for a full year while his most important colleagues (the *prostatai*) served on a board of five for only six months. However, most of what we know about the *monarchos* derives from the period of Cos's Hellenistic democracy, and even then it is possible that the post had more ceremonial than real power.[103]

Against these likely cases of potent lone officials we can set examples of magistracies rendered relatively weak by board size or by term of office. I have already mentioned the fifteen-man college of generals at Syracuse that in addition apparently suffered from demotic micromanagement.[104] At Taras, generals could serve for only one term, while at Thurii they could serve once every five years. Restrictive rules such as these made it harder, one would expect, to exercise influential leadership from office against an assertive *demos*.[105] More generally, in those democracies where we know many magistrates served six-month terms instead of one-year terms (Argos, Cos, Iasus), the effect will have been to magnify the power of the *demos* over the officials, given the briefer time for them to establish themselves in

---

[99] See Mantinea, Chapter 1.   [100] See Argos, Chapter 1.   [101] Chapter 3 for Byzantium and Cos.
[102] Chapter 1, Mantinea and the Arcadians.   [103] Cos, Chapter 3.   [104] Syracuse, Chapter 2.
[105] One should note, however, the traditions about the powerful leader Archytas at Taras, who supposedly served six or seven terms as general. See Taras and Thurii, Chapter 2.

office and the doubling of occasions on which the *demos* was able to express its preference in elections.[106] Aristotle would no doubt agree, since in the *Politics* he asserts that shorter terms and greater rotation of people through offices is more democratic: it gives more people chance to rule and lessens the odds of official corruption.[107]

Finally, there are variations in practice that suggest unusual populist approaches to *polis* governance were at work in some communities. Our sources imply that in Megara during its democracy voting in the assembly was at least sometimes done secretly.[108] Secret balloting was hardly unheard of in the ancient world – it was used often in trials at Athens and in ostracisms, for example – but we do not hear of any other case where ruling assemblies routinely resorted to it. The Athenians clearly did not consider secret assembly voting to be critical to their democracy.[109] Secret voting procedures, if indeed they were regularly employed at Megara, suggest an unusual concern there either for individual voter privacy, or, more likely, for the discouraging of bribery or intimidation in advance of important votes. Such a sensibility is very common among modern democracies but is hard to find outside judicial settings in the ancient world, making the potential Megarian concerns well worth noting.[110]

Another interesting atypical practice comes from Thurii, where the sons of all citizens were taught to read and write, with the *polis* paying for the teachers, for the explicit purpose of helping the poor participate in community affairs at a higher level.[111] This is most unusual. No other democracies about which we know did this; indeed, it seems to diverge from the normal understanding of ancient democratic education. One might glean from reading speeches by Plato's Protagoras or Thucydides' Pericles that democrats had great confidence in the political potential of ordinary citizens of the *polis* as they were, with the former arguing that all men partook to some extent in *politike arete*, and the latter claiming that the

---

[106] Argos, Chapter 1; Cos, Iasus, Chapter 3. It should be noted that the six-month terms of office in the last two are certainly attested only for their Hellenistic era democracies.

[107] 1308a13–15; 1317b23–6. See also 1261a30; 1317b19–20.   [108] Megara, Chapter 1.

[109] Though rare, secret balloting was sometimes called for in the Athenian assembly (Andoc. 1.87; Dem. 59.89–90; Hansen, *Athenian Democracy*, 94, 170). Hall argues that it was not just an issue of practicality that kept the Athenians from employing secret ballot in most assemblies, but rather the absence of any concern that democratic choices in elections and other mass meetings would be distorted by pressures that a secret ballot could thwart. U. Hall, "Greeks and Romans and the Secret Ballot," in E. M. Craik, ed., *Owls to Athens: Essays on Classical Subjects Presented to Sir Kenneth Dover* (Oxford, 1990), 191–9, at 192–3.

[110] Rome in the second half of the second century passed a number of *leges tabellariae*, though the concerns that originally prompted them need not have had much to do with democracy. See Hall, "Secret Ballot."

[111] Thurii, Chapter 2. The evidence comes from Diod. Sic. 12.12.4.

Variations

245

setting of democratic Athens made it possible for each Athenian to achieve sufficient capability in all endeavors.[112] No state-sponsored education was needed to bring about remarkably successful citizens. Josiah Ober further refines this logic: based especially on more passages in Plato,[113] he maintains that it was a "core ideological conviction" of the Athenian democracy that the institutions of the democratic city provided all the education a young person needed.[114] The Thurian law implies a different view: being a human being was not enough; growing up seeing the operation of democratic laws and procedures was not enough; instead, the poor needed the state's assistance to be able to join in governing on a more equal footing. Thus Thurii's education law is at once patronizing and egalitarian and generous. The logic is perhaps not unlike that which justified public pay for public service, which took place in a number of democracies, though it is unique for its application to education.

Last, we turn to an unusual provision at Taras. Aristotle notes approvingly that the Tarantines make property (*ktemata*) common for the use of the poor, thereby gaining the goodwill of the masses.[115] Whether the *koina ktemata* was land open for public use or other kinds of goods publicly loaned or donated at need, it represented a significant elaboration upon – or perhaps a departure from – normal democratic approaches to public welfare. It differs from public pay for public service, since no public service was immediately expected; even the Thurian law mandating literacy education aimed explicitly at improving citizenship, whereas this one offered straightforward economic assistance. The public sharing of goods for the benefit of the poor, whether along the lines of Spartan communitarianism or the generosity of rulers such as Peisistratus with his alleged loans to needy farmers,[116] tended not to be part of the program in democratic cities.[117] The indirect methods of wealth redistribution from rich to poor that one found in democracies – liturgies, *eisphorai*, public pay for public service, prejudiced jury verdicts[118] – are not quite the same thing. We may see here in Sparta's colony Taras the merging into a democratic order of a more typically non-democratic approach to public welfare.

---

[112] Plato, *Prot.* 320c–328d; Thuc. 2.37–41.   [113] *Ap.* 24c–25c; *Resp.* 492b–e.
[114] "The Athenian Debate over Civic Education," 128–56. (Quotation at 134).
[115] *Pol.* 1320b10–16. See Taras, Chapter 2.   [116] Arist. *Ath. Pol.* 16.2. Rhodes, *Commentary*, ad loc.
[117] Though hardly designed for general poverty alleviation, the Athenian democracy did offer certain limited kinds of "social security" payments to citizens: war orphans, the disabled, and the people generally during food shortages; Hansen, *Athenian Democracy*, 98.
[118] For a discussion of the redistributive aspect of such institutions at Athens, see Ober, *Mass and Elite*, 199–202.

CONCLUSION

Other variations from a putative norm (Athenian or otherwise) might be mentioned from the many examples surveyed in earlier chapters, but we need not. From what has already been discussed here it is apparent that non-Athenian democracies, while generally sharing baseline institutional and ideological features that mark them out as true *demokratiai*, nevertheless occasionally differed in their practices and tendencies. Some of the variations appear trivial, while others represent meaningful distinctions. It served Aristotle's mode of analysis to place all types of democracy along a single line going from moderate to radical, which is to say from good to bad, but we have seen the inadequacy of such a scheme. A multidimensional typology with different axes representing different aspects of democratic policy makes more sense.

A general comparison of non-Athenian examples with the Athenian one produces interesting results. As one of the arguments of Chapter 4 showed, Athens was not alone in its tendency toward democratic interventionism, and indeed one or two other more localized hegemons might have been more consistent, while the majority of *demokratiai* probably had little to do with such activism. For democratic moderation versus sheer populist domination of institutions and policy-making – what Aristotle might call "tyranny of the *demos*" – examples around Greece fell all across the spectrum, but again Athens was hardly alone in illustrating one extreme: various other states offer briefer histories nevertheless replete with episodes of demotic willfulness and violence in defense of popular prerogatives. Tales of rash and capricious decisions in the assembly and the courts come from many places other than the Pnyx and the agora – not even the reckless frenzy of the Hermocopidae aftermath or the Arginusae trial can compete with what transpired during the Argive *skutalismos*, for example. Democratic institutions to match and even occasionally exceed Athenian ones in terms of populist extremes (such as six-month terms of office) can be found outside Attica, usually in more than one *polis*. Thus not only cannot Athens be considered the only "true" democracy of the Classical world; it is far from safe to judge it the most radical one.

Not all will accept the conclusions of these last two chapters or the surveys that came before, and this is to be expected. The present study is not intended to be the final word on the subject of non-Athenian democracy in the Classical period, and especially not on comparison with the Athenian example, about which we have only occasionally been concerned. Rather, it is hoped that by focusing attention on the subject, gathering in one place much of the available information regarding non-Athenian democracies, and providing some preliminary conclusions, further debate might be sparked. The continuing modern interest in the origins of the remarkable system of government that exercises such prevalence today demands that we take a broader view of Greek democracy than has heretofore been the case, lest we confuse the history of one city-state with the history of a constitutional form. Let the discussions begin.

Data for Figures 4.1–4.4

The following dates are artificially precise extrapolations from the treatments in Chapters 1–3, produced to be data for Figure 4.1. See each city-state's entry in these chapters for discussion of its democratic chronology.

Polis	Democracy attested with a high degree of certainty Dates BC	Democracy attested with a lesser degree of certainty Dates BC
MAINLAND		
Peloponnese		
Argos	465–418; 416–323	480–466
Corinth	392–386	
Achaea	480–417; 366; 339–323	
Elis	480–365; 345–323	
Mantinea/Arcadians	421–385; 371–323	480–422
Phlius	395–379	
Sicyon		480–417; 368–366
Zacynthus	390–375	480–391
Northwest Greece		
Leucas		480–323
Central Greece		
Megara	427–424; 375–360	
Plataea	432–427	480–433
Thebes/Boeotia	480–450; 379–335	
Thessaly		406–404
WESTERN GREECE		
Sicily		
Syracuse	466–406; 357–356; 344–339	338–336
Acragas	472–406	
Camarina		461–400

Polis	Democracy attested with a high degree of certainty Dates BC	Democracy attested with a lesser degree of certainty Dates BC
Gela	466–405	
Himera	466–409	
Leontini	463–424	
Selinous	466–410	
Southern Italy		
Caulonia	445–388	
Croton	445–388	
Heraclea on Siris		433–323
Messana	400–396	466–401
Rhegium	400–387	466–401; 351–344
Taras	470–350	
Thurii	444–413	
Northwest Greece		
Corcyra	435–361	480–436
Epidamnus	436–433	
North Africa		
Cyrene	440–401	400–325

EASTERN GREECE
Aegean coast

Polis	Dates BC	Dates BC
Abdera	480–404	
Teos	480–404	
Amphipolis	437–424	423–380; 365–323
Cyme (in Aeolis)		480–323
Iasus	393–323	450–412
Aphytis		480–323
Cnidus	334–323	
Ephesus	480–412; 334–323	
Erythrae	453–387; 334–323	
Hestiaea/Oreus	475–405; 395–382; 378–357; 341–323	
Miletus	446–405; 334–323	402–335
Aegean islands		
Cos		480–323
Paros	465–412; 373–323	410–397
Rhodes	395–391; 375–355; 332–323	450–411
Eretria	342–323	446–411
Mytilene	332–323	428–405; 390–350
Samos	441–440; 412–404	
Thasos	465–411; 407–405	373–323

(cont.)

Polis	Democracy attested with a high degree of certainty	Democracy attested with a lesser degree of certainty
	Dates BC	Dates BC
Propontis		
Byzantium	390–323	477–403
Calchedon	355–323	477–405
Black Sea		
Tauric Chersonesus	424–323	480–425
Heraclea Pontica	424–365	
Istrus		440–323
Olbia	399–323	435–400

Bibliography

Ameling, W. *The Inscriptions of Heraclea Pontica.* Bonn: R. Habelt, 1994.

Amit, M. *Great and Small Poleis.* Brussels: Latomus, 1973.

Andrewes, A. "Sparta and Arcadia in the Early 5th Century." *Phoenix* 56 (1952): 1–5.

Applebaum, S. *Jews and Greeks in Ancient Cyrene.* Leiden: Brill, 1979.

Asheri, D. "Agrigento libera: rivolgimenti interni e problemi constituzionali, ca 471–446 a.C." *Athenaeum* 78 (1990): 483–501.

"Sicily, 478–431 B.C." In *CAH²*, vol. v, edited by D. M. Lewis, J. Boardman, J. K. Davies, and M. Ostwald. Cambridge University Press, 1992: 147–70.

Aubonnet, J. *Aristote Politique*, vol. ii. Paris: Les Belles Lettres, 1973.

Austin, M. M. "Greek Tyrants and the Persians, 546–479 B.C." *CQ* 40 (1990): 289–306.

Bacchielli, L. "Modelli politici e modelli architettonici a Cirene durante il regime democratico." In *Cyrenaica in Antiquity*, edited by G. Barker, J. Lloyd, and J. M. Reynolds. Oxford: British Archaeological Reports, 1985: 1–14.

"L'ostracismo a Cirene." *RFIC* 122.3 (1994): 257–70.

Bachteler, T. "Explaining the Democratic Peace: The Evidence from Ancient Greece Reviewed." *Journal of Peace Research* 34.3 (1997): 315–23.

Barakari-Gléni, K. and A. Pariente. "Argos du VIIième au IIième siècle av. J.-C.: synthèse des données archéologiques." In *Argos et l'Argolide: topographie et urbanisme*, edited by A. Pariente and G. Touchais. Paris: de Boccard, 1998: 165–78.

Barrett, W. S. "Pindar's Twelfth *Olympian* and the Fall of the Deinomenidai." *JHS* 93 (1973): 23–35.

Barron, J. P. *The Silver Coins of Samos.* London: Athlone Press, 1966.

Beck, H. *Polis und Koinon: Untersuchungen zur Geschichte und Struktur der griechischen Bundesstaaten im 4. Jahrhundert v. Chr.* Stuttgart: Franz Steiner Verlag, 1997.

"Thebes, the Boeotian League, and 'The Rise of Federalism.'" In *Presenza e funzione della città di Tebe nella cultura greca*, edited by P. A. Bernardini. Pisa: Istituti Editoriali e Poligrafici Internazionale, 2000: 331–44.

Beister, H. "Hegemoniales Denken in Theben." In *Boiotika*, edited by H. Beister and J. Buckler. Munich: Editio Maris, 1989: 131–53.

Beloch, J. *Die Bevölkerung der griechisch-römischen Welt.* Leipzig: Verlag Duncker and Humblot, 1886.

Berger, S. "Democracy in the Greek West and the Athenian Example." *Hermes* 117 (1989): 303–14.

"Revolution and Constitution in Thurii: Arist. *Pol.* 1307 a–b." *Eranos* 88 (1990): 9–16.

Revolution and Society in Greek Sicily and Southern Italy (*Historia* Einzelschriften 71). Stuttgart: Franz Steiner Verlag, 1992.

Bernabo Brea, L. "Studi sul teatro greco di Siracusa." *Palladio* 17 (1967): 97–154.

Bernardini, P. A., ed. *Presenza e funzione della città di Tebe nella cultura greca.* Pisa: Istituti Editoriali e Poligrafici Internazionale, 2000.

Berranger-Auserve, D. *Paros ii.* Clermont-Ferrand: Presses Universitaires Blaise Pascal, 2000.

Berthold, R. M. *Rhodes in the Hellenistic Age.* Ithaca: Cornell University Press, 1984.

Berve, H. *Die Tyrannis bei den Griechen*, vol. i. Munich: C. H. Beck, 1987.

Biers, W. R. "Excavations at Phlius, 1970." *Hesperia* 40 (1971): 424–47.

"Excavations at Phlius, 1972." *Hesperia* 42 (1973): 102–19.

Bingen, J. "Epigraphica (Thrace, Rhodes)." *ZPE* 46 (1982): 183–4.

Bleicken, J. *Die athenische Demokratie.* 2nd edn. Paderborn: Schoningh, 1994.

Bloedow, E. F. "The Speeches of Hermocrates and Athenagoras at Syracuse in 415 BC: Difficulties in Syracuse and in Thucydides." *Historia* 45 (1996): 141–58.

Blümel, W., ed. *Die Inschriften von Iasos*, vol. i. Bonn: R. Habelt, 1985.

Boedeker, D. and K. A. Raaflaub. *Democracy, Empire, and the Arts in Fifth Century Athens.* Cambridge, MA: Harvard University Press, 1998.

Boegehold, A. L. "Pericles' Citizenship Law of 451/0 B.C." In *Athenian Identity and Civic Ideology*, edited by A. L. Boegehold and A. C. Scafuro. Baltimore: Johns Hopkins University Press, 1994: 57–66.

Boegehold, A. L. and A. C. Scafuro, eds. *Athenian Identity and Civic Ideology.* Baltimore: Johns Hopkins University Press, 1994.

Bolmarich, S. "Thucydides 1.19.1 and the Peloponnesian League." *GRBS* 45.1 (2005): 5–34.

Bommelaer, J.-F. and J. Des Courtils. *La salle hypostyle d'Argos.* Athens: École française d'Athènes, 1994.

Borgia, E. "Gela." In *Teatri, greci e romani*, vol. ii, edited by P. C. Rossetto and G. P. Sartorio. Rome: Edizione SEAT, 1994: 471.

Bosworth, A. B. *Conquest and Empire: The Reign of Alexander the Great.* Cambridge University Press, 1988.

Brauer, G. C. *Taras: Its History and Coinage.* New York: A. D. Caratzas, 1986.

Brenne, S. "Thukydides 1, 135, 2–3 (ca. 431–395 v. Chr.): Die Ostrakisierung des Themistokles (470 v. Chr.)." In *Ostrakismos Testimonien I*, edited by P. Siewert. Stuttgart: Franz Steiner Verlag, 2002: 247–57.

Briant, P. *From Cyrus to Alexander: A History of the Persian Empire*, translated by P. T. Daniels. Winona Lake, IN: Eisenbrauns, 2002.

Brock, R. and S. Hodkinson, eds. *Alternatives to Athens: Varieties of Political Organization and Community in Ancient Greece*. Oxford University Press, 2000.

Bruce, I. A. F. "The Democratic Revolution at Rhodes." *CQ* 55 n.s. 11 (1961): 166–70.

"The Corcyrean Civil War of 427 BC." *Phoenix* 25 (1971): 108–17.

Brugnone, A. "Legge di Himera sulla ridistribuzione della terra." *PP* 52 (1997): 262–305.

Brunt, P. A. "Review: Athens and Sicily." *CR* n.s. 7 (1957): 243–5.

"Spartan Policy and Strategy in the Archidamian War." In *Studies in Greek History and Thought*. Oxford: Clarendon Press, 1993: 84–111.

Buck, C. D. *The Greek Dialects*. Chicago University Press, 1955.

Buck, R. J. "The Minoan Thalassocracy Re-examined." *Historia* 11 (1962): 129–37.

A History of Boeotia. Edmonton: University of Alberta Press, 1979.

Buckler, J. *The Theban Hegemony, 371–362 BC*. Cambridge, MA: Harvard University Press, 1980.

"A Note on Diodorus 14.86.1." *CPh* 94 (1999): 210–14.

Burstein, S. M. *Outpost of Hellenism: The Emergence of Heraclea on the Black Sea*. Berkeley: University of California Press, 1976.

Bury, J. B. and R. Meiggs. *A History of Greece to the Death of Alexander the Great*. London: MacMillan, 1975.

Busolt, G. and H. Swoboda. *Griechische Staatskunde*. 2 vols. Munich: C. H. Beck, 1920, 1926.

Carlsson, S. *Hellenistic Democracies. Freedom, Independence, and Political Procedure in Some East Greek City-States*. Stuttgart: Franz Steiner Verlag, 2010.

Cartledge, P. *Sparta and Lakonia: A Regional History, 1300–362 B.C.* 2nd edn. London: Routledge, 2002.

Cary, M. "A Constitutional Inscription from Cyrene." *JHS* 48 (1928): 222–38.

Casson, L. *Ships and Seamanship in the Ancient World*. Baltimore: Johns Hopkins University Press, 1985.

Caven, B. *Dionysius I, Warlord of Syracuse*. New Haven: Yale University Press, 1990.

Ceccarelli, Paola. "Sans thalassocratie, pas de démocratie?" *Historia* 42 (1993): 444–70.

Cerchiai, L., L. Jannelli, and F. Longo. *The Greek Cities of Magna Graecia and Sicily*. Los Angeles: J. Paul Getty Museum, 2004.

Chamoux, F. *Cyrène sous la monarchie des Battiades*. Paris: de Boccard, 1953.

Cole, T. *The Origins of Rhetoric in Ancient Greece*. Baltimore: Johns Hopkins University Press, 1991.

Cole, T. "Who Was Corax?" *Illinois Classical Studies* 16 (1991): 65–84.

Consigny, S. *Gorgias, Sophist and Artist*. Columbia, SC: University of South Carolina Press, 2001.

Consolo Langher, S. N. *Un imperialismo tra democrazia e tirannide. Siracusa nei secoli V e IV a.C.* Rome: Bretschneider, 1997.

Cordano, F. "*Phonos megistos hellenikos.*" *Atti e Memorie della Società Magna Grecia* 15–17 (1974–6): 203–6.

Le tessere pubbliche dal Tempio di Atena a Camarina. Rome: Istituto Italiano per la Storia Antica, 1992.

"Camarina città democratica?" *PP* 59 (2004): 283–92.

Costabile, F. "Strateghi e assemblea nelle politeiai di Reggio e Messana." *Klearchos* 20 (1978): 19–57.

Craik, E. M., ed. *Owls to Athens: Essays on Classical Subjects Presented to Sir Kenneth Dover.* Oxford: Clarendon Press, 1990.

Crawley, R., trans. *Thucydides:* The Peloponnesian War, rev. T. E. Wick. New York: Random House, 1982.

Crowther, C. V. "Iasos in the Second Century BC. III: Foreign Judges from Priene." *BICS* 40 (1995).

David, E. "Aeneas Tacticus, 11.7–10 and the Argive revolution of 370 B.C." *AJPh* 107 (1986): 343–9.

"The Oligarchic Revolution in Argos, 417 B.C." *AC* 55 (1986): 113–24.

Davies, J. K. *Democracy and Classical Greece.* 2nd edn. Cambridge, MA: Harvard University Press, 1993.

Demand, N. *Thebes in the Fifth Century: Heracles Resurgent.* London: Routledge, 1982.

Urban Relocation in Archaic and Classical Greece. Norman: University of Oklahoma Press, 1990.

Des Courtils, J. "L'architecture et l'histoire d'Argos dans la première moitié du Ve siècle avant J.-C." In *Polydipsion Argos* (BCH Supplement 22), edited by M. Piérart. Paris: de Boccard, 1992: 241–51.

Diels, H. and W. Kranz. *Die Fragmente der Vorsokratiker.* Berlin: Weidmann, 1951.

Dittenberger, W. and K. Purgold. *Die Inschriften von Olympia.* Berlin: Asher Verlag, 1896.

Drachmann, A. B. *Scholia Vetera in Pindari Carmina*, vol. 11. Leipzig: Teubner, 1910.

Dreher, M. "La dissoluzione della *polis* di Leontini dopo la pace di Gela (424 A. C.)." *Annali della Scuola Normale Superiore di Pisa, Classe di Lettere e Filosophia* 16.3 (1986): 637–60.

Hegemon und Symmachoi: Untersuchungen zum zweiten athenischen Seebund. Berlin: De Gruyter, 1995.

Drögemüller, H.-P. *Syrakus. Zur Topographie und Geschichte einer griechischen Stadt.* Heidelberg: Carl Winter, 1969.

Dubois, L. *Inscriptions grecques dialectales d'Olbia du Pont.* Geneva: Librairie Droz, 1996.

Ducat, J. *Les Pénestes de Thessalie.* Paris: Diffusé par les Belles lettres, 1994.

Dunbabin, T. J. *The Western Greeks.* Oxford: Clarendon Press, 1948.

Ehrenberg, V. "The Foundation of Thurii." *AJPh* 69 (1948): 149–70.

Falkner, C. "Sparta and the Elean War, ca 401/400 B.C.: Revenge or Imperialism?" *Phoenix* 50 (1996): 17–25.

Farrar, C. *The Origins of Democratic Thinking: The Invention of Politics in Classical Athens.* Cambridge University Press, 1988.

Fauber, C. M. "Was Kerkyra a Member of the Second Athenian League?" *CQ* 48 (1998): 110–16.

Figueira, T. J. *Aegina, Society and Politics.* New York: Arno Press, 1981.

——— *Excursions in Epichoric History.* Lanham, MD: Rowman and Littlefield, 1993.

Finley, M. I. *Ancient Sicily.* 2nd edn. Totowa, NJ: Rowman and Littlefield, 1979.

Fiorentini, G. "L'età dionigiana a Gela e Agrigento." In *La Sicilia dei due Dionisî*, edited by N. Bonacasa, L. Braccesi, and E. De Miro. Rome: L'Erma di Bretschneider, 2002: 147–67.

Flensted-Jensen, P., T. H. Nielsen, and L. Rubinstein, eds. *Polis & Politics: Studies in Ancient Greek History.* Copenhagen: Museum Tusculanum Press, 2000.

Flory, S. Review of Victor Davis Hanson, *A War Like No Other. How the Athenians and Spartans Fought the Peloponnesian War. BMCRev* 2006.03.40 (2006).

Flower, M. *Theopompus of Chios: History and Rhetoric in the Fourth Century B.C.* Oxford: Clarendon Press, 1994.

Forrest, W. G. "Themistokles and Argos." *CQ* n.s. 10 (1960): 221–41.

Forsdyke, S. *Exile, Ostracism, and Democracy: The Politics of Expulsion in Ancient Greece.* Princeton University Press, 2005.

——— "Revelry and Riot in Archaic Megara: Democratic Disorder or Ritual Reversal?" *JHS* 125 (2005): 73–92.

Fotheringham, J. K. "On the 'List of Thalassocracies' in Eusebius (continued)." *JHS* 27 (1907): 75–89.

Fougères, G. *Mantinée et l'Arcadie orientale.* Paris: A. Fontemoing, 1898.

Fraser, P. M. "Notes on Two Rhodian Institutions." *ABSA* 67 (1972): 119–24.

Fritz, K. von. *Pythagorean Politics in Southern Italy.* New York: Columbia University Press, 1940.

Frost, F. J. *Plutarch's Themistocles: A Historical Commentary.* Princeton University Press, 1980.

Fuks, A. *Social Conflict in Ancient Greece.* Jerusalem: Magness Press, 1984.

Gabrielsen, V. *The Naval Aristocracy of Hellenistic Rhodes.* Aarhus University Press, 1997.

——— "Naval Warfare: Its Economic and Social Impact on Greek Cities." In *War as a Cultural and Social Force*, edited by T. Bekker-Nielsen and L. Hannestad. Copenhagen: Kongelige Danske Videnskabernes Selskab, 2001: 72–89.

——— "Socio-economic Classes and Ancient Greek Warfare." In *Ancient History Matters. Studies Presented to Jens Erik Skydsgaard on His Seventieth Birthday*, edited by K. Ascani. Rome: L'Erma di Bretschneider, 2002: 203–20.

Gauthier, P. "L'inscription d'Iasos relative à l'*ekklesiastikon*." *BCH* 114.1 (1990): 417–43.

Gauthier, P. "Les cités hellénistiques." In *The Ancient Greek City-State*, edited by M. H. Hansen. Copenhagen: Munksgaard, 1993: 211–31.

Gehrke, H.-J. "Zur Geschichte Milets in der Mitte des 5. Jahrhunderts v. Chr." *Historia* 29 (1980): 17–31.

Stasis. Untersuchungen zu den inneren Kriegen in den griechischen Staaten des 5. und 4. Jahrhunderts v. Chr. Munich: C. H. Beck, 1985.

Jenseits von Athen und Sparta. Munich: C. H. Beck, 1986.

Giangiulio, M. "Gli equilibri difficili della democrazia in Sicilia: il caso di Siracusa." In *Venticinque secoli dopo l'invenzione della Democrazia*, edited by L. Canfora. Paestum: Fondazione Paestum, 1998: 107–123.

Gillis, D. "The Revolt at Mytilene." *AJP* 92 (1971): 38–47.

Ginouvès, R. *Le théatron à gradins droits et l'odéon d'Argos.* Paris: Librairie Philosophique J. Vrin, 1972.

Giudice, F. "La seconda e terza fondazione di Camarina alla luce dei prodotti del commercio coloniale." *Quaderni dell'Istituto di Archeologia della Facoltà di Lettere e Filosofia dell'Università di Messina* (1988): 49–57.

Gomme, A. W., with A. Andrewes and K. J. Dover. *A Historical Commentary on Thucydides.* 5 vols. Oxford: Clarendon Press, 1945–81.

Gorman, V. *Miletos, The Ornament of Ionia.* Ann Arbor: University of Michigan Press, 2001.

Gottlieb, G. *Timuchen: Ein Beitrag zum griechischen Staatsrecht.* Heidelberg: C. Winter, 1967.

Graham, A. J. *Colony and Mother City in Ancient Greece.* 2nd edn. Chicago: Ares, 1983.

Review of Y. G. Vinogradov, *Olbia. Gnomon* 55 (1983): 462.

"An Ellipse in the Thasian Decree about Delation (ML 83)?" *AJPh* 110 (1989): 405–12.

"Adopted Teians: A Passage in the New Inscription of Public Imprecations from Teos." *JHS* 111 (1991): 176–8.

"Abdera and Teos." *JHS* 112 (1992): 42–73.

"Thuc. 7.13.2 and the Crews of Athenian Triremes." *TAPhA* 122 (1992): 257–70.

Review of M. Jameson, D. Jordan, and R. Kotansky, *A Lex Sacra from Selinous. Phoenix* 49 (1995): 366–7.

Collected Papers on Greek Colonization. Leiden: Brill, 2001.

Grandjean, Y. and F. Salviat. "Decret d'Athènes, restaurant la démocratie à Thasos en 407 av. J.-C.: *IG* XII 8, 262 complété." *BCH* 112 (1988): 249–78.

Grieb, V. *Hellenistische Demokratie.* Stuttgart: Franz Steiner Verlag, 2008.

Griffin, A. *Sikyon.* Oxford: Clarendon Press, 1982.

Griffith, G. T. "The Union of Corinth and Argos (392–386 B.C.)." *Historia* 1 (1950): 236–56.

Haas, C. J. "Athenian Naval Power before Themistocles." *Historia* 34 (1985): 29–46.

Hall, U. "Greeks and Romans and the Secret Ballot." In *Owls to Athens: Essays on Classical Subjects Presented to Sir Kenneth Dover*, edited by E. M. Craik. Oxford: Clarendon Press, 1990: 191–9.

Hamel, D. *Athenian Generals: Military Authority in the Classical Period.* Leiden: Brill, 1998.

Hamilton, C. D. "The Politics of Revolution in Corinth, 395–386 B.C." *Historia* 21 (1972): 21–37.

Sparta's Bitter Victories. Ithaca: Cornell University Press, 1979.

Hansen, M. H. *The Athenian Ecclesia.* Copenhagen: Museum Tusculanum Press, 1983.

The Athenian Democracy in the Age of Demosthenes. Oxford: Blackwell, 1991.

"*Polis, Politeuma,* and *Politeia*: A Note on Arist. *Pol.* 1278b6–14." In *From Political Architecture to Stephanus Byzantinus,* edited by D. Whitehead. Stuttgart: Franz Steiner Verlag, 1994: 91–8.

Polis and City-State. Copenhagen: Munksgaard, 1998.

The Shotgun Method: The Demography of the Ancient Greek City-State Culture. Columbia: University of Missouri Press, 2006.

"Loren J. Samons II, *What's Wrong with Democracy? From Athenian Practice to American Worship.*" *BMCRev* 2006.01.32 (2006).

Hansen, M. H. and T. Fischer-Hansen. "Monumental Political Architecture in Archaic and Classical Greek *Poleis.*" In *From Political Architecture to Stephanus Byzantinus. Sources for the Ancient Greek Polis,* edited by D. Whitehead. Stuttgart: Franz Steiner Verlag, 1994: 23–90.

Hansen, M. H. and T. H. Nielsen, eds. *An Inventory of Archaic and Classical Poleis.* Oxford University Press, 2004.

Hansen, M. H., A. C. Hernándes, and P. Pasquino, eds. *Démocratie athénienne – démocratie moderne: tradition et influences.* Vandœuvres: Fondation Hardt, 2009.

Hanson, V. D. *A War Like No Other: How the Athenians and Spartans Fought the Peloponnesian War.* New York: Random House, 2005.

Heisserer, A. J. and R. Hodot. "The Mytilenean Decree on Concord." *ZPE* 63 (1986): 109–28.

Helly, B. *L'état thessalien.* Lyons: Maison de l'Orient Méditerranéen 1995.

"Sur les *fratrai* de Camarina." *PP* 52 (1997): 365–406.

Herrmann, P. "Teos und Abdera im 5. Jahrhundert v. Chr." *Chiron* 11 (1981): 1–30.

Hind, J. "Megarian Colonisation in the Western Half of the Black Sea." In *The Greek Colonization of the Black Sea Area,* edited by G. R. Tsetskhladze. Stuttgart: Franz Steiner Verlag, 1998: 131–52.

Hinks, D. A. G. "Tisias and Corax and the Invention of Rhetoric." *CQ* 40 (1934): 61–9.

Hinrichs, F. T. "Hermokrates bei Thukydides." *Hermes* 109 (1981): 46–59.

Hofer, M. *Tyrannen, Aristokraten, Demokraten.* Bern: P. Lang, 2000.

Hölscher, T. "Images and Political Identity: The Case of Athens." In *Democracy, Empire, and the Arts in Fifth-Century Athens,* edited by D. Boedeker and K. A. Raaflaub. Cambridge, MA: Harvard University Press, 1998: 153–84.

Hornblower, S. *Mausolus.* Oxford: Clarendon Press, 1982.

A Commentary on Thucydides. 3 vols. Oxford: Clarendon Press, 1991–2008.

How, W. W. and J. Wells. *A Commentary on Herodotus.* 2 vols. Oxford: Clarendon Press, 1912, repr. 1928.

Hüttl, W. *Verfassungsgeschichte von Syrakus.* Prague: Verlag der Deutschen Gesellschaft der Wissenschaften und Künste für die Tschechoslowakische Republik, 1929.

Huntington, S. P. "How Countries Democratize." In *Promise and Problems of Old and New Democracies*, edited by Xiaobo Lü. New York: The Academy of Political Science, 2000: 81–118.

Hutchinson, E. P. *Legislative History of American Immigration Policy, 1798–1965*. Philadelphia: University of Pennsylvania Press, 1981.

Isaac, B. *The Greek Settlements in Thrace until the Macedonian Conquest*. Leiden: Brill, 1986.

Isler, H. P. "Siracusa." In *Teatri greci e romani*, vol. III, edited by P. C. Rossetto and G. P. Sartorio. Rome: Edizioni SEAT, 1994: 33–7.

Jameson, M. "A Treasury of Athena in the Argolid (*IG* IV, 554)." In *Phoros: Tribute to Benjamin Dean Merritt*, edited by D. W. Bradeen and M. F. McGregor. Locust Valley: J. J. Augustin, 1974: 67–75.

Jameson, M., D. Jordan, and R. Kotansky. *A Lex Sacra from Selinous*. Durham: Duke University, 1993.

Jameson, M. H., C. N. Runnels, and T. H. van Andel. *A Greek Countryside: The Southern Argolid from Prehistory to the Present Day*. Stanford University Press, 1994.

Jannelli, L. "Himera." In *The Greek Cities of Magna Graecia and Sicily*, edited by L. Cerchiai, L. Jannelli, and F. Longo. Los Angeles: J. Paul Getty Museum, 2004: 188–93.

Jones, A. H. M. "The Hellenistic Age." *P&P* 27 (1964): 3–22.

Jones, N. F. *Public Organization in Ancient Greece*. Philadelphia: American Philosophical Society, 1987.

Kagan, D. "Corinthian Politics and the Revolution of 392 B.C." *Historia* 11 (1962): 447–57.

    The Outbreak of the Peloponnesian War. Ithaca: Cornell University Press, 1969.

    The Peace of Nicias and the Sicilian Expedition. Ithaca: Cornell University Press, 1981.

Kahrstedt, U. "Zur Geschichte Grossgriechenlands im 5ten Jahrhundert." *Hermes* 53 (1918): 180–7.

Kennedy, G. *The Art of Persuasion in Greece*. Princeton University Press, 1963.

Kerferd, G. B. *The Sophistic Movement*. Cambridge University Press, 1981.

Keyt, D. *Aristotle Politics Books V and VI*. Oxford: Clarendon Press, 1999.

Kinsella, D. "No Rest for the Democratic Peace." *American Political Science Review* 99.3 (2005): 453–7.

Knoepfler, D. "Un legislateur thébain chez Cicéron (*De legibus*, II xv 37)." In *Historia Testis: Mélanges d'épigraphie, d'histoire ancienne et de philologie offerts à Tadeusz Zawadzki*, edited by M. Piérart and O. Curty. Fribourg: Editions Universitaires Fribourg Suisse, 1989: 37–60.

    "La loi de Daitondas." In *Presenza e funzione della città di Tebe nella cultura greca*, edited by P. A. Bernardini. Pisa: Istituti Editoriali e Poligrafici Internazionale, 2000: 345–66.

    "Loi d'Érétrie contre la tyrannie et l'oligarchie." *BCH* 125 (2001): 195–238.

    "Loi d'Érétrie contre la tyrannie et l'oligarchie." *BCH* 126 (2002): 149–204.

Knox, R. A. "'So Mischievous a Beaste'? The Athenian *Demos* and Its Treatment of Its Politicians." *G&R* 32 (1985): 132–61.

Kritzas, Ch. "Aspects de la vie politique et économique d'Argos au Ve siècle avant J.-C." In *Polydipsion Argos* (BCH Supplement 22), edited by M. Piérart. Paris: de Boccard, 1992: 231–40.

"Literacy and Society: The Case of Argos." *Kodai Journal of Ancient History* 13/14 (2003/4): 53–60.

"Nouvelles inscriptions d'Argos: les archives des comptes du trésor sacré (IVe s. av. J.-C.)." *CRAI* (2006): 397–434.

"To proto megariko ostrakon." *Horos* 5 (1987): 59–73.

Kroll, J. H. *Athenian Bronze Allotment Plates.* Cambridge, MA: Harvard University Press, 1972.

Kwapong, A. A. "Citizenship and Democracy in Fourth Century Cyrene." In *Africa in Classical Antiquity*, edited by L. A. Thompson and J. Ferguson. Ibadan, Nigeria: Ibadan University Press, 1969: 99–109.

Lanni, A. "Judicial Review and the Athenian 'Constitution.'" In *Démocratie athénienne – démocratie moderne: tradition et influences*, edited by M. H. Hansen, A.-C. Hernández, and P. Pasquino. Vandœuvres: Fondation Hardt, 2009.

Laronde, A. *Cyrène et la Libye hellénistique.* Paris: Éditions du Centre de la Recherche Scientifique, 1987.

Larsen, J. A. O. "Representation and Democracy in Hellenistic Federalism." *CPh* 40 (1945): 65–97.

"A New Interpretation of the Thessalian Confederacy." *CPh* 55 (1960): 229–48.

Greek Federal States: Their Institutions and History. Oxford University Press, 1968.

Legon, R. "Phliasian Politics and Policy in the Early Fourth Century B.C." *Historia* 16 (1967): 329–37.

"Megara and Mytilene." *Phoenix* 22 (1968): 200–25.

Megara: The Political History of a Greek City-State to 336 B.C. Ithaca: Cornell University Press, 1981.

Leppin, H. "Argos. Eine griechische Demokratie des fünften Jahrhunderts v. Chr." *Ktema* 24 (1999): 297–312.

Lewis, D. M. "On the New Text of Teos." *ZPE* 47 (1982): 71–2.

"The Political Background of Democritus." In *Owls to Athens: Essays on Classical Subjects Presented to Sir Kenneth Dover*, edited by E. M. Craik. Oxford: Clarendon Press, 1990: 151–4.

"Mainland Greece, 479–451 B.C." In *CAH²*, vol. v, edited by D. M. Lewis, J. Boardman, J. K. Davies, and M. Ostwald, 96–120. Cambridge University Press, 1992.

"Sicily, 413–368 B.C." In *CAH²*, vol. vi, edited by D. M. Lewis, J. Boardman, S. Hornblower, and M. Ostwald. Cambridge University Press, 1994: 120–55.

Linfert, A. "Prunkaltäre." In *Stadtbild und Bürgerbild im Hellenismus*, edited by M. Wörrle and P. Zanker. Munich: C. H. Beck, 1995: 131–46.

Lintott, A. *Violence, Civil Strife, and Revolution in the Classical City.* London: Croom Helm, 1972.

"Aristotle and Democracy." *CQ* 42 (1992): 114–28.

Loicq-Berger, M.-P. *Syracuse. Histoire culturelle d'une cité grecque.* Brussels: Latomus, 1967.

Lomas, K. *Rome and the Western Greeks 350 BC – AD 200.* London: Routledge, 1993.

Lombardo, M. "La democrazie in Magna Graecia: aspetti e problemi." In *Venticinque secoli dopo l'invenzione della democrazia*, edited by L. Canfora. Paestum: Fondazione Paestum, 1998: 77–106.

Longo, F. "Agrigento (Akragas)." In *The Greek Cities of Magna Graecia and Sicily*, edited by L. Cerchiai, L. Jannelli, and F. Longo. Los Angeles: J. Paul Getty Museum, 2004: 240–55.

"Syracuse." In *The Greek Cities of Magna Graecia and Sicily*, edited by L. Cerchiai, L. Jannelli, and F. Longo. Los Angeles: J. Paul Getty Museum, 2004: 202–15.

Lotze, D. "Zur Verfassung von Argos nach der Schlacht bei Sepei." *Chiron* 1 (1971): 95–109.

"Zum Begriff der Demokratie in Aischylos' 'Hiketiden.'" In *Aischylos und Pindar*, edited by E. G. Schmidt. Berlin: Akademie-Verlag, 1981: 207–16.

Low, P. *Interstate Relations in Classical Greece.* Cambridge University Press, 2007.

Luraghi, N. "Crollo della democrazia o sollevazione anti-oligarchica? Siracusa e Rodi in Aristotle, *Politica* 5 1302b15–33." *Hermes* 126 (1998): 117–23.

Ma, J. "Peer Polity Interaction in the Hellenistic Age." *P&P* 180 (2003): 9–39.

Mader, G. "Strong Points, Weak Argument: Athenagoras on the Sicilian Expedition (Thucydides 6.36–8)." *Hermes* 121 (1993): 433–40.

Mandel, J. "Zur Geschichte des coup d'état von Euphron I in Sikyon." *Euphrosune* 8 (1977): 93–107.

Manganaro, G. "Sikelika I." *QUCC* 49 (1995): 93–109.

Manni, E. "Diocles di Siracusa fra Ermocrate e Dionisio." *Kokalos* 25 (1979): 220–31.

Markle, M. M. "Jury Pay and Assembly Pay at Athens." In *Athenian Democracy*, edited by P. J. Rhodes. New York: Oxford University Press, 2004: 95–131.

McDonald, W. A. *The Political Meeting Places of the Greeks.* Baltimore: Johns Hopkins University Press, 1943.

McKechnie, P. R. and S. J. Kern. *Hellenica Oxyrhynchia.* Warminster: Aris and Phillips, 1988.

Meiggs, R. *The Athenian Empire.* Oxford: Clarendon Press, 1972.

Meister, K. *Die sizilische Geschichte bei Diodor von den Anfängen bis zum Tod des Agathokles.* Diss. Ludwig-Maximilians-Universität, Munich, 1967.

Mejer, J. "Democritus and Democracy." *Apeiron* 37 (2004): 1–9.

Meritt, B. D., H. T. Wade-Gery, and M. F. McGregor. *The Athenian Tribute Lists.* 4 vols. Cambridge, MA: Harvard University Press, 1939–53.

Michel, C. *Recueil d'inscriptions grecques*, with 2 supplements. Brussels: Lamertin, 1900–27.

Migeotte, L. "Démocratie et entretien du peuple à Rhodes." *REG* 102 (1989): 515–28.

Minar, E. L. *Early Pythagorean Politics in Practice and Theory*. Baltimore: Waverly Press, 1942.

Minon, S. *Les inscriptions éléennes dialectales*, vol. I. Geneva: Librairie Droz, 2007.

Miro, E. de. "L'ecclesiasterion in contrada S. Nicola di Agrigento." *Palladio* 16 (1967): 164–8.

Mitchel, F. W. "The Nellos (*IG* II2 43 B 35–38)." *Chiron* 11 (1981): 73–7.

Mitchell, B. "Cyrene: Typical or Atypical." In *Alternatives to Athens*, edited by R. Brock and S. Hodkinson. Oxford University Press, 2000: 82–102.

Momigliano, A. "Sea Power in Greek Thought." *CR* 58 (1944): 1–7.

Moretti, J.-C., with S. Diez. *Théâtres d'Argos*. Athens: École française d'Athènes, 1993.

Moretti, L. "Problemi della storia di Taranto." In *Taranto nella civiltà della Magna Grecia. Atti del decimo Convegno di studi sulla Magna Grecia. Taranto, 4–11 ottobre 1970*. Naples: Arte tipografica, 1971: 47–8.

Morgan, C. *Early Greek States beyond the Polis*. London: Routledge, 2003.

Morris, I. "Beyond Democracy and Empire: Athenian Art in Context." In *Democracy, Empire, and the Arts in Fifth-Century Athens*, edited by D. Boedeker and K. A. Raaflaub. Cambridge, MA: Harvard University Press, 1998: 59–86.

Morrison, J. S., J. F. Coates, and N. B. Rankov. *The Athenian Trireme*. Cambridge University Press, 2000.

Mulgan, R. "Aristotle's Analysis of Oligarchy and Democracy." In *A Companion to Aristotle's Politics*, edited by D. Keyt and F. D. Miller, Jr. Oxford: Blackwell, 1991: 307–22.

Müller, K. "Zwei Kleroterion-Fragmente auf Paros." *AA* 1 (1998): 167–72.

Müller, R. "Sophistique et démocratie." In *Positions de la sophistique*, edited by B. Cassin. Paris: J. Vrin, 1986: 179–93.

Murray, O. *Early Greece*. 2nd edn. Cambridge, MA: Harvard University Press, 1993.

"Rationality and the Greek City: The Evidence from Camarina." In *The Polis as an Urban Centre and as a Political Community* (CPC Acts 4, Historik-filosofiske Meddelelser 75), edited by M. H. Hansen. Copenhagen: Munksgaard, 1997: 493–504.

Musti, D. "Le rivolte antipitagoriche e la concezione pitagorica del tempo." *QUCC* 36 (1990): 35–65.

"Elogio di un oplita in ana lamina di Camarina." *RFIC* 122 (1994): 21–3.

Myres, J. L. "On the 'List of Thalassocracies' in Eusebius." *JHS* 26 (1906): 84–130.

"The 'List of Thalassocracies' in Eusebius: A Reply." *JHS* 27 (1907): 123–30.

Nestle, W. "Phaleas." *RE* 38 (1938): 1658–9.

Newman, W. L. *The Politics of Aristotle*, vol. IV. Oxford: Clarendon Press, 1902.

Newskaja, W. P. *Byzanz in der klassischen und hellenistischen Epoche*, translated from the Russian by H. Bruschwitz, edited by W. Hering. Leipzig: Koehler and Amelang, 1955.

Nielsen, T. H. *Arkadia and Its Poleis in the Archaic and Classical Periods*. Göttingen: Vandenhoeck and Ruprecht, 2002.

Nielsen, T. H., ed. *Even More Studies in the Ancient Greek Polis*. Stuttgart: Franz Steiner Verlag, 2002.

Ober, J. *Mass and Elite in Democratic Athens*. Princeton University Press, 1989.

The Athenian Revolution. Princeton: Princeton University Press, 1994.

"Civic Ideology and Counterhegemonic Discourse: Thucydides on the Sicilian Debate." In *Athenian Identity and Civic Ideology*, edited by A. L. Boegehold and A. C. Scafuro. Baltimore: Johns Hopkins University Press, 1994: 102–26.

Political Dissent in Democratic Athens. Princeton University Press, 1998.

"The Athenian Debate over Civic Education." In *Athenian Legacies*, edited by J. Ober. Princeton University Press, 2005: 128–56.

Democracy and Knowledge. Innovation and Learning in Classical Athens. Princeton University Press, 2008.

O'Neil, J. L. "The Exile of Themistokles and Democracy in the Peloponnese." *CQ* 31 (1981): 335–46.

"How Democratic Was Hellenistic Rhodes?" *Athenaeum* 59 (1981): 468–73.

The Origins and Development of Ancient Greek Democracy. Lanham, MD: Rowman and Littlefield, 1995.

Osborne, R. *Classical Landscape with Figures: The Ancient Greek City and Its Countryside*. New York: Sheridan House, 1987.

Ostwald, M. *Nomos and the Beginnings of the Athenian Democracy*. Oxford: Clarendon Press, 1969.

From Popular Sovereignty to the Sovereignty of Law. Berkeley: University of California Press, 1986.

"*Stasis* and *autonomia* in Samos: A Comment on an Ideological Fallacy." *SCI* 12 (1993): 51–66.

Oligarchia: The Development of a Constitutional Form in Ancient Greece. Stuttgart: Franz Steiner Verlag, 2000.

"Athens and Chalkis: A Study in Imperial Control." *JHS* 122 (2002): 134–43.

Papageorgiadou-Banis, Ch. "Koinon of the Keians? The Numismatic Evidence." *Revue Belge de Numismatique* 139 (1993): 9–16.

Papastavru, J. *Amphipolis, Geschichte und Prosopographie*. Leipzig: Dieterich, 1936.

Pariente, A., M. Piérart, and J.-P. Thalmann. "Rapport sur les travaux de l'École française d'Athènes en 1985; Argos; the Agora." *BCH* 110 (1986): 763–73.

"Les recherches sur l'agora d'Argos: résultats et perspectives." In *Argos et l'Argolide: topographie et urbanisme*, edited by A. Pariente and G. Touchais. Paris: de Boccard, 1998: 211–31.

Pariente, A. and G. Touchais. *Argos et l'Argolide: topographie et urbanisme*. Paris: de Boccard, 1998.

Patterson, C. *Pericles' Citizenship Law of 451/0 B.C.* New York: Arno Press, 1981.

Perlman, S. "The Causes and Outbreak of the Corinthian War." *CQ* (1964): 64–81.

Piérart, M. "Argos, Cleonai, et le Koinon des Arcadiens." *BCH* 106 (1982): 119–38.

Polydipsion Argos (BCH Supplement 22). Paris: de Boccard, 1992.

"Chios entre Athènes et Sparte." *BCH* 119 (1995): 253–82.

"Argos. Un autre démocratie." In *Polis & Politics: Studies in Ancient Greek History*, edited by P. Flensted-Jensen, T. H. Nielsen, and L. Rubinstein. Copenhagen: Museum Tusculanum Press, 2000: 297–314.

Piérart, M. and J.-P. Thalmann. "Nouvelle inscriptions argiennes (I) (Fouilles de l'agora)." In *Études argiennes* (BCH Supplement 6). Paris: de Boccard, 1980: 255–78.

Piérart, M. and G. Touchais. *Argos: un ville grecque de 6000 ans.* Paris: CNRS Editions, 1996.

Polaccio, L. and C. Anti, eds. *Il teatro antico di Siracusa.* Rimini: Maggioli, 1981.

Pouilloux, J. *Recherches sur l'histoire et les cultes de Thasos*, vol. 1. Paris: E. de Boccard, 1954.

Pritchard, D. "How Do Democracy and War Affect Each Other? The Case Study of Ancient Athens." *Polis* 24 (2007): 328–52.

Pritchett, W. K. *The Greek State at War*, vol. 11. Berkeley: University of California Press, 1974.

Quinn, T. J. *Athens and Samos, Lesbos, and Chios, 478–404 B.C.* Manchester University Press, 1981.

Raaflaub, K. A. "Equalities and Inequalities in Athenian Democracy." In *Demokratia: A Conversation on Democracies, Ancient and Modern*, edited by J. Ober and C. Hedrick. Princeton University Press, 1996: 139–74.

"Zeus Eleutherios, Dionysius the Liberator, and the Athenian Tyrannicides: Anachronistic Uses of Fifth-Century Political Concepts." In *Polis & Politics: Studies in Ancient Greek History*, edited by P. Flensted-Jensen, T. H. Nielsen, and L. Rubinstein. Copenhagen: Museum Tusculanum Press, 2000: 249–75.

Raaflaub, K. A., J. Ober, and R. W. Wallace. *Origins of Democracy in Ancient Greece.* Berkeley: University of California Press, 2007.

Rabe, H., ed. *Prolegomenon Sylloge.* Leipzig: Teubner, 1931.

Rackham, H., trans. *Aristotle:* Politics. Cambridge, MA: Harvard University Press, 1932.

Rechenauer, G. "Zu Thukydides II 22,3." *RhM* 136 (1993): 238–44.

Renfrew, C. and J. F. Cherry, eds. *Peer Polity Interaction and Socio-Political Change.* Cambridge University Press, 1986.

Rhodes, P. J. "On Labelling 4th-Century Politicians." *LCM* 3 (1978): 207–11.

A Commentary on the Aristotelian Athenaion Politeia. Oxford: Clarendon Press, 1981.

The Athenian Empire. Oxford: Clarendon Press, 1985.

"The Impact of Athenian Democracy." In *CAH²*, vol. v, edited by D. M. Lewis, J. Boardman, J. K. Davies, and M. Ostwald. Cambridge University Press, 1992: 87–95.

"Oligarchs in Athens." In *Alternatives to Athens*, edited by R. Brock and S. Hodkinson. Oxford University Press, 2000: 119–36.

"Who Ran Democratic Athens?" In *Polis & Politics: Studies in Ancient Greek History*, edited by P. Flensted-Jensen, T. H. Nielsen, and L. Rubinstein. Copenhagen: Museum Tusculanum Press, 2000: 465–77.

"Nothing to Do with Democracy: Athenian Drama and the *Polis*." *JHS* 123 (2003): 104–19.

Rhodes, P. J., with D. M. Lewis. *The Decrees of the Greek States*. Oxford: Clarendon Press, 1997.

Rhodes, P. J. and Robin Osborne. *Greek Historical Inscriptions 404–323 B.C.* Oxford University Press, 2003.

Riedweg, C. *Pythagoras*, translated by S. Rendall. Ithaca: Cornell University Press, 2002.

Robertson, N. "Government and Society at Miletus, 525–442 B.C." *Phoenix* 41 (1987): 356–98.

Robinson, E. W. *The First Democracies: Early Popular Government outside Athens*. Stuttgart: Franz Steiner Verlag, 1997.

"Democracy in Syracuse, 466–412 BC." *HSPh* 100 (2000): 189–205.

"Reading and Misreading the Evidence for Democratic Peace." *Journal of Peace Research* 38.5 (2001): 593–608.

"Response to Spencer Weart." *Journal of Peace Research* 38.5 (2001): 615–17.

"Lead Plates and the Case for Democracy in Fifth-Century BC Camarina." In *Oikistes: Studies in Constitutions, Colonies, and Military Power in the Ancient World Offered in Honor of A. J. Graham*, edited by V. Gorman and E. W. Robinson. Leiden: Brill, 2002: 61–77.

"Thucydides and Democratic Peace." *Journal of Military Ethics* 5 (2006): 243–53.

"The Sophists and Democracy beyond Athens." *Rhetorica* 25.1 (2007): 109–22.

"Greek Democracies and the Debate over Democratic Peace." In *Démocratie athénienne – démocratie moderne: tradition et influences*, edited by M. H. Hansen, A.-C. Hernández, and P. Pasquino. Geneva: Fondation Hardt, 2010: 277–306.

ed. *Ancient Greek Democracy: Readings and Sources*. Malden, MA: Blackwell, 2004.

Roesch, P. *Études béotiennes*. Paris: de Boccard, 1982.

Roisman, J. "Maiandrios of Samos." *Historia* 34 (1985): 257–77.

Romilly, J. de. *The Great Sophists in Periclean Athens*, translated by J. Lloyd. Oxford University Press, 1992.

Rood, T. *Thucydides, Narrative and Explanation*. Oxford: Clarendon Press, 1998.

Rossetto, P. C. and G. P. Sartorio, eds. *Teatri greci e romani*, vols. II–III. Rome: Edizioni SEAT, 1994.

Roy, J. "Spartan Aims in the Spartan–Elean War of c. 400: Further Thoughts." *Electronic Antiquity* 3.6 (1997).

"Problems of Democracy in the Arcadian Confederacy 370–362." In *Alternatives to Athens*, edited by R. Brock and S. Hodkinson. Oxford University Press, 2000: 308–26.

"The Synoikism of Elis." In *Even More Studies in the Ancient Greek Polis*, edited by T. H. Nielsen. Stuttgart: Franz Steiner Verlag, 2002: 249–64.

Russett, B. and W. Antholis. "Do Democracies Fight Each Other? Evidence from the Peloponnesian War." *Journal of Peace Research* 29.4 (1992): 415–34.

"The Imperfect Democratic Peace of Ancient Greece." In *Grasping the Democratic Peace*. Princeton University Press, 1993: 43–71.

Rutter, N. K. "Diodorus and the Foundation of Thurii." *Historia* 22 (1973): 155–76.

Greek Coinages of Southern Italy and Sicily. London: Spink, 1997.

"Syracusan Democracy: Most Like the Athenian?" In *Alternatives to Athens*, edited by R. Brock and S. Hodkinson. Oxford University Press, 2000: 137–51.

Historia Numorum: Italy. London: British Museum Press, 2001.

Ruzé, F. *Délibération et pouvoir dans la cité grecque*. Paris: Publications de la Sorbonne, 1997.

Sacks, K. *Diodorus Siculus and the First Century*. Princeton University Press, 1990.

Salmon, J. B. *Wealthy Corinth: A History of the City to 338 B.C.* Oxford: Clarendon Press, 1984, 2nd edn. 1997.

Salmon, P. *Étude sur la Confédération béotienne (447/6–386)*. Brussels: Academie Royale de Belgique, 1976.

Salyer, L. E. *Laws Harsh as Tigers: Chinese Immigrants and the Shaping of Modern Immigration Law*. Chapel Hill, NC: University of North Carolina Press, 1995.

Samons, L. J. *What's Wrong with Democracy? From Athenian Practice to American Worship*. Berkeley: University of California Press, 2004.

Saprykin, S. Y. *Heracleia Pontica and Tauric Chersonesus before Roman Domination: VI–I Centuries B.C.* Amsterdam: A. M. Hakkert, 1997.

"The Foundation of Tauric Chersonesus." In *The Greek Colonization of the Black Sea Area*, edited by G. R. Tsetskhladze. Stuttgart: Franz Steiner Verlag, 1998: 227–48.

Sartori, F. "The Constitutions of the Western Greek States. Cyrenaica, Magna Graecia, Greek Sicily, and the *Poleis* in the Massaliot Area." In *The Western Greeks*, edited by G. P. Carratelli. Milan: Bompiani, 1996: 215–22.

Saunders, T. J. *Aristotle* Politics Books *I and II*. Oxford: Clarendon Press, 1995.

Schiappa, E. *Protagoras and Logos. A Study in Greek Philosophy and Rhetoric*. Columbia: University of South Carolina Press, 1991.

The Beginnings of Rhetorical Theory in Classical Greece. New Haven: Yale University Press, 1999.

Schleif, H., K. Romaios, and G. Klaffenbach. *Der Artemistempel: Architektur, Dachterrakotten, Inschriften*. Berlin: Mann, 1940.

Schuller, W. "Zur Entstehung der griechischen Demokratie außerhalb Athens." In *Auf den Weg gebracht, Idee und Wirklichkeit der Grundung der Universität Konstanz*, edited by H. Sund and M. Timmermann. Konstanz: Universitätsverlag Konstanz, 1979: 433–47.

"Die Einführung der Demokratie auf Samos im 5. Jahrhundert v. Chr." *Klio* 64 (1981): 281–8.

"Wirkungen des ersten attischen Seebunds auf die Herausbildung der athenischen Demokratie." In *Studien zum attischen Seebund*, edited by J. M. Balcer. Konstanz: Universitätsverlag Konstanz, 1984: 87–101.

Scott, L. *Historical Commentary on Herodotus Book 6*. Leiden: Brill, 2005.

Segre, M., ed. *Tituli Calymnii*. Bergamo: Istituto Italiano d'Arti Grafiche, 1952.

Sherk, R. K. "The Eponymous Officials of Greek Cities: v, The Register." *ZPE* 96 (1993): 267–95.

Sherwin-White, S. S. M. *Ancient Cos.* Göttingen: Vandenhoeck and Ruprecht, 1978.

Shipley, G. *A History of Samos, 800–188 B.C.* Oxford: Clarendon Press, 1987.

Siewert, P., ed. *Ostrakismos-Testimonien I.* Stuttgart: Franz Steiner Verlag, 2002.

Sluiter, I. and R. M. Rosen, eds. *Free Speech in Classical Antiquity.* Leiden: Brill, 2004.

Smith, C. F., trans. *Thucydides.* Cambridge, MA: Harvard University Press, 1920.

Snodgrass, A. "Interaction by Design: The Greek City State." In *Peer Polity Interaction and Socio-Political Change,* edited by C. Renfrew and J. F. Cherry. Cambridge University Press, 1986: 47–58.

Sokolowski, F. *Lois sacrées de l'Asie Mineure.* Paris: E. de Boccard, 1955.

Sordi, M. *La lega tessala fino ad Alessandro Magno.* Rome, 1958.

Souza, P. de. "Towards Thalassocracy? Archaic Greek Naval Developments." In *Archaic Greece: New Approaches and New Evidence,* edited by N. Fischer and H. van Wees. London: Duckworth, 1998: 271–93.

Stanton, G. R. "The Territorial Tribes of Korinth and Phleious." *Cl Ant* 5 (1986): 139–53.

Starr, C. G. "The Myth of the Minoan Thalassocracy." *Historia* 3 (1954): 282–91.

The Influence of Sea Power on Ancient History. Oxford University Press, 1989.

Ste. Croix, G. E. M. de. *The Origins of the Peloponnesian War.* London: Duckworth, 1972.

"Political Pay outside Athens." *CQ* 25 (1975): 48–52.

The Class Struggle in the Ancient Greek World. Ithaca: Cornell University Press, 1981.

"Trials at Sparta." In *Sparta,* edited by M. Whitby. New York: Routledge, 2002: 69–77.

Storey, Ian. "Thrasymachus at Athens: Aristophanes Fr. 205 (*Daitales*)." *Phoenix* 42 (1988): 212–18.

Strauss, B. S. "Athenian Democracy: Neither Radical, Extreme, Nor Moderate." *AHB* 1.6 (1987): 127–9.

Stylianou, P. J. *A Historical Commentary on Diodorus Siculus Book 15.* Oxford: Clarendon Press, 1998.

Svoronos, I. N. "ΤΑ ΠΗΛΙΝΑ ΕΙΣΙΤΗΡΙΑ ΤΟΥ ΘΕΑΤΡΟΥ ΤΗΣ ΜΑΝΤΙΝΕΙΑΣ." *Journal International d'Archéologie Numismatique* 3 (1900): 197–228.

Tacon, J. "Ecclesiastic *Thorubos*: Interventions, Interruptions, and Popular Involvement in the Athenian Assembly." *G&R* 48 (2001): 173–92.

Taeuber, H. "Androtion *FgrHist* 324 F 6 (ca. 340 v.Chr): Die Einführung und erste Anwendung des Ostrakismos (488/7 v.Chr)." In *Ostrakismos-Testimonien I,* edited by P. Siewert. Stuttgart: Franz Steiner Verlag, 2002: 401–12.

Talbert, R. J. A. *Timoleon and the Revival of Greek Sicily, 344–317 B.C.* Cambridge University Press, 1974.

Taylor, C. C. W. *The Atomists: Leucippus and Democritus.* University of Toronto Press, 1999.

Tod, M. N. *A Selection of Greek Historical Inscriptions to the End of the Fifth Century B.C.* Oxford: Clarendon Press, 1933.

Tomlinson, R. A. *Argos and the Argolid.* Ithaca: Cornell University Press, 1972.

Touchais, G. "Chronique des fouilles et découvertes archéologiques en Grèce en 1980: Rhodes." *BCH* 105 (1981): 862–3.

Tréheux, J. "Koinon." *REA* 89 (1987): 39–46.

"La 'prise en considération' des décrets en Grèce à l'époque hellénistique." In *Du pouvoir dans l'antiquité: mots et réalités*, edited by C. Nicolet. Geneva: Droz, 1990: 117–27.

Trojani, M. "Le antichità." In *Il teatro antico di Siracusa*, edited by L. Polacco and C. Anti. Rimini: Maggioli, 1981: 34–46.

Tsetskhladze, G. R. *The Greek Colonization of the Black Sea Area.* Stuttgart: Franz Steiner Verlag, 1998.

Tuplin, C. "The Date of the Union of Corinth and Argos." *CQ* 32 (1982): 75–83.

"Timotheus and Corcyra." *Athenaeum* 72 (1984): 537–68.

Unz, R. K. "The Chronology of the Elean War." *GRBS* 27 (1986): 29–42.

Vinogradov, Y. G. *Olbia: Geschichte einer altgriechischen Stadt am Schwarzen Meer.* Konstanz: Universitätsverlag Konstanz, 1981.

Vinogradov, Y. G. "Zur politischen Verfassung von Sinope und Olbia im Fünften Jahrhundert v.u.Z." In *Pontische Studien: Kleine Schriften zur Geschichte und Epigraphik des Schwarzmeerraumea*, edited by Y. G. Vinogradov. Mainz: von Zabern, 1997: 165–229.

"Ostrakismos als strenges Kampfmittel für Demokratie im Lichte des neuen Funde aus Chersonesos Taurika." In *Gab es das griechische Wunder?*, edited by D. Papenfuss and V. M. Stroka. Mainz: von Zabern, 2001: 379–86.

Vinogradov, Y. G. and S. D. Kryžickij. *Olbia: Eine altgriechische Stadt im nordwestlichen Schwarzmeerraum.* Leiden: Brill, 1995.

Vinogradov, Y. G. and M. I. Zolotarev. "L'ostracismo e la storia della fondazione di Chersonesos Taurica." *Minima Epigraphica et Papyrologica* 2 (1999): 111–31.

Vlastos, Gregory. "Isonomia." *AJPh* 74 (1953): 337–66.

"ISONOMIA POLITIKH." In *Isonomia. Studien zur Gleichheitsvorstellung im griechischen Denken*, edited by J. Mau and E. G. Schmidt. Berlin: Akademie-Verlag, 1964: 1–35.

Vollgraff, G. "Ad titulos Argivos." *Mnemosyne* 58 (1930): 20–40.

Walbank, F. W. *A History Commentary on Polybius*, vol. v. Oxford: Clarendon Press, 1957.

Walker, E. M. "Democracy in the Empire." In *CAH*, vol. v, edited by J. B. Bury, S. A. Cook, and F. E. Adcock. Cambridge University Press, 1927: 471–2.

"The Political Situation in Boeotia in 457 B.C." In *CAH*, vol. v, edited by J. B. Bury, S. A. Cook, and F. E. Adcock. Cambridge University Press, 1927: 469.

Wallace, M. B. "Early Greek 'Proxenoi.'" *Phoenix* 24.3 (1970): 189–208.

Wallace, R. W. "The Sophists in Athens." In *Democracy, Empire, and the Arts in Fifth-Century Athens*, edited by D. Boedeker and K. A. Raaflaub. Cambridge, MA: Harvard University Press, 1998: 203–22.

Wallace, W. P. "Kleomenes, Marathon, the Helots, and Arkadia." *JHS* 74 (1954): 32–5.

Wallinga, H. T. *Ships and Sea-Power before the Great Persian War*. Leiden: Brill, 1993.

Weart, S. *Never at War: Why Democracies Will Not Fight One Another*. New Haven: Yale University Press, 1998.

"Remarks on the Ancient Evidence for Democratic Peace." *Journal of Peace Research* 38.5 (2001): 609–13.

Welwei, K.-W. "'Demos' und 'Plethos' in athenischen Volksbeschlussen um 450 v. Chr." *Historia* 35 (1986): 177–91.

Wentker, H. *Sizilien und Athen. Die Begegnung der attischen Macht mit den Westgriechen*. Heidelberg: Quelle and Meyer, 1956.

Westermark, U. and K. Jenkins. *The Coinage of Camarina*. London: Royal Numismatic Society, 1980.

Westlake, H. D. *Thessaly in the Fourth Century*. London: Methuen, 1935.

"Athens and Amorges." *Phoenix* 31 (1977): 319–29.

"Rival Traditions on a Rhodian Stasis." *MH* 40 (1983): 239–50.

Whibley, L. *Greek Oligarchies, Their Character and Organisation*. London: Methuen and Co., 1896.

Whitby, M. "The Union of Corinth and Argos: A Reconsideration." *Historia* 33 (1984): 295–308.

White, Stephen A. "Thrasymachus the Diplomat." *CPh* 90.4 (1995): 307–27.

Whitehead, D. *Aineias the Tactician*. Oxford: Clarendon Press, 1990.

From Political Architecture to Stephanus Byzantinus. Sources for the Ancient Greek Polis. Stuttgart: Franz Steiner Verlag, 1994.

Will, E. *Le monde grec et l'orient*, vol. 1: *Le Ve siècle (510–403)*. Paris: Presses Universitaires de France, 1972.

Wolski, J. "Thémistocle était-il promoteur de la démocratie athénienne?" *Acta Antiqua Academiae Scientiarum Hungaricae* 32 (1989): 43–9.

Woodbury, L. "The Date and Atheism of Diagoras of Melos." *Phoenix* 19 (1965): 178–211.

Wörrle, M. *Untersuchungen zur Verfassungsgeschichte von Argos im 5. Jahrhundert vor Christus*. Diss. Erlangen-Nurnberg, 1964.

Wuilleumier, P. *Tarente des origines à la conquête romaine*. Paris: de Boccard, 1939.

Yunis, H. "The Constraints of Democracy and the Rise of the Art of Rhetoric." In *Democracy, Empire, and the Arts in Fifth-Century Athens*, edited by D. Boedeker and K. A. Raaflaub. Cambridge, MA: Harvard University Press, 1998: 223–40.

Zahrnt, M. *Olynth und die Chalcidier*. Munich: C. H. Beck, 1971.

Zoepffel, R. "Aristoteles und die Demagogen." *Chiron* 4 (1974): 69–90.

Index

Printed in the United States
By Bookmasters